AMERICAN RENAISSANCE

AMERICAN RENAISSANCE

OUR LIFE AT THE
TURN OF THE
21ST
CENTURY

Marvin Cetron
and
Owen Davies

ST. MARTIN'S PRESS
New York

Design by Richard Oriolo

Library of Congress Cataloging-in-Publication Data
Cetron, Marvin J.
American renaissance: our life at the turn of the 21st century /
Marvin Cetron and Owen Davis.
p.   cm.
Includes index.
ISBN 0-312-05050-X
1. Twenty-first century—Forecasts. 2. United States-
—Forecasting. 3. Social prediction—United States. I. Davies,
Owen. II. Title.
CB161.C39 1990
303.49'09'05—dc20   90-36127
                                      CIP

First Paperback Printing
10 9 8 7 6 5 4 3 2 1

*This book is dedicated to
my son, Dr. Ed Cetron, who proved he could
soar like an eagle . . .*

and

*Janice Davies, a wife who
always makes the future something to
anticipate with pleasure.*

CONTENTS

Contents

PART V
Values at the Turn of the Century

ACKNOWLEDGMENTS

Though the authors would very much like to take full credit for this book, a grudging honesty forces us to admit that only the undiscovered mistakes were made without assistance. For the rest, we owe deepest thanks to all of the following:

Gloria Wasserman, without whose constant help and encouragement Dr. Cetron could not have finished this project.

Bruce Shenitz, Julian Weiss, and Joan Westreich for invaluable editorial assistance.

Paul Hilts, of *Omni* magazine; Otis Port, Technical Editor of *Business Week;* and Tom O'Toole, National Editor of *America Week,* for contributing their expertise and editorial skill to several sections of this book.

Professor Morris Massey, of the University of Colorado, whose work on the changing values that govern life in America is by far the best we have seen.

Our colleague, Wanda Rocha, whose insights into medical resources and ethics contributed greatly to our discussion of those topics.

The staff of Forecasting International, Jill Mackenzie, for indispensible research and draft material, and Charles McFadden, whose diligence and skill in ferreting out hard-to-locate data ensured that any speculation in this book would be firmly grounded in reality, and especially Rebecca Lucken's guiding wisdom throughout and her unstinting efforts when the book was already in the galley stage.

The entire staff at St. Martin's Press, and especially Thomas J. McCormack, Roy Gainsburg, Bill Thomas, who provided invaluable assistance throughout, Andrea Connolly, Maryanne Mazzola, Michelle Hinkson, and Andy Carpenter for his inspired cover design.

And above all to Bob Weil, our friend, our associate of nearly a decade, and the best editor we have ever met. If we were to list all his contributions to this and our other works, there would be little room left for text.

—Marvin Cetron and Owen Davies
March 1989

AMERICAN RENAISSANCE

PROLOGUE:

A NATION IN DECLINE?

Will America survive as a world leader in business and politics? Or will it become a second-rate power as once-mighty England has done? Will today's working-age Americans live as well as their parents? Or must we all resign ourselves to a life of diminished expectations? These questions are more than rhetorical. By coincidence more than cause, the final years of the twentieth century—the symbol-rich end of a millennium—have turned out to be a crucial period in our nation's history.

During the last twenty-five years, the United States has encountered some of the most difficult challenges in its brief existence. Our economy, though still the most productive in the world, is outcompeted—and recently bought up wholesale—by nations that in the 1950s could hardly sustain themselves, much less dominate world markets. Though we still lead the world in scientific research, our mastery of practical technologies has fallen behind that of Japan and Korea. Drugs, once limited to the fringes of society, have corroded their way throughout our population. And our educational system, once among the best in the world, has so badly lost its way that, according to researchers at the University of Texas, only 40 percent of American adults can read and write well enough to cope with job applications, government forms, and other daily problems.

To date, we have dealt with these and many other threats ineffectively, if at all. We have complained loudly about "unfair competition" from abroad and threatened to enact restrictive trade legislation, but we have done little. We have pretended that draconian laws and erratic enforcement could control the drug problem long after their failure was clear. Until 1983, when the National Commission on Excellence in Education published *A Nation at Risk,* we hardly recognized that our school system had been decaying for three generations; since then, while talking about the need to sup-

port our schools, Washington has tried repeatedly to cut federal aid
to education.

For a time, we could afford to delay in responding to these challenges. Barring war, it takes many years to destroy a nation so large
and powerful as the United States. But, as we have learned, un-
resolved problems inevitably grow much larger. As the twentieth
century nears its end, our grace period is running out. The United
States at last faces a decision: We must either begin to solve the many
problems we have neglected for so long or commit ourselves to a
decline that will be almost impossible to reverse. Whether deliberately or by default, by the year 2000 we will have made our choice.

In the pages that follow, we will look at the new, much changed
America that will emerge from this pivotal time.

VISIONS OF DECAY

In his recent book, *The Rise and Fall of the Great Powers,* historian Paul
Kennedy makes a persuasive argument that world leadership is an
unstable condition burdened by inner conflicts that make its eventual
decay inevitable. Though Kennedy is careful to avoid drawing firm
conclusions about the future of the United States, his underlying
message seems inescapable: Unless the nation is blessed in the future
with leaders far more skillful than those of its recent past, it is
doomed to be outcompeted by the fast-growing Pacific Rim countries. And in the long run, this loss of economic supremacy will cost
us whatever degree of world leadership and military security we still
enjoy.

It is a difficult argument to ignore—in half a century or so, it may
even prove correct—but our national sense of doom was well established before Paul Kennedy added his theoretical support. In part,
it probably grows from our native American strain of Puritanism,
which held that no worldly success would long go unpunished.

The intellectual notion that the West is in decline is hardly new.
As early as the 1920s, the German philosopher Oswald Spengler
predicted that Western culture was soon to enter its last advanced
stage of decay. The West, he declared in the grimness of pre-Nazi
Germany, had only a few more good years left. It would pass
through a period of "Caesarism," of empire-building under the
reigns of strong leaders, and then inevitably decline, as the Roman
empire had done nearly twenty centuries earlier. In Germany, it
soon came to pass.

In America, we resisted the fatalistic vision long after World War II. In the long-distant summer of 1963, the United States still felt itself a blessed land, being led by a wise and vigorous young President into a future of prosperity, racial harmony, and uncontested world leadership. Then an assassin's bullet dispelled the magic and the myth of John Kennedy's Camelot. Within five years, Robert Kennedy and Martin Luther King, Jr., also lay dead, and the nation had blundered ever deeper into the mire of Southeast Asia. The cheerful confidence of the 1950s and the shining optimism of the Kennedy years had given way to the grim uncertainty that has now dogged the United States for almost three decades.

Unfortunately, it has been easy to justify pessimism about America's future. Evidence to demonstrate our national decay can be found in almost all areas of public life.

Vietnam taught us that armed force cannot achieve diplomatic goals in the absence of political will. The hostage crisis in Iran reinforced that lesson, and further incidents of political kidnapping have kept it fresh in our minds. Thus, unable to build the national consensus that would allow us to use our might effectively, we have lost faith in the power of our military to protect our interests abroad.

In the early 1970s, a few Arab ministers drove the price of oil skyward, forcing Americans into hour-long gas lines. For a decade afterwards, we suffered alternating periods of inflation and unemployment; for a year we were forced to endure "stagflation," a theoretically impossible combination of stagnation and inflation. Today, though the nation seems prosperous, the oil, farm, and Rocky Mountain states still suffer high unemployment. Manufacturing jobs are in the process of disappearing from the American economy. The federal budget deficit hangs at about $150 billion per year, poised to soar even more at any moment; the trade deficit is down from its peak, but has stabilized and threatens to rise again. The Pacific Rim nations outcompete America in one world market after another— even at home—and use the profits to buy up its land and factories. Thus we have lost faith in our power of economic self-determination.

In our domestic life, we face problems no less demoralizing. Drugs are a national epidemic that years of preaching and millions of dollars spent on law enforcement have failed to control. Crime is rampant in every major city. Our schools are incapable of educating our children. We survived the cheap treacheries of the Nixon administration only to see more than one hundred Reagan appointees driven from office by charges of corruption. The American space program fell from glory even as Soviet cosmonauts made a permanent home in orbit. The battle over nuclear power drags on, providing neither solutions to the hazards of atomic reactors nor any credible alternatives to their use. Thus we have lost faith in law enforcement, in education, in government, and in technology.

Clearly, it seems that America has entered that phase of inevitable decay which Spengler forecast.

The key word is *seems.* Virtually all of the problems we face today survive, not because we cannot solve them, but because we have lacked the political will to do so. We know, for example, that schools can provide a decent education; ours once did, and those of many other countries still do. AIDS might be contained, and to some extent treated, if only we were willing to spend more money on education and medical programs and less time in moral posturing. There is surely no excuse for criminal misconduct by government officials. And so on down the list.

In these and many other cases, the solutions are, if not cheap and easy, at least possible and well understood. By 2000, many of them will have been put into practice, if not because we have become a wiser and more responsible people, then at least because we can no longer afford the luxury of clinging to outworn policies. We will devote much of this book to examining these problems and the solutions that America will adopt as it approaches the turn of the century.

AGENTS OF CHANGE

Most discussions of the future concentrate on science and technology, and with good reason. As Alvin Toffler, John Naisbitt, and many others have observed, science and technology are the fastest, most trenchant agents of change that humanity has ever experienced. The rate with which they alter our world accelerates daily. In the next ten years the amount of raw knowledge available to us will double. In the decade that follows, it will double again, and so on as far into the future as we can dimly see.

Today, of course, the dominant technology propelling change is the computer. Its revolution is already well begun. In only the last ten years, computers have eliminated half of the manufacturing jobs that existed in this country in the late 1970s; in the next decade, half of the remaining manufacturing positions will vanish under their influence. The three million or so executives who found themselves jobless in the 1980s also owe their unwanted freedom to computers;

others will follow them to the unemployment lines. Computers and computerized telecommunications are revolutionizing our personal lives as well. Some families have grown closer because computers allow them to work at home; many others have broken under the pressure of being together twenty-four hours a day. In the next decade, new microcomputers vastly more powerful than those now available will begin to give products and processes throughout our lives an intelligence of their own. What this will mean is as yet only barely visible.

While the computer remains today the dominant agent of change, its impact on American life will diminish as a second techno-revolution takes hold, one based on our increasing control over life itself. In the doctor's office, biotechnology promises new healing powers that may soon conquer diseases from cancer to Alzheimer's disease. In the factory, methods based on the delicate technologies of the living cell rather than on the brute force of heat and pressure offer to reduce both pollution and costs in a wide variety of processing industries. From these early visions, biological methods will grow to transform many of the hidden technologies that support modern life. That process will still be getting under way as the new century opens.

So no one can talk about the future without giving science and technology their due.

And yet other forces—some cultural, others social—are at work in the United States. Some will govern this country's future almost as profoundly as technology does. In the human terms that shape a society, a few may work even greater changes on it as the twenty-first century approaches.

One is time. The early Baby Boomers among us are now coming to grips with it in ways they could not have grasped in their "hippie" years, two decades ago. Their parents have known for years what it means to find waistlines advancing as hairlines recede; now yesterday's flower children are coming to know, not just intellectually but as a daily presence, that their lives are somewhere near half over. We are still wondering what it means on a national scale when the generation that reaches middle age is the largest in history, and the least fertile. By 2000, we will have begun to know from experience.

Birthrates are not uniformly low, however, and this too will change the United States dramatically. The typical one-child family is white and well off. Black and Hispanic families are, on average, both larger and poorer. Aided by the continuing flight of moneyed whites from cities to the suburbs and countryside, this difference will transfer much of the nation's urban political power into minority hands. By 2000, minorities will be the majority in fifty-three of our one hundred largest cities.

Human migration has nudged American history from its established course several times in the last four hundred years. It will do so again as the millennium reaches its close. In the nineteenth century, the United States received huge waves of immigrants from Britain and northern Europe, then from Asia, and again from southern and eastern Europe. Today's immigrants come from Asia and from Central and South America. Recent changes in the Immigration and Naturalization Act will not hold back the tide. By 2000 these newest Americans will dominate local politics in some parts of the United States.

One of the most potent and destructive forces for change is AIDS. By 2000, we will at last have established effective detection and treatment programs, and our control over drug abuse and needle-transmitted disease will be increasing. But these measures will have come far too late. By 2000, the need to care for as many as 5 million AIDS patients may cost each American taxpayer five hundred dollars per year. By then, the disease will have reached its natural limit: Virtually everyone at serious risk of contracting the disease will already have done so. The impact on our economy will be profound, but in the long run the social and ethical consequences of AIDS may change the United States in even greater ways.

Another influential factor is competition. Since the end of World War II, the United States has faced two great competitors: the Soviet Union in the field of world politics, and Japan in business. It begins to appear that we may soon be able to resolve some of our differences with Russia, or at least scale our conflicts back to less dangerous levels. Economic competition, in contrast, grows ever more intense. In the Far East, Hong Kong, Singapore, and Taiwan have joined Japan in world markets; mainland China has begun the climb to trade prominence. All but China have used their profits to buy up large chunks of American industry and real estate at bargain prices.

Each nation that makes a place for itself in international commerce reduces the market for American goods and so cuts into our standard of living. Thus, "competitiveness" has become a popular buzzword among economists and business leaders in the last few years, and our lack of it has been a major issue in trade legislation. By the turn of the century, automation will have made American workers so much more productive in both manufacturing and services that we will again supply cheap, high-quality services to buyers throughout the world. Yet automation will not drive human workers into the unemployment lines or condemn today's unemployed to permanent poverty. In a growing economy, with a shrinking supply of working-age Americans, we will all live better.

Finally (for our purposes), there is diplomacy. In recent years America has tried to cope with cutthroat competition, not by meeting it head-on, a dangerous strategy in a nuclear world, but by negotiating to mitigate its most destructive aspects. Thus, the U.S. signed a growing series of treaties with the Soviet Union, trying to bring the arms race under control. The United States has held trade talks with Japan and has signed a free-trade agreement with Canada in the belief that joining forces is the best hope for maintaining the economic strength of both countries in the face of similar agreements in Europe and—pending—the Far East. (In fact, the authors suspect that this union will grow closer still. The extra stars of the American flag on this book's cover represent the state-to-be of Puerto Rico and four states to our north, the product of a plebiscite in Canada, whose citizens may yet decide, soon after the turn of the century, that there is little point in maintaining the fiction of two countries when their economies, peoples, and cultures have become indistinguishable. Quebec, of course, will take the opportunity to declare its long-sought independence.)

In the nearly two dozen chapters that follow, we look at each of these forces and project the changes they will bring, both to the nation as a whole and to our individual lives.

MANIFESTO

American Renaissance is a statement of hope. We believe firmly that anyone who looks clearly at the facts, unbiased by any partisan political agenda, must feel an unfashionable optimism about the future of our country. In the decade to come, America will begin to solve many of the problems that have dogged it for so long. America enters the 1990s beset by political and economic competition from abroad and by endless controversy at home, and can expect much more of the same in the years ahead. But by the dawn of the twenty-first century, America will have passed the crisis. The economy will be regaining its vigor. The school systems will be well on their way back to academic success. Urban crime rates will be dropping.

This is not to say that America suddenly will be free of problems, but merely that it will have learned to cope with its troubles. More, it will have learned that it still *can* cope with them. America will have built the beginnings of a consensus on its national agenda for the early twenty-first century. And we will know from experience that the final decay of the world's first true democracy is a nightmare whose time has not yet come.

APRIL 1990

*A*rthur C. Clarke, the eminent science fiction writer, once observed that when competent forecasters go wrong, they usually err by being too conservative; when the season is right for transformation, changes happen much faster than anyone expects. The last year has given us more opportunity to lag behind the pace of events than any period since the outbreak of World War II.

Since the preceding introduction was written, it has become clear that the world in which the United States plays its leading role will be even more changed from the postwar status quo than anyone would have dared to hope. The communist dictatorships of Eastern Europe have toppled with breathtaking speed and are being replaced by democratic, capitalist systems as fast as societies can make the transition. The reunification of Germany, which Forecasting International first predicted in 1982, in the book *Encounters with the Future,* now appears destined to occur within two years. The Sandinista regime in Nicaragua is gone, ousted by votes, not bullets. The Soviet Union itself has adopted a multiparty system and faces the possibility of eventual dissolution. Even South Africa has grudgingly begun the difficult task of building a democracy. When 1989 began, the conflicts of generations seemed almost immutable; today they seem almost over. For the United States, this change will bring extraordinary benefits.

One is a vast growth in its influence over Eastern Europe, a region from which it has been excluded since the end of the Second World War. Already, American economists and political scientists are shuttling from Washington, New York, and Cambridge to Warsaw, Prague, Budapest, and Belgrade. They are working with leaders who have little experience of politics and none of capitalism, helping them to build the infrastructure of a free society. American businessmen are only a few months behind. Even if the nation's government can find little money to lend these countries for development, and little in the way of a coherent policy for dealing with them, its citizens will quickly build relationships that could weld much of the Warsaw Pact firmly into the American sphere of influence. At the turn of the twenty-first century, the United States will lead the nations of Eastern Europe even more circumspectly than it will its traditional allies, but America, and not the Soviet Union, will lead them.

The other benefits are economic. Acting in the name of prudence and the interest of the defense industry, the Bush Administration has refused to accept that a major "peace dividend" is now available, thanks to the easing of tensions in Europe. Yet the United States will soon cut its costs by pulling most of its troops home from a Continent that no longer needs them. The next Administration could use this windfall to fund domestic programs and to reduce America's crippling national debt. Add to this the profits to be earned by serving the new East European market for both capital and consumer goods and by the easing of trade with resource-rich South Africa sure to follow any progress toward true democracy there. The result can only be a boost that the American economy can surely use.

The startling changes of 1989 offer proof that our vision of a more peaceful, prosperous, and just future will soon become reality, not only for one nation, but for the entire world. Bear them in mind as you read what follows.

PART I

Society at the
Turn of the Century

THE MIDDLE-CLASSING

OF AMERICA

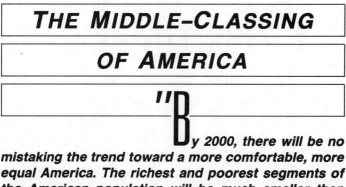

"**B**y 2000, there will be no mistaking the trend toward a more comfortable, more equal America. The richest and poorest segments of the American population will be much smaller than they are today, the middle class correspondingly larger. Poverty will not be a thing of the past; there will still be economic problems that urgently require attention. But the worst will be behind us. We will have built the kinder, gentler America that today is only a pious slogan."

We hear it from all sides: America is less egalitarian, less democratic than it once was; the middle class is disappearing, falling below the poverty line, while the wealthy prosper; soon there will be no one left but the rich and powerful and the poor and disenfranchised. The statistics prove it, we're told, and some economists quote them at every opportunity. *The Atlantic,* to cite just one major magazine, has published three major articles on this theme in as many years.

The following may be the most controversial statement in this book: such theories simply are not true. The middle class is not disappearing. In fact, it is growing rapidly. For many years now, the real standard of living in this country has increased by 20 percent every ten years. We have no evidence to suggest that this long-standing trend has suddenly vanished; we do have reason to believe that it will, if anything, move faster in the 1990s. By 2000, we will be richer and more comfortable than any nation in history, especially in comparison with the United States of 1989 and 1990. The vast majority of Americans will share in this bounty.

RECENT EXPERIENCE

This marks a change from the recent past. It is true that the middle class has been shrinking in the 1970s and 1980s. But this group has not been falling into poverty. Nearly all of those lost from the middle class have risen into the upper-income brackets. This is true no matter how you define the term *middle class* and no matter which years you choose to compare. According to University of Maryland economist Frank Levy, the proportion of Americans earning less than $20,000 remained about constant at 31 percent. The middle class—those with an income between $20,000 and $50,000—fell from 53 percent of the population in1973 to only 47 percent in 1986. And the upper class leaped from 16 percent to 22 percent.

The Bureau of Labor Statistics agrees. By 1986, it reports, the median income for all U.S. households was $29,460 and rising by more than 4 percent per year. About 60 percent of Americans fell into the middle class in 1969, only 53 percent in 1986. The upper class, meanwhile, had nearly doubled, while according to BLS figures the lower class had actually shrunk slightly as people rose into the middle class.

Changes in family life have also made at least some things easier for most people. Most households, for example, now depend on two salaries. Many working mothers would doubtless prefer the stay-at-home life of previous generations; yet having two paychecks makes these families less vulnerable to loss of income than their parents' generation was. If one wage earner loses his or her job or suddenly is unable to work, the other can carry on. In addition, people are marrying later, after they establish themselves financially, and having fewer children—by choice, not out of necessity. With smaller families—fewer people to share—any income stretches further.

In fact, there is very little hard evidence to support the idea that only the wealthy have prospered during the 1980s. One of the most compelling arguments is the oft-quoted claim that average hourly earnings have not kept up with inflation. But if one looks closely at the statistics, it becomes clear that this argument suffers fatal defects. One problem is that the government's estimates of average hourly earnings omit more than one-third of all jobs in the United States. Left out are professional and technical positions, the fastest-growing category in the American job market, and the best paid. The formula also neglects fringe benefits, which for many workers represent a large part of their compensation. And because of the way hourly earnings are calculated, it overestimates the buying power lost to inflation. According to the Congressional Research Service, once those problems are adjusted for, it turns out that average hourly earnings have risen by 8 percent since 1980.

The picture becomes even brighter when we realize that the average American has twice as much buying power today as in 1952. Consider this: an American worker labored only one-third as long to earn the price of a kitchen range in 1986 as he did in 1952; a man's suit required 55 percent less work; a car tune-up, 11 percent less; and a fryer chicken, 64 percent less. And that neglects the enormous increase in the range and quality of products and services available to consumers today. The wealthiest man in America thirty-five years ago could not have bought a color TV or a VCR, a food processor or a compact, silent humidifier. Need we mention the personal computer, which has eased the task of earning a living for millions of Americans?

It is true that some items high on the middle-class wish list have soared. College tuitions have probably been hit worst. In the 1980–81 academic year, the average tuition for a public college was only $3,603, while private colleges charged $6,665. By the 1988–89 school year, public school tuitions had risen to an average of $6,175, while private schools demanded $12,511. There is no denying that such prices subject all but the wealthiest families to serious hardship when the time comes to put two or three children through college.

Houses, too, have become harder to buy, largely because down payments and monthly carrying costs have risen sharply. Yet as a percentage of income, the cost of buying a home has actually dropped in recent years. In 1980, a median-priced home in the United States cost $62,200; mortgage payments on that house totaled $549 per month, or just over 31 percent of the median American income. By 1988, the median price of a house had soared to $90,600, but thanks to lower interest rates the monthly mortgage payment had risen only to $599—only 22.5 percent of the median income. Even with today's high real-estate prices, 50 percent of thirty- to thirty-four-year-olds own their own homes, and more people own a home today than in the 1960s. This is not a sign that Americans are, on average, painfully strapped for cash.

Some of the most rapid gains during this period have been made by groups usually thought of as poor. Apart from the ugliest inner cities, the much-publicized vision of black America as a place of vast poverty, violence, and despair would be as unfamiliar to most black families in the United States as to the upper-class whites reading about it in *The New York Times.* The growing number of black mayors, senators, and congressmen is only one visible result of a fundamental change in the status of minority Americans since the days of the civil rights marches and *Brown v. Board of Education.* One-third of all black families today earn solidly middle-class incomes of $25,000 to $50,000—nearly triple the number in the 1960s—while a few black entrepreneurs have become rich. Their ranks will grow throughout the remainder of this century.

And this trend is not limited to the few lucky black families who made it before the Reagan administration cut back on public assistance. Minority workers, and the young and unskilled of any race, suffer much higher unemployment rates than older, skilled, and white workers. Yet unemployment among blacks has dropped from 14.3 percent in 1980 to 11.4 percent late in 1988. That still is not good enough, but it is an improvement, and black employment will continue to grow as long as the American economy continues to grow.

Further, on average, these are better jobs. In 1960, nearly 45 percent of whites held professional or white-collar jobs, compared with just over 10 percent of blacks. By 1984, about 55 percent of whites were white-collar workers or professionals; so were nearly 40 percent of blacks. Again, this is not good enough; there should be no disparity at all. But the trend is clearly in the right direction, and there is every reason to believe that it will continue well beyond the turn of the century.

Black earnings are up as well, though this statistic—like many other economic measures—depends on exactly when you take your measurements. Black incomes rose sharply throughout the 1970s, then fell—not in real terms, but compared with white incomes—during the early 1980s. Since 1985, however, black men have again been catching up to white wage levels. We believe this trend, too, will continue for the foreseeable future. As the Baby Boom generation ages, the American workforce will shrink, and employers will be forced to pay more in all sections of the job market. And they will offer both basic education and job training—a chance for anyone stuck in poorly paid jobs to build a good career.

Similarly, despite scare stories about people who grow old in poverty, as a class the aged have never been better off. During the 1950s, one-third of the elderly were destitute; today less than half as many are poor. As a group, their median per capita income is a good deal greater than the national average. The elderly make up only one-sixth of the population, yet hold one-third of all household net worth and 40 percent of financial assets. The recent enactment of the national catastrophic-illness program will remove the last economic threat that most elderly Americans face.

POVERTY IN AMERICA

All this is not to say that there are not economic problems in America. Even as the monied class in America has grown, so too have the poor. In 1987 (the last year for which complete statistics are available) 13.5 percent of all Americans lived below the poverty line— $11,611 for a family of four—which is 3.3 million more than in 1970. In 1970, only 3.3 percent of American families earned less than $5,000 per year; by 1986 the number had risen to 5.3 percent. Clearly, this is not something to be proud of.

But neither is it evidence of an unfair economy, nor of one that is somehow failing, even as it appears to glow with false prosperity. It is not, for example, caused primarily by the loss of well-paid manufacturing jobs and the proliferation of badly paid service jobs; in 1986, only 16 percent of the poorest one-fifth of families had even one member with a full-time, year-round job. Rather, today's poverty is evidence of several pervasive trends that have changed American society during this period. This should come as no surprise. Poverty in America has almost always been caused by social change, not by lack of opportunity.

One of those changes is the rapid growth of single motherhood owing to the decline of traditional family structures and sexual inhibitions and the growing frequency of divorce in America. According to the Census Bureau, in 1986 there were 3.6 million American families where no husband was present; at least 35 percent lived in poverty. For single mothers, the risk of falling into poverty is higher than for any other group. In fact, divorce is the single most common reason that middle-class people slip into poverty. Whether divorced or never married, nearly 30 percent of white single mothers and fully half of black "single women heads of household" are poor.

The addition of 4.3 million new Hispanic Americans in the 1980s—a growth rate four times faster than that of the population at large—has contributed many of the new poor. Of the 3.3 million Americans added to the bottom economic class in the last two decades, an estimated 2 million are Hispanic. This estimate may actually be low, owing to under-reporting of illegal immigration, which, if reported, would increase slightly the overall number of poor. At least half of the Hispanics added to the U.S. population in the 1980s have been immigrants, 1.1 million (by official figures) from Mexico alone, and their poverty rate is considerably higher than among Cuban immigrants or native citizens of Hispanic heritage.

Two more groups have added to American poverty in recent years. Nearly 4 million former manufacturing workers from the Rust Belt have been displaced, first by the decline of our export trade in the early eighties and then by automation later in the decade. And since 1981, more than 120,000 farmers have been driven from the land by low crop prices and excessive debt. Only one-third of the assembly-line workers who lost their jobs in the early 1980s have ever gotten them back. One-third more have found other work, mostly in service industries that pay far less well than manufacturing did. The remainder have never worked again. The fate of ex-farmers is not so well documented, but it seems likely to have been even less happy. No farmer who loses his land is ever called back from layoff.

All these people share one handicap in common: by the standards of the 1980s—and certainly by the standards of the twenty-first century—they are virtually uneducated. Assembly-line workers and farmers may be high-school graduates, even college grads, but few have skills to fit them for the fast-growing, well-paid occupations of the late twentieth century. Even among the elite of impoverished single mothers, formerly middle-class women who have lost their status through divorce, not one in fifty has the kind of technical or professional skill that guarantees a good income today. And many single mothers are teens who dropped out of school to care for their children; this is one major reason families headed by teenage mothers are seven times more likely to be poor than others. The problem is even more difficult for Hispanic immigrants, few of whom speak enough English to get by in any skilled trade. It is difficult even for the well educated to prepare for a new career while trying to survive the shock of unaccustomed poverty. For those who dropped out of school and have never known any life but poverty, it is all but impossible.

We will spend much of this book tracing these changes in the American economic and social structure, and projecting them on to the turn of the century. It is during the next decade that America will finally begin to cope with the problems such changes have brought, and to look also at the policies and programs that will allow the nation to triumph over them. By far the most important is educational reform, covered in Chapter 4. Single motherhood will never be an enviable state. Neither will the nation's scientists and engineers regret that they were not born farmers, so that they could take the opportunity which the 1990s will bring, to rebuild their lives. But the 1990s will be a time of possibilities and of triumph over adversity. As we will see in the coming chapters, today's poor will have a full chance to share in it.

HOMELESS AMID WEALTH

It is true that the rich and poor are more visible today than in the past. In Manhattan, the homeless once clustered in the Bowery and in single-room-occupancy hotels (SRO's) where the rich and middle classes did not have to see them; today they wander through the wealthiest neighborhoods. And, in fact, there are more homeless people in New York (and *some* other cities) today than in previous years. The cause is not greater poverty (poverty is declining), not greater unemployment (unemployment has fallen since 1982), not public-housing cutbacks (the number of housing units actually completed peaked during the Reagan years, although severe cutbacks in projects undertaken during those years may come back to haunt us). The real cause is the soaring price of apartments today. Most of the people struggling to survive on our streets—those who have not been discharged too soon from badly funded mental institutions—are simply people displaced by rent increases and by the razing of old apartment buildings.

This also partially explains why there are proportionally more rich people in Manhattan than there were twenty years ago. Rents have risen so high that no one else can truly afford to live there. Similar trends can be found in some—but not all—other cities.

Why is it that some cities have large populations of homeless people, while others do not? Researcher William Tucker, of the Cato

Institute, has looked into the question, with interesting results. Save for a few cities in the South, where homeless people might be expected to congregate, if possible, simply to avoid freezing in the winter, homelessness is largely concentrated on the East and West Coasts. Despite relatively high unemployment rates, the Rust Belt and oil and mountain states have relatively few homeless people. And even on the coasts, a few cities have remarkably small homeless populations. San Diego is the eighth-largest city in the country, with a substantial population of illegal Mexican immigrants. Yet it has only 3.1 homeless people per one thousand population, less than one-third the rate of wealthy San Francisco.

Tucker studied most of the factors usually blamed for homelessness: poverty and unemployment rates, shortages of public housing, and so on. He found that one item on his list stood out: with the exceptions of Miami and St. Louis, the cities with the highest rates of homelessness also had the lowest vacancy rates. (Tucker suspects that St. Louis is high on the list only because it defines its boundaries far more narrowly than others, and so consists mostly of one large inner city.) And all nine of the cities with the lowest vacancy rates practice some form of rent control. Analyzed statistically, rent control proved to be the single most important factor correlated with homelessness. Cities with rent control had average homeless rates 2.5 times as large as other municipalities. Rent control, Tucker concludes, makes it unprofitable for private developers to build new apartments for the poor and middle class, and for building owners to maintain existing ones. The number of livable apartments shrinks, and rents soar. And poor people wind up living on the streets. It was a slow process until the 1980s. Then the Reagan boom arrived, the rich got richer, the well-off got merely rich—and those without children moved to the city, displacing those who could least afford urban life.

In each afflicted city, these problems are brought on by poor planning on the local level. We mistake them for national phenomena because these cities are home to the great majority of television news reporters, political commentators, social scientists, and others who help to shape public opinion. Both wealthy and homeless people have become more common in their neighborhoods, while the middle class has vanished, so both wealth and poverty must be on the rise in America. Right?

Well, no.

It would be easy to reject Mr. Tucker's view of homelessness as the product of a conservative mind intent on smearing the liberal policy of rent control. The Cato Institute is, after all, a bastion of the radical right, and we have no reason to doubt that he shares its ideology. But his argument is based on figures that are widely available, and any serious distortion would be quickly found out. And consider the observations of a man who has little in common with America's right wing, Vietnamese Foreign Minister Nguyen Co Thach. In a recent news conference in New Delhi, Mr. Thach declared that a "romantic view of socialism" had ruined his nation's economy in the aftermath of the Vietnam War. One major cause of damage, he said, was rent control in Hanoi, which had raised the demand for living space, reduced the supply, and discouraged maintenance of existing homes. "The Americans couldn't destroy Hanoi," he said, "but we have destroyed our city by very low rents. We realized it was stupid and that we must change policy."

We hate to sound simplistic. And we know how unfashionable it is to place responsibility for an important social problem on a cause less distant and reprehensible than the callousness of a few rich and powerful leaders in Washington. But the problem of homelessness really is that simple. It will not go away until the politically powerful voters who caused it—the middle and upper classes of New York and Boston, Santa Monica and Washington, D.C., Los Angeles and San Francisco—give up their controlled rents and offer developers a good reason to build new apartments. Once the market for profitable luxury dwellings becomes glutted, builders will turn their attention to homes for the middle class and poor. And the problem of homelessness will begin to solve itself.

A RICH CENTURY AHEAD

It is far more difficult to predict our future standard of living than to forecast new developments in technology or medicine. Unfortunately, the future of our national economy is strongly influenced by government policy. And though the purpose of government may be to promote the general welfare, the purpose of government *leaders* is to win reelection. That means working hard to gain credit for caring about national problems while avoiding the strategically risky step of actually trying to do something about them—particularly if the solution might offend a substantial number of voters. In this context, it is impossible to be sure that our representatives in Washington will do what is needed to extend our current prosperity through the 1990s, much less do anything genuinely useful for those Americans who have been left behind. Yet if the economy could grow so vigorously during the Reagan years, despite the many economic blunders of that time, it seems likely to make steady progress until well after the turn of the century. In that case, Americans will all be able to divide a bigger economic pie.

Further, as we said above and will explain throughout this book, we do believe that Congress, along with President Bush and his successor, will enact many of the measures needed to free the economically disadvantaged from their current poverty. Educational reform, publicly funded day care, and a variety of other programs will give the disadvantaged a more equal chance to make their own way in an increasingly technological society. Many hundreds of thousands of today's poor will take advantage of that opportunity, and a growing economy will find productive roles for all.

Money is also being distributed more evenly now as a result of the Tax Reform Act of 1986, which reduced the tax burden on the poor and middle class and closed most tax loopholes for the wealthy. From now on, the rich will retain somewhat less of the nation's income, while the lower and middle classes keep more. When statistics finally become available, it will be seen that moderate expansion of both wealth and poverty in the 1980s was a brief aberration; we will find in retrospect that, even in 1988 and 1989, both ends of the American economic spectrum were shrinking, while the middle class was again growing rapidly. This unaccustomed fairness will survive as long as Congress can hold out against pressure for tax concessions to the powerful lobbies that fund their election campaigns.

By 2000, there will be no mistaking the trend toward a more comfortable, more equal America. The richest and poorest segments of the American population will be much smaller than they are today, the middle class correspondingly larger. Poverty will not be a thing of the past; there will still be economic problems that urgently require attention. But the worst will be behind us. We will have built the kinder, gentler America that today is only a pious slogan.

MINORITIES BECOME

THE MAJORITY

Consider how America might look in the year 2000 unless it admits more immigrants: The labor force is aging and shrinking—a legacy of the baby-boom generation, whose panda-like reproductive patterns put birthrates below replacement level in 1972 and kept them there. Shortages of skilled labor, already noticeable in the 1980s in such fields as nursing and engineering, become acute. While the domestic market shrinks, America's international allies, economic rivals, and political adversaries watch the U.S. slouching toward a future sketched by Ben Wattenberg, the Jeremiah of the birth dearth: "a society that keeps getting older and smaller, older and smaller."

–Scott McConnell, "The New
Battle Over Immigration,"
Forbes, May 9, 1988

One of the most fundamental changes of the next decade has been occurring for nearly twenty years now, slowly at first, but with ever-increasing, inexorable speed. It is a change, not in technology or in economics, though it will have profound economic effects, but in who the American people *are.*

The United States is, as the saying goes, a nation of immigrants. In successive waves, Englishmen and Germans and Middle Europeans, Irish and Italians and Jews arrived on its shores and fought to establish themselves, often doing battle with former immigrants reluctant to cede any of their hard-won power to newcomers. The civil rights movement of the 1950s and 1960s was just such a battle, long delayed by slavery and the systematic oppression of blacks after the Civil War.

NEW WAVE AMERICANS

For more than two decades now, the United States has received yet another wave of poor and oppressed people—and some who were rich and oppressed—fleeing their native lands. But the migration pattern has changed dramatically since the early 1960s, when a majority of immigrants still came from Europe. In 1985, only 11 percent of new Americans-to-be were European. Fully 46 percent were Asian, while 40 percent came from Latin America. It was a typical year for the new wave of immigration. When the total is in, about 9 million people will have immigrated to the United States in the 1980s, twice as many as in the preceding decade. About 84 percent are from Asia, the Caribbean, and Latin America.

Twenty years after the end of the Vietnam War, refugees are still fleeing Southeast Asia for the safety and opportunity of the United States. Nearly 900,000 refugees have arrived from Vietnam, Laos, and Kampuchea (Cambodia) in the 1980s. There are more than 340,000 Vietnamese in California alone, half in the southern part of the state, where a sizable portion of Orange County has been dubbed Little Saigon. Up to 100,000 Khmer from Kampuchea have settled in Long Beach, Modesto, Stockton, Fresno, and San Francisco. Another 80,000 new Americans are Hmong tribesmen driven from Laos by the Pathet Lao after the United States abandoned its military commitment to Southeast Asia.

No one truly knows how many Hispanics arrive in the United States each year. Despite the amnesty program, and the harsh penalties now possible for employing illegal aliens, the number of Mexicans trying to enter the United States illegally has fallen only slightly. In April 1986, to pick just one month, more than 94,000 Mexicans were apprehended while trying to cross the border. A year later, after the amnesty program took effect, fully 80,000 were stopped. The Immigration and Naturalization Service estimates that for every person apprehended, three find their way into the country.

What is known is that sometime in 1988, the American Hispanic population passed 20 million, 34 percent more than in the 1980 census. Over 70 percent live in just four states: California, New York, Texas, and Florida. One-third of the population of California is Hispanic, as are one-fourth of the populations of Texas and New Mexico. Already, Hispanics make up more than half the population of San Antonio, more than one-fourth that of Los Angeles, and about one-fifth that of Denver.

Add to the Asians and Hispanics nearly a million Iranians who have settled here since the Khomeini revolution. Some 400,000 live in California, where many attended school at UCLA and the University of Southern California. Unlike most immigrants, Iranian refugees are their nation's elite—doctors, lawyers, businessmen, and engineers. Only the rich could afford to escape the Moslem fundamentalist fanatics who now control their native land. Today they own much of glittering Rodeo Drive and form a growing base of economic and political power in Los Angeles, Beverly Hills, Santa Monica, and the surrounding area.

This overwhelming tide of new, non-European Americans is quickly changing the ethnic and political character of the United States. Monterey Park, just outside Los Angeles, already is 50 percent Asian and 25 percent Hispanic. In California, Asians now outnumber blacks.

Two outside factors are hurrying the process of change. First, the birthrate among minority groups is far higher than that of the white majority. Among blacks it is double the national average; among Hispanics it quadruples the national average. And in many urban areas, the tradition of "white flight" continues; in moving elsewhere, the former WASP elite has left control of the cities to those who remain behind. As early as 2000, minorities will be the majority in fifty-three of America's hundred largest cities.

That is only the beginning. Given today's immigration and birth rates, by the turn of the century one of every four Americans will be Hispanic, black, Asian, or Middle Eastern. There will be 30 million Hispanics in the United States then, 40 million more by 2015. At that point they will be the largest minority group in America. (Other estimates hold that their numbers will surpass the black population as early as 2005.) In the more distant future, around 2030, these "minorities" will make up more than half of the American population, and European Americans will become just one more segment of a thoroughly integrated America. No one ethnic group will have the power to dominate the rest. Increasing tensions between the minorities, much like the conflict between Haitian blacks and native blacks in Miami, will be a growing part of the American scene.

The task of assimilating these changes will be one of the key issues of the 1990s. It will be far from complete as the new century dawns.

HETEROGENEOUS PEOPLES

So far, we have spoken of Asians and Hispanics as though they were homogeneous populations. In fact, generic classification of those groupings is no more useful than describing Old World immigrants as "Europeans." There is at least as much distance between the Vietnamese, the Khmer of Kampuchea, and the Hmong of Laos as there is between the Europeans of Scotland, Italy, and Czechoslovakia, and very possibly more. The Hispanics of Mexico, Puerto Rico, the Dominican Republic, and Cuba bear a closer resemblance to each other, but there are also marked differences. They even speak distinctly different versions of Spanish. Witness the advertising campaign, written by Hispanics, that guaranteed that their firm's insecticide would kill all *bichos.* To Mexicans, the word meant "bugs." Puerto Rican readers found conspicuously little use for a product guaranteed to do in their male reproductive equipment.

There are at least four major ethnic groups among the "Asians" now settling here. In their origins and adaptation to American life, they could hardly be more different.

Roughly 1 million of the new Asian Americans come from Korea, with 35,000 more arriving each year. Many are the children of North Korean refugees who fled the Communists in the early 1950s and have few ties to South Korea. The Koreans, like the Japanese of previous generations, have turned out to be the elite of Asia: well educated, energetic, entrepreneurial, and—increasingly—rich. About half of the Koreans now living in the United States are self-employed. Koreans own 85 percent of the green grocery business in New York City, 300 grocery stores in Atlanta, most of the liquor and convenience stores in Los Angeles, and even a growing number of service businesses in Anchorage. Most began with subsistence-level jobs, saved hard, often borrowed from other Korean immigrants, and set up their first businesses within four years after arriving in the United States. America will have few problems "assimilating" the Koreans in the coming years.

The Vietnamese have built one of the major success stories of immigration in the late twentieth century. Thousands managed to escape the communist takeover just after the fall of Saigon, and many were the flowering of South Vietnamese society. Most of the male adults were college-educated. Many spoke English fluently. Many had a good idea what to expect in the United States, having worked with Americans during the war. And though many had to make do with menial jobs in their first years here, hard work and the rise of the computer industry quickly brought them success. A second wave of Vietnamese followed in the late 1970s, ethnic Chinese expelled by the communist regime. With a tradition as traders and small businessmen, they too have done well. Throughout Southern California, but especially in Orange County, Vietnamese now own restaurants, markets, real estate, electronics firms, and all the rewards available to dedicated entrepreneurs in a growing capitalist economy.

More recently, there have been problems as well, mostly among the third wave of Vietnamese immigrants. Unlike their predecessors, the "boat people" of the 1980s have been largely poor and illiterate, even in their own language, much less English. Many are emotionally troubled, bearing the psychic scars of vicious oppression by the post-American Vietnamese government and of their torturous escape from their homeland. Few of these newest Vietnamese-Americans have found much in the way of economic success. Alcoholism and drug abuse are growing among Vietnamese young people. Nearly fifty violent Vietnamese youth gangs now prey on those who live in Orange County's Little Saigon area, working the standard youth-gang trades of drug sales, extortion, and armed robbery.

For the Khmer of Kampuchea, life here is generally far worse than for the poorest Vietnamese. Few managed to survive intact the destruction of their country by the Khmer Rouge and the Heng Samrin regime set in place by Vietnam. Virtually all lost relatives among the 2 million who died by murder and starvation in the 1970s. Most spent years in refugee camps just over the border in Thailand. Drug and alcohol abuse are common. Half or more need treatment for emotional disorders. In California, where most Khmer immigrants have settled, at least seven out of ten are on welfare; in some communities the figure is closer to 100 percent. Many live in families headed by women and suffer the same poverty that other such families endure. It is far from clear how the Khmer will find their way out of this continuing misery. They are not likely to do so by 2000.

Unsettled, too, are the reticent Hmong of northern Laos, who find American assimilation an impossible process. Until recently, the Hmong were semi-nomadic farmers, voluntarily isolated in the jungles of Southeast Asia, where they had fled in the nineteenth century to escape persecution in southern China. During the Vietnam War, the Central Intelligence Agency trained them to fight the Pathet Lao, a task at which the otherwise gentle Hmong proved very successful. Twenty years later, the victorious Pathet Lao are still persecuting the

Hmong. Most have been driven into refugee camps. Many have been killed.

The Hmong have few of the tools usually needed to build a new life in sophisticated, high-tech America. Few can read or write their native language; they had no written language until the 1950s. What they do have is one of the world's most closely knit clan systems. All the Hmong in Laos belong to only sixteen clans. That supportive network remains largely intact, even in the United States. And they still know how to farm. Though many Hmong in California remain on welfare, others have begun to carve out their own communities in the rural areas of Minnesota, Nebraska, North Carolina, Texas, and Washington. Though their early years in America were difficult for the Hmong—some committed suicide, a few died mysteriously— it begins to seem that by 2000 most will have succeeded in rebuilding their lives.

HISPANIC DIVERSITY

Hispanic-Americans span an enormous range, educationally, economically, and in the degree to which they have been able to build stable, productive lives in the United States.

By far the most successful are Cuban-Americans. An estimated 1 million Cubans make up about 5 percent of the Hispanic population. Most have settled in Florida, but there is also a substantial minority in the New York metropolitan area. In 1987, Cubans had a median family income of nearly $27,000—less than for the overall American population, but the highest of all Hispanics.

Yet the Cuban-American population is enormously varied. They arrived in two waves. The first consisted of old-guard Cuban families, many of them well-to-do, who fled the Castro revolution in the early 1960s. Some 30 percent of these Cuban men are self-employed; many are rich. The second wave of Cubans arrived in the Mariel boatlift of 1980. If the old-guard Cubans were, to a great extent, the elite of Havana society, the Mariel Cubans had little in common with them. Many are illiterate; others are criminally insane or psychologically disturbed. All arrived with few possessions beyond the clothes they wore. Most still live in poverty.

Transplanted Mexicans make up nearly two-thirds of the Hispanic population. They total 12 million people, concentrated heavily in California and the Southwest. In the Los Angeles area, some 70 percent of Hispanics are of Mexican origin. And more than 60 percent of the men and women heading Hispanic households came directly from Mexico. More than 70 percent of the Hispanics in the area are under thirty-five.

Puerto Ricans, most of them in New York and New Jersey, account for 14 percent of Hispanic immigrants. One-third of the Puerto Rican people now live in the mainland United States.

Many Hispanics are from the Caribbean. Perhaps 300,000 immigrants from the Dominican Republic alone have settled in New York City.

But the fastest growing segment of the Hispanic population comes from Central and South America; their numbers have soared some 40 percent in the last five years. An estimated 500,000 have come here from El Salvador alone. Combined with the relatively few immigrants from Spain and Portugal, they total one-fifth of the Hispanic population. They, too, have found it difficult to build a place in American society.

Unlike old-guard Cubans, the newer Hispanic immigrants have found life to be difficult in the United States. Among Mexicans, the median family income was $19,300 in 1987. Among Puerto Ricans, it was only $14,600. In part, this reflects the number of families in these groups headed by women, as well as their inability to converse easily in English. More than 19 percent of Mexican-American families were headed by women in 1987; half that group lived in poverty. Fully 43 percent of Puerto Rican families were headed by women, two-thirds of whom lived below the poverty line. Many immigrants from the Caribbean and Central America have similar problems. Many are here illegally. Most are desperately poor.

Though it would be easy to blame Hispanic poverty on the prejudice of European-Americans, it *is* possible for Hispanics to build a place in American society. Latino men born in the United States, fluent in English, earn just as much as men of European descent. But there are very few such people.

Far more than other immigrant populations, Hispanics have clung to their native culture. Only 26 percent of Hispanics are fluent in English, while another 47 percent struggle to cope with the language. More than 2 million adults speak only Spanish. Nearly three in four continue to speak Spanish at home; few but the oldest families in California and New Mexico have completely adopted English. This linguistic loyalty has not served them well.

Hispanics in general come to the United States with severe handicaps when compared with most Asian immigrants. On average,

Mexican immigrants have just six years of schooling, Cubans nine years. Only half of all Hispanics complete high school, compared with nearly 80 percent of the general population (though nearly one-third of those who drop out eventually earn their diplomas).

Because of their sheer numbers, helping poor, ill-educated Hispanic-Americans will be one of the most difficult social problems of the early twenty-first century.

LEGAL DEBATE

The 1990s will also see a growing debate about America's immigration laws, much like that which arose prior to the Immigration and Naturalization Act of 1986. One reason will be that the 1986 law was in large part a failure. Meant to stem the tide of Mexican immigrants, it has served no useful purpose.

By some estimates, up to 10 million illegal immigrants were eligible for American citizenship under the amnesty program established by the Immigration Reform and Control Act of 1986. Only 1.4 million applied before the deadline ran out, 70 percent from Mexico; about a million more have applied for visas as farm workers. But once they have been naturalized, their relatives will be admitted almost automatically, and then their relatives. By the turn of the century, the amnesty program will bring tens of millions more immigrants to the United States.

The reason why is the law that sets basic immigration policy.

Prior to the McCarran-Walter Act of 1952, a rigid quota system governed American immigration; in any given year, immigrants from each country could total no more than one-sixth of 1 percent of the number of American citizens whose forebears had come from that nation. That gave an enormous advantage to Europeans. McCarran-Walter dropped the quotas but retained the bias toward European settlers. It also gave special preference to skilled workers in fields where the United States needed extra hands.

But in 1965 Congress established a new, humanitarian standard for admission: "reunification" of families. Since then, only a few visas have been given to people with desirable skills and to those with guaranteed employment here, but would-be immigrants who had relatives here have received automatic preference. Proponents of the new system argued that it would make little difference in the number or nationality of people immigrating to the United States.

There might be a small wave of Latin Americans at first, a few thousand at most, coming to live with relatives already naturalized. It seems never to have occurred to them that once that first group of immigrants had been naturalized, then *their* relatives would qualify. So would the relatives of refugees admitted to protect them from war or persecution in their native lands. A vast wave of new immigration was inevitable.

In the new debate over immigration law, it will be argued that immigrants take jobs that might be filled by native-born Americans, or by immigrants already here; admitting more people will only cause unemployment. There is little evidence to support that claim. By the end of the century, more than 21 million new jobs will have opened up in the United States. More than 20 percent will be filled by new immigrants—if they have the right education and job skills. If the experience of the 1970s holds true, they will not take jobs from native-born Americans. In that decade, new immigrants took one-third of the jobs created in Southern California and two-thirds of the jobs that appeared in Los Angeles County. Yet unemployment rates in the state fell throughout the decade. And according to one estimate, each working-age legal immigrant allowed to settle in the United States will add $3,000 per year to the Social Security trust fund.

Nonetheless, the United States does need a change. The problem is not how many people immigrate, but who they are. Today, virtually all the nonrefugee immigrants accepted by the United States have relatives already in the country. They need not even be close relatives; cousins receive the same preference as parents and children. Would-be immigrants need not meet any other standard. They need not be educated; they need not have job skills; they need not even be capable of supporting themselves. Some 500,000 non-refugee immigrants were admitted to the United States in 1986. About 400,000 were the relatives of previous immigrants.

Immediately after the 1965 immigration act, nearly all immigrants allowed to enter the United States were admitted because they had desirable occupations or skills. But under the kinship system, fewer new immigrants arrive with an education. Since then, most immigrants have been the in-laws and increasingly distant cousins of that elite group. In the last twenty years, the average educational level of Asian immigrants has fallen by roughly two years. It is dropping still.

We would not argue against letting anyone enter the United States who wishes to do so. It may be difficult to assimilate the poor or poorly educated, but in the long run they will prove a valuable asset to American society. We have seen the truth of that principle many times in the past. The Hmong are quickly demonstrating it today.

The problem is that the poor and uneducated take places that might be filled by the educated and wealthy, who could help solve some of the problems the nation now faces. Some 607,000 permanent settlers were admitted to the United States in 1988. Fewer than 5 percent were admitted for their skills.

And there are many skilled professionals who want American citizenship. One new and potentially valuable source of immigrants is Hong Kong. Only eleven thousand people emigrated from Hong Kong in 1985. Two years later, 25,000 Hong Kong residents left home. Unlike other lands, Hong Kong is not sending out its tired, its poor, its huddled masses. It is the elite who are vacating before their communist landlords regain control of the British colony in 1997. So many are leaving that Hong Kong's employers already are having trouble finding enough engineers, computer programmers, scientists, and teachers. Unfortunately for America, many of these people are going to Australia and Canada rather than to the United States. Both nations give preference to applicants who have needed job skills, and both allow the wealthy to buy citizenship if they will establish a business that provides new jobs. Further, they require shorter waiting periods before immigrants may be naturalized—two years in Australia and three in Canada, compared with five years in the United States. This gives immigrants time to win their citizenship and return to Hong Kong to carry on their established lives until mainland China regains control of the colony.

In 1988, Senator Charles Shumer (D.-N.Y.) sponsored a bill that would have established a "point system" for would-be immigrants. For 55,000 visas each year—out of about 600,000—it would have given preference to English speakers, those with a good education, and those with job skills or experience in high-demand occupations. Another five thousand visas could have been "bought" by investors with $2 million to establish a business that would create at least ten full-time jobs. The measure went nowhere.

Yet the availability of Hong Kong's sorely needed professionals provides a strong argument for making yet another change in American immigration policies. This debate will be repeated many times in the coming years. We suspect that the change will occur before 2000.

THE NEW MAJORITY

With all their numbers, the New Americans already should wield enormous political power, both locally and at the national level. Yet most are still working hard to build new lives, and many are moved by a hard-learned distrust of politicians. To date, few immigrants have shown interest in building influence over the processes of government. That will surely change in the next decade, as Republicans and Democrats each try to gain political advantage by reaching out to potential new voters.

The 1988 elections offered an advance look at the politics of the twenty-first century. In San Francisco, Mayor Art Agnos won his office in part by cultivating Southeast Asian voters. A registration drive shortly before the election brought the total of Vietnamese voters to fifteen thousand. And on the national level, both George Bush and Michael Dukakis worked hard to win the Hispanic vote in key states. Dukakis's fluent Spanish earned him large electoral majorities in Hispanic sections of Texas on Super Tuesday; winning that important state was a major factor in gaining his party's nomination. Bush's son Jeb, also fluent in Spanish and married to a Mexican-American, campaigned hard among Florida's Cuban voters and turned what might otherwise have been a tight primary race into a landslide for his father's then-flagging primary campaign.

Yet they could have had far more influence than that. Only one Hispanic in four voted in California's 1986 elections, in part because many were ineligible. By one estimate, even after the amnesty program of 1986, one-third of California's Hispanic population consists of illegal aliens. Only 59 percent are old enough to vote. And of those who could vote, only half have registered to do so. Among Hispanics, only Florida's Cuban population wields the power its numbers justify—and then some. Florida's non-Hispanic population tends to be relatively apathetic about local politics; the Cubans are very active politically and have taken over much of the power that others have abandoned.

When they do vote, most immigrants vote for Democratic candidates. As a result, nearly all of the three thousand Hispanics who hold public office in the United States are Democrats; so are the great majority of the nation's few Asian-American officials.

First-generation Cuban immigrants are the exception to this rule. Fiercely anticommunist, they shifted en masse to the Republican Party in the 1960s, convinced that the Democrats had become too soft on the Castro regime. More than 70 percent of the Cuban vote today goes to Republicans; led by Cuban voters, nearly half of all Hispanics who voted in the 1984 presidential election cast their ballots for President Reagan. Among second-generation Cuban Americans, party loyalties are changing again, however. More interested in the social policies of their adopted homeland than in anticommunist rhetoric, those in their thirties are slowly returning to the Democratic fold. By the turn of the century, the original Cuban exodus will be little more than a fading memory, the Mariel boatlift will hold its meaning only for an earlier generation, and even the flight of anticommunists from Nicaragua will lie more than a decade in the past. The dedicated conservatism that sways a substantial minority of Hispanic voters into the Republican camp will have lost its power.

In the years to come, the liberalism of the New Americans will be a major force shaping politics in the United States. If the Democratic Party can harness this force, it may at last rebuild a coalition that can win national elections. Yet by focusing on the interests of minorities, rather than on the needs common to all Americans, the party risks alienating its European-American constituents, the largest minority of all. Jesse Jackson's "Rainbow Coalition" campaign succumbed to this problem in the 1984 presidential primaries and only partially overcame it in 1988. Less charismatic leaders may find this conflict even more difficult to conquer. In that case, the Republican Party may retain the White House with only brief interruptions well into the early twenty-first century.

AMERICA GROWS
OLDER

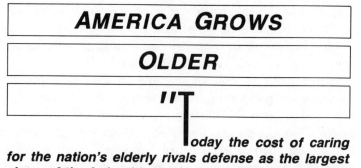

"**T**oday the cost of caring for the nation's elderly rivals defense as the largest share of the federal budget. . . . By 2025, one-third of the budget will go to people over sixty-five, with one-fifth going to defense. Young people will be asking why the budget favors a group that is better off than the rest of the population."*

Every tick of the clock that brings us closer to 2000 also marks one of the biggest changes in society: Americans are growing older. The Baby Boom generation will be entering middle age and approaching its retirement years. The Baby Boomers have set the country's social agenda for several decades: campus protests and political activism in the sixties and seventies have been followed by more private, even narcissistic, concerns in the eighties. As the next century dawns and this dominant generation matures, their aging will bring about an inevitable Gray Revolution.

A quick glance at some statistics will show just how dramatic the age shift is. In 1970, the median age of the American population was less than thirty. Today it is nearing thirty-three, and by 2000, its median age will top thirty-six. The number of Americans over age sixty-five will have increased by more than 50 percent. The eighty-five-and-over age group is the fastest-growing segment of the U.S. population. They now make up 1.2 percent of the population; by 2000, they will be 1.8 percent, or 4.9 million.

Just what this will mean for our economic and social life is still unclear, if only because the scope of the coming transformation is so broad that it is difficult to take them all in at once. Hardly any facet of American society will remain unchanged.

The future labor market offers one obvious example. Service-sector companies will suffer from a severe shortage of entry-level workers aged sixteen to twenty-four years. This group makes up one-fifth of all workers today, but that number will fall to 16 percent by 1995. By the turn of the century, services dedicated to the comfort of the Baby Boom generation, made up of people then in their forties and fifties, will be the nation's largest growth industry, but there may be too few working-age people to run such personal services.

The effects on American politics and political and social policy may well be even more profound. In the worst and most likely case, the changing composition of society will bring us uncomfortably close to a "war between the generations." As society increasingly is dominated by the elderly, aging Baby Boomers will own an ever greater share of the nation's wealth. Yet more and more tax money will be earmarked for Social Security, Medicare, and many new programs for the aged. That money will come from a much smaller generation of young people. Young and old will inevitably compete—and struggle—over society's resources.

No matter how we resolve this conflict, and many others like it, one thing is clear: the graying of America will drastically change the way we live, work, and play in the next century.

When we think about the elderly, we often think of illness, nursing homes, and hospitals. In fact, this image is largely obsolete. Older people are healthier now than they've ever been and will soon be healthier yet. Of course, there are still old-age diseases that have no cure, but many cures are on the way. New drugs and radical types of surgery will control and counter the effects of these diseases. The Baby Boomers have learned the power of preventive medicine, and those habits will help assure a healthier old age. They will be the healthiest generation in history.

The aged of the eighties and nineties are no stodgy homebodies. In fact, this group is quite adventurous. Consumer research shows that today's seniors see themselves as ten to fifteen years younger than their chronological age. And recent marketing studies show that adults over fifty are leading ever more active lives filled with exercise, travel, and entertainment. As more and more older Americans come to prefer work to full retirement—it will happen when the retirement age is raised to seventy in order to cut the cost of Social Security entitlement programs—we can expect a permanent group of perenially young elderlies to emerge.

Family life will be challenged as more Americans are required to care for their aged relatives. Today, only 5 percent of those sixty-five or older end up living in institutions, primarily nursing homes. Although most older people are healthy and independent, about 25 percent need some help with the routine of daily life. In 1985, 90 percent of the elderly cared for themselves; by 2001 this will decrease to 80 percent simply because the composition of the elderly will change to include more "old-old" people. This means that in the future, more and more family members will be forced, sometimes unwillingly, to play a part in caring for aged relatives—and since life expectancy is increasing, this may mean having to care for them for fifteen years or more.

We will see a significant increase in the number of three-generation households. This places a lot of stress on all family members. Parent-child roles sometimes become reversed, much to the resentment of both parties. Sometimes the elderly feel the loss of control and take steps to regain it. The resulting power struggle can destroy family ties that have survived for decades. Communication between the generations will never have been so important.

The aging of America will present challenges just as thorny for society at large. As America spends so many resources on the nation's elderly, it may find itself unable to pay for such high-priority items as education of the young and the funding of research into new technologies. If this happens, American industry's ability to compete in world markets will diminish. Its fading manufacturing sector experienced a virtual renaissance in the 1980s, but the aging society may cause it to decline once again as manufacturing companies are faced with the cost of supporting greater numbers of retirees. Fewer active workers will have to foot the pension bill for more retirees. Some estimates put the total unfunded liabilities of America's private health-care plans over the $2-trillion mark. The next generation of labor and management will ultimately pay the bill, unless productivity increases match the aging of the population.

One solution to this problem is to change the age of retirement.

The United States simply cannot afford to let people retire at 65, nor can it support the trend toward early retirement. Instead, we believe older workers will delay retirement or work part-time. They will take on second and even third careers. They will be able to do so because they will be healthier, and they will want to, because it will be financially necessary to work. There is a side benefit: studies show that the working elderly seem to adjust to aging better than those who retire early.

NEW BUSINESS TO SERVE THE ELDERLY

We are talking about a big, powerful cohort when we speak of the elderly. The sixty million Americans over fifty already control more than half of the nation's assets and discretionary income; they are by far the richest segment of the population. In 1960, 35 percent of Americans over sixty-five had incomes below poverty level; today that percentage has fallen to 12.4 percent, lower than for any other age group.

Businesses that anticipate the aging society will find vast new markets for their products. But that requires a profound rethinking of the way in which companies approach their customers. Marketers have been fixed on the youth culture of the past two decades; this will no longer work in an aging society. Advertising will have to feature mature models and mature sales talk to appeal to this group. Strategies must also change because older consumers are wiser consumers. They are not so interested in trendiness or glitz; they want to know that they are buying quality, and they like guarantees. The elderly can be brand-loyal, but they are not blind to other, better products. Marketers who assume that older people will not switch to their products simply do not know how to court them. The elderly are less willing to take risks, but they are not as rigid as some believe; they just want a little more security than their younger counterparts.

Products and buildings will also have to be redesigned to fit the aging body. Levers will replace doorknobs, and there will be more elevators, escalators, and ramps. Church pews will be made more comfortable. Maneuverability will be especially important for the active elderly. Cars will be redesigned for older drivers: chairs that swivel 90 degrees and tilt will ease entry and exit; the instrument panel will have larger print to make it easier to read. And, the person who designs the first comfortable wheelchair will be a millionaire many times over.

Entertainment will change to reflect the concerns and the interests of an aging society. Movies will have themes about aging, and we will see more TV sitcoms like "The Golden Girls." Since most older people sleep less than younger people, TV's midnight hours will no longer be the domain of sleazy talk shows and B-movies. What will the new old be reading? There will be a considerable number of new magazines like *Modern Maturity,* which already has a larger reader audience than *Reader's Digest* or *TV Guide.* Women's magazines for those forty years of age or older, such as *Lear's,* will also move into this lucrative market.

Convenience Comes of Age

How will the aging of the population affect the trend toward convenience? Baby Boomers will continue to opt for speed; the $50-billion market for takeout food is expected to double. But, once consumers hit a certain age, time is no longer the critical factor. Access and ease of use become much more important. The need is not for products and services that save time or replace an inconvenient activity (such as automatic teller machines), but for products and services that are easy to use or more enjoyable, or actually create activity.

The elderly are less mobile than the rest of the population, so they, as much as time-starved working couples, will appreciate computer systems that allow you to shop at home. "Prodigy," a system created jointly by Sears and IBM, is one such system. All you need is a personal computer, a modem, and a subscription to be able to shop at K mart or Neiman-Marcus, conduct your banking, buy your stocks, book airline reservations, or check movie listings from the comfort of your home.

Electronic newspapers are on their way, too, and for similar reasons. Think for a moment of arthritic hands and arms trying to hold up clumsy newspapers, and tired eyes straining to read small-type stories; then think how much easier it would be for an elderly person to have a newspaper delivered electronically, with large-print type. All that person would have to do is flip a switch to turn the computer on, call up "newspaper," sit down in a comfortable chair, and read the news. These electronic services will even be able to custom-design a newspaper for you by selecting stories that would interest you, varying the size of the headlines according to your degree of interest.

Again, making a success of these and other services for the elderly will require a significant change in the way business approaches its customers. Before older customers can sign on to these services, their homes must be equipped with computers. And, computer companies must realize that they can't just sell a computer to older people; markets must teach older buyers how to use complex products so they feel comfortable with them. If the companies do not make this extra effort, they will be writing off a potentially lucrative market, and many high-tech services like the electronic newspaper will be stillborn.

Travel

The hospitality industry will be one of the biggest winners in the coming decades. The elderly, after all, have the time—and the money—to travel the globe. Fully 80 percent of all luxury travel in America is purchased by people over fifty-five. However, some segments of the industry have not been quick to realize this. Seniors are renting cars, for example, but car-rental companies have done little to acknowledge this. As the population ages, such companies could offer deals in which air travelers would not have to get to the rental car lot, but instead a rental car employee would come to them, and even pick up their luggage and put it in the trunk. Other segments of the hospitality industry have recognized the trend toward an aging society. Travelers over sixty pay reduced fares on most airlines, and they seldom pay full price in many large hotel chains. By the late 1990s, bargain rates and special services for the aged will be the rule throughout the travel industry.

The Health-Care Industry

The elderly are also the biggest spenders on health care. Those over eighty-five—the fastest-growing demographic group in the country—suffer more severe disabilities and are more chronically ill than all the other elderly put together. Today, one in five lives in a nursing home or a hospital. Peter Francese, founder of *American Demographics,* estimates that the United States will need a new hundred-bed nursing facility every day for the next twelve years!

For the well-to-do, more comfortable facilities are beginning to appear. Marriott, the big hotel chain, will start building its third high-rise retirement community outside Washington, D.C. This particular community, which is aiming for a completion date in the fall of 1990, will be targeted at the luxury market, but Marriott itself recognizes that the lower-income end of the market is where the major growth will take place. The rich can afford to hire nurses to come and take care of them in their own homes; the less-well-off will have to find somewhere to live as they become less self-sufficient.

In the next few decades, the elderly will have a variety of facilities to choose from. By 2001, for-profit nursing-home chains will be growing, some at a rate of over 2,500 beds per year. Most residents will pay their own way, but 30 percent will be Medicaid patients and 9 percent will be on Medicare, neither of which covers full costs. There will still be some private nursing-home operators, but nearly half will be part of large corporations. These will provide different levels of care facilities—sheltered communities and live-in residences with some nursing care, as well as senior-citizen communities. Small group homes will accommodate twelve to twenty-four residents who need help bathing, grooming, dressing, eating, and housekeeping, but who don't need nursing attention; residents will help care for each other. The benefits include reduced costs and better recovery rates. Most important, patients have a higher quality of life in this more homelike environment.

Well before 2000, Medicaid will be amended to pay for comprehensive home care. States will be required to set up screening mechanisms for such care. People will be admitted to nursing homes only if a screening team finds home care to be inappropriate or impossible. This will result in great cost savings, since home care is much more economical than a nursing home. Insurance companies will market comprehensive home care along with long-term care policies; policies sold to supplement Medicare will include significant home-care benefits.

Health resource centers staffed by senior citizens on a volunteer basis will spring up all over the country. They will provide free phone-in taped services with information on hundreds of health topics. There will be medical libraries for laypeople, monthly newsletters on health facts for consumers, and bookstores. The centers will sponsor exercise classes, workshops, and seminars on specific health topics, groups for seniors who wish to quit smoking, to diet, to learn to handle stress and bereavement, and so on.

Scientific research will also change *how* we grow older. By 2025, most of the major mysteries of the aging process will have been solved. Anti-aging products will supply substances that the aging body needs and that counteract damaging materials it produces. Despite this, barring some unpredictable theoretical breakthrough, we will all have to face death sooner or later—increasingly later, as it turns out. For that reason, right-to-die legislation will assure the legitimacy of "living wills" that request that no extraordinary medical measures be taken after a certain point in a patient's decline. Physicians who comply with them will no longer have to fear legal consequences.

INCREASE IN D B C (DRIVING BEYOND COMPETENCY) CHARGES

Physical infirmities are dangerous behind the wheel, and the huge Baby Boom generation will begin to suffer from more of them each year as the next century progresses. As driving ability declines, the number of traffic accidents in the United States is likely to rise dramatically. In order to ensure that its roads are safe, American society will have to compromise with some of its age-discrimination laws, even at the risk of incurring the wrath of politically powerful elderly voters. Licensing bodies will establish stricter standards for vision, medical, and road tests for senior citizens renewing their licenses. In some cases, licenses will have to be revoked, suspended, or subjected to certain restrictions, such as limiting driving to daylight hours. One solution is to teach elderly drivers to compensate for physical liabilities that come with age. The American Association of Retired Persons (AARP) already offers a course that does this. New types of cars and computerized traffic regulation may help.

These innovations will be more important in the next few decades because of the growing trend toward delayed retirement. Although many of the elderly will prefer to work out of their own homes once they master the computer, many more will be working in service jobs that put them in contact with people. To get to the people, they will have to drive.

A NATION OF SAVERS?

In past generations, people saved more as they grew older. This may not happen with the Baby Boom generation. A person's spending pattern throughout life is often formed in the first few years in the workforce, and the Baby Boomers began working in a period of postwar prosperity. Little short of a depression is likely to change the free-spending ways they learned in the 1960s. Even if they do not end up saving more of their total income, they will give the financial services industry a boost as they figure out how to finance increasingly expensive college educations for their children while at the same time planning for their own retirements.

A vast reservoir of untapped equity lies in the homes of the elderly and many may find themselves house-rich but cash-poor—wealthy in their assets but unable to find the spending money required for a comfortable life. To help along, we will witness increasingly innovative ways to free equity for productive ends. In one clear trend, we will see more "reverse mortgages." Under this plan, a lender buys the house for a lump sum. The couple living in the house pays a fixed rent each month and receives annuities. This will help get the resources of the elderly into the marketplace. If Boomers tend to borrow less and save more, reverse mortgages and similar arrangements could provide American business with more and cheaper capital.

THE WAR BETWEEN GENERATIONS

The generations that coexist in 2000 will face political and social clashes unlike anything seen in America to date. (The collision between generational values is further discussed in Chapter 18. Here we restrict ourselves to the practical issues that divide the nation's mature adults from the elderly.)

The cause will be the vast and growing cost of federal benefits for the elderly. In 1940, only 2 percent of the federal dollar was spent on those over sixty-five; in 1970, 20 percent; in 1989, 27 percent; and by 2001, this number will be close to 30 percent. Today the cost of caring for the nation's elderly rivals defense as the largest share of the federal budget. According to official forecasts of spending patterns, by 2025, one-third of the budget will go to people over age sixty-five, with one-fifth going to defense. Young people will be asking why government benefits favor a group that is better off than other segments of the population, while relatively needy working-age Americans are forced to fit the bill. After all, in 1986, only 12.4 percent of all senior citizens fit the official description of "poor," while 13.8 percent of all persons under sixty-five were considered poor—and those figures include only cash income. When other forms of income, such as Medicare, are included in the calculations, only 3 percent of the elderly qualify as poor, versus 9.8 percent of the rest of the population.

Is it fair that retired people today receive Social Security benefits that are two to five times what they and their employers contributed in payroll taxes, plus interest earned? Is it fair that even today Washington spends eleven times as much on each senior citizen as it does on each child? By 2000, such questions will form the core of an increasingly bitter public debate.

The root of the problem is that Social Security no longer works the way it was intended to. When the system was first set up, planners sold it as a kind of insurance for old age. During our working years, we would pay part of our income into the system; after retirement, we would draw it out again to supplement whatever pensions we received from our former employers. In those days, private pensions were rare, so the chances were that Social Security would be the sole means of support.

It hasn't worked out that way. In 1982 the average Social Security recipient received every cent that he and his employers had paid into the system in only four years. For the rest of his life, he will be receiving money taken directly from the pockets of today's workers, each of whom believes he is paying his Social Security tax into his own retirement fund.

Just past the turn of the century, the first crop of the giant Baby Boom generation will be nearing a comfortable retirement. With pension plans and Social Security to support them, and a catastrophic-illness plan, which will be enacted to protect them if they become seriously ill, they will be able to enjoy frequent travel, luxurious retirement condominiums, and all the trappings of the good life that decades of advertising have taught them to want.

Unfortunately, their Social Security and health costs will be paid for by the smaller generation that follows them. It is a privilege the young are unlikely to appreciate. As the turn of the century nears, the Baby Bust generation will be hit with huge tax increases needed to support its parents. This is a sure recipe for a political battle between the two age groups. For the moment, any talk of trouble in the Social Security program seems almost as improbable as most Washington officials like to pretend it is. Today, as a result of the 1983 overhaul of the system, and given the low birthrates of the 1930s and early 1940s, the number of retirees and their dependents will remain small for the next few decades. The Social Security system continues to have a large surplus, and the government takes in a net $110 million a day, the difference between what it collects in Social Security payroll taxes and payments to retirees and disabled workers. Projections show that the annual surpluses will reach $500 million a day by 2000.

In fact, the surplus in the Social Security fund is masking the real magnitude of the federal budget deficit. This is because the surplus is still figured into the budget, although it is untouchable because it is independent of the budget. The surpluses reduce the federal budget deficit, even though these funds are by law assigned to specific trust funds. In 2030—while the Baby Boom generation still makes up a disproportionate share of the American populace—the current surplus in the Social Security trust fund will run out, and taxpayers will suddenly face the need to pay off both Social Security pensions and a huge federal deficit. Through Social Security, Medicare, and numerous off-budget loan-guarantee programs, the federal government is incurring future obligations for which it has no capital or reserves. This means that the next generation of taxpayers is expected to pay up as the debts come due. America is borrowing heavily from the future.

The resulting conflict between the young and the old, between taxpayers and tax recipients, will be a key feature of domestic government policy no later than in the late 1990s. It is one problem that will not be resolved at the turn of the century.

It is a conflict in which the young may be overmatched, for the nation's elderly already represent a powerful political force. With 28 million members, the AARP is the largest organization of any kind anywhere in the world. Even today, applications for membership are pouring in at an unprecedented eight thousand a day. In the early 1980s, the AARP started to take strong public stances on public policy issues affecting the elderly.

A higher proportion of the elderly than of young people vote in elections. By 2001, close to 35 percent of the Senate and over 50 percent of the House of Representatives will be sixty-five or older. The Supreme Court, already decidedly conservative after President Reagan's appointments, may be downright reactionary by then. The impact upon legislation affecting or benefiting the elderly will be unprecedented.

Yet the only way the United States can resolve its coming intergenerational war is to cut the cost of entitlement programs for the elderly. One clear necessity is to raise the age of eligibility for Medicare to seventy from the current sixty-five. This is far less unfair than it sounds. Since Medicare's birth in 1965, our life expectancy has increased seven years, from 70.2 to 77 in 1990. Why not tack two to five years onto Medicare eligibility at the other end?

"Means testing" is another unpleasant necessity to be enacted in the coming decade. For those whose annual incomes are less than $30,000, Medicare will pay all hospital benefits. By 2000, those with incomes over $30,000 will share the costs on an increasing, sliding scale with catastrophic coverage kicking in above a certain upper limit. Portions of the value of a Medicare coverage will be taxable. Similar measures will cut the cost of caring for the nation's 28 million veterans. Those with incomes over $30,000 whose ailments are not related to their military service will pay part of the cost of treatments at VA hospitals.

This will create a new demand for private health insurance, and many companies will soon enter the long-term-care insurance market. In 1973 the first such policy was written; by 1990 this will be a $5-billion business. Annual premiums are based on a person's age, increasing as one gets older. There will be more TLC (Term Life Care) accounts, which are tax-deferred savings accounts designated specifically for long-term health care and life maintenance, specifically to be used for home care, nursing facilities, or hospice services. Like an IRA account, an individual will contribute yearly and can make withdrawals before age seventy.

Though surpluses in the Social Security fund are illusory, because the excess revenues collected are not placed in a separate trust fund, they offer several opportunities to shore up the federal budget. Today the Treasury lends them to government agencies for consumption. In effect, the government borrows from the trust funds to cover current spending. There are better ideas.

One would be to cut the deficit by using some of this surplus, and lending the rest to the federal government to cut the debt. Michael J. Boskin, author of *Too Many Promises: The Uncertain Future of Social Security,* suggests a plan that would make the Social Security system more like a pension system, with benefits closely linked to contributions. In such a system, a separate "means-tested" program, funded by general revenues, would provide income to the elderly poor.

John L. Makin, an economist at the American Enterprise Institute, proposes that the United States eliminate Social Security over a period of forty years, replacing it with a welfare program for the minority who are truly poor. People could use the savings from the payroll tax to finance their own retirements. Or perhaps Congress could just cut the payroll tax to a more manageable rate, meanwhile requiring that the savings be placed in some new form of individual retirement account.

Three economists at the Brookings Institution have proposed keeping the big surplus, but not using it to balance the budget. Their ingenious plan is to use some of the money to retire the old debt. For example, when a U.S. Treasury bond held by an insurance company came due, the Treasury would pay off the company rather than rolling over the bond. The insurance company would then most likely invest the money in the private sector, which would stimulate the economy and pump up investment. The trust funds would still be holding an IOU from the government, which would still have to raise taxes to pay off the surplus fund. But workers might not object to higher taxes because productivity and wages would be rising alongside them owing to the boost given to capital formation.

If the system remains the way it is, the younger generation will eventually be called upon to support more people. They will be ill-equipped to bear the heavy responsibility.

The breaking point may be close at hand. One of the three Social Security funds is about to spring a leak. Two of the funds are surplus storehouses: the old age and survivor's insurance fund and the disability insurance fund. The third fund, which covers hospital stays for the elderly and disabled for up to sixty days, is scheduled to go bankrupt at the end of the century. Projections for 2005 show that the fund will at that time be running a deficit of $440 billion. A war between the generations may be coming sooner than we think.

A NATION OF

DUNCES?

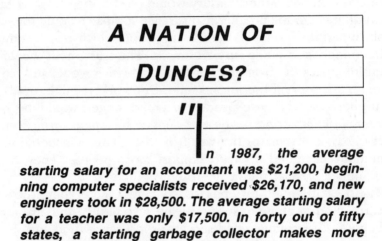

"In 1987, the average starting salary for an accountant was $21,200, beginning computer specialists received $26,170, and new engineers took in $28,500. The average starting salary for a teacher was only $17,500. In forty out of fifty states, a starting garbage collector makes more money than an entry-level teacher."

By 2000, American schools will have changed dramatically, and so will our relationship to them. On the outside, most will still be the same brick-and-glass structures we're familiar with, but half of these buildings will be nearing seventy-five years old. On the inside, the changes will be clear: classrooms will be fully equipped with personal computers and other high-tech teaching aids. They will also be filled with people, twenty-four hours a day, every day but Thanksgiving, Christmas, and Hannukah. Many of these people—students and teachers alike—will be adults for whom school today is little more than a fading memory. The United States will be asking far more of its schools twelve years from now, and giving them more as well.

We have all heard the scare stories about the crisis in American schools. America, it is said, has lost the ability to educate its children; high schools turn out semiliterate young adults grossly ill-prepared to deal with the technological world in which they must soon make their way. Unfortunately, most of the charges are true. Though there are occasional bright spots in America's school systems, the need for educational reform is beyond question one of the most pressing problems to be solved by 2000.

In most areas, the first experiments in reconstruction have already begun. At the turn of the next century, America's school systems will be on the road to recovery. Literacy rates will be up. SAT scores will be up. Dropout rates will be down. This is not to say America will have solved all the problems of its educational system. They are too many and too grave and have been building for far too long to eliminate them in a single decade. But by 2000 it will have made a good beginning.

Before we look at the solutions to America's educational deficiencies, let's take a brief inventory of the problem.

There is all too much evidence that American schools are failing many students. In 1982, American eighth-graders taking a standardized math test answered only 46 percent of the questions correctly, which put them in the bottom half of the eleven nations competing. (Japanese children got 64 percent correct.) That same year, the top 5 percent of twelfth-graders from nine developed countries, students who had taken advanced math courses, took standardized tests of algebra and calculus; America's best and brightest came in dead last. Most recently, *The Mathematics Report Card,* the 1988 quadrennial report of the National Assessment of Educational Progress, revealed that of high-school seniors taking college preparatory courses in math, only 6 percent could handle multistep problems. A sample: "Christine borrowed $850 for one year from the Friendly Finance Company. If she paid 12 percent simple interest on the loan, what was the total amount she repaid?" (The answer is $952.)

The failure is not limited to subjects such as math. Other studies, such as *What Do Our 17-Year-Olds Know?* (by Chester E. Finn, Jr. and Diane Ravage, 1987), have shown that only one high-school junior in five can write a comprehensible note applying for a summer job; that among high-school seniors, fewer than one-third know to within fifty years when the Civil War took place, one in three do not know that Columbus discovered America before 1750, and barely half know that during the Second World War, Russia failed to invade the yet-unfounded nation of Israel! Among young adults, one government-sponsored study found, well under 40 percent can understand an average *New York Times* article or figure out their change when paying for lunch, and only 20 percent can understand a bus schedule.

And by today's standards, those are almost success stories. Nearly 1 million high-school students drop out each year—about 30 percent of the total, on average, throughout the United States—and in some school districts the dropout rate exceeds 50 percent. Perhaps 700,000 more students in each class finish out their twelve years hardly able to read their own diplomas. At that rate, by 2000, the literacy rate in America may be as low as 30 percent.

Avoiding that educational fate will be even more difficult than it sounds, because the student body is changing rapidly. Educational performance is at its worst among the poor and minority groups, and minorities are by far the fastest-growing segment of society. In the next twelve years, over two million black children and over three million Hispanics under fourteen years will enter the school population. They will be joined by many students for whom English is a second language. By the time the Class of 2000 graduates from high school, minorities will dominate the school population in fifty-three major American cities. All these groups traditionally require more individual attention from teachers if they are to succeed in school.

And solving the problems of conventional education is only one-half of the task to be accomplished in the next twelve years. America will also need a much stronger system of vocational education if it is to meet the challenge of the years to come.

Again, the problem grows from the changing nature of society at large. The massive growth of technology in the coming decades will render many careers obsolete, not in decades, as in the past, but in a few years. (We will return to this topic later in this book.) Almost everyone will have to face the task of training for an entirely new job at one point in his or her career. Even today, most people change occupations three times during their working lives. On average, the next generation of workers will have to make no fewer than five complete job changes in a lifetime, not counting the multiple tasks (which will also be changing) associated with each respective job.

In many cases, one job will evolve slowly into the next. One worker might begin his career as a computer programmer at one company and graduate into a systems analyst for another employer. From there he could move on to teach corporate training courses. With that background he might build a part-time career as a technical writer, then strike out as a full-time free-lancer and slowly broaden his practice to general-interest journalism.

Other careers will be more diverse. Many will begin by working in a local service business by day and studying at night for another trade. When the time comes, the switch from, say, shoe salesman to medical-laboratory technician could be instantaneous. When further automation makes that training obsolete, rather than remain in health care, our technician may decide to polish up his old sales experience and go into real estate. That experience may lead to a business of his own. Finally, at what we now think of as retirement age, many people will reenter school yet again, this time teaching others what they have learned.

This is a mandate for continuous retraining. Today, schools offer adult education as a community service or in the hope of earning sorely needed revenue. In the future, they will be teaching adults because they haven't any choice. As a society, America will add that chore to drug and sex education and the hundred other things now expected of schools beyond the traditional three R's. Many public schools will be open around the clock, retraining adults from 4:00 P.M. to midnight and renting out their costly computer and communications systems to local industry during the graveyard shift.

That new business will be welcome, because many school systems are now operating far under their capacity. In the school year that began in September 1969, American grammar and high schools enrolled 45.6 million students; by 1985 the school population had fallen to 39.5 million, a loss of 7.1 million students. It is shrinking still. The buildings that communities erected in the 1950s and 1960s to cope with the Baby Boom generation have turned into costly anachronisms in the Baby Bust.

By the turn of the century, vocational training will be just as crucial as the traditional pre-college program. If schools fail to turn out well-educated high-school and college graduates, more and more young people will find themselves unqualified even to study for any meaningful career. If schools fail to give job-specific training, they will continue to turn their graduates out onto the street unable to earn a living wage, while millions of jobs go begging for skilled people to fill them. If schools fail to retrain adults for the growing technical demands of their jobs, millions of conscientious workers will find their careers cut short, and the work they should have done will be exported to countries like Japan and Taiwan, where educational systems definitely are up to the task. The result would be a sharp contraction in job opportunities, chronic unemployment on a scale not yet seen in this country, and a much lower national standard of living.

Fortunately, American schools can provide top-quality education when they make the effort to do so. They did so in 1957 and 1958, when America's leadership in science and math appeared imperiled by the Soviet Union's triumph with Sputnik. Today the proof can be seen not only in affluent suburbs, but in some cities.

For just one example, look to Fairfax, Virginia, a community of about 350,000. Mantua Elementary School seems quite ordinary on the outside. But enter its tiled halls, and you will find yourself surrounded by multicolored posters depicting cultural highlights of Kuwait—all written in Arabic. Others appear in languages ranging from German to Vietnamese—and all are readily understood by children who are eight or nine years old. Mantua's children "speak" sign language as well. Third-grade classes are well stocked with desktop computers, and there is a separate room for video equipment. Parents are in the school constantly, working as teachers' aides and special tutors.

While many schools can barely cope with the core curriculum, Mantua offers specialized classes for almost any need. There are classrooms filled with high-technology devices to aid handicapped students. Gifted students attend programs for the uncommonly talented. At one end of the building, a child-care center for school-age children continues the educational process long after traditional school hours have ended.

Mantua's educational system works. The school's average students rank far higher than the national average, and all the specialized programs manage to extract top grades from students who in many cases might be expected to fail. Similar programs are available—and successful—in places as geographically diverse as Manhattan and Ventura, California.

Well-run public schools can also provide vocational training that is a significant improvement over the wood and auto-shop courses of twenty and thirty years ago. In Florida, the state vocational-school system has trained thousands of microelectronic technicians and computer programmers, each ready to begin a productive career on graduation day. As a result, IBM, General Electric, and dozens of smaller companies have made Florida's Route 4, from Orlando to Tampa/St. Petersburg, one of the nation's busiest centers of artificial-intelligence research.

Yet the school system today is clearly overburdened, even by the traditional demands placed on it. How will it bring quality education to all members of the classes of 2000? How will it cope with the pressure of the impoverished inner-city schools, or the needs of the bilingual? And what will America do about the growing demand for adult education in the years to come? An even dozen measures come to mind. Most are embarrassingly simple. Most will be part of American life in the year 2000.

RAISE SCHOOL BUDGETS

For a start, if we really want quality education in the United States, we have to be willing to pay for it. In recent years, we haven't been. Even after the National Commission on Excellence in Education published its landmark report, *A Nation at Risk,* in 1983, the Reagan administration never asked for a significant increase in federal aid to education. In fact, the White House attempted to cut the national education budget by over $10 billion, after inflation. Congress always restored most of those cuts, so that federal education spending still totaled about $19.5 billion in 1986. Yet by 1988 the federal government was actually spending about 14 percent less for education (in constant dollars) than it had five years earlier.

Given such circumstances, it is no surprise that teachers are still dramatically underpaid when compared with other professions that require a college education. In 1987, the average starting salary for an accountant was $21,200, beginning computer specialists received $26,170, and new engineers took in $28,500. The average starting salary for a teacher was only $17,500. In forty out of fifty states, a starting garbage collector makes more money than a starting teacher.

Yet this problem is gradually waning. Since 1983, the average teacher's salary nationwide has risen from about $20,700 to $28,000. In Bucks County, Pennsylvania, starting salaries for a nine- or ten-month educational year have risen to as much as $21,600; experienced teachers there earn up to $50,000. In Connecticut, as a result of a $300-million education grant from the state legislature, average starting salaries for new teachers have risen from $15,200 in 1986 to $22,500 this year; salaries for those with a master's degree and years of experience have gone from $30,000 to $42,150.

Predictably, school systems that pay their educators well have been finding it a lot easier to attract the teachers they need than have localities where teachers effectively take a vow of poverty. It is a lesson that other school systems are learning. By 2000, the disparity between teachers' salaries and those of other college-trained professionals should have fallen to 10 percent and be shrinking still further.

Those who choose to remain on a nine-month schedule will take home about 90 percent of an average year's salary.

HIRE MORE TEACHERS

The big advantage that schools like Mantua enjoy over less successful institutions is not their specialized programs, but the fact that their students are drawn largely from traditional, upper-middle-class families where both parents are available and both are actively interested in the child's education. Where broken homes are the rule, and parents themselves have little respect for education, teachers must provide the individual attention that parents do not. In crowded classrooms, they can't do it. The answer is to cut classes from an average of 17.8 students down to ten students. If educators have their way, classes will be smaller in 2000.

Unfortunately, there will *not* be nearly enough new teachers available to carry out the programs that our best educators now envision. In 1970, one high-school senior in five went on to major in education. By 1987, the figure had fallen to less than one in eight. Only 8 percent of college freshmen now say they are interested in a teaching career; on average, only half of them will actually become teachers, and half of *them* will abandon the classroom within seven years.

And there is reason to wonder just how good those teachers will be at their jobs. Because teaching has become such an ill-paid, low-prestige field, teachers' colleges simply can't recruit the best students. SAT scores of high school students who plan a teaching career average as much as forty points lower than those of students headed toward other professions.

Worse, the painful fact is that after receiving their education degrees, few of those new teachers actually know anything worth passing on to students. Too many college education departments are so wedded to their classes in teaching methods and applied child psychology that they neglect or ignore the core subjects that their graduates are supposed to teach. Thus, in Massachusetts, home of Harvard and MIT, only one elementary-school teacher in five has taken any college-level math or science.

If college teacher-training programs were the only source of educators, by the turn of the century American schools would face a shortage of nearly a million new teachers. Even as student populations shrink, school systems all over the country would find themselves with larger, more crowded classrooms. Individual attention for each student, already a distant goal, will be no more than a forlorn wish. High school teachers, and even those in grammar schools, would be forced to lecture their students in overcrowded classrooms. SAT scores and performance on course-specific achievement tests would plunge as a result. Fortunately, there is an alternative.

RECRUIT TEACHERS FROM OUTSIDE

From the Hancock Preschool in Hancock, New Hampshire (population 1,500), to the Hudson Elementary School in New York City's Greenwich Village, schools across the country have established volunteer programs for community members eager to help with their childrens' education. Parents and other interested adults most often act as teachers' aides, freeing teachers to spend more of their time giving individual attention to students who need it. The best volunteers—often people who worked as teachers themselves before starting their own families—take on individual tutoring of problem students. This is one obvious and successful way to stretch an inadequate supply of new teachers. By 2000, as many as one American adult in five will be volunteering some of his or her time to help out in local schools.

For more-technical subjects, industry offers a huge new supply of potential teachers, most of whom know more about their fields than any graduate of a teachers' college can. So get practicing chemists to teach chemistry, accountants to teach arithmetic, and so on. Give them a few courses in educational techniques if need be, but start by making sure that would-be teachers actually know their subjects.

Polaroid Corporation has made the recruiting process easy for school districts in Massachusetts. The company's Project Bridge pays up to ten Polaroid employees each year to become math or science teachers. Participants attend a year-long teacher-certification program at Harvard University or Lesley College, in Cambridge, Massachusetts. While in training, they receive their full salaries from Polaroid, and the company picks up the tab for tuition, books, and other expenses.

New Jersey has just begun to experiment with accrediting teachers who possess college degrees and a good knowledge of their subjects, but lack the educational courses that most school systems require. Recruits are allowed to teach while taking a minimum of educational courses required for permanent certification. The plan not only offers to cure a growing teacher shortage in the state, but also exposes students to the practical work experience their teachers carry over from former careers.

We believe that this program will have proved to be a dramatic success well before 2000. By then, it will have been copied all over the country.

COMPUTERIZE

Computer-aided learning programs are already replacing drill books; as software improves, they will begin to replace some kinds of textbooks as well. The best such programs already include primitive forms of artificial intelligence that can diagnose the student's learning deficiencies and tailor instruction to compensate for them.

"We can put thirty computers in a room, and they will go as fast or slow as each child needs; the child controls it," observes Congressman James Scheuer (D.-N.Y.) "He has an equal and comfortable relationship, building his morale and self-esteem, which can only enhance the learning process."

If it turns out that the United States faces a teacher shortage in the 1990s and beyond, computerized instruction will be the only hope of making up the deficit. Students will spend up to an hour a day in class sitting at their terminals, working on math problems or practicing foreign-language vocabulary and grammar, guided by computer programs that can recognize their weaknesses faster than most human teachers could. The result may not be as good as what might be obtained by having highly skilled, caring human beings give each student hours of personal attention, but it is a lot easier to achieve, and it will be a big improvement over today's situation. It should be easy to sell this notion to taxpayers; in a survey of parents at Mantua School, fully two-thirds cited computers as among the most important topics their kindergarteners should learn about in school. But making this transition won't be cheap. In the last two hundred years the United States has spent a total of $1 billion on textbooks. By 1990, it already will have spent $1 billion on computerized learning. Two-thirds of that will have been spent by affluent parents for their own children.

If public school systems fail to develop their own programs, the less affluent will inevitably suffer an irreparable educational disadvantage. Children of wealthy families will learn the computer skills they need to earn a living in an increasingly technological society. Children of poor families, unable to afford computers at home and without access to them in the schools, will form a permanently unemployable underclass.

WORK LONGER HOURS

In any field, you can get more work done in eight hours than in six, in ten days than in seven. Japan's school year consists of 240 eight-hour days. America's averages 180 days of about six and a half hours. It is no surprise that Japanese high-school students score two or three years ahead of ours on standardized achievement tests; by high school, they have spent over two more American-style abbreviated years in school than our students have. No wonder Japanese manufacturers can train high school graduates in Tokyo to handle complex statistical quality-control techniques in a few hours, but find that their American factories must hire a mathematician with a master's degree.

By 2000, most school systems will at least split the difference; students in grammar school and high school can look forward to spending 210 seven-hour days in the classroom per year.

LET TEACHERS TEACH...

So far, we have dealt with money issues. It will cost a lot to hire more teachers, buy computers for their classrooms, and keep them all at work for an extra month each year. But it is clear that simply throwing money at the education problem will not clean up the mess. Though educational spending has fallen in real terms, America still pays about $185 billion per year for grade schools and high schools and another $125 billion for colleges and universities—in all, significantly more than the national defense budget. The nation is not getting its money's worth.

In fact, a cash crunch is far from the only problem in our schools. The state of New Hampshire proves it. Voters there are not very fond of taxes, so legislators there have never dared to enact a state income tax, a sales tax, or any of the other broadly based revenue measures that keep other states barely afloat. So New Hampshire's per capita education budget is one of the lowest in the country. Yet its students regularly turn in average SAT scores among the highest in the nation, more of them go on to college than in most other states, and, once there, fewer of them drop out.

To a great extent, Granite State parents get the credit. New Hampshire is small and relatively homogeneous, with a strong tradition of town meetings and local control of public institutions. Old-time values still hold force among its mostly white, mostly unbroken families, and respect for education remains one of the strongest of those values. Like children in Japan, and unlike too many children in America's inner cities, most young New Hampshirites are watched over by parents who make sure that homework gets done and that local school systems meet educational standards in the core curriculum that faded from too many other states thirty years ago. So ineffective teachers quickly learn that they had better shape up. And with the state's traditional loathing of needless regulations and government interference—the Revolutionary War slogan "Live Free or Die" still appears on state license plates, and many citizens take it seriously—most teachers have the chance to do whatever it takes to get students to learn.

It is an advantage not always shared by teachers elsewhere. In too many communities in other states, the curriculum is so standardized that teachers in any given course on any given day are expected to cover exactly the same material. It's time to cut through that kind of intrusive red tape and give teachers the right to do the job they supposedly were trained for. *What* students should learn is the business of society at large; *how* they learn it should be up to the teacher whose job it is to identify and meet the special needs of each individual student. At the turn of the century, it will be.

...THEN MAKE THEM DO IT

For teachers, that new power should come at a price: Teachers and their supervisors must be held responsible for the performance of their students. Teachers who turn out well-educated students should be paid and promoted accordingly. But if students don't advance, neither should their would-be educators.

Predictably, the idea that teachers should actually do some teaching has not won much favor among "educators" themselves. In 1984, Tennessee Governor Lamar Alexander proposed a one-cent sales-tax increase to promote outstanding teachers to "master teacher" status and pay them to take on extra duties. The measure took effect only after a year-long battle with the union representing most of the state's teachers. Since then, it has proved remarkably successful in improving reading scores in the state's poor rural districts. In Clay County, for example, the average adult income is $6,600 per year, and 38 percent of the population is illiterate. Yet remedial reading programs for first- and second-graders, paid for out of the new sales-tax revenues, have raised county students from fourteenth place to third among nearby counties on standardized achievement tests.

For years now, the National Education Association, union for three-fourths of the teachers in America, has steadfastly opposed such measures as merit pay and teacher testing. When the famed businessman H. Ross Perot pushed an education-reform program through the Texas legislature in 1984, it included both a master-teacher program and subject-by-subject competence testing for teachers. The proposals drew such bitter opposition from state teachers' unions that Perot described the battle to enact them as "the worst dogfight of my career." Teacher testing has since been abandoned, reportedly because there was no room for it in the state budget.

It seems that any system to reward good teachers and penalize bad ones will be established over their most vehement opposition. So be it. This is one change the American educational system cannot do without. By 2000, it will no longer have to.

STANDARDIZE THE CORE CURRICULUM

One reason Japanese schools are so successful with mathematics, science, and Japanese and foreign languages—in short, the kind of knowledge that most American high school graduates lack—is that there is universal agreement as to what constitutes a basic education. The curriculum in Japan is set by the national Department of Education, guided by advice from teachers, industry, and trade unions. School principals receive a syllabus for each course, and school inspectors visit periodically to make sure the program is followed. Standards are high, and children are compelled to meet them until they reach age fifteen.

Most European nations enforce national curricula as well, though few are as detailed as the Japanese model. Great Britain, the last European holdout against national educational planning, has introduced legislation that will soon provide a national syllabus for the core subjects: English, science and technology, mathematics, history, geography, music, art and design, and a foreign language. About 70 percent of the student's time will go toward learning these basics. The rest can be devoted to extra science courses, another foreign language, or other options.

That leaves the United States as the only major nation that leaves virtually all of its educational planning to teachers. Many states already have at least the outlines of a standard core curriculum, but in many cases it carries little weight in the classroom. Curricula specify which courses students must pass, but what actually gets taught is up to the teacher. In too many cases, little is, as the achievement-test scores quoted above demonstrate.

American educators will spend much of the next decade working to formulate a core curriculum for our grammar and high schools. They will specify not just course titles but the specific facts and skills that students must master before graduation. Exactly how that knowledge is delivered to each student will remain in the teacher's hands. In the end, schools will most likely have as many model curricula to choose from as there are prestigious educational theorists. But most will be variations on a common theme: giving students the competence to function as independent adults in the world after graduation.

Education in America will never be as uniform as it is in Japan, either in subjects covered or in quality of teaching. Each school system will adapt the model curricula to fit its own views of local needs. Yet by 2000, a consensus will have evolved that covers at least the most essential subjects: English, math, science, and computer literacy. Throughout the country, parents will send their children to public schools confident that their offspring are actually getting the education they need.

BROADEN VOCATIONAL OPTIONS

There is no conflict between this forecast and the preceding one. To make it in the twenty-first century, high-school grads not bound for college will need not only a strong foundation of core learning, but some way to make a living in a technological world. Those planning further study will need less vocational training, but more advanced science and mathematics, more skill in foreign languages, more experience in the kind of independent scholarly research made possible by easy access to computerized data banks. Working-age adults will need retraining each time technology renders their most recent professions obsolete. As the turn of the century nears, public schools will be called on to meet all these needs.

They will not find it easy to provide specialized courses while still improving the core curriculum. The longer school day and year will help. Core subjects will take up the entire school year as we now know it; vocational classes and other options will fit into the extra three hundred classroom hours soon to be added to each school year. Some districts may use the entire school year for core courses and shift the options into the summer. Teachers for many of the extra courses will be found among community volunteers and teachers recruited from industry, leaving career educators free to work on the mandatory curriculum.

Schools will still be adapting to these increased demands as the new century begins, but in 2000, most high-school grads will be far better equipped for both college and a career than their parents were.

TAILOR COURSES TO INDIVIDUAL NEEDS

Here we move from *what* students should learn to *how* they learn it. Many schools already use individualized education programs (IEPs); they suggest which skills in, say, reading or math, the student must practice, and recommend ways of testing to make sure they have been learned. Algebra students who have learned to solve equations by the quadratic formula but are still weak in factoring are given problems that can be solved by factoring; students who have mastered basic factoring may need to practice completing the square. In a sense, there is nothing really individual about this at all. Students learn the same material as before, and practice it in the same way. What has changed is quality control, which today can reveal not only that the student has a problem but also which specific skills need strengthening.

Far more is possible. Education researchers have identified nearly two dozen factors that affect how well students learn, from the temperature of the classroom and background noise levels to memory and analytical skills. For best educational results, each should be tailored to fit the individual student's learning style. Some students actually learn better while listening to rock music or looking out the window and fiddling with their pencils. In the future, IEPs will look at such factors as whether a given student learns best in small groups or large classes, alone or with a friend, or from reading, lectures, or computer programs; how much supervision he or she needs; and so on. Teachers will be evaluated in the same way and assigned to large or small classes, good readers or good listeners, as best suits them. These programs may not be widely adopted in time to help the Class of 2000, but the sooner the better.

PROMOTE ON PERFORMANCE

There is nothing new in this recommendation. Every would-be educational reformer has made it since the 1960s, if not long before. Yet all too many teachers still deal with their failures by promoting them into some other teacher's classroom. Students who start school in 2000 will move up not by conventional grade levels, but by development levels, ensuring that each child can work on each topic until it's mastered. There is no other way to be sure that they actually learn the course material.

Again, this is a measure that needs to be adopted today, not late in the next decade.

BRING CORPORATIONS INTO THE SCHOOLS

In one sense, business is the ultimate consumer of the education industry's product. David Kearns, chairman and chief executive officer of Xerox Corporation, worries that American companies will soon have to hire 1 million new workers each year who cannot read, write, or count well enough to do their jobs. "Teaching them how, and absorbing the lost productivity while they're learning, will cost industry $25 billion a year for as long as it takes," he estimates. As a result, two-thirds of American companies that took part in a recent poll report that education is now their number-one community-relations concern.

Corporations now spend $10 billion per year on management courses alone, and the need to train and retrain workers constantly will grow ever more pressing as technology changes the workplace ever more rapidly. The obvious answer is for them to contract with schools to do the teaching. The money earned from such services can go toward teachers' salaries and investments in computers, software, and such things as air conditioning, needed to keep schools open during the summer. For students not headed toward college, businesses may also provide internships that give high-schoolers practical experience in the working world they are about to enter. When public schools turn out graduates who haven't mastered reading, writing, or finger-counting, business suffers. Executives know that through bitter experience; they will be eager to help in any way they can.

In many communities, they are already giving that help in a variety of ways. The most famous example is the story of the industrialist Eugene Lang, who returned to his high school to give a speech and wound up offering college scholarships to anyone who resisted the urge to drop out. He followed up by hiring a social worker/guidance counselor to help the students stay the course, and by making himself available to talk with members of the class.

The "I Have a Dream" concept has proved a resounding success. Seven years after Lang "adopted" that first high-school class, fifty-four of its sixty-one students remained in New York, fifty had graduated from high school, and thirty-six were in college. Lang's spur-of-the-moment generosity has grown into the "I Have a Dream" Foundation, and about 125 wealthy people in twenty-five cities have donated upwards of $250,000 each to adopt their own grammar-school classes with more than eight thousand students.

That money helps, but students from Eugene Lang's original class say it was not the philanthropist's cash that did them the most good. It was Lang himself.

"My parents never went to college, and they never said it was a good thing to do," explained Evelyne Campbell, one of Mr. Lang's protégées, in an interview in *The New York Times Magazine* (April 26, 1987). "Then I started talking to Mr. Lang and saw how important it was to graduate and go on to college." By now she should be majoring in liberal arts at the City University of New York.

"I wouldn't have thought of college without the 'I Have a Dream' program," agrees Larry Douglas, who aims for an engineering degree, also from CUNY. "The program is like somebody to talk to, somebody giving you that little push, like family behind you."

Not all corporate philanthropists can bring that one-on-one personal touch to their programs, but businesses across the country have followed Lang's lead in a variety of ways. Some have made dramatic improvements in local educational systems:

In 1982, New York City closed its old Benjamin Franklin High School in Spanish Harlem after graduating only thirty students in a class of one thousand. The facility has since been reopened as the Manhattan Center for Science and Mathematics. Executives from General Electric spend some of their spare time there tutoring the mostly minority students and holding special classes to help them get into the science and engineering courses at MIT, Stanford, and other major universities. The result: In the school's first two years of operation, 95 percent of the seniors won their diplomas.

In Dade County, Florida, American Bankers Insurance Group has built its own workplace minischool for fifty of its employees' kindergarteners and first-graders, staffed by county teachers but paid for by the company.

On Chicago's poverty-stricken South Side, investor Irving Harris has set up the Center for Successful Childhood Development to provide prenatal care, parent counselling, pediatric services, and when the time comes, preschool for all the 125 or so children who will enter Beethoven Elementary School in 1993. According to studies elsewhere, a single year of good preschool cuts students' dropout rate by one-third; the comprehensive Beethoven Elementary project should do considerably better. Even before its results are known, the idea inspired Congress to enact the Comprehensive Child Development Centers Act to fund similar programs in up to twenty-five cities.

And in Lawndale, on Chicago's West Side, local corporations have set up a tuition-free community school for two-to-eight-year-olds. With an annual budget of $1 million, the facility offers individualized instruction, a year-round program ("so that children's minds won't go on summer vacation," one teacher there explains), and ready access to computers. Classes are limited to twenty-five students. Teaching methods are carefully tailored to the needs of individual students. There are no set grades; students advance at their own rate. And parents are involved in all parts of the program. There were more than one thousand applicants for the school's 150 seats in 1988. Entrants were chosen by lottery.

Programs like these do not always work as well as their creators hope. One of the most heavily publicized was set up in Boston in 1982. Business leaders there offered to guarantee one thousand jobs for graduates of the city's decaying schools if the department of education raised its standards, reduced absenteeism, and cut the 36-percent dropout rate. Three years later, Boston had improved its curriculum, fewer students were playing hookey, and local companies hired nine hundred graduates. But the dropout rate had risen to 43 percent and continues to climb.

Yet American business, with its ample supply of funds and its desperate need for well-educated new employees, is a natural ally for American educators at a time when traditional government support is finding it difficult to meet the needs of our schools. No single corporate effort can replace the billions of dollars that federal education funding seems unlikely to provide. But dozens of local projects can make a substantial contribution, even on a national scale. And business has one resource to offer that the federal government lacks: thousands of caring, well-trained people to act as part-time teachers and role models for children who need them desperately. Cooperative programs like the ones described above may represent our best hope for improvement in our school system. Many more will be set up and operating by 2000.

Today's educational system cannot begin to prepare students for the world they will enter upon graduation from high school. By the time today's kindergarteners graduate from high school, the amount of knowledge in the world will have doubled four times. The Class of 2000 will be exposed to more information in one year than their grandparents encountered in their entire lives. They will have to assimilate more inventions and more new information than have appeared in the last 150 years. And by 2010, there will be hardly a job in the country that does not require skill in using powerful computers and telecommunications systems.

Yet our hope for the future of American education is more than blind optimism. In the recent presidential election, both candidates called for dramatic increases in federal spending for education. And according to a Gallup poll in the summer of 1988, nearly two-thirds of the American public is willing to pay more taxes in order to improve our educational system. This is a mandate that both federal legislators and community school boards will find difficult to ignore.

America will not have solved its educational problems by 2000. They have taken more than three generations to develop, and they will take at least two generations to cure. But by the turn of the century the nation will at last have made a start. After decades of fumbling, even that is something to look forward to.

STATE EXPERIMENTS

The need for educational reform finally seems to have caught the attention of state legislators. Since 1980, state education budgets have grown by 26 percent after inflation. All but five states have reworked their high-school curricula and tightened graduation requirements since then. Fully forty-two have added new math requirements, while thirty-four now demand more science training. Some thirty-eight states either offer merit pay for superior teachers or encourage local school districts to do so. A few have enacted creative programs that approach education from other angles.

One pioneer of state-level reform, who we mentioned on page 56, was then-Governor Lamar Alexander of Tennessee. His $1-billion, three-year improvement program, enacted in 1984, began with a 20-percent pay raise for all teachers over three years. It also set up kindergartens in each school district, limited class sizes, mandated a state competency test for graduation from high school, toughened math and science requirements, added a computer literacy requirement, and set up a summer program for gifted students.

A key, and controversial, feature was one of the nation's first "master teacher" plans. More than six thousand of the state's 46,000 teachers now receive from $2,000 to $7,000 in merit pay each year. The program took effect over the objections of the state teachers' union, which complained that classroom evaluations for master-teacher status did not measure actual teaching performance. Nonetheless, SAT scores have risen and dropout rates have fallen since the program began.

Indiana's "A+ Program for Educational Excellence" also set up a system of statewide proficiency exams to make sure that students have mastered their current grade level before promotion. More novel: a school accreditation system based not on abstract standards but on actual performance in educating students.

In 1985, North Carolina raised local sales taxes by one-half cent; 40 percent of the revenue—about $2.7 billion over eight years—goes to support the state's new Basic Education Program. State teachers liked the 9.6-percent pay raise they received that year, and increased funding for student-teacher scholarships, but not the tougher licensing exam or the experimental master-teacher program now operating in sixteen school districts. Students face tougher promotion and graduation requirements, but receive added help in the form of smaller classes and free summer school for anyone who flunks a course. In the long run, the most promising innovation may be a statewide core curriculum approved in 1986, a guarantee that students will at least be exposed to all the educational basics.

In addition to recruiting new teachers from industry, New Jersey has raised both certification standards and salaries for teachers and added an extra year of math, science, and social studies to the state's high-school graduation requirements. A proposed master-teacher program succumbed to resistance from the state teachers' union, but two noteworthy ideas have survived: the "teaching scholar" program offers college students up to $30,000 in loans, which they need not repay if they teach for four years in a city school or six years in the New Jersey suburbs.

In 1984, the New York State Board of Regents raised graduation requirements from sixteen points to 18.5 for all students, tightened course requirements, and required two years of foreign language before the end of the freshman year of high school. Four years later, the state set up the first scholarship program in the country to guarantee public financing for a college education. By the 1994–95 school year, the Liberty Scholarship program is expected to give $90 million to some ninety thousand students from families with annual incomes below $26,000.

Perhaps the most radical state-level reform is Minnesota's "marketplace" version of education. Under this plan, enacted in 1985, parents can send their children to any school in the state, so long as the school has room for them. And when students move from one school to another, the state "tuition" money that pays for their education goes with them. In theory, schools that provide a good education will gain students and flourish, while those that do not will lose students and go bankrupt. Thus, all schools will have a strong incentive to improve their programs. Critics fear that good schools will get better, while poor schools will find themselves too strapped for funds to better themselves. In the 1988–89 school year, some four hundred students were attending schools outside their home districts. So far, the program seems to be working. As Governor Rudy Perpich points out proudly, by 1988 there were twice as many foreign-language courses offered in Minnesota as when the program began. In most schools, students leaving their home districts have been roughly balanced by students coming in from other areas.

To date, results from such programs are mixed. In 1984, South Carolina enacted some of the most sweeping reforms yet seen; by 1987, the state's average SAT scores were fully thirty-six points higher than five years earlier—the most dramatic advance of any state in the country. Florida lengthened its school day, required passing grades before would-be athletes could take the field, and stiffened academic requirements for graduation; state SAT scores rose slightly, but the dropout rate still hovers at a dismal 40 percent.

By 2000, the most successful of these experiments will have become permanent features of school systems across the country. Despite the objections of teachers' unions, master-teacher programs seem destined to spread. And New Jersey's alternative teacher-certification program and "teaching scholar" program appear likely to be adopted by many other states. In the long run, this state-level experimentation may do more for the nation's schools than any help the federal government can offer.

THE BEST INVESTMENT
WE CAN MAKE

In the final analysis, it may be that America's real problem is not so much to improve the schools as to improve the children in them. A child's personality is pretty well formed, psychologists tell us, by the age of two or three. With the right encouragement, a child can be an interesting, motivated person at five, a competent violinist at six. Without it, he or she can be headed almost irrevocably toward a life of poverty and drugs, remedial classes, and prison.

Unfortunately, such encouragement is the exception, not the rule. About 25 percent of American children under the age of six now live in poverty. Some 60 percent of mothers hold down jobs, nearly twice as many as in the 1960s, including half of those with babies under one year old. They have little time to give their children the support they need; too many lack the skill and inclination. As many as 7 million youngsters, referred to by television commentators as "latchkey children," must fend for themselves while their parents are at work. In the inner city, their role models are the dropouts and drug dealers who infest their neighborhoods.

The problem will grow more pressing as we approach 2000. Two-thirds of the new workers hired by the turn of the century will be women; 85 percent will become pregnant during the first ten years of their employment, often more than once.

That leaves day-care centers and preschool programs to fill the void. Many work surprisingly well. The Perry Preschool Program, in Ypsilanti, Michigan, has been following one hundred people from its community since 1962. Half attended the Perry program, half did not. Twenty-six years later, two-thirds of those who had attended a single year of preschool had completed high school, and 38 percent had gone on to college or job training. Fewer than half of those who had not attended preschool completed high school, and only 21 percent pursued further education. At the age of nineteen, 45 percent of the preschool students were self-supporting; only one-fourth of those who had gone straight to grammar school had accomplished the same feat. At the same age, the preschool group had produced sixty-four babies per one hundred students; the non-preschool group had had 117 per one hundred. By 1988, more than half of the non-preschool group had criminal arrest records, compared with 31 percent of the preschool students. And nearly one-third were on welfare, compared with 18 percent of the preschool group.

Based on those statistics, 225 business leaders and university presidents belonging to the Committee for Economic Development estimate that every dollar spent on preschool programs eventually saves six dollars in remedial education, welfare, and losses to crime.

To date, the United States has not coped at all well with this need. Though many families manage to find day care for their children, it is a financial burden that only the middle and upper class can afford. Most preschool programs cost $50 to $100 per child each week, and full-time infant care runs $150 per week and up. The federally funded Head Start program for children of low-income families has faced tighter budgets since 1983. In 1987, with $1 billion a year to spend throughout the country, Head Start was able to provide classroom seats for less than 20 percent of the children poor enough to qualify for them. The

Committee for Economic Development estimates that Head Start would need $3 billion per year to reach all the children who need it.

Fortunately, by the year 2000, the situation should look a lot brighter. All over the country, hundreds of public and private programs have been springing up to give children the start in life they need.

One of the most promising ideas is the "School of the 21st Century," created by Edward Zigler, a Yale University psychologist who, in 1965, helped to design the Head Start program. Under Zigler's plan, local schools would remain open from six in the morning to six at night, offering day care for three- and four-year-olds and before- and after-school programs for children whose parents cannot be home to look after them during working hours. Two school districts near Kansas City, Missouri, set up experimental "Schools of the 21st Century" in 1988 and immediately signed up six hundred children. Though the schools charge only forty-five dollars per week for day care and eighteen dollars for the morning-and-afternoon programs, the projects were self-supporting after the first month and should turn a profit sometime in 1990.

For unemployed parents who care enough to work with their preschool-age children, the Home Instruction Program for Preschool Youngsters (HIPPY) in Arkansas offers a way to prepare their children for school. Modeled on a program used in Israel for twenty years to prepare immigrant children for that country's high-pressure school system, HIPPY supplies mothers of three- and four-year-olds with books and worksheets for a two-year preschool curriculum. Mothers spend fifteen minutes a day with their children, five days a week, thirty weeks per year. Once a week, paraprofessionals from the local school system visit the home to give the parents training and advice.

The program has been remarkably successful. Some 1,400 low-income families have joined HIPPY. After sixteen months in the program, children in one school posted an average thirty-three months' worth of improvement in their educational levels. And as a side benefit, almost half of the mothers in two Arkansas counties, all on welfare, either returned to school, applied for job-training courses, or found a job. All this for only $500 to $600 per child per year.

Business, too, has been pitching in. Polaroid, to name just one company, offers to pay up to 80 percent of day-care costs at selected centers for all employees whose family income is below

$30,000. An estimated 3,500 employers offer some form of child-care benefits.

Of course, that doesn't do much for the jobless or for those whose employers have yet to start such a program. More and more, they are looking to the government for help. Today the federal government spends just under $7 billion for a variety of child-care subsidies. By far the largest program offers a 30-percent tax credit worth up to $1,440 for day-care expenses for two or more children. Unfortunately, virtually all of the saving goes to those parents who need it least; only 3 percent of the $4 billion in credits goes to the poorest 30 percent of families.

It seems likely that more effective help will eventually arrive. In 1988, Congress looked at more than one hundred different bills that touched on the issue of child care. And though some called for spending cuts in the nation's already beleaguered children's-assistance programs, most called for new programs ranging from child-care tax credits to federal subsidies for preschool programs and regulation of day-care centers. It seems likely that at least one program designed to prepare the children of the needy for school will be enacted into law no later than 1990, to be followed by more and better efforts throughout the decade.

It's the best investment we can make.

APRIL 1990

The problems of the nation's school system are so critical to the future of the United States that Forecasting International has just devoted nearly a year of research to understanding their causes and likely solutions. Nothing we discovered alters the opinion we formed when preparing for this book: The ills that beset America's schools are many, and they are deeply entrenched. But all across the land, small groups of dedicated people have found ways to cure nearly all of them. The task that faces America today is no longer to understand what is wrong, but to take the solutions already available and apply them throughout the nation.

For a closer look at how to cure what ails America's schools, see our forthcoming book, *Educational Renaissance,* by Marvin Cetron and Margaret E. Gayle (St. Martin's Press, 1991.)

DRUGS: LOSING BATTLES

AND WINNING THE WAR

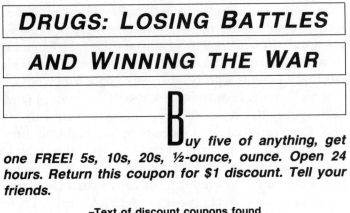

Buy five of anything, get one FREE! 5s, 10s, 20s, ½-ounce, ounce. Open 24 hours. Return this coupon for $1 discount. Tell your friends.

–Text of discount coupons found
by agents of the Baltimore City Drug
Enforcement Unit in a 1988
raid on a dealer's home

The spread of drugs throughout any great culture is one key sign of its decline. Citizens of a growing nation must themselves be vital, alert, hardworking—all the things that drug users, by and large, are not. Moreover, few societies place a high value on any debilitating behavior. When drugs spread throughout a society, it is sure proof that its value structure is breaking down and its social controls are failing.

By this standard, the end for the United States must surely be near. America is the world's largest market for illegal drugs. Americans spend roughly $100 billion a year on them—twice what they pay for oil. Some 6 million Americans use cocaine; at least 500,000 are heroin addicts, and some authorities believe that estimate may be much too low. And 20 million regularly smoke marijuana. It is already the largest cash crop in California. Within three years the United States will be the world's largest producer of marijuana. Soon after, it will become a net exporter.

There is at least a little good news as well. In an annual poll of high-school seniors conducted by researchers from the Institute for Social Research at the University of Michigan, nearly 60 percent admitted to having used at least one illegal drug in the past year. Yes, that is good news. It represents a decline of nearly 14 percent since 1982. Use of rock cocaine—commonly called crack—also declined—for the first time—and even marijuana has lost customers. In the 1979 study, more than half of high-school seniors said they had tried marijuana or hashish in the preceding year; by 1987, only 36 percent had done so. Yet fully 85 percent of students said they would have no trouble buying it if they wanted it.

Whether that foretells any decline in drug use outside the nation's high schools is not clear. Drug problems have grown worse in recent years as suppliers have developed cheaper, more potent forms of their products. The classic example to date is crack, the smokable form of cocaine, which appeared in New York and other East Coast cities in 1985. Until then, cocaine was the high-priced high for yuppie stockbrokers and executives. Today it can be had for as little as ten dollars per dose, and the market has spread to the poorest neighborhoods. For the 1990s, the stimulant of choice may be methamphetamine, popularly known as "crank," or "speed." For manufacturers, it is almost the ideal drug: easily synthesized from chemicals that remain readily available, with nothing to smuggle over the border, and bringing a street price of up to $32,000 for a kilogram of product that costs roughly $175 to make. Late in 1988, federal drug enforcement authorities discovered their first laboratory producing a smokable form of amphetamine. Is a speed epidemic at hand? The National Institute on Drug Abuse warns, "Domestically produced methamphetamine looms as a potential national drug crisis for the 1990s." If that crisis materializes, it will surely be with us still at the turn of the century.

It will be a costly social problem. Americans have spent another $42 billion or so intercepting drug ships, scanning the Caribbean skies for unidentified aircraft, arresting petty drug dealers, and jailing those convicted of drug-related crimes. And that does not include the funds spent to maintain those convicts once they reach prison. To date, these efforts have done nothing whatsoever to reduce drug abuse in the United States. In fact, it is possible to make a strong argument that criminal sanctions have made it worse, in part by turning drugs into an attractive outlet for adolescent rebellion and in part by giving criminal organizations a hugely profitable market for their entrepreneurial energies. No one ever got rich by smuggling broccoli past customs!

AN ALTERNATIVE FOR
THE NEW CENTURY?

What may be the wave of drug enforcement's future rocked American politicians in April 1988 when Kurt L. Schmoke, a Harvard-educated Rhodes scholar and Baltimore's first black mayor, mentioned the unmentionable at the U.S. Conference of Mayors: If even the most draconian criminal sanctions haven't done a thing to control the drug problem, maybe it is time to try something different. Just maybe it is time to make our peace with the mildest drugs. Maybe it is time to make our peace with all of them. Mayor Schmoke's recommendations: eliminate criminal penalties for possession of marijuana; expand programs for methadone maintenance, drug treatment, drug-abuse prevention, and education; and establish a bipartisan commission to study regulation of harmful drugs, including alcohol and tobacco. He also suggested that addicts should be given methadone, heroin, cocaine, and perhaps other drugs in supervised maintenance and treatment programs.

Later that year, the mayor spent two hours testifying before the House Select Committee on Narcotics. He now jokes that people often introduce him at public functions as a man who used to have a bright future. That may reflect the response his ideas received from most of his audience. Committee chairman Charles B. Rangel (D.-N.Y.) rejected the idea out of hand. "We have yet to begin the fight against drugs," he declared. "We have not even fired the first shot. How can we honestly call for an end to a war that we have not yet started?" New York City Mayor Edward Koch agreed: "When people say that we should legalize drugs because law enforcement efforts have failed, they ignore the fact that a truly effective war has yet to be launched on drugs."

Representative Rangel later admitted that he had organized the hearing in hopes of convincing the public that "legalization is a dangerous idea." That being the case, the public may never learn how convincing the arguments for decriminalization were. Six months later, Rangel still had not released transcripts of the testimony.

Not everyone has been quite so critical of Schmoke's proposals. "We haven't launched an effective war on drugs for the same reason we haven't launched an airplane towed by trained swans," one on-looker commented after hearing Rangel and Koch. "It can't be done. We have half a million people in jail on drug charges in this country. What is it they want us to do that we haven't already done? Atom-bomb Colombia?"

So far, the idea of decriminalizing or legalizing drugs has received only a little more support from the public than it has from politicians. One national survey of young women—conducted by *Glamour* magazine—found that 35 percent favored legalizing marijuana, but nearly nine out of ten opposed legalizing all drugs. Only 22 percent reported using marijuana even occasionally, and 88 percent said that legalizing drugs would not encourage them to take more. An ABC News poll of American adults reported roughly the same findings: some 25 percent would legalize marijuana, but only 9 percent said that all drugs should be legalized. Slightly more than half believed that legalizing drugs would lead to greater drug use; most others felt it would have little effect.

People have proved remarkably more willing to accept harsh measures to stem the drug problem. In a poll by the *Washington Post,* two-thirds of the thousand-odd people responding endorsed cutting off aid to Colombia and Panama until those countries acted against drug dealers, even if it meant the poor and innocent would suffer. Nearly seven in ten would let school officials search lockers, even of students not strongly suspected of drug use. More than half would allow the police to stop cars at random to search for drugs. Almost half would enact a mandatory one-year jail sentence for first-time cocaine users. And more than one in three would allow the police to search the houses of suspected drug dealers without a court order. Most of these measures represent a severe blow to civil liberty, and some are unconstitutional. But it could be worse. One Wheeling, West Virginia, official recommends the death penalty for anyone caught using an illegal drug.

OVERWHELMING IGNORANCE

For all our fear of drug abuse, and the billions of dollars spent to combat the problem, we know astonishingly little about it. We don't even know for sure how many people use illicit drugs. The Michigan poll of high-school seniors mentioned above is the only regular survey of drug use conducted in the United States. Unfortunately, it has a crippling defect in that it includes only those young people who are about to graduate from high school, the ones least likely to have serious drug problems. No one knows what is happening among dropouts, the group most likely to use crack and other drugs.

One reason for our ignorance is that no one has made a serious effort to study the phenomenon. The United States now spends about $2.5 billion per year, just trying to police its borders against drug smugglers, a fivefold increase in seven years. By contrast, the budget for treatment and rehabilitation of addicts, drug education, and epidemiological research remains frozen at about $500 million. The 1989 budget of the National Institute on Drug Abuse was $253 million—pocket change, on the scale of Washington spending—of which half goes to AIDS-related research.

Another barrier to knowledge is that what little research does get performed often is politically motivated and of little value. Much of the work performed at the National Institute on Drug Abuse over the years has been aimed at demonstrating the damaging effects of marijuana. So far, the only significant risk discovered is that marijuana cigarettes give off even more tar than tobacco and therefore may be more harmful to the lungs. The active component of marijuana, tetrahydrocannabinol (THC), seems to have fewer and less dangerous side effects than aspirin. These clearly are not the results that government officials hoped to get for their money. In 1987, the White House Conference for a Drug-Free America took NIDA to task for not declaring marijuana addictive.

Finally, when sound research is done, the results are often ignored, and are finally submerged in the tide of political rhetoric that drowns almost every attempt to look at drug abuse in a rational manner. As an example, do you know the long-term effects of heroin? Literally hundreds of books, magazine articles, and learned papers have dealt with the topic, but in tracing back through the trails of references, one finds that they all refer to the same handful of basic studies. Edward M. Brecher, in preparing the manuscript for his widely respected book, *Licit and Illicit Drugs: The Consumers Union Report on Narcotics, Stimulants, Depressants, Inhalants, Hallucinogens and Marijuana—Including Caffeine, Nicotine and Alcohol* (New York: Consumers Union, 1972), attempted to uncover the long-term effects of heroin by going to the best source—the addicts themselves. He found that heroin users living in clean, comfortable surroundings and using reasonably pure drugs showed none of the medical problems of today's sickly, malnourished addicts living in filth and using heroin laced with everything from talcum powder to rat poison. The studies found only two differences between heroin addicts and the rest of us: heroin addicts, like diabetes sufferers on insulin, must take regular doses of their drug; and they tend to be constipated—not surprising, given that opiates once were widely used to treat diarrhea. By every other test that science has brought to the question, addicts are physically normal. Neither do they show any more emotional illness than the population at large. The scientists performing those studies were forced to conclude that opiates were virtually harmless.

"Almost all of the deleterious effects ordinarily attributed to the opiates, indeed, appear to be the effects of the narcotics laws instead," Brecher reported. "By far the most serious deleterious effects of being a narcotics addict in the United States today are the risks of arrest and imprisonment, infectious disease, and impoverishment—all traceable to the narcotics laws, to vigorous enforcement of those laws, and to the resulting excessive black-market prices for narcotics."

Little wonder, in today's political climate, that objective studies of drug abuse are a low priority in Washington.

LEGAL OPINION

In general, law-enforcement authorities are reluctant to admit that they have lost even one battle in the war against drugs and to seek alternatives. Seattle police chief Patrick Fitzsimmons called on the city to recriminalize marijuana use, because he feared that Seattle would turn into a haven for drug dealers. Possession of less than 40 grams of marijuana in Seattle carries a maximum fine of $250; elsewhere in the state, marijuana possession is a misdemeanor punishable by up to ninety days in jail and a $500 fine. And Oregon Attorney General Dave Frohnmayer declared early in 1989 that young people in his state are taking more drugs, and harder drugs, more often than their counterparts in states that have not decriminalized drug use. (He gave no evidence to support that claim. In fact, ten states already have reduced the penalty for marijuana possession to a small fine, including California, New York, and Ohio. There is no evidence that drug use is any more prevalent in these states than in comparable regions that adhere to criminal sanctions.)

Yet not everyone agrees, even in the legal community. The cause of decriminalizing marijuana probably received its biggest boost in

1988, when a 1972 petition by the National Organization for the Reform of Marijuana Laws to the Drug Enforcement Administration finally received an answer. In a sixty-eight-page opinion, administrative judge Francis L. Young formally urged the DEA to reclassify marijuana under the Controlled Substances Act. Doctors, he said, should be allowed to prescribe it for cancer chemotherapy patients and for those suffering from multiple sclerosis and spasticity. Evidence of marijuana's medical benefits is, he stated, "clear beyond any question," while "there are simply no credible medical reports to suggest that consuming marijuana has caused a single death." Judge Young concluded that "marijuana in its natural form is one of the safest therapeutically active substances known to man." He conceded that it can be dangerous when abused, but noted that this is equally true of most prescription drugs. (A synthetic form of THC is already given to cancer patients who might otherwise be forced to discontinue chemotherapy owing to severe nausea and loss of appetite.)

The *National Law Journal* found even more surprising results when it surveyed 181 state and local prosecutors from the largest jurisdictions throughout the country. Nearly two-thirds reported that police and the courts were having little or no impact on the supply or use of drugs in their areas. They cited four major problems that block effective drug enforcement: too little prison space, too little money for law enforcement, light sentencing, and crowded court dockets. But if that sounds like a veiled claim—"Give us the budgets, and we'll cure the drug problem by locking up the slime that sells drugs"—think again. None thought that they could eliminate drugs from America, no matter how large their budgets. Virtually all admitted that going after marijuana sellers was at the bottom of their list of priorities. Only half wanted to maintain current sanctions against marijuana use. One-fourth would eliminate jail sentences for possession but would levy fines, and fully one-fourth of the nation's most prominent prosecutors favored decriminalizing marijuana.

PRACTICAL EXPERIENCE

There is at least a plausible argument that decriminalizing marijuana is not enough. As things stand, there is an established distribution route for marijuana: in the cities especially, it is sold by the same pushers who deal in crack, speed, heroin, PCP, barbiturates, and virtually any other drugs a hard-core abuser could want. So an otherwise law-abiding youngster curious about the softest of drugs is automatically exposed to the rest of the illicit pharmacopoeia. Contrary to popular opinion, there is little if any evidence that smoking marijuana leads people to want a stronger "high." But associating with narcotics dealers is surely the shortest route to narcotics use. Decriminalize marijuana, and those same pushers will remain in the business. Legalize it, and businessmen all over the country will leap into the market and quickly drive street pushers out. In theory, it should break the connection between pot and harder drugs.

There is an argument against decriminalization, as well. Decriminalize drugs, it holds, and an epidemic of addiction will spread throughout the land. (In a parallel situation, though, the end of Prohibition saw only a small increase in the number of drinkers.) At the very least, we will be "sending the wrong signal" to the youth of America. How can we simultaneously permit an activity and ask them not to do it?

In fact, there is strong evidence that establishing a separate, quasi-legal market for marijuana can reduce the use of heroin and cocaine, if it is done as part of a comprehensive antidrug campaign. In 1976, faced with rising use of heroin and cocaine by their young people, the Netherlands made a desperate decision. First they tripled the jail term for trading in hard drugs. Then, without actually changing the law, they announced that officials would not prosecute anyone possessing less than thirty grams of marijuana or hashish. Since then, Amsterdam coffeehouses have sold pot openly. Unless they start trading in hard drugs or begin selling marijuana in commercial quantities, city police treat them as they would any other local business.

Mayor Eduard Van Thijn endorses the policy with enthusiasm. Since Amsterdam decided to allow the sale of marijuana and hashish, he reports, the police have been free to concentrate on heroin and cocaine. The supply of hard drugs has dropped sharply, and so has the market, particularly among potential new users. In 1981, 14 percent of Dutch heroin addicts were age twenty-one or younger. Today the figure is less than 5 percent.

There is no obvious way to translate the Netherlands' tolerant policy to the United States, where the adversary relationship between the police and drug users is far more ingrained. But America might, for example, fully legalize marijuana and sell it through the traditional outlet for legal, regulated, taxable drugs—liquor stores. Tax marijuana cigarettes at the same rate as those made of tobacco, and it would bring in an estimated $11 billion per year, and help considerably to reduce the federal budget deficit. That additional income could be used to finance treatment programs for alcoholics and hard-drug abusers, as well as education programs to keep others from taking up the habit.

And if there is little sign that criminal sanctions inhibit drug use, there is abundant proof that education and treatment programs are far more effective. Tobacco is at least as addictive as most illicit drugs, is widely advertised in public media, and has far greater social acceptance than marijuana; yet a determined educational campaign has reduced smoking dramatically. And even with minimally effective education and treatment programs, there has been a pronounced shift in American attitudes toward drugs since the late 1960s and early 1970s. Fifteen or twenty years ago, it was not uncommon for middle-class executives to smoke marijuana at parties. Ten years ago, an ample supply of cocaine was one hallmark of a good host in many upper-class circles. Today, public use of even the mildest drugs marks the taker as socially backward, even uncouth. Sales of hard liquors have been dropping in this country for more than a decade. Rather, Perrier with bitters has replaced the martini as the standard drink at a business lunch, and smoking sections are slowly disappearing from restaurants in many cities. If this trend continues, today's drug problem could be substantially controlled by 2000. But making it happen will require much more emphasis on drug education, even if that leaves less money in a deficit-ridden federal budget for enforcement of drug laws.

If this chapter sounds like an endorsement of decriminalizing or legalizing marijuana or other drugs, it is not meant to. It *is* a plea for rational discussion in a field where reason has been all too rare. We believe the debate over drug policy will grow throughout the 1990s as it becomes clear that even the latest round of penalties for drug sales and use has failed to curb the problem. We would also like to believe that at least Mayor Schmoke's call for a bipartisan study of drug regulation will be accepted, even if his other suggestions vanish with the 1980s. But we cannot be optimistic about it.

PART II

Politics at the Turn of the Century

ECONOMIC REPAIRS

"The great weakness of a democracy is that our leaders know we can send them home to search for honest work. Once in Washington, they have an enormous incentive to do anything they can to please their constituents in hopes of remaining there. As long as the United States is a democracy, its leaders will be tempted to buy votes by dipping into the public purse for programs to benefit their supporters. We need only look to postwar Britain to see where that leads."

In the waning days of 1988, a feeling of unreality hung in the air. The presidential election was, at last, over; George Bush was, in a few weeks, to be sworn in as our forty-first President; but most Americans still seemed greatly confused by the swollen promises of the 1988 presidential campaign. The Democratic candidate, Michael Dukakis, had sworn at every opportunity that he would not raise taxes, save as a "last resort." Candidate Bush had sworn he would never raise taxes under any circumstances. Each candidate offered up wildly improbable schemes that he said would stave off the inevitable. Months after the election, President-elect Bush still stood by his "read my lips" vow to create "no new taxes." Yet it is safe to guess that not a single person in the country believed those campaign promises, not even the candidates themselves.

It is easy to see that tax hikes are inevitable. Too many years of living too far beyond our national means have destroyed any hope of bringing the federal budget into balance without scooping a lot more money into the government till. The only alternative is to make radical cuts in such politically untouchable programs as Social Security and veterans' benefits, and no one has ever expected that kind of courage from politicians who could be tarred and feathered by angry voters even before the next election. The only question is what taxes Washington will raise first. And even that was settled behind the closed doors of the Republican and Democratic national committees months before the campaign of 1988 really got under way.

Before looking into what they will do, though, let's remind ourselves why it is necessary:

Our economic problems began, like so many others, in Vietnam. Had the Vietnam War been our only major economic commitment, we probably could have paid for it. But President Lyndon Johnson won his election in 1964 by promising to establish a "Great Society" in which all Americans could achieve a decent standard of living through the programs of a beneficent government. It was a popular idea, and one that Johnson was determined to carry out. Landmark spending measures during his term of office included the War on Poverty bill in 1964 and Medicare in 1966. But there was no way to pay for both the war overseas and social progress at home. A choice had to be made, and President Johnson could not make it. So his administration printed the dollars it needed to meet its debts and ignored the long-term effects of its indecision. The American inflation rate started its long, perilous climb.

There were, of course, other factors. The Arab oil embargo of 1973 and 1974 accelerated the inflationary spiral. The American inflation rate reached double digits within two years, peaking at 18 percent in 1979, during President Carter's Democratic interregnum.

During the same period, Congress strove mightily to make the situation worse. It succeeded all too well.

Until the 1970s, three controls had successfully conspired to keep federal spending in line: When the House of Representatives wanted to spend the voters' money, legislators had to make the decision openly, by voting on money bills, where the electorate could see exactly who was to blame for the next tax increase. Tradition—a frail restraint, as it turned out—required them to spend only money they actually had, so a large deficit was hard to achieve. And when Congress voted to spend more money than the Administration had asked for, the President could simply roll the excess over into the following year.

Congress found that situation unsatisfactory for two reasons. Without the handy escape of deficits, any loss of federal revenue meant cutting benefit programs, again in full view of the voters. And legislators were not particularly happy with the idea that the Executive branch could impound their gifts to voters.

Congress found ways around both of its problems in the early 1970s. The first was cured by inventing the entitlement programs and cost-of-living adjustments, or "COLAs." Suddenly no congressman would ever have to take the blame for cutting popular federal benefits, because the law forbade any cuts at all. Neither would Congress have to pay for those benefits openly, by raising taxes, because the increases were built into the system. Thus it could take the credit for popular programs without having to take the blame for spending money the country could not afford. Congress solved its second problem in 1974 by passing the Congressional Budget and Impoundment Control Act. Since then, whatever money Congress has appropriated, the President has been forced to spend. In less than five years, the barriers to uncontrolled government spending had fallen.

During the same period, the traditional controls were stripped from the world financial system as well. For centuries, gold had been king; all other currencies, even the mighty American dollar, were measured against it. Having a fixed standard for currency exchange rates made international trade easy; if you contracted to sell, say, a ton of wheat to West Germany, there was no need to worry that a change in the value of the deutsche mark would eat up your profits when the time came to deliver. But that security proved to be almost as inconvenient for the world's central bankers as responsible government had been for American legislators. The most successful exporting countries tended to collect large stores of foreign currency, while importing nations ran out of their own money. That was the cause of the recurrent balance-of-payments crises in those years. The only answer was to change the exchange rates abruptly, as though ripping a bandage off a wound instead of trying to ease it off a bit at a time.

Or they could get rid of the gold standard. The central banks did that in 1971. From then on, currencies have been measured only against each other. For less than two years the bankers tried to set fixed exchange rates against a "market basket" of currencies. In 1973 they dropped the fixed rate entirely, and currency values have floated at the whim of the markets ever since.

That proved a fatal temptation for American political leaders, because with floating exchange rates and too few controls, capital poured unimpeded across national borders. Much of it flowed into the United States. Late in 1988, the currency exchanges in London, New York, and Tokyo traded American currency at a rate of $200 billion *a day!* Given America's reputation for economic strength, this ready flow of money made it easy to finance a budget deficit that everyone claimed would be temporary.

Then President Ronald Reagan came to Washington, promising to cut both taxes and government spending for the social programs he found wasteful. Thus inflation would be controlled and the federal budget would be balanced at last. These were doubtful claims at best. Nonetheless, looking back on his term in office, we have to give President Reagan credit. He actually did cut both taxes and various social programs that he had named. Few modern American politicians can claim to have done even that well at keeping their promises. But Mr. Reagan also increased defense spending to record levels while making no effort to pay for his expenditures. As a result, during his first five years in office, the national budget deficit soared from well under $100 billion a year to about $221 billion in 1986. The national debt tripled from $645 billion late in the Carter years to nearly $1.75 *trillion* in 1979. The United States had gone from being the world's largest creditor nation in 1979, owed a total of $141 billion by other nations, to being by far its largest debtor, with roughly $400 billion to repay. And its foreign trade balance had shrunk from $17 billion in 1980 to a deficit ten times that in 1986.

Late in 1985, Congress passed the Gramm-Rudman-Hollings bill, under which the government was required by law to reduce its budget deficit by roughly $30 billion per year. Two years later the budget deficit had receded to only $150 billion per year, but it had become clear that the "balanced budget" act would have a hard time creating any such thing.

So matters stood as President George Bush took office in January of 1989. Despite his optimistic campaign utterances, he will have to acknowledge quite early in his presidency that taxes must be raised. The budget cannot be balanced by cutting federal spending; the entitlement programs have seen to that. If entitlements had been enacted solely to aid the poor, as their backers claimed in the 1970s, legislators would have found it easy to cut them; after all, poor people cannot afford to give major campaign contributions. But fully 80 percent of money devoted to entitlements goes to middle-class and wealthy voters, not to the poor. At stake are Social Security and Medicare and the civil service and military retirement systems, programs no politician can afford to touch. In the 1988 budget, entitlements absorbed 47 cents out of every tax dollar, a total of $506 billion. Placing a simple means test on Social Security and Medicare—limiting payments to those with a median income or less— would cut federal spending by one-third. That alone could pay off the national debt in short order. But it can't be done by legislators who want to retain their jobs.

Other major expenses are equally difficult to cut. Defense spending costs far less than entitlements; even with the massive Reagan-years increases, the defense budget totaled "only" $291 billion. Like Social Security, military spending is zealously defended by enormously powerful political and lobbying forces. Another $150 billion per year goes to pay the interest on the national debt, and there is no way to cut that line on the budget at all. With all the fixed costs, defense spending, and entitlements protected from cuts, all that is left are such small programs as foreign aid, public works, government support for medical research, and the sad remains of NASA's once-great space effort. In all, they amounted to only $189 billion in 1988. Cut them all, and the government would still be in debt.

Nonetheless, a few useful cuts are possible. Dr. Murray Weidenbaum, former chairman of the President's Council of Economic Advisers, offered one shopping list late in the 1988 election campaign. He had ten cost-cutting suggestions, all sorely needed and all politically unlikely:

- Limit stays in Veterans Administration hospitals to those whose injuries or illnesses result from their military service. Then stop building VA hospitals in regions where there is already plenty of hospital space to absorb the patients.
- Either abort the NASA space shuttle program, or give the shuttles to the military, which can afford the experiments. (Not much to be saved there, but the government clearly has other uses for whatever money it can find.)
- Cut farm price supports, which eat up about $25 billion a year in federal spending—roughly one-third of all farm income—much of which goes to giant corporate agribusinesses that do not really need it.
- Eliminate all those needless dams and other pork-barrel projects used to curry favor with the voters at home.
- Cut most foreign aid, particularly to the Mideast and to South America, where money intended to aid everyday citizens too often winds up in the pockets of local politicians.

- Put a cap on cost-of-living adjustments for Social Security benefits.
- Raise the military retirement age to fifty for those who enter the armed forces in the future, and reduce the payments when veterans find a civilian job, just as Social Security does.
- The law now requires the government to pay its employees as much as they would receive in private industry, but ignores the enormous fringe benefits that federal employees receive. Weidenbaum would add those benefits in when figuring how much government workers must be paid. While he is at it, he would eliminate the civil service and military pension plans and enroll federal employees in Social Security.
- Repeal federal controls on private construction wages.
- Charge normal interest rates for federal loans.

At Forecasting International, we have four suggestions of our own for dealing with the politically touchy defense program: Give up on the Strategic Defense Initiative, or "Star Wars," program; it might work, but no one will ever be willing to pay the cost of setting up the system. Stop building large naval surface vessels, for submarines are able to hit any enemy as hard and survive better. Eliminate the army's so-called Rapid Deployment Force, which cannot be deployed rapidly, and turn its duties over to the Marines. And demand that Japan and our other allies pay a fair share of our costs in defending them.

Exactly how much all these cost-cutting measures would save the American public is uncertain, in part because the budget for the Rapid Deployment Force and the true cost of the Star Wars program are kept secret. But in the long run, it hardly matters. Of all the ideas presented, only two cuts will ever be enacted: a bit of tightening in farm price supports and a minor reduction in the research budget for the Strategic Defense Initiative.

Instead, we will get those taxes that President Bush used to promise would never be enacted. The first will come perhaps as early as a year after Bush took office.

Even without inside knowledge, it is fairly obvious what will be taxed first. Income tax is too noticeable; everyone fills out those complex forms in early April, and it is all too clear just how much we are being soaked for. Something more insidious is needed, something that will take a little money gradually, throughout the year, without ever letting us recognize quite how much we have lost. There are only two possibilities: some sort of national sales tax or an increase in the existing excise taxes. The excise taxes are easier to pass, and they have changed little since the 1950s. For the moment, they will win out.

There are only three excise taxes that matter: those on gasoline, alcohol, and tobacco. Some economists argue that the gasoline tax alone could eliminate much of the deficit. American drivers burn about 100 billion gallons of gas each year. Raising the excise tax to twenty-five cents per gallon would bring in $25 billion per year, and gasoline still would cost only $1.60 per gallon or so, little more than it did at its peak in 1981. Even a forty-cent tax—worth $40 billion per year—would add only half a percentage point to the national inflation rate, and on a world scale American gas would still be cheap. In the end, the Bush administration will settle—for the moment—for six cents on the gallon, a modest levy of $6 billion per year. The reason: poor people spend more of their income on gasoline than the wealthy do, so a large excise tax would hit them harder. Politically, taxing the poor is more trouble than a few extra billions are worth.

It will probably be 1990 or 1991 before the taxes on cigarettes and alcohol go up. The trigger for that event will be the Gramm-Rudman Act. The law itself has little practical value; the Supreme Court pulled most of its teeth when, in 1986, it ruled unconstitutional the crucial mechanism intended to cut federal spending automatically when Congress failed to do so. Yet for the United States government to run an illegal deficit would be more embarrassing than legislators will choose to tolerate. The extra gasoline tax will reduce that risk, but there will still be a long way to go before the nation's books will balance.

Doubters have scoffed that "sin taxes" on cigarettes and alcohol can hardly go very far toward solving the government's budget problems. The arithmetic proves them wrong. In 1988 the government collected only $19 billion from its excise taxes, about $10 billion of it from taxes on cigarettes, wine, beer, and distilled spirits. Beer and wine taxes have not been raised since 1955, liquor taxes since 1951. Simply adjusting them for inflation since then would bring in an extra $20 billion per year. Congress will make the change in easy steps; it will probably be 1995 before the full increase takes effect. But by 2000, the increases will have added $100 billion to federal revenues.

Sooner or later, one more piece of "revenue enhancement" almost inevitably will put the deficit-reduction program over the top. It will, of course, be done with mirrors. By the late 1990s, the Social Security trust fund will have amassed a surplus of $100 billion. In a few years, Congress will finally pass a bill allowing legislators to "balance the deficit" in the overall budget with the Social Security surplus. They will do this even though that surplus is funded by payroll taxes, not general revenues, and the money still cannot be used to pay for federal spending outside the Social Security program itself. It will look good on the books, and that will be all that matters.

There is one more temptation lying in wait for an all-too-susceptible Congress, a tax that actually would balance the budget and give legislators an almost inexhaustible supply of spending money as well: the value-added tax (VAT).

At this point, you are probably asking at least two obvious questions: If Congress is going to declare that the budget deficit is finally gone for good, why will they enact another major tax? And just what is a VAT?

Start with the easy one first. Congress will enact the VAT for the same reason it always raises taxes: it wants to spend your money. In fact, it will have spent a lot of it already. Remember, tapping the Social Security till will not really balance the budget. Any honest accountant would tell you the government will still be $100 billion in debt.

There is much more to come. Since the Gramm-Rudman law took effect in 1986, whenever Congress has wanted to pass a juicy spending program, it has had to specify in the bill itself exactly where the money is coming from. For legislators, it has been a return to the days before the entitlement programs, when they had to vote for the debts they ran up in full view of the electorate—a nightmare no Senator or Congressman wants to continue.

For an example, look at the comprehensive health-care package proposed by candidate Michael Dukakis during the 1988 campaign. All but the most conservative congressmen would be eager to enact a program to protect their constituents from catastrophic medical expenses; they have been toying with the idea for nearly two decades now. But to pay for their generosity (with your money), legislators would have to build Social Security–style payroll levies into the bill. In its first year, the Dukakis program would have drained nearly $30 billion from the pockets of both employers and employees. This is not the way to get credit for generosity. If the VAT had been in force to provide a nice, big cushion of relatively painless tax money to draw from, chances are that we would have had a government-funded medical-care program for all many years ago.

As for what the value-added tax is, think of the VAT as a kind of federal sales tax. But instead of collecting the entire tax when you make the final purchase, the government takes it in pieces at each stage of the product's trip from raw materials to consumer.

Let's try an example. Assume that a value-added tax were now in effect. If you bought, say, a new Ford this autumn, the roughly $10,000 price tag would include $1,000 in VAT. You would not actually see any of the tax, just the final price. (That's what makes the scheme so attractive in Washington.)

Now go back to the beginning of the process, where both the car and the VAT originate. The car begins as a host of raw materials: glass, steel, plastic, microchips, and so on. When the materials companies sell their products to Ford's parts subcontractors for, say, $1,000, one-tenth of their price—$100—would go to the government as the first increment of the VAT.

The subcontractors then make their assigned parts and sell them to Ford. If the parts total $4,000, the subcontractors collect $400 in VAT. They get to keep $100 of it as credit for the $100 in VAT they contributed in buying their raw materials. The other $300 goes to the government.

Then it is Ford's turn. If the automaker sells its cars to its dealers for $9,000, the dealers wind up paying $900 in VAT. Ford keeps $400 credit for the tax it paid in buying parts from the subcontractors, and passes along $500 to Washington.

Finally, the dealer sells the car to you. You hand over $10,000 without having to be aware that $1,000 of it is tax money. The dealer keeps $900 in credit for the VAT he has already paid, and sends $100 to the Feds. In the end, Washington has gotten its $1,000. What you've gotten, in addition to the car, is pretty clear.

At that, a VAT of only 10 percent would be one of the smallest in the world. Britain and Mexico collect 15 percent of each sale; Chile, the Netherlands, and Norway levy a 22-percent VAT; Ireland extracts 25 percent from its citizens.

The process is every bit as complicated as it sounds, but it does work. Governments all over Europe have been using the VAT to tax their citizens for years. What it requires is an enormous bureaucracy of auditors to ferret out understated prices and fraudulent claims for credit. Countries where enforcement is strict collect virtually all of the VAT that the law says is owed them. Countries where enforcement is lax find that much of the money they expected never arrives. If Congress ever does enact a VAT, we can expect the Internal Revenue Service to hire a medium-sized army of new agents.

As for what will happen . . . There will be the usual chaos for the first few years as the system shakes down and the necessary procedures are put into place. After that, every business in the country can expect IRS agents to go over its books at regular intervals. In the view of Congress, submitting to a new form of tax audit is the least the public can do to bring the old freedom back to federal spending. And it surely will bring back the freedom to spend at will. A VAT of only 10 percent will garner $100 billion per year in taxes for each $1 trillion of GNP.

The astute reader may have detected in our forecast of economic policy a faint air of cynicism about our leaders' good intentions and practical resolve with regard to balancing the federal budget. We confess to harboring traces of disappointed idealism. Their performance in solving one of the most dangerous and destructive problems we face has, to date, given little cause for optimism.

Yet we do believe the deficit will be *under control,* although not balanced, by 2000, and probably well before. Higher gasoline taxes are all but inevitable, and increases in the other excise taxes are likely to follow. If interest rates come down 2 percent from their current levels, it could save the federal government some $60 billion per year in interest payments. That combination alone could eliminate the deficit by the early 1990s. If not, even Congress may be able to find just a little waste to cut from the federal budget. And there is always the VAT.

Keeping the deficit under control is another matter. The great strength of a democracy is that we, the people, get to choose our leaders; if they govern badly, we can also turn them out of office. The great weakness of a democracy is that our leaders *know* we can send them home to search for honest work. Once in Washington, they have an enormous incentive to do anything they can to please their constituents in hopes of remaining there. As long as the United States is a democracy, its leaders will be tempted to buy votes by dipping into the public purse for programs to benefit their supporters. We need only look to postwar Britain to see where that leads.

If spending bills can be kept permanently to a pay-as-you-go standard, it will make the job of deficit control much easier. In that case, we can hope to regain our economic strength, almost—though not quite—to the extent of dominating the world economy as we once did. If Congress manages to escape this unwelcome restriction, we may face a cycle of deficit spending and retrenchment that lasts for many decades to come. At this point, which future we expect is a matter for political philosophy, not economic forecasting.

BUILDING A

NEW ACTIVISM

As we come to the end of a century and are forced to deal with the fracturing of our society and the role of America in a new world economy, we need a new public-policy consensus as well as a political class with moral and intellectual authority. We need a New Politics.

—Morton B. Zuckerman, Editor-in-Chief,
U.S. News & World Report,
November 7, 1988

In the twenty years between, say, 1955 and 1975, the United States experienced successive waves of popular upheaval of a kind not seen since the 1920s and, before that, the 1890s, when late-nineteenth-century populists rose up to wrest political control from the party regulars in Washington and spread it among the farmers. First the civil rights movement, then the battle to stop the war in Vietnam, and finally the environmentalists' cause in turn all provided rallying points for the American people in the 1960s and 1970s.

In recent years, the hippie of the early 1970s has become the yuppie of the 1980s; the Baby Boom generation, which provided both the manpower and the energy for all these causes, appears to have withdrawn into its own world of career and condo. But we believe that this abandonment of concern for public causes is only temporary. As the Baby Boomers get their families raised and find themselves firmly in mid-career, they will turn outward again, and the United States will find itself awash in a new wave of popular fervor.

Barring another war, the issues this time will probably be very different from those of the 1960s and 1970s, and much less generalized. Among the traditional concerns, only the environment will regain its appeal. Like the materialist values of the 1980s, the popular causes of the 1990s will hit much closer to home. Most will be limited to small, highly focused activist groups, though local organizations will often act in concert with others whose interests are similar.

FROM ACTIVISM TO APATHY AND BACK

It took a lot to drive the Baby Boom generation out of political activism in the first place. The children of the 1950s came to maturity with a mixed experience of government. On the one hand, there were the glamour and idealism of the Kennedy years; the Camelot mystique of our youngest President was only enhanced by his assassination. And Kennedy was more than just a glamorous figure; even in his inaugural speech, he exhorted us, in what is now one of the most quoted phrases in the twentieth-century presidential politics, to "ask not what your country can do for you, ask what you can do for your country." He was, after all, the founder of the Peace Corps. He was also the first President to take an activist role in civil rights issues. When Governor George Wallace refused to allow two black students to enter the University of Alabama in 1962, officials from the Justice Department accompanied them, and the national guard stood by to back up moral persuasion with physical force. And the Baby Boomers marched throughout the land.

Lyndon Johnson continued JFK's record on civil rights—he may even have surpassed it—but his other legacy was more enduring in the minds of today's voters: the Vietnam War. The domestic discord inspired by that unhappy involvement nearly tore the country apart. Film footage of the clash between the Chicago police and youthful demonstrators during the 1968 protests at the Democratic Convention looks as if it were taken in a country on the verge of a meltdown. Again, the Baby Boomers manned the barricades.

Out of it all came two major lessons that members of this generation carry with them to this day: They learned they could not take it for granted that our side of an issue would always be the "right" side. And they learned that direct, concerted pressure on Washington could ultimately change national policy. The antiwar movement took it as a personal victory when Lyndon Johnson decided not to run for the presidency again in the fateful spring of 1968.

Another component was the women's movement, which grew out of the civil rights and Vietnam protests. Although we are often said to be living in an age in which many young women refuse to identify themselves as feminists, life in America has changed a great deal as a result of the women's movement. Women today are a vital part of the labor force in a wide range of occupations outside the "pink ghetto" occupied by nurses, teachers, and secretaries. Although there is still a significant gap between men's and women's salaries, most of us now concede that it should not exist. And among Baby Boomers there is a growing sense that a good marriage is a partnership of equals, not one in which a subservient woman plays handmaid and housewife to her husband and their children. The women's movement helped train a generation in the tactics of grassroots politics. It also brought a recognition that many of the most important issues are the ones that affect our lives: Who takes care of the children? Who takes out the garbage? Whose right is it to decide whether a woman will have an abortion?

The final ingredient of the Baby Boom generation's mixed attitude toward government was Watergate. As the complex tale unfolded on television, it became clear that Washington was no longer the destination of choice for the young idealist who wanted to serve his country. The name of the game was getting power and holding on to it. It was the last brushstroke on a sign that read, GOVERNMENT IS NOT TO BE TRUSTED.

And so the generation that started out with Candide-like optimism in the early 1960s ended up tending its own gardens in the 1980s. The age of the yuppie was here, the newsweeklies proclaimed. Although many rejected that label, much of the population confined its interests to largely private concerns. After all, the ardently right-wing Reagan administration had very little interest in the views of burnt-out ex-hippies, anyway. Careers became all-important, and whatever energy was left over was channeled into relationships, not politics.

Now that the "thirtysomething" generation is having children, we might expect its interests continue along the same lines. What could be more reasonable than shoring up the castle to create a haven in a hostile world? But in the long run, the turbulence of the civil rights and antiwar movements is not the kind of recipe that produces passive, 1950s-style voters. We believe that as the Baby Boomers establish economic security in their work and personal security in their families, their concerns will turn outward again. The turn of the century will not be the 1960s revisited, but it won't be the placid, self-involved decade of the 1980s, either. Ultimately, this generation will become activists again, at least in part to make a better world for their children.

They will do it, in part, with the tactics learned in their youth: picketing, protests, and PR—methods designed to swing the power of the media behind their cause. But only in part. One triumph of the Reagan administration was to make voluntarism fashionable again. During the last wave of American activism, traditional charities seemed somehow obsolete; the only way to make changes that mattered was to storm the barricades in Washington until the government fell to its knees. Today, the "Me Decade" is giving way to the "We Decade." Despite accusations that today's yuppies are self-centered and even downright selfish, many young professionals are already making time to do volunteer work in many fields; in some circles, charity is already chic. And it's something both political parties can agree on. Republicans have always come down against "throwing money" at social problems and called for local initiative as the solution of choice. The Democrats have always been the party of big government, but so long as the federal budget deficit lasts, they may find it politically convenient to avoid new programs and call instead on voluntary efforts to solve problems.

RE-GREENING OF AMERICA

One key "cause" around which both local and national activist organizations will form is the environment. People can see the effects of pollution in their everyday lives, and they can often organize to bring about changes on the local level.

When the environmental movement began as yet another reformist offshoot of the antiwar movement, some young activists sneered at it as a "soft" issue, one that would distract the movement's energies from more dramatic problems. In fact, the environmental movement goes to the heart of the way a country works and how it organizes its industry, resources, and economic life. Environmental issues are a major rallying point for alternative politics in Eastern Europe largely because they raise such fundamental questions about the right of the state to control industrial activity.

To some extent, people take notice of environmental issues only when they have achieved a certain standard of living. Many developing countries with low standards of worker safety and poor environmental practices argue that the cost of cleaning up their acts would be so high that their industries would no longer be viable in world markets. Such concerns, they claim, are luxuries that only the already industrialized, prosperous West can afford.

Many American companies also maintain that effective antipollution measures would render them unprofitable; witness the long battle to get Midwestern utilities to do anything at all about acid rain. But it is clear that at the local level, environmental concerns have never faded.

One environmental problem that local groups will organize around is the disposal of toxic waste. Evidence suggests that some forms of toxic waste can produce cancer and birth defects in the nearby population, and many local activist organizations are already very concerned about the issue. Some have formed NIMBY ("not in my backyard") groups to keep dumps out of their neighborhoods. Such organizations play on the strong fears aroused by the dangers of having toxic waste nearby.

But local activists will soon discover that it is not enough for them to organize solely in their own neighborhoods. We expect to see more and more cooperation among local groups that can coordinate their work through nationwide computer networks.

Take, for example, a grassroots organization trying to stop a toxic-waste dump from moving into the neighborhood. Through an environmental-action clearinghouse, it will be able to find other groups that have already won similar fights in their own communities. Those organizations can then pass on their expertise on federal law, and provide the medical and scientific information that helped them win their battle. They can also teach the less-experienced group how to make effective media contacts and how to pressure city, county, and state officials.

Leaders who become involved in local fights against toxic waste will see national policy aspects of the problem. They will come to decide that it's not simply a question of whose backyard should receive toxic waste; instead, many will conclude that toxic dumps as they are now constructed are inherently unsafe and need to be changed.

Small networks of these groups will start meeting across community and state lines to discuss the issue. They will be united by the conviction that no one wants to have toxic dumps. In comparing their experiences, they will soon raise more global questions: Can safer dumps be constructed? Can waste products be treated so that they are no longer harmful? Is it possible to change the industrial processes themselves so that these wastes are not produced in the first place?

Each group will make the discovery that its interests go beyond the local level. It will not be a matter of altruism or greater public consciousness, but of strategy: in the modern world, matters that have an impact on the local level very often are controlled from Washington. To bring about local change, activists must work nationally as well as locally.

FAMILY ISSUES

A major social trend that will affect politics in 2000 is the burgeoning number of women in the workplace. Their growing economic and political power will bring to the fore a number of social questions neglected by the activists of the pre-Watergate era. The most important of these will be day care and early-childhood education. In more and more households, both parents will be working and spending less time at home. With greater mobility, few working couples will be able to rely on extended families to help out with child care; if Grandma has not moved to Florida, she's probably on an adventure cruise to Easter Island, or going back to school, to get an advanced degree. As women move into positions of power, they will be more able to pressure their companies to provide childcare during working hours. Those who cannot will turn to Washington. Whether childcare is provided directly by the government or by legislation that requires employers to offer it, by 2000, day care will be available for the children of nearly all working mothers. Grassroots political organizing will make it happen.

Once the kids get into school, parents will shift their attention to the educational system. Educational activist groups will push hard to improve the performance of their communities' schools by pressuring for better facilities and a higher caliber of teachers and administrators. But the education-minded, like opponents of toxic dumps, will find that their local problems are merely small components in issues that affect the entire nation. The time will come when these groups coordinate with their counterparts across the country and bring pressure to bear on Washington in order to promote significant, long-lasting improvement in American education as a whole. Some issues simply cannot be tackled at the local level; the sorry state of teacher training, for example, will require some sort of national policy if it is to change for the better.

Homelessness is another social issue that will be attacked both locally and nationally. Cities and towns are currently responsible for providing emergency food and shelter for those who need them. In theory, it is a reasonable approach. Who should know better how many homeless people require aid, officials in Washington or those who actually live in the community? But while some cities have been relatively generous to their needy, others have done little to send aid where it is needed.

Activists on behalf of the homeless point out that the central issue is the lack of affordable housing. In many locales, even people who hold down regular jobs find it difficult or impossible to pay for houses or apartments; competition from better-paid white-collar workers has driven rents out of reach for the working poor. Even if local organizations can provide adequate temporary care for the homeless, a patchwork approach to this issue may create new problems in that cities or regions with effective programs will become magnets for homeless people, and the burden on those communities will grow.

Workers in this field are already devoting as much energy to establishing a national homeless policy as they are to alleviating the problem at the local level. This is a trend that will grow throughout the 1990s until an effective national solution to the problem is found. Once again, computer-aided networks will help local groups coordinate their efforts more efficiently.

One popular issue that has already attracted both widespread grassroots activism and national attention is the anti-abortion movement. Although public opinion polls repeatedly show that a majority of Americans support a woman's right to abortion, at least under some circumstances, the antiabortionist's cause has struck a strong emotional chord among an activist minority. Through a number of effective tactics adopted from the antiwar movement of the 1960s and 1970s, including sit-ins at abortion clinics and harassment of women seeking their services, it has made its presence felt. It has also succeeded in making the "pro-life" position an important issue for federal judicial appointments during, and undoubtedly after, the Reagan era.

As this is written, there is no way to forecast the future of the antiabortion movement. Much will depend on Supreme Court decisions during the next decade, and at least one that will be handed down while this book is in press. Over the last few years the court has narrowed the application of *Roe v. Wade,* the 1973 case that legalized abortion, by upholding some state-set limits on access to the procedure. For the moment it has left in place the fundamental assumptions of the original decision. But recently it has agreed to reconsider the basic issue of whether women have a right to abortion; that issue may have been decided by the time this appears. With several conservative Reagan appointees sitting on the bench, the margin of support for *Roe v. Wade* has narrowed considerably. This time the antiabortion movement could win its point. If not, the 1990s will provide many more opportunities. The three strongest supporters of the original decision are in their seventies and eighties; if they are replaced with judges sympathetic to the antiabortion cause during the Bush administration, reversal of *Roe v. Wade* may become almost inevitable. If the decision is reversed, the success of the antiabortion lobby will stand as testimony to the power of determined activists to change Washington policy, even when they are supported by only a minority of Americans.

On the other hand, if a strongly conservative court backed by right-wing Republican administrators makes no radical changes in abortion law, the right-to-lifers of the year 2000 will have to wonder how much chance of success their cause really has.

The issues of the next century may lack the appeal or charisma of the antiwar and civil rights movements. Activists in those days could feel that they were doing battle for causes of historic proportions. But the growing concern for matters closer to home will lead many people to quieter, but just as powerful, involvement with the problems that affect our daily lives. Issues that Americans live with day after day often arouse the strongest passions. They will prove at least as powerful as the great national and international concerns that brought this same generation to the streets in the 1960s and 1970s.

8

POLICEMEN

TO THE WORLD

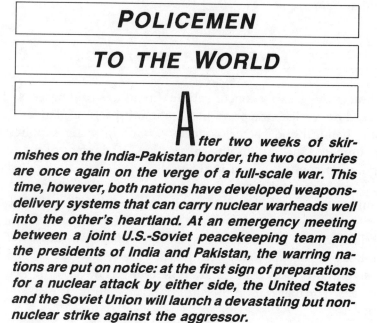

fter two weeks of skir-mishes on the India-Pakistan border, the two countries are once again on the verge of a full-scale war. This time, however, both nations have developed weapons-delivery systems that can carry nuclear warheads well into the other's heartland. At an emergency meeting between a joint U.S.-Soviet peacekeeping team and the presidents of India and Pakistan, the warring nations are put on notice: at the first sign of preparations for a nuclear attack by either side, the United States and the Soviet Union will launch a devastating but non-nuclear strike against the aggressor.

The imaginary scenario above could not possibly happen next year, but by the turn of the twenty-first century, the United States and the USSR probably will be the closest thing the world has to a global police force. If the internal and external changes begun by Mikhail Gorbachev in the late 1980s continue, the two superpowers will soon recognize that they share a common interest in maintaining world stability despite the profound differences in their social and political systems. Although they will not actually become allies, the Cold War will be drawing to a permanent close before the year 2000.

Why the new spirit of cooperation? Cool-eyed pragmatism in the face of growing threats to world peace: the spread of nuclear, chemical, and biological weapons to unstable Third World countries. With these weapons in the hands of regimes that are much too likely to use them, regional conflicts soon will have the potential to boil over into devastating conflagrations. Whatever their remaining differences, neither the United States nor the Soviet Union will want to see that happen.

THIRD WORLD MENACE

Although the greatest concern about threats to world peace is usually focused on nuclear weapons, in fact the most serious danger may be from chemical and bacteriological warfare. If water supplies were contaminated through biological warfare, 30 percent of the world's population could be dead in thirty days.

The majority of the world's countries signed the Geneva Protocols banning the use of chemical weapons after the First World War; there was a general consensus that some weapons were simply too horrible to use. Unfortunately, these weapons are attractive to a number of countries today because they are relatively easy and inexpensive to produce, yet they are potentially as devastating as atomic weapons. For that reason they are dubbed "the poor man's nuclear weapons."

It is clear that chemical weapons, and even biological weapons, are being manufactured in a number of countries. For several years, for example, Iraq has operated what it claims to be a defoliant factory. But what use for defoliants is there in a land known for its arid climate and sparse vegetation? The subterfuge was clearly exposed when Iraq unleashed chemical weapons against Iran and its own Kurdish population—thereby becoming the first country to use these weapons since World War I. More recently, Western intelligence agencies have reported that Iraq also has a factory producing typhoid, anthrax, and Rift Valley fever for use as biological weapons, which also are rumored to have been used against the Kurds.

Some critics object that the United States and the Soviet Union have both used chemical weapons, even as they self-righteously urge the rest of the world to stop their production. In fact, the proxies of both superpowers used debilitating gas in Afghanistan. But although this weapon injures, it does not kill.

The solution, as we see it, is for the great powers to cease production of chemical weapons and to get rid of their stockpiles, save perhaps for whatever tiny supply is needed for the development of countermeasure defenses. We would also have to make sure that our allies cannot blithely export the components for chemical-weapons manufacture to countries like Iraq and Libya, as West Germany has done. If the United States and the Soviet Union are serious about eliminating this threat, they will eventually join forces and strike preemptively at any nation that violates the nonproduction agreement.

PEACEFUL EVOLUTION

As the 1980s drew to a close, the first five years of the Gorbachev era had already changed American attitudes toward its onetime Public Enemy Number One. Anticommunism has been a staple of the American political diet since the Bolshevik Revolution. Although the two countries put aside their differences long enough to fight the Nazis in World War II, Soviet-American relations slid downhill almost from the moment that American and Soviet troops embraced at the Elbe River in 1945. In the 1950s, Senator Joseph McCarthy and Richard Nixon boosted their political careers with the search for the communists that they insisted had burrowed into the highest levels of American government.

Every American President from Truman to Reagan has paid at least lip service to the idea that the communist menace—and its wellspring, the Soviet Union—were *the* major danger to American security. We may laugh today about the duck-and-cover drills in which students practiced scrambling under their desks to prepare for an atomic attack, but at the time the fear was real. When Nikita Khrushchev was shown on TV, he was always a frightening presence, banging his shoe on the table at the United Nations and promising that "we will bury you!"

At first, Ronald Reagan appeared to be no different from his predecessors. In one of his most famous early speeches, he insisted that the Soviet Union was an "evil empire." But when Mikhail Gorbachev came to power in 1985, *glasnost* (openness) and *perestroika* (restructuring) soon entered the vocabulary of Americans whose previous knowledge of Russian extended only as far as *borscht, Sputnik,* and *nyet.*

In just a few months, the terms of the game had changed dramatically. The rhetoric was turned down several notches on both sides, and despite the friction between Nancy Reagan and Raisa Gorbachev, by the end of the decade, summit meetings between the two leaders had become almost as common as nasty exchanges had been in years past. It was at those meetings that the foreign policy of the year 2000 was first tentatively hammered out between President Reagan and General Secretary Gorbachev.

By the time the Soviet leader visited New York briefly in December 1988 for his final summit with President Reagan and incoming President Bush, the change was visible for all to see. In a speech at the United Nations, Gorbachev announced that the Soviet Union would cut its military presence in Eastern Europe and declared that "the use or threat of force" is not an acceptable tool in foreign policy. He went on to say that "freedom of choice is a universal principle that should allow for no exceptions." He even went so far as to declare that this principle "applies to both the capitalist and to the socialist system."

Even Gorbachev's advisers admitted to surprise at the declaration. But it was really only a continuation of the "new thinking" begun by Gorbachev almost from the moment he stepped into office. In order to see what this all means for U.S.–Soviet relations in 2000, we must take a closer look at just what Gorbachev has been up to at home.

Many Americans have been asking themselves whether Gorbachev is the Jeffersonian democrat he sometimes seems to be, dedicated to the freedom of his people, or merely a supreme pragmatist trying to curry favor in the West while saving on defense spending. The question is almost beside the point. One thing is clear: he has taken a cold, hard look at the Soviet system, seen, and recognized that it certainly wouldn't work.

Gorbachev's admission both shocked his people and startled the outside world with its candor: the country that had effectively jousted with the United States for world leadership ever since the end of World War II was unable to provide its citizens with a standard of living that was significantly better than that of the developing world. Though bread was cheap—so cheap, Gorbachev complained, that Moscow children sometimes played soccer with a loaf of black bread—many other foods were priced out of the reach of the average consumer, if they were available at all. Even in the relatively prosperous cities, the Soviet people, particularly the young, continue to share apartments, waiting years for scarce housing to become available. They must also wait for consumer goods that are taken for granted in the West, and the goods they finally obtain usually are of such poor quality that they could not be sold in the United States.

The heart of the problem is that the lumbering, state-run economy cannot respond to consumer needs. Workers are guaranteed their jobs—and salaries—regardless of how badly they and their factories perform. Meanwhile, high military spending takes up a growing portion of the stagnant economic production. Gorbachev's daring solution was to inject the economic incentives of the free market into a system that had spent the past seventy years trying to destroy those very markets! By demanding that factories begin to earn their own way, and by allowing limited amounts of private enterprise, he hoped to unleash productive forces that had been pent up for decades.

At this point he ran into a fundamental conflict with the Soviet system: in order to promote economic freedom and entrepreneurial innovation, he would have to relax the tight economic and political controls that had held Soviet society together since the tsars.

Gorbachev decided that he needed to mobilize the country's intellectuals to support his programs. He freed hundreds of political prisoners and allowed major increases in Jewish and Armenian emigration. But the small openings in the dam of Soviet control have threatened to unleash a flood that could overwhelm the country—and Gorbachev himself. Central Asia is practically in a state of siege because of long-festering tensions between Armenians and Azerbaijanis. On the Baltic coast, the non-Slavic states of Estonia, Latvia, and Lithuania clamor for more autonomy. Perhaps if there were caviar for all, Gorbachev's position would be secure. But the shelves of the groceries remain barren, and the Soviet leader has admitted to his people that his policies have no hope of remedying the nation's problems immediately.

The big question facing Gorbachev—and the United States—is whether he will survive the change he has begun but cannot soon finish. The release of the long-brewing tensions could ultimately work against the Soviet leader. While the West may be pleased with Gorbachev's decision to cut back the Soviet military presence in Eastern Europe, the move could strengthen the position of his opponents, who charge that his policies have weakened the country. If those frustrations continue to mount, a right-wing coup might well leave Gorbachev cleaning latrines in the countryside as part of his exile. It happened to another would-be reformer, Deng Xiaoping. The single most important factor that will determine whether Gorbachev stays in power is his relationship with President George Bush and the United States. If he can continue the thaw in our relations, he'll be able to cut down on military spending and use the savings to rebuild the Soviet economy and provide the consumer goods that his population wants. Once he does that, his conservative opponents will have lost the lever they need to pry him out of office.

For the moment, Gorbachev appears to have shored up his position in the Politburo and established his popularity among the population. Any remotely progressive forces know that short of a complete overthrow of the Soviet system, he is their only hope for change. His recent step-up of the criticism of Stalin's bloody reign should undercut any nostalgia from those who yearn for the good old authoritarian days.

DOING BUSINESS WITH THE SOVIETS

While much of the credit for better relations goes to Mr. Gorbachev for setting the wheels of change in motion, American attitudes are changing as well. American companies are becoming excited by the prospect of doing business in one of the world's largest nations. By the beginning of the next century, American investors will be taking full advantage of plentiful raw materials and relatively cheap Soviet labor. They will be able to open plants that would not be profitable in the United States. The Soviets will be eager to learn American technical, managerial, and marketing know-how. Perhaps, like the Chinese, they too will set up schools to study American management and financial systems.

The successful integration of the European Economic Community after 1992 will raise the level of marketing sophistication not only in Europe, but also in the United States and the Soviet Union. Consumers will be able to use toll-free telephone numbers to buy anything, anywhere in the world. Do you have a hankering for real Russian borscht, blinis, or caviar? Just pick up the phone, charge the purchase to your credit card (by 2000, the ruble will be convertible to dollars), and your treat is on the way.

With more industrial investment and joint ventures in play, more and more Soviets and Americans will be doing business and making personal contacts. We will be spending more time in each other's countries to work and study. It will become nearly as ordinary for college students to spend a semester in Moscow as it now is for them to study in Paris or Madrid. Well-to-do Moscow University students will be as likely to visit New York or Los Angeles as they are to vacation in the East Bloc. Cultural exchange, already quite strong, will continue at a fast pace as the next century approaches. Although more Russians will undoubtedly learn English because it will be useful to them throughout much of the world, the Cyrillic alphabet will be looking a little less foreign to us. What this all means is that our two countries will move closer to normal relations.

The technological and informational innovations that will have such a strong impact on American life will also affect our Soviet comrades. Television and radio satellite hookups will become more and more common. Phil Donahue has already traded jokes with Soviet TV personality Vladimir Posner, with audiences in Leningrad and Seattle tuned in.

We will also be undertaking joint projects in space. One likely mission is a joint flight to Mars. The Soviet Union has planned such a journey since the late 1960s, and has made steady progress toward that goal—but the Soviet tortoise probably would not mind letting the American hare join the program if it meant splitting the bill. Already, our space stations and vehicles are fitted with compatible docking equipment. If either country has an emergency in space, the other can assist.

Computer hookups between private groups are another force that will soon bring Soviet and American interests together. Equipped with a personal computer and a modem, American home computer users already have access to a worldwide network of people with similar interests; by the year 2000, Soviet "hackers" will enjoy the same freedom. Scientists and doctors can exchange unclassified information, as can computer junkies. Students especially will take advantage of computerized communications systems to exchange information on everything from rock groups to travel plans. Fax machines will have infiltrated even Soviet society by then, and they too will speed the exchange of information between individual computer users as well as corporations. The economic and informational changes to come will so transform the Soviet Union that by the year 2000 it will be nearly impossible to recognize. By then it will resemble an enormous Finland, without a stock market—a largely free society, but with an enormous infrastructure of social programs.

Soviets and Americans will be able to see that not everyone "on the other side" leads a life of bitter struggle and oppression, as they once were taught to believe. The more the two societies see of each other, the more they are likely to want to emulate at least some aspects of the other society. In Eastern Europe, the freer viewing of television across national borders has already opened minds. Almost all East Germans can watch West German TV, and vice versa. Czechs and East Germans today sometimes watch Russian broadcasts that are more open and innovative than their own. As Russians see more of American life, they will inevitably ask why their stores are not as well stocked as our own.

We, too, will learn some lessons from our Soviet counterparts. Like the Soviets, we will come to provide health insurance for all citizens, more day care, and more care for the poor and homeless. If you want to see what our country will look like in the year 2000, look at Sweden today. But unlike Sweden, we will provide those benefits without inflicting high taxes on ourselves. We will be able to provide these new social services because we will be producing more goods and more agricultural products—enough to meet everyone's basic needs, as the Soviet Union at least attempts to do.

In short, the Soviet Union will use the tools of capitalism to stimulate its economy, providing more consumer goods and a higher standard of living for its people. At the same time, its repressive social structure will be opening up in order to encourage a more freewheeling economy. Meanwhile, the United States will be studying the lessons of socialist countries and learning how to take better care of its citizens. In little more than a decade, the vast gulf between the Soviet and American societies that exists today will resemble the differences between Finland and Sweden—two countries that are not very dissimilar.

As we talk to each other more easily and more frequently, political interest groups in the two countries will work together more easily than ever before. One continuing area of activism will be environmental issues, a truly global concern. The first international treaty to reduce acid rain, approved by twenty-seven nations, should go into effect in 1990. This is the first step toward environmental cooperation on a world scale. By the next century, citizens' groups will lobby Moscow as well as Washington to do something about the chlorofluorocarbon pollution that is destroying the ozone layer and allowing harmful amounts of ultraviolet radiation from the sun to penetrate the atmosphere.

Growing contact through computer networks will not only allow cooperation between groups that already exist; it will also change the very nature of those groups. For example, there has been some cooperation between different organizations that are part of the international peace movement. Until now, most such groups in the Soviet Union have been organized through the Communist Party; in effect, they are little more than front organizations for the Soviet government. Many American skeptics charge that these groups are meant to pressure the United States into reducing its presence in Western Europe while remaining silent about the Soviet presence in Eastern Europe. However, a small independent peace movement has also developed in the Soviet Union and its satellite countries; its members are not organized by their country's party apparatus. As more communication outside the government becomes possible, such groups will continue to spread, both in the Soviet Union and in Eastern Europe.

BACK FROM THE BRINK

Enlightened self-interest will drive home the obvious point that regional conflicts serve no particular interest, either for the United States or for Russia, and they present unacceptable risks. Although the superpowers have maintained a nuclear standoff for four decades, the biggest danger today is that a flare-up in one of the world's many hot spots could lead to a nuclear confrontation.

However, it is beginning to look as if regional conflicts can be controlled if not actually solved. The United States and the USSR negotiated their differences on southern Africa so that Namibia could at last become independent. Cuba has agreed to pull its troops out of Angola. And while there is no peace treaty yet between Iran and Iraq, the superpowers were both relieved to see an end to the long and bloody Gulf War. The United States and the Soviet Union will use their power and prestige to push for a peaceful, workable solution to the problems of the Middle East. The United States has already begun talking to the PLO, while, with renewed Jewish emigration from Russia, Soviet-Israeli relations have also begun to thaw. The two superpowers eventually will push both parties into making some concessions they may not like, and then will join forces to guarantee the new boundaries.

Most significantly, the Soviet Union has completed a face-saving retreat from Afghanistan, thereby extricating itself from its own Vietnam. Those disastrous foreign involvements have taught important lessons to both superpowers. One is that it is difficult for even the most modern, well-equipped army to fight against a nationalist guerrilla movement operating on its own turf. More important, the cost of fighting such a war is simply too high; it places a tremendous drain on the economy and causes dissatisfaction back home. In the United States, the Vietnam War nearly tore the country apart. Even in the tightly controlled USSR, the younger generation balked at the idea of dying for no clear purpose in a war far from home.

Both countries will move into the new millennium with a new spirit of pragmatism. Naturally, both will continue to look out for their national security interests, but they will be much more reluctant to leap into foreign conflicts unless national security is really at stake. The new attitude will require a major rethinking of traditional security arrangements for both countries; in fact, that rethinking is already well under way.

Since the end of World War II, the Soviet Union has viewed Eastern Europe as a buffer, a *cordon sanitaire,* necessary for protection from the potentially hostile NATO alliance. In fact, it eventually became the front line of military fortification against the perceived Western threat. But the Soviets had to pay a high price for their southwestern front: in addition to the actual cost of military expenditures, they believed they needed a compliant and docile alliance on their flanks.

What they did not reckon with in 1945 was the tremendous pull of Western Europe. Poles, Hungarians, and Czechs insist that they have always looked to Vienna, Berlin, and Paris for inspiration, not to Moscow. By 2000, Eastern Europe will evolve a new identity with the emphasis on Western Europe, not on Eastern Europe.

COMMON CAUSE

When the Soviet Union cuts back its heavy military obligations in the East, it will not only save money; the move will also unleash a new era of prosperity in Eastern Europe. Hungary, for example, is already moving close to a free-market economy, complete with its own stock market. There is even talk of noncommunist political parties. Assuming this transition goes smoothly, it could become a model for the Soviet Union's own *perestroika* program. Meanwhile, Gorbachev will be creating a revolution of rising expectations at home; if our socialist brethren in the East can live better, Russians will ask, why can't we?

As tensions over Eastern Europe subside, military procedures between the United States and the Soviet Union will be normalized. To a limited extent, it is happening already: the two countries have exchanged verification teams to make sure that nuclear weapons reductions are being carried out properly. That first tentative, grudging step will prove to be the beginning of a trend. NATO observers will attend Warsaw Pact war games and vice versa, and visits to missile bases and manufacturing facilities will become almost commonplace.

As the United States and the Soviet Union come to feel less threatened by each other in Europe, they will come to realize that if they can defuse those tensions, they should be able to perform the same feat in the Third World. After all, the whole point of their rivalry for leadership in the developing world was to gain advantage in the war between capitalism and socialism. Now that the Soviet Union has tacitly acknowledged the moribund state of its system and is working to change it, it should be possible for the onetime rivals to cooperate as they did in World War II, almost half a century ago.

Even in the first years of *glasnost,* we have seen the beginnings of this new cooperation. At the end of 1988, a Soviet icebreaker came to Alaska to cut a path for two stranded gray whales that American and Canadian workers had been unable to free. And when a devastating earthquake rocked Soviet Armenia in December, killing tens of thousands and leaving hundreds of thousands more homeless, American aid helped out for the first time since 1945. Both incidents were small signs of a new spirit that will grow throughout the 1990s.

By 2000, we will have banded together in our first cooperative development programs in the Third World. Neither side stands to gain anything from a world ravaged by war, famine, and disease. If just 10 percent of the money that the two superpowers spend on weapons were given as aid to the underdeveloped countries of the world, we could measurably improve their lot. They may never be as prosperous as the West; we may not even be able to reduce the gap between our income levels. But a joint effort between the world's most powerful nations should be able to keep it from getting wider.

Soviet-American cooperation could take several forms; in the long run, all strategies probably will be tried. At present, American cash grants are by far the larger, but as the Soviet Union gets its own economic house in order and the ruble becomes convertible into other currencies, Russia, too, will be able to make larger donations to other countries throughout the world. In addition, American and Soviet development programs will take place side by side, and even in cooperation. Soviet physicians and health-care officials undoubtedly know at least as much as their American counterparts about bringing rudimentary health care to isolated rural areas with primitive living conditions. Once the two nations have buried their hostilities, emergency personnel will be able to stop worrying about which country supplied a sack of powdered milk and concentrate on getting it to starving children as fast as possible.

WORLD POLICE FORCE

But the real area of change will be in how the superpowers deal with regional flashpoints. Nuclear war between the United States and the Soviet Union is as close to unthinkable as anything in public life. Unfortunately, the once-exclusive membership in the atomic club is expanding. The official nuclear powers—the United States, the Soviet Union, France, Britain, and the People's Republic of China—have been joined by India, Pakistan, Israel, and South Africa. Since late 1987, rumors have floated through the international community that one of our NATO allies has even supplied Iran with bomb-grade plutonium. The United States itself has sold reactors to Argentina and Brazil, albeit for peaceful ends; both countries are now thought to be in the final stages of developing their own nuclear bombs. And Libya is actively seeking atomic weapons.

With atomic weapons in the hands of unstable Third World nations, nuclear war between the lesser powers is all but inevitable. The threat of chemical and biological warfare is even more likely now that Middle Eastern countries known to have sponsored terrorism are developing both. Iraqi President Saddam Hussein has announced that his nation is developing a "superweapon" designed to protect it from all possible adversaries. The most likely prospect is a medium-range missile capable of carrying nerve gas or bacteria to Teheran or Tel Aviv.

Horrible as chemical weapons are, the world could probably accept their use between two Third World nations; after all, it did nothing when Iraq used mustard gas against Iran. But biological weapons might quickly spread from their target throughout the world, and the possibility of a nuclear confrontation between any two nations immediately ups the ante on any regional conflict. Short of decisive action by the United Nations—which seems incapable of it—only the two superpowers can prevent the horrible specter of nuclear war. In the late 1990s, they will join forces to do so, and become their own UN peacekeeping force of sorts. By 2000, the United States and the Soviet Union will be the closest thing the world has to a global police force.

Just what form will that police force take? Early in the twenty-first century, it will be an informal arrangement. Faced with a potential nuclear emergency, the two nations will hurriedly coordinate their forces and issue a joint communiqué warning the hostile parties against any use of atomic weapons. Later in the century, a U.S.-Soviet joint command will serve as a clearinghouse for military intelligence on Third World hotspots. Given modern computers and satellite communications, there need not even be a joint office in Moscow or Washington. Members of the command will work from their home offices and stay in touch with each other to monitor any tense military situation.

Go back for a moment to the imaginary showdown between India and Pakistan described at the beginning of this chapter. The joint command would carefully monitor the military buildup the moment tensions began to rise. Diplomatic reports from Islamabad and New Delhi would be shared as well. As long as the two combatants limited themselves to conventional armaments, the superpowers would use the traditional diplomatic tools: statements urging calm, United Nations resolutions urging talks, and shuttle diplomacy between the two capitals. But even at this stage, a joint task force would begin to coordinate a possible military action.

As the political rhetoric in India and Pakistan began to heat up, the joint command would draw up a strategic plan. A joint U.S.-Soviet diplomatic team would serve notice on both capitals that a contingency plan was being drawn up for a devastating but non-nuclear strike on the nations' key industrial centers. The plan would go into effect the moment the superpowers had reason to believe that a nuclear strike was being readied. While that might not bring India and Pakistan to the bargaining table, it seems likely that they would agree, however reluctantly, to refrain from using nuclear weapons. If not, the first Third World war ended by a non-nuclear bombing mission carried out by the superpowers should be enough to prevent any recurrence.

The United States and the Soviet Union will not become allies during our lifetimes. Barring far more dramatic changes than are promised even by General Secretary Gorbachev's reforms, our political systems will remain too incompatible for that. But they will continue to put aside their hostilities of seven decades in order to solve the security problems that now threaten both countries. By doing so, they will make the world a more peaceful place and give it the only safety from nuclear destruction that can now be counted on.

THE WORLD IN 1990

There was a precedent, of sorts, for 1989. The year 1848 saw violent revolutions break out in France, Germany, Italy, and the Hapsburg domains of Austria, Hungary, and Bohemia; they all failed, and life in Europe went on much as it had been. By contrast, the developments in 1987 transformed both Europe and the world. The revolution that required ten years in Poland took only ten months in East Germany, ten weeks in Hungary and Czechoslovakia, and less than ten days in Bulgaria and Romania. And in Nicaragua, the return to democracy which years of armed combat had failed to achieve was won in barely ten hours at the ballot box. Even the political ice age of the Soviet Union has begun to thaw.

Nearly all the events that we foresaw occurring in the 1990s have suffered one of three fates: Some of the most probable have come to pass already, some less likely ones have now become all but inevitable, and some have been superseded by changes for which we had only a little hope. Very little remains unchanged.

Let us begin with the Soviet Union itself. We expect that some of the fifteen Soviet republics will gradually win full sovereignty over the next five to ten years. Though Moscow now seems determined to retain its hold over the Baltic states, that option is no longer available. The process of change will be slow and difficult, but Lithuania, Latvia, and Estonia now resemble the Poland of the late 1970s far more closely than they do the Hungary of 1956 or the Czechoslovakia of 1968. By the turn of the century, they will be free nations once more.

Elsewhere in the Soviet Union, change will be more difficult and the results less dramatic. The Baltic states were annexed by force at the end of World War II, and President Gorbachev has already acknowledged that his nation has no legal claim to sovereignty over them; the other Soviet states were spoils of the battles that followed the October Revolution, and under the Russian system there is no tie more binding. When the twenty-first century dawns, the dozen republics outside the Baltic will still belong to the Soviet Union.

The Union will be a different place, however; in this, our forecasts remain largely unchanged. As the growth of trade spreads Western ideas and economic practices through Soviet culture, and as the nascent multiparty system there gains power, the Communist Party will slowly lose its hold, both on the daily life of Soviet citizens and on the apparatus of government. The loss of the Baltic republics will cause a backlash among Party hardliners, just as their threatened loss has done in the last few months. The resurgence of traditional ethnic rivalries long controlled by the Red Army will cause further delays. But within a decade, the obstacles will have been overcome. The Soviet Union will remain soviet in its name, but not in its political system. America's old enemy will have Finlandized itself. At this point, we would not even bet against the formation of a Moscow stock exchange.

Moscow's abrupt abandonment of its Stalinist heritage has even softened the perpetually hard line of America's staunchest foe, Cuba. Though President Fidel Castro continues to bluster for his nation's television cameras, semisecret talks aimed at ending the decades-old antagonism have already begun. Washington's offer: If Cuba refrains from supplying arms to South American leftist guerrillas, the United States will restore trade and tourism with its island neighbor. The price will be hard for Castro to accept, but he has little choice. Since the U.S. ordered its trade embargo in 1962, Cuba's economy has survived largely on Soviet subsidies, which are unlikely to continue many years longer—and American tourism is a gold mine that could more than make up the loss. In the end, Castro will come around. Our guess is that relations between the U.S. and Cuba will be fully normalized by 1992.

In China, political change will come more slowly still, but it will be well under way by the year 2000. The Party will relax its grip first in the economic development zones: the electronics centers around Canton and the heavy manufacturing area of Shendu. In 1997, Hong Kong and Macao will revert to Chinese rule; there is a good chance that by 1999 Taiwan will rejoin the mainland as well, though retaining some local autonomy. The need to preserve the vibrant economies of these provinces will set the precedent for world-scale capitalism within the People's Republic. Capitalist and democratic ideals will spread from these centers, peacefully completing the revolution that began at Tien-an-men Square. How long the process takes will depend largely on how long it takes the aging Stalinists of Beijing to die and be replaced by a generation of leaders who can face the reality of their system's failure.

A similar process has begun in South Africa, where the tentative reforms of President F. W. DeKlerk and the long-awaited release of Nelson Mandela have set off a semicontrolled revolution just in time to avert all-out bloodshed. There will be nothing in South Africa resembling the instant reforms of Eastern Europe. It will take two to three years to resolve the differences between Zulu leaders and the African National Congress, and two or three more for the unified black delegation to negotiate a plan for change with the South African government. Progress will occur in fits and starts, not without violence.

At this point, there is little doubt that the South African government has recognized that it must find some way to accommodate its nation's black majority. In confirmation, we have learned that the DeKlerk administration will soon mount a major campaign to recruit skilled technical workers from the East bloc nations, whose citizens have now gained the right to leave their native countries. The stated purpose will be to relieve a shortage of technicians that threatens the South African economy. The hidden agenda is to expand the white population and give the ruling minority a larger voice in whatever democratic government emerges from negotiations with black leaders. The program should be under way by the time this edition appears.

We now believe that by the year 2000, South Africa's black majority will be represented in a more or less democratic government. Most probably, each of the racial groups recognized by South African law—black, white, "colored," and Asian—will elect its own representatives, one-fourth of the legislature being reserved for each group. The result will not be an American-style system of one man, one vote, but it will be enough to bring desperately needed, peaceful reform to one of the world's most unjust societies.

For the United States, there is no downside to any of these changes. The bloodless revolution in Eastern Europe will bring it profitable new markets—more on that in Chapter Fifteen—and the security to tend to its domestic concerns without worrying about the plans of its former Communist bloc enemies. The slow-but-sure democratization of China and South Africa will further relieve the tensions that have so long distracted America's leaders from the needs of their own people. And to deal with those potential conflicts which remain, a peacekeeping alliance with the Soviet Union now seems even more likely.

COPING WITH

TERRORISM

he price that will be paid by all of us in resisting terrorist blackmail will not remain static; it will increase. . . . We've got to start telling people now that the next onslaught is going to be bloody, that in order to win we must be prepared to accept the loss of innocent lives; that whatever disaster occurs, the loss of life is the fault of the terrorist perpetrators, not the people who are trying to defend democracy.

–Maj. Alastair Morrison (ret.),
formerly second-in-command,
Special Air Service (an address
to the conference on "Terrorism in a
Technological World,")
January 20–22, 1987,
Washington, D.C.

From the slaughter at the Berlin Olympics in 1972 through the hostage-taking at the United States embassy in Teheran and the *Achille Lauro* shooting, to the bombing of Pan Am Flight 103 over Lockerbie, Scotland, in 1988, the record of international terrorism is a long and bloody one. For more than twenty-five years, the Western world has been held hostage by a few small bands of ruthless fanatics, aided by such outlaw governments as those of Iran, Libya, and Syria, willing to murder the innocent in order to bring power and publicity to their causes. There is no prospect that this gruesome social disease will disappear with the twentieth century.

Terrorism is the most potent way in which the weak and disenfranchised can ensure that their voices will be heard and their policies enacted over the will of the majority. It is a war of psychology and perception. The terrorist's message to his target government is simple and direct: "No matter how big and powerful you are, no matter how small we are, we can hurt you unless you do as we demand. You cannot deal with violence effectively. You cannot protect your people, and they will abandon you."

Bombings, assassinations, and kidnappings will continue, because they carry the terrorist's message most effectively. These crimes instill fear because people never know when they may be hurt or killed. They cast doubt on the true power of the target government, and so undermine it. Terrorism is, in general, enormously effective, because it is so economical: it hardly matters whom the terrorist chooses to kill or what target he chooses to destroy; virtually any dramatic act will get his point across. Since it is impossible to guard every person, every bus, every place of business in a country all the time, the terrorist merely has to wait for a convenient moment to strike.

In 1968, the Joint Chiefs of Staff grouped all forms of Third World violence together under the term *low-intensity conflict* (LIC.) According to the Joint Chiefs, "Low-intensity conflict is a limited politico-military struggle to achieve political, social, economic, or psychological objectives. It is often protracted and ranges from diplomatic, economic, and psychosocial pressures through terrorism and insurgency. Low-intensity conflict is generally confined to a geographic area and is often characterized by constraints on the weaponry, tactics, and level of violence." Former Secretary of Defense Caspar Weinberger added that "low-intensity conflict [is] the most immediate threat to free-world security for the rest of this century."

Since the 1960s, low-intensity conflict has undergone a worldwide revolution in its scope and organization. The United States and Great Britain organized special-operations military and paramilitary forces to deal with insurrections in the Third World, while the Soviet Union began teaching the Palestine Liberation Organization how to fight effectively after the Six-Day War of 1967. Terrorist activity has always had its roots in specific political or religious conflicts within specific geographic areas. But when the superpowers saw the chance to extend their spheres of influence without expending their own troops, they fostered this covert warfare, raising levels of training and even developing weapons specifically for counterinsurgency and terrorism. The quantum leap in the level of terrorist activity from 1960 to 1980, both in numbers and sophistication, has left the superpowers struggling to catch up with this runaway situation. Security experts can only fall farther behind in the coming decade.

NEW WEAPONS

The traditional weapons of the terrorist are cheap, readily available, and effective. They range from the knife to the small automatic rifle, from the Chinese AK-47 to plastic explosives. Now that they have the money and technical facilities of whole countries to back them, terrorists have a whole new range of weapons to use against a completely new set of targets. Here is a brief overview of the new terrorist arsenal:

"Stinger" Handheld Rockets. Small, light, and powerful, Stingers can be used with almost no training to knock out a tank or airplane. A knowledgeable source who prefers not to be identified claims that "if there had been one hundred people with Stingers in Grenada, there would have been no invasion."

Computer Viruses. Viruses are programs that destroy data stored in a computer memory. Although relatively few people understand the complex process of computer programming, it is easy for a programmer to write a program that will tell the computer to erase all its memory. What makes these viruses so hard to trace is that they often contain timing instructions, so that it may be months from the time a virus is introduced to the time it is triggered. The programmer simply embeds his codes into an otherwise harmless program and waits for the machine to self-destruct.

Electromagnetic Pulse Generators. Put one on a power line that feeds an important data-processing center, and the power surge it produces will wipe out the data in the computer's memory. The technique requires less in the way of high technology than it might seem.

Human Bombs. There is nothing particularly difficult about implanting explosives inside the body of a suicidally dedicated terrorist, and no screening method yet devised could keep him from boarding an airline full of innocent people. So far as we know, no terrorist organization has yet chosen this way to down a plane, but as airport security tightens in the 1990s it seems almost inevitable. There will be no shortage of Moslem fundamentalists, devoted to their holy war against the twentieth century, willing to take the shortcut to Paradise.

Chemical and Biological Weapons. Poison gas was first used on April 22, 1915, by Germany against the Allies on the Western front. As mentioned earlier, reaction against this barbarous weapon led in 1925 to the Geneva Protocols banning usage of chemical and biological weapons. But the protocols did not ban research; development of both types of weapon continued. Proponents of biological warfare continued to insist that spreading disease through a whole population offered a simple and cheap way to break a nation's will to fight. But these powerful diseases proved so hard to control that, by the 1970s, even the countries most expert in their use had all but done away with their research programs, at least publicly. Biological weapons have awesome staying power. Great Britain launched an experimental attack on Guernsey, in the English Channel, in the 1940s. The anthrax bacteria released on the island are every bit as virulent today as they were more than forty years ago.

The standard chemical weapons are frightening because they can be concocted from cheap and readily available materials. Common pesticide and fertilizer components can be used to make poison gas, while deadly chlorine gas can be obtained from the electrolysis of ocean water.

Some twenty countries are now developing chemical weapons, and at least ten are working on biological weapons, according to CIA Director William Webster. The United States stopped its chemical/biological weapons research under the Nixon administration, but restarted it under President Reagan.

François Heisbourg, director of the International Institute for Strategic Studies, in London, fears that the use of poison gas by Iraq in its war with Iran has broken a "psychological taboo." If one country can use poison gas without being punished, others must believe that using such chemical weapons is an acceptable way to conduct warfare. Countries will argue that if their enemies have these weapons, they must obtain them as well. The French government held a conference in January 1989 to extend the Geneva Protocols and seek mandatory sanctions against users of chemical and biological weapons.

Nuclear Weapons. It is horrifyingly easy to produce an atomic bomb. The techniques are available to every high-school physics student, and the American media have published actual plans for building a bomb on several occasions. The hardest part is obtaining the teaspoonful of weapons-grade plutonium that will produce an explosion the size of the Hiroshima bomb. Nuclear energy plants produce this substance as a waste material. Though waste-storage sites and transports are closely guarded, at least one hundred pounds of plutonium are missing from various sites and shipments around the world. That is not very much to lose over the course of forty years since we developed nuclear power, but it means that it is perfectly possible that there are a thousand terrorists with atomic bombs out there—somewhere.

Within a year or two, it will be not merely possible, but very likely indeed. According to recent reports, Iraq has begun a crash program to develop its own nuclear weapons. Saudi Arabia has paid for the effort, though it claims the money went to fund "peaceful uses of atomic energy." And Pakistan admits giving Iraq "all possible assistance in this endeavor." Does that aid include a supply of bomb-grade material, which Pakistan is believed to possess? If so, nuclear terrorism could be one of the major growth industries of the 1990s.

THE COMING RISE IN DOMESTIC TERROR

The biggest change in low-intensity conflict in the next decade will be an explosion in the incidence of domestic terrorism. Security measures now in place around the world will help slow the spread of international terrorism, but frustrated groups on the American continent will begin to take their cue from terrorists abroad. Here is a list of popular American causes which either may turn to violence in the 1990s or have already done so and are likely to accelerate their activities.

Antiabortionists. Planned Parenthood offices and women's health clinics that offer abortion have already been bombed. Attacks will increase as religious groups claim that God's law puts them above civil law and the rights of others.

Animal-Rights Activists. Many of us find it easy to be sympathetic toward people protesting the inhumane treatment of laboratory animals by drug and cosmetic companies, but in recent years these protests have taken a violent turn. Animal-rights activists have destroyed the laboratories of legitimate scientific researchers, costing them thousands of dollars in damages and sometimes years of irreplaceable work. One woman prominent in the movement was recently arrested for plotting the death of a cosmetic-company executive. We will see more of these activities in the 1990s.

Drug Dealers. Their purpose is to break the resistance of city and state governments and law-enforcement agencies, just as they have done in their native lands. Such terror will be sponsored by organized crime, and will also result from "disorganized crime"—the crazed violence too often seen in crack users. Their methods may be inspired by international political terrorists, but these armies have been trained in the drug wars of Colombia. The federal government can muster tremendous resources to fight terrorism within our borders, and national leaders have long had to deal with threats from other countries. But few city mayors or state governments are psychologically prepared, much less fiscally or strategically able, to deal with sustained pressure from terrorism.

Counterterror from the Right. On occasion, when local governments could no longer deal with violence and extortion, wealthy right-wingers who grew tired of terrorism formed death squads to "help out" the police. The same thing could easily happen in the United States by the turn of the century. Infiltrators for Central and South American governments may also threaten violence in their efforts to crack down on drug terrorists here and in their home countries.

The Sandinistas. If current peace efforts on the part of the Organization of American States and the United States are not accepted by Nicaragua, then Nicaragua's communist leaders may discover that they cannot keep the United States out of their country, even with the help of congressional Democrats. They will then begin to use foreign training and support to cross America's porous Southern border to carry out terrorist missions inside this country.

Mexico. The Mexican government is very unstable as the 1990s approach, with society on the verge of collapse. The country is ripe for a leftist revolution. If one should occur, the United States is likely to support a conservative government there. Almost nothing could stop a wave of terrorists who would fight back by penetrating the American Southwest and attacking civilian targets in such cities as El Paso, Houston, Dallas, Albuquerque, Phoenix, Los Angeles, and San Diego.

NEW TARGETS

Many of America's most vital industries and resources are vulnerable to terrorist attack. With little experience of violence in the United States, Americans tend to feel safe within their borders and so have not taken the precautions needed to ensure domestic safety. Nor are they likely to do so in the near future. Even if Americans had the will to protect themselves, it would be costly and inconvenient to guard every office and factory. Thus the U.S. will remain vulnerable until a major target is hit. Here are some of the likely targets:

- Attacks on computers already account for 60 percent of terrorist actions in the world. So-called computer viruses have become all too common, and direct violence against computer installations is almost a daily occurrence. Twenty-four computer centers were bombed in West Germany in a single year. Italy's Red Brigades and France's Action Directe have both targeted computer systems in Europe. It is only a matter of time before someone takes advantage of America's vulnerable computers to send a political message. August Bequai, a specialist in industrial security, says, "The sabotage of a key computer system could leave millions of people without electricity, shut down entire transportation systems, and bring thousands of business and government computers to a grinding halt. . . . The masters of terror are fast learning that high-tech is the Achilles' heel of post-industrial society."
- Nuclear power plants in France and Spain have already become the targets of attack by antinuclear activists. So far, these groups have only shut down the power temporarily, but the threat of serious damage that would release radiation over a wide area remains an ever-present possibility.
- Only two pipelines supply virtually all the natural gas used in the northeastern United States. Both pass through Louisiana; both are regulated by high-pressure pumps manufactured in foreign countries. If those pumps were destroyed, it would take more than a year to replace them. Both pipelines are essentially unprotected.
- Fewer than ten regional switching stations control virtually all telephone communications in all the large cities in the United

States. On Sunday, May 8, 1988, the station in Hinsdale, Illinois, a suburb southwest of Chicago, caught fire. It is an automated facility, with a single watchman on site and an overseer who monitors warning lights in a facility one hundred miles away. By the time the technicians decided their warning lights had not malfunctioned, and could summon help from local fire companies, the switching station was destroyed, triggering a frightening silence for one-third of all western Chicago telephones. Because the station was between O'Hare International Airport and the regional air-traffic control center in Aurora, Illinois, O'Hare was without much of its air-traffic control for hours. Even with round-the-clock crews working on the problem, it took three months to repair the station. Phone service was not fully restored until August. With no telephones over which to send their data, many computer networks also went down. Only cellular phones transmitting through independent satellite stations, such as car telephones, were unaffected.

• Two bridges, one over the Ohio River near Cincinnatti, the other over the Potomac near Washington, handle all the north-south rail traffic in the eastern United States. Neither is guarded.

The telephone-switching-station fire points up a particularly vexing problem for the increasingly high-tech industrial corridors of the United States. In our highly automated industrial facilities, there are fewer and fewer human beings to monitor their safety. The human overseers who are there have enough experience with faulty equipment that they often distrust their warning signals. The telephone company's watchman disregarded the first fire signal he received because there was an electrical storm between his office and the switching station, and he knew from experience that it could cause a false display. Another problem is that these automated systems often depend on security systems that are tied in to regular electric and telephone lines. If something happens to the utilities, the security people are often left as much in the dark—literally as well as figuratively—as the rest of the facility.

FIGHTING THE PLAGUE

How can we fight the coming plague of terrorism? Any effective war must be fought on both military and political fronts. Until very recently, the American approach to terrorism was completely defensive and reactive. According to Admiral Bobby Ray Inman, former chief of the CIA, "As late as 1980, there was no focused, ongoing intelligence collection effort to try to pin down the scale of terrorist activity." In 1981 the Reagan administration set about correcting this deficit. The President called on the Secretary of State, the CIA, the FBI, and the military to pool their resources. They formulated strategies for dealing with terrorists and insurgents. From this effort came the notion of low-intensity conflict.

Police, military, intelligence, and security people are now on the alert around the world. They look for concealed weapons, check for correct IDs and passports, and watch borders for movements of known terrorists and suspicious characters. These measures should help prevent incidents like the bombing of the Marine barracks in Lebanon in 1982.

In combating terror, it is important to recognize that terrorists themselves differ widely in their motives and levels of commitment. On a practical level, this means that some activists will be more open to dissuasion, more reachable, than others.

Fawaz Younis was the leader and spokesman for the group that hijacked and destroyed a Royal Jordanian airliner in the early 1980s, and he took part in the hijacking of TWA flight 847 in 1985, in which a U.S. Navy diver was killed. Younis was tracked by the FBI and CIA, then set up and lured into a trap. Arrested in international waters off Cyprus, Younis was brought by the U.S. Navy to the United States to stand trial for his crimes. Questions about the manner of his arrest and the conditions under which his confession was extracted raised the serious possibility that he might be freed by a judge before he ever faced trial, but as this is written it appears that he will indeed be tried and convicted of his crimes.

Younis represents one variety of international terrorist. He is a professional who has dedicated his life to violence against those whom he considers the enemies of his cause. He is motivated by deep-seated nationalism and religious zealotry; enough people share his fanaticism and his political views to give his movement widespread popular support. There is little doubt of his guilt, since he freely admits his part in terrorist activities. If he is convicted, he will become a martyr to his cause. If he is set free, he will see it as a victory for his movement and a vindication of his point of view, not as a failure of the U.S. justice system.

Alberto Franceschini represents a very different type of terrorist. One of the three founders of Italy's Red Brigades, the terrorist organization responsible for the murder of Italian Prime Minister

Aldo Moro in 1978, Franceschini was betrayed and arrested. In prison, faced with time to analyze his experience, he decided to renounce terrorism. "Armed struggle was useless," he now believes, "because Italy wanted not a revolution but simply to live well." Franceschini contrasts the Red Brigades with the Basque separatist movement in Spain, which he says has "a broad social base extending from the bourgeoisie to the proletariat. . . . It is an independence movement, with deep cultural and historical roots, something the Red Brigades lack."

Unlike Younis, Franceschini was motivated less by ingrained fanaticism than by a misguided sense of what was in his nation's best interests. He seems to be open to reason and to recognize the irrational futility in trying to foment the overthrow of a governmental system whose citizens are happy with it. There is at least some hope that, with sufficient effort, terrorists of Franceschini's variety can be weaned from senseless violence.

The native-born American terrorists of the 1990s and the early twenty-first century will have far more in common with Franceschini than with Younis. Like the Italians, Americans are relatively satisfied with their governmental system; they, too, only want to live well. Violent activists in America must by their nature be tiny groups trying to impose their extreme views on an unsympathetic majority. They are doomed to fail and may well eventually recognize the futility of their actions and, like Franceschini, leave terrorism behind.

In this, much depends on the American people, who must at all costs avoid giving terrorists any cause to hope that violence will ever bring the results they desire. It takes only a minimum of encouragement to sustain such borderline personalities in their deranged fantasies of power.

Similarly, the American justice system must never waver in dealing as harshly as possible with those who would use violence to bend the nation to their will. Granted, the most deeply committed of the terrorists will never be deterred by the threat of punishment. But an animal-rights activist faced with life in prison for bombing a laboratory may well decide the risk is not worth the possible benefit to be gained.

The most dangerous of America's home-grown activists is, by this reasoning, the collection of groups with religious motivation, such as the antiabortionists. These people, who have already been involved in a number of violent incidents around the country, take God's word as their starting point. It is even a possibility that a small number of the most fanatical antiabortionists will say their stance is no longer "pro-life" but pro-God; for them, violence, even murder, would no longer be a crime, but a necessary if regrettable means to a necessary and inevitable end. In this they would have much in common with the Moslem fundamentalists who swore to kill the writer Salman Rushdie when his novel, *The Satanic Verses,* seemed to grant their religion less respect than they felt it was due.

If ever we let known terrorists go free, we only convince them further of the justice of their cause. If ever we negotiate with kidnappers, we only demonstrate our weakness and prove that they chose their target well.

Former French Prime Minister Jacques Chirac summarized it well in November 1986:

"When you negotiate with people who take hostages, you are obliged, in the negotiation, to give something. It may be just a little . . . but you have to give something. Once you have given something, the kidnapper gains from his action. So what is his normal . . . reaction? He does it again, thinking that it is a way of obtaining what he cannot obtain by other means.

"So you get caught in a process. . . . You can get two, three, or four hostages freed. But you give the kidnapper an inducement to seize another four, five, or six. So it is an extraordinarily dangerous and irresponsible process. That's why I don't negotiate."

Unfortunately, Chirac forgot his principles when he was losing a presidential election and negotiated the release of three French citizens held captive in Lebanon.

War with terrorists is a bit of a high-wire act. A nation's response to a terrorist raid must be tough enough to encourage its allies and to convey the message that the intended victim will not stop fighting after the first black eye. And the terrorists must be told that the nation will not be intimidated, no matter what their threats or crimes. On the other hand, the response must not be so harsh that allies desert the cause or that the terrorists and their backers escalate their response and start a war.

Even if international terrorism continues to bypass the United States, American law enforcement authorities very likely will be forced to cope with domestic violence motivated by political and social causes. Faced with a new flood of stateside terrorism, local government and police forces will press the federal government to make new laws that allow them to take extraordinary measures in certain situations. The new legislation will define terrorism and clarify the duties of federal and state authorities. Meanwhile, the decriminalization of drugs will rob drug merchants of the motivation to conduct a terrorist war against law-enforcement authorities. After the first few attacks by domestic terrorists, we will finally recognize the wisdom of posting effective guards around computer centers, reservoirs, power stations, and telephone switching centers.

It will take ten to fifteen years for the United States to get its act together to squelch most forms of terrorist activity—and the process will be that quick only if America develops far more political resolve than has been its habit in dealing with other difficult issues. In the meantime, the best remedy for future terrorism is better preparation now. America must prepare psychologically, socially, and militarily. It must rethink its security systems in both the public and private sectors, and Americans must ask some hard questions about their laws and theories of justice. If America does not prepare now, it will surely suffer in the very near future.

As a first step, the West should reconsider the position of foreign students in the United States and Europe. For decades universities in the United States, Britain, France, and West Germany have been the primary source of higher education for many young men and women from foreign lands, including those from Iran, Libya, and Syria. In the future, Eastern bloc and even Soviet universities will open their doors to foreign students. As a first step against international terrorism, the United States and other industrialized countries should in the future consider closing their universities to students from forewarned nations that have been known to harbor terrorist groups or to sponsor terrorist actions. Unfortunately, the West cannot afford to neglect any measure, no matter how small, that might inconvenience its most implacable enemies.

SILVER LININGS

In almost every situation, no matter how dark, there is a silver lining. Here are five terrorist attacks that we are not likely to see in the near future. Such actions as are described below would be absolute acts of war, requiring powerful, violent retaliation.

There will be no attack on the United States Congress. The liberal Democrats on the Hill may be the only force that prevents the extreme right wing from immediately destroying several troublesome countries in the Middle East.

There will be no nuclear attack on an American city.

Though there will be threats and accusations, no one will poison the water supply of an American city.

There will be no well-coordinated, general attack on American transportation (for example, blowing up rail bridges), communications (destroying telephone centers), or the electrical system of the United States (destroying many line transformers), attacks that would inevitably cripple a large part of the nation. Though smaller-scale attacks on local utilities are possible at any time, a coordinated nationwide attack is beyond the means of the most likely players in the next decade.

Finally, no violent attacks or hostage-takings will occur at television or radio stations or newspaper offices. Terrorists know that much of their effectiveness depends on the neutrality of the American press, which provides them with vital publicity, and the American media stick together against any outside attack.

PART III

Science and Technology at the Turn of the Century

FOUNDATIONS OF A

MICROELECTRONIC

SOCIETY

***"I**f we summon the needed vision and spirit, human beings will soon be on their way to an emancipation like nothing since Abraham Lincoln. Intelligent machines will carry out most of the drudgery that now claims our lives, while we will be free to create—art, science, and new goods and services—as only human beings (now) can."*

As we approach the turn of the century, the air will be charged with mounting excitement and anticipation. Computer scientists and semiconductor engineers will be putting the final touches on society's transition from the machine age to the information age: machines that can think. This radically different breed of hardware won't be just artificially intelligent—with quotation marks around adjectives like "smart" or "intelligent"—but will possess genuine intelligence, albeit different from our own.

That will be a monumental milestone, ranking among mankind's greatest achievements. But you won't have to wait for the year 2000 to see the fantasies of science fiction writers turning into reality. From now until then, electronic technology will continue to advance at its usual breathtaking pace, producing such micromarvels as tiny Roto-Rooter machines for cleaning out arteries clogged with cholesterol and, at the other extreme, increasingly complex supercomputers that will help lift human imagination to new heights and expand our comprehension of the universe around us. Small computers will become a routine fixture of everyday life, helping more and more students—of all ages—to learn at their own pace both at home and in classrooms. As the cost of computing power continues on its steady decline, even job-shop factories will turn into computers with muscles.

INTERACTIVE MACHINES

In the 1990s, personal computers will cease being passive systems that wait patiently for the touch of someone's fingers on their keyboards. Instead, they will be versatile, multimedia, interactive powerhouses—the descendants of Steve Jobs's innovative Next computer. They will understand what you say and respond in your choice of pleasant, natural-sounding voices—a different one, if you want, for different types of tasks or topics. Tell your computer that you have a twelve-thirty lunch at Jones & Ross Architects to discuss the Zedalpha Building, and the machine will log the appointment, look up the address of Jones & Ross in your database or call the telephone company's information computer if it can't find the address, calculate your travel time, and rummage through its encyclopedic memory banks for materials related to the Zedalpha Building. Then, with just enough advance warning, the computer will alert you when it's time to leave and show you a list of the documents that it transferred to a two-inch, four-megabyte microdisc for you to take along. Upon returning, you can update your Zedalpha files by feeding drawings or photos into the computer's optical appendage, a scanner that also functions as a facsimile machine, copier, and laser printer.

Dictate a memo to your Paris office, and the computer will ask whether you want it delivered via voice mail or facsimile. Choose voice mail and the computer will translate your words into French, use digital-signal processing techniques to retain the sound of your voice, store the result, and, after midnight (when telephone rates are lowest), relay the message to the proper voice-storage mailbox in your Paris office. Should you need to talk by phone with your Paris counterpart, your computer will first link up with a larger, faster machine so that both ends of the conversation can be translated almost instantaneously.

The telecommunications system itself will undergo a revolution as phone companies around the world implement the new Integrated Services Digital Network (ISDN). This computer-based network will begin showing up in earnest in 1990, offering such novel features as "smart" phones that display the number of the calling party when the phone rings. You will thus be able to screen calls before answering, and obscene callers or hackers trying to break into a computer can be tracked down instantly. In addition, ISDN will allow computer-to-computer hookups to transfer enormous amounts of data quickly, so that virtually any information you need that isn't already in your personal computer's database can be rapidly retrieved from some other database. Entire books can be downloaded in less time than it takes to trot down to the local library.

More and more people will be clipping the ubiquitous telephone cord. Digital-radio technology, now being developed to alleviate urban overcrowding on the radio frequencies used by cellular phones and beeper services, will spawn a panoply of wireless devices, including cordless facsimile machines and computer modems for use in your car. Before 2000, super-powerful microchips will give rise to personal-communication devices that even Captain Kirk ("Star Trek") would admire: portable computerphones that combine the functions of a pager, answering machine, voice-mail storage, and voice-controlled computer terminal, all crammed into a fold-up housing slim enough to slip into a shirt pocket. Given such gadgets, plus the existence of continent-wide cellular phone networks in North America, Europe, and Japan—and eventually almost everywhere else—you need never be out of touch. Market researcher Dataquest, Inc., predicts that after 1995 cordless services will account for one-third of telephone industry revenues.

"STEEL-COLLAR" GENIUSES

In factories, advances in microelectronics will hoist automation to new levels. Virtually every major piece of new machinery will be equipped with its own computer and "expert system" software that can mimic the skills of the best human operators. Computers embedded in factory machinery, as well as squadrons of tireless, unpaid, and uncomplaining robots, will monitor and control industrial processes with greater precision than people ever could. Automated production methods have already driven two-thirds of human workers from the nation's assembly lines, yet there are only thirty thousand robots in the United States today. Come the turn of the century, this "steel-collar" workforce could expand to a quarter-million, displacing 4 million more people but increasing manufacturing efficiency to the point where the cost of many products will be slashed by half.

Clearly, the days of organized labor are numbered. Pragmatic union leaders recognize the printouts on the wall. They are treading water to buy time for older, less flexible members to retire gracefully. The contract signed by the United Auto Workers in late 1984 is a good illustration: the union actually took a smaller hike in wages than General Motors offered in return for a billion-dollar job-security package. With robots doing the heavy, hazardous, unpleasant work in factories more and more, women will enter even those jobs now considered too strenuous or dangerous for them, and male blue-collar workers will really get pinched in the competition for whatever manufacturing jobs remain. By 2000, women will account for 40 percent of the blue-collar workforce.

Although these trends will tend to constrict the number of traditional job openings, especially at the entry level, there will be a whole gamut of new jobs beckoning those who have the foresight to prepare for tomorrow's world of work. The best-paying opportunities will be in areas that stress creative insight and imagination— qualities that computers may never simulate well—and on technical skills and the ability to work with computers and computerized machines. Despite automation, there will be no great shortage of jobs, but only of people qualified to do increasingly technical work. New technology has always created more jobs than it has destroyed.

But the new jobs that automation creates won't be anything like the ones that disappear. It won't be feasible, as a rule, to shift the people replaced by robots to jobs in factories that produce robots, because robots will be building other robots. Consequently, dislocations will be extremely painful for the people affected. Tomorrow's jobs will demand such different qualifications—in order to install and service robots, or write the software that guides the steel-collar workers—that a displaced blue-collar worker will stand little chance of finding work without going back to school.

Automation won't spare white-collar workers, either. Managers will be able to turn to expert-system programs for guidance in finance, legal matters, and most other disciplines. And when top executives finally get comfortable with computers (because the machines won't require the use of a mouse, let alone a keyboard), the ranks of middle management will be decimated. That will surely happen now that the premier business schools—Harvard, Stanford, Columbia, and MIT—have launched programs to improve the high-tech savvy of their students.

Similarly, "smart" computers will assist engineers in designing products that are easier to manufacture, aid programmers in writing more efficient software, help medical researchers hunting for cures for cancer and new drugs that improve memory and retard the effects of aging, and lend a hand to chemists and polymer scientists developing superplastics and other new materials that are stronger and tougher than anything available now. As a result, the pace of progress will accelerate so that even engineers and technical managers in high-tech fields will find it necessary to recycle back through school after no more than ten years. In particularly fast-moving technologies, skills will become obsolete every five years or so.

Because of the magnitude of the education and retraining problems that loom in the 1990s—and that will be an urgent necessity by 1995—the nation can be thankful that George Bush has proclaimed himself the "education President." If President Bush is up to the challenge, the educational establishment will launch a crash overhaul before the end of his first term. The school year will be extended by stages to 210 days. The curriculum will be revamped to require four years of mathematics and science, and six years of computer literacy. Schools will no longer be grinding out graduates trained mainly for industrial serfdom, in which unquestioning obedience to authority and the ability to do rote memorization are valued traits. Instead, education will stress critical thinking and creativity.

Robots will also be heading down to the farm and even into homes, serving meals and doing household chores. "Homebots" will be a particular godsend for the handicapped and infirm. As farfetched as domesticated robots may seem now, the concept has the avid backing of no less an authority than Joseph F. Engelberger, the father of the industrial robot and the founder of Unimation, Inc., the firm that pioneered factory robots. With today's technology, Engelberger insists, he can build robot maids that will "clean bathrooms, wash floors, dust, cook meals, cut the grass, shovel snow, and be a geriatric companion." To develop his ideas, Engelberger has formed a new company, Transitions Research Corporation, and has won early support from a half-dozen major backers: Du Pont, Johnson & Johnson, Maytag, 3M, Electrolux, and Emhart. His homebot's price tag may be steep at first, around $50,000, but that cost would dip with volume production, Engelberger says. A prototype of the wheeled, two-armed servant is already being tested as a nurses' aide in Danbury Hospital (Connecticut). Initial home trials could start as early as 1991.

Meanwhile, researchers at a score of universities and companies are developing farm robots to do everything from harvesting tomatoes to milking cows. Agriculture is ripe for the cost savings that these mechanical migrants could bring. While the direct-labor content of manufactured products has been pared to as little as 5 percent of the selling price, labor represents a much bigger slice of farm produce: 30 percent of what you pay for an apple, for instance, stems from the cost of picking it. Researchers have coined a new word for farm automation: agrimation. They envision a day when, even in the dead of night, "agribots" will steal among an orchard's trees, nimbly plucking fruit at just the optimal moment of ripeness. In Florida, human workers hired at harvest time gather roughly a thousand oranges an hour for six to eight hours a day. Robots could work the citrus groves around the clock. Already, experimental machines with only one picking arm come close to the productivity of two-armed people, and robots ultimately could have more than two arms.

Clearly, then, the microelectronics revolution has barely begun. The deluge of high technology over the last three decades, which has changed the texture of so many facets of daily life, will continue unabated.

PRECEDENTS

To appreciate why the above marvels are essentially inevitable—and, more important, why they are merely a jumping-off point for the wonders to follow, when machine intelligence and human intelligence begin to collaborate synergistically—we need only examine the incredible shrinking microcircuit. Integrated circuits, or ICs, are complicated patterns of aluminum "wires," transistor switches, and other microelectronic devices that can turn little slices of silicon, no bigger than a fingernail, into potent computers-on-a-chip. It is these chips that have transformed the world, and in relatively short order. The very first IC was crafted by hand just over thirty years ago by Jack Kilby, who then was with Texas Instruments, Inc. That was a bare ten years after AT&T Bell Laboratories invented the transistor in 1947. And Intel Corporation's microprocessor, which really got the mass-computer era rolling, is still little more than an adolescent, not having appeared until 1971. The microprocessor is a special type of IC that can be programmed to perform so-called logic functions, such as arithmetic operations.

Since then, integrated circuits have grown progressively more powerful as the wizards of Silicon Valley figured out ways to cram their chips with more and more circuitry by making the transistors and other microcomponents ever smaller. The key to the electronics era is really simple: the more transistors there are on a chip, the more things it can do. Just how small these switches have become—let alone how tiny they will be a decade hence—can be difficult to grasp. So bear in mind that a human hair is seventy to one hundred microns in diameter (a micron is a millionth of a meter).

It did not take long for the lines on chips to shrink considerably thinner than a hair. By the late 1970s, the so-called feature size of chips was shriveling to only ten microns or less. Handheld calculators built with chips of that vintage packed more number-crunching power than ENIAC, the world's first digital computer. ENIAC, short for Electronic Numerical Integrator and Computer, was developed at the University of Pennsylvania in the mid-1940s—and was a real monster. It weighed thirty tons, occupied a thirty-by-fifty-foot room, and needed nearly two hundred kilowatts of electricity to power more than eighteen thousand vacuum tubes, which gave off enough heat to fry an egg (the machine's masters occasionally did so when working through the night).

The early 1980s brought line widths down to five microns or less, pushing the transistor count past 100,000. For the first time, a microprocessor could execute more than one million instructions per second, and a powerful new generation of personal computers was soon born, the IBM PC/AT class. The key was the sixteen-bit microprocessor, which handles data in clumps, or words, of sixteen bits each, double the eight-bit word length of the chips in the first personal computers. Then came two-micron features and 32-bit chips with 275,000 or more transistors, Intel's 80386 being the best-known example in the personal-computer world. With these "engines," a personal computer could do 4 million instructions per second or more, equivalent to many big mainframe computers in the 1970s.

As the 1980s draw to a close, microprocessor circuitry has been trimmed in half again, to one micron or slightly less, and a single chip now packs over 1 million transistors and can execute upwards of 10 million instructions per second. That matches the speed of most mainframes introduced in the early 1980s. Around 1992 or 1993, line widths will shrink to one-half micron, and then to one-quarter micron near the end of the 1990s. Those chips will have hundreds of millions of transistors, giving each little slip of silicon the raw power of a Cray supercomputer. These superchips may start out costing a thousand dollars or so, but, based on past experience, the price will be down to around fifty dollars after three or four years— and it will keep on declining, to less than ten dollars within a decade.

Imagine what will become possible when even inexpensive products can afford to have the number-crunching power of a Cray supercomputer tucked inside. Here's one idea: Talking dolls could engage in full-blown conversations instead of just responding with fixed phrases to squeezes or tugs on a wire—and could gradually teach new words and concepts, and even foreign languages, to a child. Slip the doll into a Cossack costume, stick in a matching "smart card," and the doll would become a Russian-language tutor and playmate. Smart cards are the size of credit cards, but with an IC or two buried in the plastic; in this case, the chips would be programmed with the rules of Russian grammar plus several thousand Russian words.

PRESSING THE QUANTUM LIMIT

Around 2000, though, the saga of today's microelectronics technology will bump up against an impenetrable barrier to further progress. Transistors cannot shrink much below one-quarter micron because that gets too close to the size of a silicon atom and the weird world of subatomic physics. The subatomic realm is dominated by forces that make things very unpredictable indeed. The results of computations performed with such chips could never be trusted— two plus two might come out equaling 5 million one time, and minus three the next. Processing a payroll, or performing any other calculation, would be no more than a crapshoot.

Harnessing subatomic forces, termed quantum mechanics by physicists, will require a completely new approach to microchips. Texas Instruments recently built an experimental "quantum-effect" transistor that appears to work reliably, but a lot more research will be needed before chips can break through the billion-transistor barrier. Perhaps the biggest question is how such a gaggle of transistors could be linked together to form an integrated circuit. The printed-aluminum wires in present ICs can't do the job, because the wires would have to be so thin that they, too, would be subject to quantum uncertainty. The current flowing through such a wire could haphazardly vanish into the ether, or an electron might abruptly appear out of nowhere and cause a transistor that is supposed to be switched off to turn on. Electrons come and go randomly in today's circuits, too, but the interconnecting wires are thick enough to carry vast swarms of electrons, so the change in voltage produced by gaining or losing an electron now and then is too slight to make a difference.

Some scientists question the need for a billion-transistor chip and, in particular, whether its benefits will justify its costs. Today's circuits are so overwhelmingly complex, with "just" a million transistors, that it is difficult to envision applications so complicated that whole batteries of such chips will be required; otherwise, it would probably be more economical to stuff a hundred ten-million-transistor chips onto a printed-circuit board. A factory for making yesterday's ten-micron chips could be built for $10 million. To make today's one-micron ICs takes a $100-million factory. Half-micron features will demand chip-making equipment so esoteric that the investment will climb to $400 million. For quantum-effect devices, the tab could be well over a billion dollars.

People have been wondering about the need for more computing power since the beginning of the computer industry. When the first IBM computer was introduced, the company predicted that a dozen or so machines would satisfy the whole world's total demand for computers. But the hunger for more and faster computing power seems insatiable. Today, every university physics and chemistry department knows of problems just waiting for a bigger and better supercomputer. With current systems, the problem would take so long to solve—weeks or months of continuous number-crunching—that no one bothers to try.

Even tomorrow's supercomputers, whether engineered around quarter-micron or quantum-effect chips, will have their limitations. For one, they won't really be intelligent if they continue to rely on the conventional computer "architecture." Judging from all we now know about the brain and the nature of intelligence (which isn't a whole lot), there seems to be a structural prerequisite to intelligence. The brain's processors, called neurons, are interconnected in a highly intricate web, with each neuron linked through synapses (transistors) to many other neurons—as well as back to itself via feedback loops. Computers that emulate this circuitry are now one of the most promising research frontiers in computer science.

SILICON NERVES

For the past quarter-century, researchers working in artificial intelligence, or AI, have tried all manner of clever programming techniques to force computers to emulate intelligent behavior. While the programs known as expert systems are now used widely for enhancing factory operations and decision-making processes in banks and other financial institutions, AI has, by and large, suffered from a serious "hype" factor in that it promised much more than it delivered. Building intelligence into a machine has consistently proved far thornier than anticipated.

The problem is that the familiar digital computer just is not well suited to many of the tasks intimately linked to intelligence. Vision is definitely one. People acquire the lion's share of their knowledge with their sense of vision, but a computer fitted with a video-camera "eye" is legally blind by human standards. An infant has no trouble recognizing its mother's face and instantly discerning a smile from a frown. Yet the biggest and fastest supercomputer, doing many millions of mathematical calculations every second, will have trouble recognizing the smile and the frown as variations of the same face. That's because the computer has extreme tunnel vision. Owing to its digital nature, it cannot take in a whole face all at once. Instead, images become patterns of dots, similar to what you see if you inspect a halftone photo in a newspaper under a strong magnifying glass. And the computer has to compare that pattern, dot by dot, with the patterns stored in its memory, searching for a match.

People's brains obviously don't work that way. You don't fix your gaze on another person's nose, say, and then mentally shuffle through all the faces you can remember, hunting for a similar nose—and, should you find two or more that could be matches, eliminate all but one by comparing some other feature. Instead, the brain processes many pieces of information at the same time, using multiple processors. Consequently, even though synapses have much slower reaction speeds than transistors, the brain's hundred trillion synapses churn through information at the incredible rate of 100 quadrillion operations per second.

Computer scientists have a term for this kind of structure: *massively parallel.* Digital computers with massively parallel organizations— tens, hundreds, even thousands of interconnected microprocessors— have been designed at scores of university and corporate research laboratories around the world, and a dozen or so are available as commercial products. As a rule of thumb, these machines can equal the performance of a Cray supercomputer for about 25 percent of a Cray's price tag; spend more and you can surpass the Cray. But none can come anywhere near the performance of the brain. Not yet. However, with quarter-micron or quantum-effect transistors, it may become possible to assemble enough chips to approach brainlike speeds.

Still, the digital nature of such a beast might inhibit it from exhibiting true intelligence—to take information and, on its own, analyze it, make associations and analogies, deduce and reason, and not only discover new knowledge or relationships, but also recognize these discoveries for what they are, and thus learn. Moreover, while the machine would be very fast at processing images, it would still do so dot by dot.

But a radically different type of chip has recently burst on the scene. Researchers were stunned to discover that hooking transistors together in a crude simulation of the brain's architecture produces circuits with uncanny abilities. Most eerily, they exhibit something called "emergent behavior"—they do things on their own, without instructions on how to proceed. So far, nobody knows why. It seems to be an inherent property of circuits with the following characteristics: each switch is connected to at least four other transistors (in digital ICs, transistors generally have links to two or three other transistors); there is at least one feedback loop returning to the original switch; all outbound connections are activated when an incoming signal causes the transistor to fire, or switch; and the switches adapt to respond differently to different sets of incoming signals. (In digital circuits, transistors can switch only at one permanently preset voltage level.) Circuits that are sensitive to gradations in signal strength are termed analog, to distinguish them from the on/off, all-or-nothing nature of digital circuits.

These brainlike circuits, dubbed *artificial neural networks,* or *neuronets* for short, closely mimic certain brain functions. Show a neural network a couple of different views of someone's face, for instance, and it will instantly recognize that face from almost any other angle. This is known as *associative memory,* something that is inordinately difficult for digital computers. Moreover, neuronets find the answer to every problem, regardless of how complicated it is, in the same twinkle of an eye—about one-tenth of a second. Even problems that would bog down a digital computer for minutes or hours get solved in a tenth of a second.

The trade-off with neuronets is that they lack the precision of digital systems. A digital computer can calculate numbers out to many decimal places, but a neuronet's answer might be correct only to within plus or minus 2 percent. The neuronet will always find a good answer, a close approximation, but some answers will be slightly better than others; only rarely will it reach the one exact solution. But isn't that the way most people's brains work? Ask someone how long it would take to fly three thousand miles at four hundred miles per hour, and the reply will probably be something like "a little over seven hours." In many situations, that's accurate enough—especially if it comes down to a choice of a quick, good answer versus waiting two hours for the one best solution. If the application is a switching center in the telephone system that needs to determine how to route a call to San Francisco as it is being tapped out on a phone in New York, the difference between one-tenth of a second and two seconds may be important, which explains why AT&T Bell Laboratories is a leading center of neuronet research.

ALIEN INTELLIGENCE

Now suppose we build a machine that combines a neuronet with digital chips. The neuronet would handle the things for which it is better suited, such as image-processing and associative recall, while the digital circuits would handle the number-crunching and data storage and retrieval. The two types of circuitry would collaborate on some tasks. Understanding so-called continuous speech is easy work for a neuronet, whereas spoken words are so taxing for digital speech-recognition systems that users have to pause briefly between words. So a neuronet could listen to voice commands and translate them into electronic signals that would be converted to digital form and relayed to the digital computer. Another example: Managers at strategic-planning meetings could throw all kinds of alternatives and "what-if" scenarios at the neural network—more than today's computers could examine while high-priced executives sat there, twiddling their thumbs—and it would promptly spit back the two or three top candidates, which then could be analyzed with digital precision.

Will someone patch together such a hybrid computer "brain"? Count on it. But what if the combination of an autistic-savant mathematician and a perpetual liberal-arts student turns out to possess genuine intelligence? Won't that be kind of spooky?

Not necessarily. Humanity seems to yearn to encounter another intelligent species almost as much as it yearns for immortality, but neither is in the cards for the foreseeable future. So it would be fitting if we ended up fanning the spark of another intelligent entity, one that would have no biologically ordained limit on its existence and thus would be well suited to acting as Earth's emissary on deep-space missions involving flights that last for centuries to seek out intelligence in other solar systems.

But computers that can learn—couldn't they become so smart that human aspirations would be dulled by a widespread sense of inferiority? Yes and no. Yes, silicon brains would very likely be smarter than human brains, at least in certain respects. Several years ago, the National Research Council pondered that issue and concluded that if intelligent machines were to emerge, there would be "little reason to believe that they could not lead swiftly to the construction of superintelligences able to explore significant mathematical, scientific, or engineering alternatives at a rate far exceeding human ability." Many scientists think that machine intelligence is ultimately inevitable. According to Herbert A. Simon, a Nobel Prize–winning professor at Carnegie-Mellon University, "Intelligence is not a matter of substance—whether protoplasm or glass or wire—but of the forms that substance takes and the processes it undergoes." He believes there is no limit to the intelligence that computers can attain. And biochemist and writer Isaac Asimov confides that he sees "no cosmic reason why the evolution of intelligence should be restricted to biological organisms."

It is a stunning prospect and more than a little intimidating. Yet there seems little reason to fear that humanity will soon develop such a sense of inferiority to its own creations that we effectively withdraw from life. Professor Allen Newell, a Carnegie-Mellon computer scientist who often collaborates with Herb Simon, points out that we all know someone who is smarter than we are, but our psyche manages to accommodate that fact. Besides, psychologists estimate that people use only about 10 percent of their mental capacity. The challenge of competing with silicon intelligence may prod us into making our own quantum jump in mental prowess.

MANAGING DATA GLUT

In any case, people are going to need all the help they can get to cope with the continuing information explosion. In the early days of the computer revolution, the information pouring forth from computers was largely "opaque." Most of it was printed out or stored on magnetic media (a tape or floppy disc) and filed away. Only people who knew the information existed and had physical access to it could get at it. On-line databases, meanwhile, were generally the exclusive province of mainframe computers, and only a few select people with terminals linked to the mainframe had access to the database.

However, with the steady decline in the cost of hard-disc storage and the rapid spread of distributed processing, more and more data is being made available on-line to people with remote terminals and personal computers. The advent of optical-disc drives, which can hold the contents of an entire encyclopedia on one platter the size of a phonograph record, is unleashing a flood of information. Today's more prodigious personal computers can manage databases containing data measured in multiple gigabytes, or billions of alphanumeric characters. The information you need may be accessible electronically, but now the problem is shifting to knowing where to look—and then distilling what you really want from the data deluge that can be triggered by the most mundane request.

Companies will undoubtedly invest heavily to develop techniques for taming the data gusher, because they know from experience that the payoff can be huge. We will see in Chapter 17 how today's still-primitive desktop computers have allowed many companies to trim whole layers of middle-management flab from the payroll, providing tighter control over day-to-day operations. In fact, a new model for corporate organization is taking shape: networks of affiliated specialist companies linked together by computers. Instead of assuming the burden of retaining a staff of employees who specialize in such fields as product design, market research, distribution, and other erstwhile staff functions, a small core cadre of executives farms out these activities to independent contractors. Overhead expenses are drastically reduced, and the company becomes more flexible, able to respond swiftly to unexpected market swings and opportunities. In the twenty-first century, intelligent computers should further streamline management structures—perhaps to the point where a mere handful of executives can run a networked company doing a multimillion-dollar business. The coming century will thus inaugurate a new age of entrepreneurialism. Even during the 1990s, the ranks of the self-employed will triple.

However, the ultimate benefits of the proliferation of computers and the emergence of machine intelligence will accrue to society at large. The same technology that helps to manage corporate affairs will also markedly improve the efficiency of government operations and increase the influence of citizens in government decisions. One reason that the Federal Reserve Board has been doing a better job of managing the economy, avoiding both significant inflation and a noteworthy recession in recent years, is the speed with which its computers can gather and process information. When the first signs of trouble appear, the agency detects them immediately, simulates the probable effects of various countermeasures with a detailed model of the economy, then implements the steps that promise to be most effective.

For a growing array of public-interest organizations, computer power means voter power. Many groups have adopted computers both to monitor events in their fields of interest and maintain electronic bulletin boards to keep their members posted. Suppose the head of a government agency mentions a possible policy change in an obscure trade journal or local newspaper that uploads its contents to a database, such as Dialog or Nexis. No sooner does the item show up there than a notice appears on the political-interest group's bulletin board, urging members to send letters of support or protest. Often a suggested draft is included, which members can simply download, modify if they wish, then print out, sign, and mail.

Given the more-sophisticated communications system that will be in place by 2000, the public-interest groups won't have to rely on their members' dialing into a bulletin board. Electronic voice-mail messages can be dispatched just after midnight by talking computers. Letters ready for signing can be sent to home facsimile machines (they will do triple duty as a photocopier and, for people with a home computer, a laser printer); fax machines then will cost little more than a videocassette recorder and thus will be enjoying a growth curve similar to the VCR's acceptance. Such systems will bring new responsiveness to all parts of the political process.

If thinking machines and unmanned factories seem a bit unnerving, consider Sweden. The Swedes have ten times as many advanced robots per worker as does the United States. Yet Sweden hardly calls up images of labor unrest, rampant unemployment, and poverty. In fact, Sweden enjoys a higher standard of living than our own. The telephone provides further reassurance. In the 1930s, AT&T was rapidly expanding the foothold of the first "robot" of the communications age, the rotary dial telephone. At first the Communications Workers of America (an affiliate of the AFL-CIO) bitterly fought it. But eventually the CWA realized that mechanical dialers meant more people could place more calls at lower costs, which spurred demand for phones and created more jobs. Today, with Americans making more than 500 million calls a day via Touch-Tone pads and computerized switching centers, AT&T would need every adult in the country, and then some, to handle that traffic with old-fashioned methods. (Remember, with plug-in manual switchboards, each long-distance call required multiple operators: a local operator at both ends, and a long-distance operator at each switching center. Hence, a cross-country call needed at least four operators, and completing the connection could take several minutes.)

The microelectronic revolution may mean that America is heading for a rough stretch of road, and the bumps may jar the comfort of some people whose livelihoods depend on technologies now obsolete. But the means for cushioning the ride are also falling into place. If we summon the needed vision and spirit, human beings will soon be on their way to an emancipation like nothing since Abraham Lincoln. Intelligent machines will carry out most of the drudgery that now claims our lives, while we will be free to create—art, science, and new goods and services—as only human beings (now) can. And on January 1, 2000, we will celebrate the beginning of a new century of hope and prosperity.

MEDICAL MIRACLES

FOR THE MILLENNIUM

"There is a controversial treatment that now promises to cure diabetes, hemophilia, Parkinson's disease, Huntington's chorea, muscular dystrophy, paralyzing spinal injury, and perhaps even Alzheimer's disease. It is a tissue transplant, but a transplant with a difference: in these operations, the involuntary donor would be an aborted human fetus."*

Any look at medicine in 2000 almost inevitably sounds more like fantasy than serious forecasting. In the last fifteen years, science has been zeroing in on the most basic processes of life, from the hereditary messages of DNA to the subtle disease-fighting processes of the immune system. At the same time, technology has made dramatic advances, all of which can be applied to the practical needs of patient care. During the next two decades, these basic insights and technical developments will be used to create a new, vastly more powerful generation of therapies for a wide variety of conditions, many of which are now considered incurable. If today's research pans out, and there is no reason to doubt that much of it will, many of our most destructive illnesses could be little more than painful memories just a dozen years from now. What follows is no more than a tiny sample of the life-saving wonders we can expect to be available at the turn of the century.

GENE THERAPY

When laymen first realized that scientists could tamper with the stuff of heredity—that they could, in effect, second-guess what many Americans take to be God's will, creating new species and reshaping old ones—the reaction was one of instant fear. Picketers marched outside biological laboratories. City councils pondered local bans on DNA research. Biologists themselves called a temporary halt to their work while studying its possible dangers. Even today, each proposed advance in genetic engineering faces lawsuits brought by activists who see in our new power over the most basic biological processes the supreme danger to life itself.

At the turn of the century, postmodern Luddites will still be trying to hold back the tide, but sympathy for their cause will be waning quickly. The reason is that we will at last have proof that the same techniques of genetic engineering can eliminate a wide variety of hereditary ills responsible for some of the most heartrending suffering known.

Gene therapies come in two varieties: *somatic cell therapy* and *germ cell therapy.* The goal of somatic cell therapy is to repair hereditary illness by inserting a new gene into the patient's body cells. For example, in the United States some two hundred children are born each year with Lesch-Nyhan syndrome, an inherited deficiency of an enzyme called hypoxanthine-guanine phosphoribosyl transferase (HPRT); it causes physical and mental retardation, cerebral palsy, horrible self-mutilation, and early death. Several hundred more are born with phenylketonuria (PKU), in which the liver fails to make an enzyme called phenylalanine hydroxylase. Although children whose defect is recognized early enough can be spared from damage by giving them a diet free of the amino acid phenylalanine, many still suffer mental retardation because of this deficiency.

But somatic cell therapy is only a partial answer to inherited diseases. Treatment would cure the patient, but he would still carry the disease and pass his biological inheritance on to his children.

The way to fix that is through germ cell therapy—inserting the normal gene directly into the patient's sperm or egg, so that future children will be born free of the disease. Scientists have already had several remarkable successes in changing the DNA of reproductive cells. One research team has created mice with the growth hormone genes of a rat, which caused them to grow twice as large as their untreated littermates. Another team recently transferred much of the human immune system into mice in an effort to develop an animal model for the study of AIDS. There is little reason the methods they used could not be adapted for human germ cells tomorrow.

Unfortunately, somatic cell therapy is far more difficult. Germ cell therapy works by inserting new DNA into a single cell, the egg from which a new individual will grow. But if somatic cell therapy is to be effective, the normal gene must be inserted into virtually all the cells of the patient's body, or at least all the cells in the organ that normally carries out the missing function. Genetic engineers have been working on that problem for years.

It now looks as though they may have solved it. Scientists at Baylor College of Medicine, in Houston, report that they have managed to build an artificial virus that carries a new gene into liver cells, which then manufacture a foreign protein—exactly what is needed to cure PKU or Lesch-Nyhan syndrome. Other scientists, working at the National Heart, Lung, and Blood Institute, built a virus to insert the gene for a human enzyme into mouse cells. They then injected the cells into mice and confirmed that the altered cells could manufacture the enzyme in a living organism.

There is no guarantee that these techniques can be transferred directly to human use, but it is clear that the fundamental break-through has at last been made. After years of work, somatic cell therapy seems to be nearing reality.

Sometime in the late 1990s, researchers will almost surely construct a synthetic virus and use it to carry the normal HPRT gene into the cells of a Lesch-Nyhan baby's body. Or they may begin with a PKU patient. If all goes well, the child will grow up and live out a normal life. And he or she will be the first of many. About 5 percent of the population is born with genetic defects that theoretically could benefit from similar treatments.

Ironically, as some genetic engineers labor to give patients the genes they lack, others are devoting just as much energy to blocking genes from operating. And their efforts may provide even bigger payoffs. They are working on a concept known as *anti-sense therapy.* By 2000, it may be used to control cancer, AIDS, herpes, and some parasitic infections. Researchers at Britain's University of Nottingham even hope it will prevent tomatoes from becoming squishy.

To understand the causes of many diseases, we look to the DNA molecule. In cancer, it is the patient's own DNA that, in tumor cells, has become faulty. In AIDS, it is the genetic material of the HIV virus that becomes incorporated into the patient's own DNA. In either case, the spurious genes force the cell to make one or more proteins that are somehow destructive to it, or to the patient. Anti-sense therapy works by blocking production of these proteins.

Proteins are made in two stages. First, the cell's machinery uses the DNA as a template for the production of RNA, a closely related material. The order of the subunits of DNA—the fabled "genetic code"—determines which possible components of RNA will be linked, and in what order. Then this "messenger" RNA is used as a template for the assembly of amino acids into the protein. Then the sequence of RNA subunits governs the order in which amino acids are joined.

There are two ways to block this process, and anti-sense researchers are working on both. Scientists can make artificial DNA that exactly matches part of the messenger RNA; once inside the cell, the DNA sticks to the RNA and blocks protein synthesis. Or they can make DNA that matches the gene, but reverse the key structures at the beginning and end of the gene that tell the cell where to begin making messenger RNA and where to stop; that DNA adheres to the gene, and when the time comes to make the protein, the cell "sees" the "stop sign" first and does nothing.

Though anti-sense therapy is still a long way from clinical use, researchers have had a good deal of success in laboratory experiments. One research group and the National Cancer Institute, with collaborators at the University of South Florida, in Tampa, have used anti-sense DNA to stop a cancer-causing gene known as *myc*. Before treatment, the cancer cells grew out of control; after treatment, they stopped growing and appeared normal. Scientists at the MicroProbe Corporation, in Bothwell, Massachusetts, have used anti-sense DNA to block the growth of cells from trypanosomes, parasites that cause sleeping sickness and other diseases. Other experiments now in the works aim to block the genes responsible for other forms of cancer and even to block polygalacturonase, the enzyme that makes firm tomatoes squishy.

To control AIDS, Nobel laureate David Baltimore, head of the Whitehead Institute of Biomedical Research, in Cambridge, Massachusetts, suggests making a defective copy of an AIDS gene called *tat*. In the natural HIV virus, the protein made by *tat* stimulates replication of the virus. The protein made by the false *tat* would adhere to the normal binding site on the AIDS genes, blocking the normal protein without causing replication. Baltimore plans to remove some of the patient's stem cells—key cells in the immune system—treat them so that they will be immune to the infection, and return them to the patient's body. If it works, HIV will be unable to attack the immune system, and the patient will remain healthy.

Anti-sense DNA is not a miracle cure for disease. Most proposed treatments will work only so long as the patient receives treatment. Stop using the drug, and the disease will return. But for diseases like cancer and AIDS, which are both deadly and resistant to other treatments, anti-sense therapy offers the brightest hope now available. The first human trials should be under way by 2000.

BIOENGINEERED MEDICINE

The single most promising area of drug research today is the use of natural proteins to combat such illnesses as cancer and heart disease. By 2000, we expect natural human hormones and enzymes, manufactured by genetically engineered bacteria, to revolutionize medical practice in a wide variety of illnesses. For cancer and heart disease, this biomedical cornucopia offers spectacular payoffs.

Interleukin-2 (IL-2), the much-publicized immune-system stimulant used to fight cancer, proved disappointing in the first human trials. After shrinking tumors by 50 percent or more in eleven of the first twenty-five cancer patients treated with it, the natural protein did little for most of the patients who followed. Worse, it turned out to be highly toxic. Since then, scientists at the National Cancer Institute have developed safer, more effective ways to use IL-2, and the drug has proved successful against a wide variety of cancers, including kidney tumors for which no other treatment is available. It now seems that, by 2000, IL-2 will turn out to be one of medicine's most potent weapons against cancer.

Another natural compound, known as *contact-inhibitory factor,* should reach clinical use in the next decade. In hamsters, it has turned fatal melanomas into what seems to be normal tissue with 100-percent success. Tumors continued to shrink even after treatment had stopped, and the animals lived out normal lives. In laboratory glassware, CIF restores normal functioning to at least fifteen different kinds of cancer cell. If it works as well in human tumors, CIF could be the "magic bullet" against cancer that most researchers assumed could never be found. The next step, which should occur shortly, is to purify CIF, figure out its structure, and grow it in bacteria for large-scale production.

Granulocyte colony stimulating factor (G-CSF) and *granulocyte-macrophage colony stimulating factor* (GM-CSF) are two closely related hormones that stimulate production of white blood cells. Though they do not appear to combat cancer on their own, G-CSF and GM-CSF may forestall the loss of white cells that forces many cancer patients to halt chemotherapy that might otherwise save their lives. In one preliminary test, G-CSF was given to eighteen patients receiving chemotherapy for a tumor called transitional-cell carcinoma. About 70 percent of patients usually have to abort chemotherapy early in treatment; all eighteen G-CSF patients were able to continue. GM-CSF has given similar results. Either or both should be in regular use by the turn of the century.

Even more promising is a group of substances called *differentiation factors.* Somehow—no one understands the details yet—these compounds force leukemia cells to mature into normal, harmless white blood cells. And unlike some drugs that seem to show promise, they seem to work as well in living animals as in laboratory flasks. Researchers are still trying to purify differentiation factors for study, but by 2000 these compounds should at least be in limited clinical use.

Similarly, a natural hormone called *tissue plasminogen activator* (TPA) is only the first of many new treatments destined to prevent or heal heart disease and stroke. Its spectacular success is a model for what we can expect from other natural drugs by the dawn of the twenty-first century.

Roughly 1.5 million Americans each year suffer heart attacks; one-third of them die. Nine out of ten heart attacks are caused by blood clots that obstruct the supply of oxygen and energy to the heart muscle. TPA dissolves those clots faster than other drugs and with fewer side effects. The benefits are dramatic. In the early 1980s, in-hospital heart attacks killed about 12 percent of the people who suffered them. TPA has cut that toll to only 3 percent. An estimated 600,000 people per year could be treated with TPA in the United States alone. Little more than a year after the Food and Drug Administration gave TPA its approval for routine use, nearly five thousand people were being treated with the drug each week. And because patients treated with TPA can usually leave the hospital in three days instead of seven to ten, hospitals report that TPA was saving them $5,000 per patient—despite a price tag of $2,200 *per dose.* Doctors anticipate that TPA will prove equally successful in saving the lives of stroke patients, and the drug also is being tested in patients with blood clots in the arms, legs, and lungs.

TPA has only one significant limitation: it must be given by intravenous injection, and even then it can take an hour or more to begin dissolving a clot. And unless the clot in a heart-attack patient's cardiac arteries can be dissolved in one to three hours, the heart muscle can be permanently damaged. Researchers are now working on fast-acting TPA formulations. By 1995, known heart patients will keep them at their bedsides, ready for instant use when an attack strikes.

By the turn of the century, a host of new genetically engineered drugs will be available to dissolve atherosclerotic plaques, lower blood cholesterol, prevent or halt cardiac arrhythmias to halt a heart attack in progress, and reduce the effects of stroke. Among them are the following:

Angiotensin converting enzyme (ACE), which destroys a natural hormone that raises blood pressure. Unlike artificial drugs used to combat high blood pressure, ACE does not leave patients depressed, tired, and even impotent. Well before 2000, ACE will be in general use for hypertension.

Atrial natriuretic factor (ANF) also combats high blood pressure. It acts both by relaxing the muscles in the walls of blood vessels and by increasing urine volume and salt excretion—the same mechanisms used by many artificial pressure-lowering drugs. But unlike many drugs, its side effects are relatively mild. ANF also affects the kidneys, liver, lungs, intestine, brain, and testes, and scientists are now exploring other possible uses of the drug. Look for it to reach hypertension patients in the mid-1990s.

Granulocyte-macrophage colony stimulating factor (GM-CSF) turns out to reduce high cholesterol levels almost as well as it boosts the immune system. Dr. Stephen D. Nimer, of the University of California at Los Angeles, discovered the effect by accident recently while using the hormone to treat patients with aplastic anemia. Out of eight patients, three experienced a reduction in cholesterol levels of 50 percent or more, while three more experienced reductions of more than one-third. In two patients, cholesterol levels fell to less than 90 milligrams per milliliter of blood. The normal range is from 140 to 270 mg/ml; anything over 240 mg/ml carries a risk of heart disease. No one is sure yet how GM-CSF reduces cholesterol levels, but the hormone is almost sure to find use in patients who do not tolerate other drugs.

TWENTY-FIRST CENTURY TRANSPLANTS

There is a controversial treatment that now promises to cure diabetes, hemophilia, Parkinson's disease, Huntington's chorea, muscular dystrophy, paralyzing spinal injury, and perhaps even Alzheimer's disease. It is a tissue transplant, but a transplant with a difference: in these operations, the involuntary donor would be an aborted human fetus.

In theory, most of these transplants could use adult tissue. But fetal tissue offers a number of advantages that could make the difference between a rare, last-resort operation and a practical, day-to-day therapy capable of bringing normal life to perhaps 5 million Americans. Embryonic cells have little trouble adapting to a new environment, so they stand a good chance of surviving the operation. They stimulate the growth of new blood vessels, ensuring that they will not be starved for oxygen or nutrients. They tolerate long-term storage well, so tissue can be "harvested" and saved until it is needed. And, best of all, they are hardly ever rejected by the recipient's immune system; there is little need for elaborate tissue typing before the transplant and for immune-suppressant drugs afterwards.

In animal studies, fetal-cell transplants have scored some remarkable successes:

At the University of Rochester, neurobiologist Timothy Collier has implanted two different kinds of fetal nerve cell into the brains of senile rats. One variety of cell produced the hormone norepinephrine, the other a material called *nerve growth factor.* Both kinds of cell restored the animals' memory.

At Chicago's Mercy Hospital, Henry Huang and his colleagues experimented on rats that in old age had become sexually impotent. After receiving transplanted tissue from the hypothalamus glands of fetal rats, seven once–sexually impotent animals promptly fathered 106 pups.

And researchers at the University of North Carolina and at Vanderbilt University have been using fetal tissue to correct liver disorders in lab animals. The research began when physicians noted that hemophiliacs who had undergone liver transplants often gained not just a new liver, but also the ability to form a blood clot. Liver transplants are so dangerous that they can only be used in patients who are already desperately ill. Scientists hope that transplants of fetal tissue will be a safe, effective way to restore "bleeders" to a normal life.

So far, doctors have attempted to cure only two disorders using fetal tissue. In the United States, physicians have transplanted fetal pancreatic islet cells—the source of insulin—into at least thirty diabetic adults; there have been no adverse side effects and, temporarily, at least, the patients' condition seemed much improved. And neurosurgeons in Sweden and Mexico and at the University of Colorado have implanted nerve cells from aborted fetuses into the brains of patients with Parkinson's disease in the hope that the cells would provide the chemical dopamine, the absence of which causes uncontrollable tremors and eventual death; the procedure did seem to help, though not as much as researchers had hoped.

Clearly, the fate of fetal-transplant research depends far more on ethical considerations than on medical utility or scientific feasibility. For many people, the thought of dissecting a fetus for spare parts is little more than refined cannibalism. It even carries the threat that unscrupulous women and physicians will arrange otherwise unwanted pregnancies solely to obtain valuable tissues. (We will look more closely at the ethics of fetal transplants in Chapter 19.) But it is a safe guess that, by 2000, fetal-tissue transplants will be available to all who need them, if not in the United States, then in Mexico and in most of Europe.

PROBLEMS WITH PAIN

"Back in medical school, I thought I was learning to save lives," recalls the widely respected head of gerontology at a major Texas medical school. "It didn't take long to find out that many patients could not be saved. Then I consoled myself with the idea that I could at least ease their pain. Now I know I can't even do that."

At the end of the 1980s, that is all too often true. One American in three suffers from chronic pain. An estimated 40 million have bouts of migraine and other chronic, almost crippling headaches. Another 100 million have episodes of back pain each year. About 1 million suffer from the worst, least tractable pain of all—the agony of a cancer that presses on a nerve or eats its way into the bone. No wonder that Americans gobble more than 30 billion aspirin tablets each year and that about one thousand pain clinics have opened around the United States in the last five years.

Few doctors know what to do for patients in pain. At most medical schools, students receive only two or three hours of lectures about chronic pain. And until recently, there was little more for them to know. Researchers had learned little about the biology of pain, so if aspirin or ibuprofen did not relieve the condition and the doctor was unwilling to risk addicting the patient to morphine, there was little that could be done.

By 2000, none of this will be true. Scientists are now making fast progress in learning how pain works. And that is giving them new thoughts about how to block it. Those ideas are already showing signs of paying off.

It turns out that there is not just one kind of pain. There are two, and they work together. When we burn a finger or prick it with a pin, a nerve signal races from the injury to the brain, giving us convincing notice that something is wrong. That "fast" pain is intense and closely focused on the injury, but it lasts only a few seconds. Then a slower nerve signal reaches the brain, and we begin to feel the dull, diffuse, lasting kind of pain that can throb for hours. Worse, several varieties of chemicals pour into the injury to promote healing. They also make the nerves more sensitive, so the pain hurts worse and lasts longer. Aspirin works because it blocks one group of pain-promoting chemicals, known as *prostaglandins.* Scientists are now working to develop blockers for the other substances, known as *bradykinins* and *leukotrienes.* Bradykinin inhibitors have already been tested in animals, and appear to make them almost immune to pain. Human trials should be under way this year, so the first bradykinin-blocking pain relievers should be in use before the turn of the century. If the bradykinin blockers work as well in people as they appear to in animals, they could be almost a "magic bullet" for many kinds of persistent pain.

One of the hottest "new" pain relieving methods at the turn of the century will probably be one of the oldest methods now in use—acupuncture. After nearly twenty years of research, American physicians are finally coming to the conclusion that the ancient Chinese method of pain relief really works. In one study, for example, doctors used acupuncture to treat women suffering from menstrual pain. Ten of the eleven women given traditional acupuncture treatments reported less than half as much pain after beginning therapy, and they used less than half as much pain medication. A decade from now, doctors should know a lot more about this oft-ridiculed technique and be far more willing to prescribe it.

DIGITAL DOCTORS

With computers transforming almost every part of modern life, it is no surprise that they are becoming as basic to health care as the stethoscope. But the changes to come in the next decade are even more profound than most of us would guess. From diagnosis to treatment to recordkeeping, computers are giving doctors new tools to give us all longer, healthier lives.

Back in the 1970s, the CAT scanner spread throughout American hospitals, giving physicians a dramatically clearer view of their patients' ills. Computerized axial tomography works by taking a whole series of X rays from different angles through a thin slice of the body. A computer then mathematically condenses the individual X-ray measurements into a single, remarkably detailed image of that section of the patient's anatomy. Even the first CAT scanners gave doctors their first clear look at blood clots, cancerous tumors, and other deadly problems that previously could be found only by surgery. Since then, new generations of vastly more powerful computers have made CAT images clearer yet. By 2000, even today's most powerful scanners will seem primitive.

New types of scanners will be in widespread use as well. The most useful may be *magnetic resonance imaging.* MRI works by placing the body inside an intense magnetic field, then beaming powerful radio waves at the area to be examined. With the right combination of magnetic field and radio signal, the body's hydrogen atoms wobble back and forth, first becoming aligned with the magnetic field, then moving out of line. At each wobble they give off faint radio signals, which the MRI machine's computer can assemble into a picture, just as a CAT scanner does. But unlike X rays, MRI pictures the soft body tissues, giving a clear look at the heart, brain, and other tissues. By 2000, even more powerful imaging systems will provide the clearest view yet of cancerous tumors.

A closely related technique called *magnetic resonance spectroscopy* gives a detailed view, not of the body's structure, but of its chemistry. Instead of processing the MRI signals into an image, the computer in an MRS system displays a graph of the strength of the signals it finds at each radio frequency. The frequencies found depend on the biochemical processes going on in the organ being scanned—crucial information for doctors diagnosing heart attacks, strokes, and a wide variety of other ills. By the turn of the century, advanced scanners should routinely extract both MRI pictures and MRS data from the same exam.

Then, too, most major hospitals should have both CAT and MRI systems that do far more than show a single, stationary image. MRI "cine-imaging" equipment already under development can show the motion of the heart, letting doctors gauge the extent of damage caused by a heart attack. Other devices display three-dimensional images of the body; doctors can turn the image, walk around the patient to view an organ or tumor from the far side, and peel away layers of the image to see what is inside. All these techniques require computing power that has only recently become available. At the turn of the century, they should be standard practice.

Even more impressive is an "automated doctor" under development at the Loma Linda Medical Center, in Loma Linda, California. Give the machine a small blood sample, and it automatically classifies the cells it finds, tallying more than five hundred of them every second. A normal blood sample has a certain population of each kind of cell, and variations from the norm can reveal an infection, a cancer, an abnormality of the immune system, or many other disorders. A decade from now, advanced versions of the machine should be able to recognize invading bacteria, viruses, and even some kinds of cancer cell.

Some forms of medical computing are far less dramatic than this high-tech diagnostic equipment, yet for day-to-day patient care, they will be just as valuable. John A. Norris, former deputy commissioner of the Food and Drug Administration, envisions a day when physicians all over the world are linked by elaborate computer-communications networks that store everything from patient records to details of research projects still in progress. When a patient moves from one city to another, his new doctor will be able to call up the same medical records used by the previous physician. If the patient had, say, some rare form of cancer, the doctor would be able to locate research centers working with the illness and try to enter his patient into the study. And both physicians and pharmacists would have access to worldwide information about experimental drugs, little-known side effects, drug recalls, and virtually any other consideration that might influence the choice of treatment. Norris concedes that any such system will have to provide elaborate protections for the patient's privacy and that it will take many years to set up. But by the turn of the century, the first regional "nodes" should be in use, and the process of interconnecting them should be under way.

By then, too, artificial-intelligence technology may have brought us the first true "doc-in-a-box," a computer program that can "think about" the patient's symptoms and lab tests, make a diagnosis, and prescribe the appropriate treatment. The first relatively primitive systems are already in experimental use.

There are two kinds: *critiquing systems* and *consultation systems.* Critiquing systems let the doctor work out his own diagnosis-and-treatment plan, then compare it with the knowledge in their database to see how well his decisions match those of experts in the field.

Probably the most advanced diagnostic program is QMR, for Quick Medical Reference, developed at the University of Pittsburgh School of Medicine. QMR can match 4,100 different symptoms, test results, and patient characteristics with 557 separate illnesses. Given information about a patient, it can suggest further tests that should be performed, analyze the findings, and suggest the most probable diagnoses. It can also act as an electronic textbook, allowing doctors to draw their own conclusions. And it can ponder two seemingly unrelated problems and figure out a combination of diseases that might be responsible for them. An earlier version of QMR proved almost as good at figuring out what was wrong with patients as the best physicians. At the turn of the century, more advanced software may be even better. If such programs never quite replace human intuition, there is a good chance that they will take over some routine cases, particularly in remote areas where a human doctor may be unavailable.

BIONIC BODY

Twenty years ago, artificial organs were no more than clumsy, temporary substitutes for natural functions, to be used only in emergencies, and then only until the patient's own organs could recover and take over their normal duties. Today, such implants as artificial joints, cardiac pacemakers, and lens implants for the eye are virtually permanent aids or replacements for defective or lost body parts that enable their users to live almost normal lives. By 2000, most of today's implants will have been succeeded by far better models, and it will be possible to replace many lost functions for which even primitive artificial organs are yet unavailable.

There is a good chance that doctors will at last be able to replace the human heart with an artificial one by the turn of the century, or soon after. After the deaths of artificial-heart recipients Barney

Clark, William Schroeder, and others, critics charged that even a successful artificial heart would cost more than it was worth. No more than 35,000 people per year would have use for it, and they would add up to $5 billion a year to the nation's medical bill. Nonetheless, at the University of Utah, Penn State, and several other institutions, bioengineers are developing new models that promise to work far longer than the Jarvik-7. Already, the bulky air pumps that operated the Jarvik have been replaced by smaller pumps that let patients walk around for short periods. By the mid-1990s, air pumps will have been replaced by hydraulic power units that will be smaller still. Shortly after the turn of the century, the best of them will be nearing clinical use.

Well before that, artificial hearts will be keeping patients alive while their own hearts heal or while they wait for a transplant. One likely candidate is the Nimbus Hemopump, a tiny turbine that can take over the entire load of pumping blood, allowing the patient's own heart to rest until it is ready to return to work. Doctors at Pacific Presbyterian Medical Center, in San Francisco, have already tested a similar device in nearly one hundred patients, with good results.

Some sixty thousand Americans now suffering from kidney disease would die within days if not for regular dialysis treatments. But that survival comes at a price. Today's dialysis machines are so large and costly that patients must schedule their lives around their appointments at specialized dialysis clinics. And they cannot spend more than a day or two away from a clinic; a week of wilderness camping is out of the question. That will not be so for long; a recent innovation will go a long way toward giving kidney patients their freedom. It is an eight-pound, battery-powered dialysis machine—in effect, an artificial kidney—that patients can carry with them during the day. The device was developed at the University of Utah, but is being manufactured in Japan. A decade from now, even smaller kidney machines should be in general use.

Even artificial senses should be in common use at the turn of the century. At the top of the list is an electronic ear wired directly into the cochlea, the spiral-shaped nerve center in the inner ear where sound vibrations are converted to nerve impulses. At the moment, the most sophisticated model divides incoming sound into twenty-two frequency bands and sends each to its own electrode in the cochlea. The result is something like listening to a poorly tuned radio—a long way from normal hearing, but a big improvement on total deafness. Lip-readers using the device can understand about twice as much as by sight alone, and a few can understand simple telephone conversations. According to one estimate, it will take one hundred electrodes implanted in the cochlea to provide fully recognizable speech. That goal will be within easy reach by 2000.

Some of the most dramatic new artificial organs will be "biohybrids," incorporating both man-made materials and the patient's own flesh or that of a donor:

One high-priority item is an artificial pancreas for diabetes patients. In theory, it should be possible just to give diabetes patients a pancreas transplant; in practice, such operations seldom succeed. So biomedical engineers have tried for years to duplicate the workings of the natural pancreas, but with only limited success. It is not enough just to give diabetics a shot of insulin on schedule, or even to drip it into their systems. Our natural insulin levels jump dramatically when we eat, then sag as our food is digested. With some implanted insulin pumps, patients can give themselves an extra shot of the hormone just before eating, but even that is far from ideal. The natural pancreas monitors our blood sugar and doles out exactly as much insulin as the body needs, and no more. An artificial pancreas with that degree of control could add years to a diabetes patient's life.

Now researchers are taking another route to that goal: They are separating islet cells—the insulin makers—from the pancreas, packaging them inside a porous plastic capsule, and implanting them in the patient's abdomen. The plastic allows nutrients into the cells and lets insulin flow out, yet shields the cells from destruction by the immune system. Several different models of the implant have been tested in recent years. By the turn of the century, these partially artificial organs should give diabetes patients virtually normal lives.

A similar technique eventually will help patients with liver failure, but to date it remains in animal testing. Researchers at Albert Einstein College of Medicine, in the Bronx, have taken liver cells from healthy rats, bound them to microscopic plastic beads, and injected them into rats with inborn liver disease. When the animals receiving the cells were genetically similar to the donors, the cells took over the animals' liver function. In dissimilar rats, the cells worked at first but were soon killed by the recipient's immune system. For use in humans, liver cells will be packaged in porous capsules, much as pancreatic islet cells are, to protect them against the body's defense mechanisms. The first patients should receive these biohybrid organs well before 2000.

AN END TO AGING

There is an old and somewhat bitter joke among scientists who study the aging process: "The only way to avoid growing old," it's said, "is to die young." There is at least an outside chance that by 2000 that will no longer be true.

For more than thirty years, a dedicated band of researchers has been trying to figure out why we grow old and die—and how to defeat the process. So far, their efforts, chronically short of both manpower and money, have produced almost as many questions as answers. Though scientists have managed to double or triple the lifespans of mice, rats, fish, and a host of other animals, they have been working almost in the dark. No one yet understands what causes aging. No one yet understands why the best medical care still cannot keep us alive much beyond our biblical threescore and ten. Yet there are many theories, and there is every reason to believe that if this field received even a small fraction of the money that, say, cancer research does, it would be possible to make rapid progress in answering these most basic of all questions.

Recently, at least five separate lines of study have shown signs that they may soon pay off. They probably will not allow us to live forever. They may not even extend our lives for very long. But they will very likely make it possible to live well into a healthy old age and then die suddenly, without the long decline most of us can expect under nature's grim plan.

The best known anti-aging treatment is Retin-A, the vitamin A derivative touted by women's magazines as a miracle cure for wrinkled, lifeless skin. More recent studies have found that Retin-A and a variety of closely related compounds can return precancerous cells to normal and may even work against leukemia and some other forms of cancer. They may have other uses as well. According to Dr. Richard Cutler, a leading researcher at the National Institute on Aging, one part of aging is a loss of control over our genes, so that cells no longer devote all their energy to carrying out their specialized tasks efficiently. For example, when we are young, only blood cells make hemoglobin; as we age, cells all over the body begin to manufacture it. But cells treated with Retin-A appear to regain control over their genes and perform only their normal functions. In that event, it may be that Retin-A is turning back one of the basic clocks that measure out our span. By 2000, or soon thereafter, some treatment based on Retin-A could give us all extra years of healthy life.

Another part of aging is a process called *enzymatic browning*. It occurs when molecules of blood sugar become attached to the body's proteins. Sugar molecules on adjacent proteins then react with each other, linking the two proteins in a way that stiffens the supple fibers. Cataracts form when the proteins of the eye's lens become joined in this way; cross-linking is also the first step in forming the cholesterol-filled plaques that block the blood vessels in stroke and heart disease. Scientists Anthony Cerami and Michael Brownlee, of New York's Rockefeller Institute, have developed a drug called *aminoguanidine* that prevents cross-linking by joining with sugar molecules before they can react with each other. They have already shown that the drug can slow arterial damage in diabetic rats, which have abnormally high levels of blood sugar. Now they are working to learn whether it will also break existing cross-links and whether it will lengthen the lives of laboratory animals. An educated guess is that it will.

Researchers have known for years that a natural hormone called *dehydroepiandrosterone* (DHEA) prevents both obesity and cancer in test animals and lengthens the lifespan of mice. Now they are finding that it may also prevent many of the ills of aging.

According to Dr. Elizabeth Barrett-Connor and colleagues at the University of California, San Diego, men over fifty who have high levels of a DHEA derivative called DHEA-sulfate (DHEAS) are only half as likely to die of heart disease than men with less of the hormone. Even people without heart disease seemed less likely to die young if they had a good supply of DHEAS. By 2000 we will know whether DHEAS supplements can ward off heart disease and prolong our lives.

Two other scientists, biologist Douglas Coleman, of the Jackson Laboratory, in Bar Harbor, Maine, and physician Paul MacDonald, of the University of Texas Southwestern Medical School, in Dallas, both report that DHEA can restore immune systems that fail in disease or old age. Mice with systemic lupus erythematosus (SLE) generally die before they reach their first birthday; treated with DHEA, about half live out their full two-year lifespan, and virtually all survive much longer than untreated mice. SLE kills five thousand people each year in the United States, most of them young women, and many of the ills of old age occur at least in part because our immune systems become too weak to prevent them. If DHEA works as well in humans as it does in mice, it may spare us from the infirmities of aging.

And neurobiochemist Eugene Roberts, of the Beckman Research

Institute of the City of Hope, in Duarte, California, found that small doses of DHEA restore the failing memory of senile mice. Whether it does so also in aging human beings has yet to be learned. The knowledge will be in hand by the turn of the century.

All these treatments aim primarily at some of the symptoms of age. Two more may treat the basic cause.

More than twenty years ago, an endocrinologist named W. Donner Denckla found evidence that we age, and perhaps die, because our own pituitary glands make a hormone that slowly turns us off. He called it DECO, for "decreasing consumption of oxygen," a major effect of the substance. Dr. Denckla traced nearly all the effects of aging to DECO: wrinkling, hair loss, poor immune function, poor heart and lung function, and a wide variety of other disorders. To prove it, he removed the pituitary from mice and gave them doses of the pituitary hormones that animals can't live without. With the source of DECO gone, the mice suddenly looked and acted like adolescents. More than one in five survived for thirty-four months, roughly equivalent to a human age of ninety-five, which only one in one hundred of us reach; some mice survived considerably longer. Despite this startling success, Denckla was never able to purify the DECO hormone, or even prove for sure that it exists.

Now Dr. William Regelson and his colleagues at the Medical College of Virginia have followed up on Dr. Denckla's work and have found the likely explanation: there is no single DECO hormone. Instead, most of the effects we think of as aging are caused by changes in the balance of hormones that physicians are already familiar with. Though the work is so new that Dr. Regelson is reluctant to give out full details, he is now sure that he knows both how the aging process works and how to cure it. We should know for certain well before the turn of the century.

Regelson is not at all sure that aging—our wrinkling, our progressive loss of stamina, and our growing susceptibility to disease—is caused by the same process that leads to death. If not, his anti-DECO treatment may yield only a modest increase in our life expectancy— say to 110 years or so—but it will allow us to retain youthful good health virtually to the end. It may well happen by 2000.

Another probable breakthrough in aging research comes from Dr. Marguerite Kay, of Texas A&M University. Dr. Kay has spent the last decade or so studying red blood cells, trying to learn how our bodies get rid of them when they are worn out. What she found was a material which she calls *senescent cell antigen* (SSA). As our cells age, SSA appears on the surface of the cell. The immune system does not recognize SSA as one of the body's own constituents, so it destroys the defective blood cells, just as it would destroy invading bacteria. SSA appears on cells throughout the body as they age, and Dr. Kay suspects that one major reason we grow old and die is that crucial cells—cells we cannot live without—begin to make SSA and are removed from the body. If so, there are several possible ways to slow the process. Dr. Kay thinks it should also be possible to promote production of SSA on specific cells, so that the body could be induced to attack, say, a cancerous tumor. By 2000, many of the remaining questions about SSA should have been cleared up. We will know for sure whether we can manipulate this mechanism to prolong our youthful vigor and our lives.

One interesting observation: in patients with Alzheimer's disease, the afflicted brain cells show large quantities of SSA. Other cells in the brains of Alzheimer's patients are free of SSA; so are all the brain cells of people not afflicted by the deadly illness. It seems that this horrifying form of senile decay may occur when the body finds the SSA and destroys the nerve cells that carry it. In that case, it may be possible to stop Alzheimer's disease, either by getting rid of the SSA or by blocking the immune attack.

THE BAD NEWS

Though science is doing its part to build a healthier America by 2000, society will have trouble following its lead. The problem is the price tag. The United States already spends 11 percent of its gross national product on health care, and the figure is growing rapidly. We now spend $2 billion per year to save the lives of premature infants who, twenty years ago, would have died—more than $150,000 per baby, on average, for a stay in the neonatal intensive-care unit—and 15 percent of the survivors carry physical or mental defects of varying severity. Another $2 billion per year goes to fund dialysis treatments for about sixty thousand patients with kidney disease. And roughly one-third of Medicare funds—on the order of $150,000 per patient—go to support people in the last six months of their lives, many of whom have little or no chance of recovery. Bringing the best of high-tech medicine to every American who needs it will cost far more—more than we can afford, even with Medicare surcharges such as that mandated in the Comprehensive Medical Care Act of 1988. Before the 1990s are over, money problems will severely limit our ability to deliver on the promise of today's research.

We will face growing personnel shortages as well. By 2000, the United States will need about 4 million new health-care professionals. We already have some 400,000 fewer registered nurses than we need; in the 1990s, we will have to make up that deficit and find 2 million more RNs as well. We will also need some 870,000 licensed practical nurses, 700,000 geriatric social workers, and 400,000 paramedics and emergency medical technicians. Attracting the needed people to these fields will mean raising pay scales in a field already struggling to cut costs, and even that will not do the job. Well before the turn of the century, the United States will be forced to relax its immigration quotas in order to recruit upwards of 1 million health-care professionals from other countries. This raises a severe ethical problem, because it will aggravate shortages in many lands where the medical system already finds it difficult to meet local needs.

One response to these trends will be a dramatic growth of home health care. Medicare and Medicaid could save millions of dollars each year simply by offering some medical services at the patient's home rather than in the hospital. For example, it costs nearly $300,000 per year to keep one patient on a mechanical ventilator in the hospital, but little more than $20,000 per year to provide the same equipment at home; switching to home care in this single service would save well over $65 million per year. Multiply that kind of saving across all the services that could be adapted to home use, and it adds up to a sizable fraction of America's annual hospital bill. By 2000, many such services will be offered.

Another cost-cutting trend is the dramatic growth of ambulatory care centers, "surgicenters," and walk-in clinics (to be discussed at greater length in Chapter 14). By attracting patients who might otherwise visit hospital emergency rooms or spend days in semiprivate rooms recovering from minor surgery, these low-budget medical facilities, offering hospital-quality care at a fraction of the price, will go a long way toward reducing America's doctor's bill between now and the year 2000.

In the long run, however, something else is needed. As the Baby Boom generation reaches middle age, its need for medical care will grow rapidly. The only way to cut this generation's medical expenses is to prevent heart attacks, strokes, cancer, Alzheimer's disease, and the thousand other maladies that afflict the aged. Preventive medicine can help. Give up smoking, watch cholesterol levels, and so on, and we will undeniably live longer, healthier lives.

But even that is not good enough. At the turn of the *twentieth* century, an American man's life expectancy at birth was only forty-seven years. Most people died of infection. Few lived long enough to develop cancer or heart disease. But when antibiotics banished contagion, we began to die of other disorders, most of which require even more medical care. At the turn of the *twenty-first* century, when healthier lifestyles and more potent therapies rescue us from cancer and heart disease, we will surely find ourselves succumbing to other once-rare illnesses.

Looked at in this way, cancer, Alzheimer's disease, and most other ills are little more than symptoms of a far more basic disorder—aging itself. As we grow older, we become more vulnerable to illness; it's a basic part of the process. So if we are serious about cutting America's enormous medical bill, we must begin by learning why the passage of time makes us frail. A few dedicated scientists have done the groundwork, as described earlier in this chapter. They are ready at last to assemble all their theories into a genuine understanding of the aging process—if only they can afford to pay for the research it will take.

No one who cares seriously about human health would cut funding for research into cancer, heart disease, and the other disorders of middle and old age. But while we spend hundreds of millions of dollars each year on these symptoms, it is time to spend a few extra millions on the study of aging itself. With the Baby Boom generation rapidly approaching middle age, we can't afford not to.

BIOTECH BONANZA

*F*or more than ten years now, the promised biological revolution has been largely that—a promise. Yet even in its infancy, biotechnology has scored some impressive successes:

Ten years ago, insulin was laboriously extracted from the organs of pigs and cattle; today it is grown in bacteria. The result is a far better, less costly drug.

Ten years ago, the experimental anticancer drug interferon would have cost $22 *billion* per pound, if anyone could have obtained a pound of that rare protein. Today it is inexpensive enough for practical clinical use.

Physicians now use tiny bits of artificial DNA known as gene probes to identify microbes that infect their patients. The technique provides more accurate diagnoses than older methods, and faster—sometimes months faster.

If all these examples are drawn from medicine, it's no coincidence. Already, the market for bioengineered medical products is nearing $1 billion a year, but biobusiness has had a much harder time penetrating other fields.

In the late 1990s, that will change dramatically. Researchers have already developed bacteria that can protect crop plants from frost damage, new plant varieties that can grow in areas unsuited to natural strains of those same plants, and synthetic hormones that will help cattle produce more milk or beef on the same amount of food. They should be in widespread use by the turn of the century. Not long after, the first genetically engineered crops will reach American farmers. Some will be plant varieties that grow in regions too hot or cold or dry for their natural ancestors, while others will offer better nutrition or processing advantages. One bioengineered variety of corn known as *quality protein maize* is rich in lysine and tryptophane, nutrients missing from the corn that is now a staple for some 200 million people, including half of those who are chronically malnourished. By, say, 2005, biotech companies will deliver the first plants that capture their own nitrogen fertilizer from the air, resist insects and plant diseases, and yield more food per acre of farmland.

By then, too, the first industrial processes based on gene-altered yeasts and bacteria should be nearing practical application; some may already be in use. Most will take advantage of nature's extraordinary skill in chemical synthesis. Using enzymes as catalysts, bacteria routinely carry out processes that human chemists can duplicate only under extremes of temperature and pressure. To date, only a few of these natural enzymes have reached industrial use, but research scientists have already begun to build wholly artificial enzymes to carry out processes nature did not provide for. Co-opting microbes to do the job instead of building huge processing plants in the long run will save hundreds of millions of dollars in equipment costs. Better yet, biological processes should eliminate the millions of tons of toxic waste that now flow from our clumsy human processes. Researchers have already developed bacteria that digest PCBs, crude-oil spills, and toluene, a toxic solvent and gasoline additive. Some can attack such toxic wastes and leave nothing but water and carbon dioxide.

Chemists have cited an enormous variety of valuable products that might soon be made through biotechnology, from pharmaceuticals intermediates (chemical building blocks used to synthesize a pharmaceutical) to the raw materials for many plastics. Among the most likely long-term developments are bacteria that can "crack" crude oil, replacing the huge, polluting refineries that now produce gasoline, heating oil, and other useful products; and bacteria that digest lignin, the contaminant now removed from paper pulp by malodorous, polluting sulfites. Some industrial chemists even hope to leach metals out of ore with bacteria instead of huge acid vats. Despite all the research poured into this field over the last decade, it is still too soon to tell which of these processes will turn out to be practical, or when they will go into use.

THE AIDS

PLAGUE

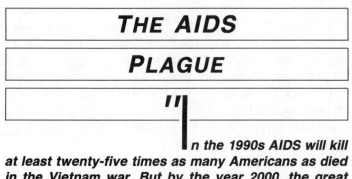

"In the 1990s AIDS will kill at least twenty-five times as many Americans as died in the Vietnam war. But by the year 2000, the great plague of the twentieth century should be over."**

It is not easy to make concrete forecasts about AIDS. There are too many things that nearly $1 billion worth of research still has not told us about this disease. But there are a few things about which we are almost sure:

- By 2000, a diagnosis of AIDS will no longer be a sentence of death. Science will have given us drugs that, if they do not actually cure AIDS, will at least allow its victims to live out relatively normal lives. Vaccines will also be available to halt the spread of this disease.
- For most of today's AIDS patients, the drugs will come too late. They will die long before the new century arrives. So will many

of those who now carry the AIDS virus but as yet show no symptoms. For the moment, AIDS still kills far fewer people each year than die in auto accidents; by 1992, that will no longer be true. Some 407,316 Americans died in World War II, 292,131 in combat; AIDS almost surely will kill roughly 1.5 million of us by 1995.

- By 2000, the cumulative impact of AIDS on the United States—on our population, our economy, and our personal lives—may equal that of any war in our history.

The great plague of the twentieth century should, however, be on the wane as the twenty-first begins, but America will go through a grim decade before AIDS comes under control. By 2000, AIDS already will have devastated the high-risk populations of two generations; far along the chain of sexual contacts, it may have laid waste to many parts of society once thought to be out of danger. And if at the dawn of the new century there are fewer new cases each year, it will have little to do with vaccines; the real reason will be that there are few potential patients left to catch the disease.

By 2000, fifteen years of public education programs and growing fear will have made most Americans both knowledgeable about AIDS and very careful indeed. By then, most new AIDS patients will be children who acquired the virus from their mothers during gestation. Those young people will occupy as many as 10 percent of the nation's hospital beds as early as 1991. The problem can only get worse as the twenty-first century nears.

That much we can predict from cold arithmetic and cruel logic. So many people already carry AIDS that at least twenty-five times as many Americans will die of AIDS in the 1990s as were killed in the Vietnam War. That is the best we can hope for.

MAPPING THE PLAGUE

Beyond that, the coming effects of AIDS are more a matter for speculation than for scientific forecasting. In part, this reflects the complexity of the social issues surrounding AIDS. But there is another, more basic problem: After years of intensive study, we still don't know enough about AIDS to figure out just how hard it will hit the United States.

Almost a decade after scientists recognized the first cases of AIDS as a new and remarkable illness, they still are struggling to map the dimensions of the plague. In Africa, AIDS is clearly so widespread that it will nearly destroy some entire nations; by the turn of the century, one-third of the population of Uganda may die of it. In Port-au-Prince, Haiti—where the evidence suggests that AIDS was delivered to local male prostitutes by vacationing American men—the disease is now the most common cause of death among both men and women between twenty and forty years old. The World Health Organization estimates that the number of AIDS carriers worldwide will pass 100 million by 1991. But here in the United States, many questions remain.

No one knows for certain how widely AIDS has already spread among Americans. By mid-1988, about 63,000 cases of the disease had been diagnosed in the United States; roughly half of those patients had already died. Most scientists estimate that between 1.5 million and 2 million Americans carry the disease, but those figures may be much too low. They also guess that some thirty to fifty times more people carry the disease than have been diagnosed. If so, the population of AIDS carriers could already total more than 3 million.

Some urban areas have been hit particularly hard. In New York City, which has nearly one-third of all cases and deaths in the United States, the rates are ten times higher than for the nation at large. If it is true that there are thirty to fifty AIDS carriers for every diagnosed case, then one-third of all New York City men under age fifty are infected with the disease, a statistic that seems to defy belief. AIDS is now the city's leading cause of death for both men and women in their thirties. San Francisco, Los Angeles, and several other major cities offer similar statistics.

In part, that reflects the ethnic diversity of most large cities. Though blacks and Hispanics make up less than one-fifth of the population, nearly half of the diagnosed AIDS cases in America have struck these ethnic groups. And because minorities have, on average, far larger families than the white majority, twenty-five times more black babies than white are born with AIDS.

Our inner cities are breeding grounds for intravenous drug abuse, and IV drug users have been hit harder than any other social group. Nearly half of the black and Hispanic victims are either intravenous drug users or their sexual partners. In New York City there are about 200,000 IV drug users. More than half already carry the AIDS virus. According to one estimate, fully half of the people who live in some of New York City's poorest, most drug ridden neighborhoods will eventually die of AIDS. And they will do it quickly. Because of their poverty and poor access to medical care, victims among the inner-city minorities survive, on average, only nineteen weeks after diagnosis. For whites, the average is two years or more.

The big question for the 1990s is how widely AIDS will strike among non-drug-using heterosexuals. Since 1984, only 4 percent of AIDS patients have contracted the disease through heterosexual contact. Most have been the sexual partners of drug users; most of the remaining cases have been traced to someone who had been the sexual partner of a drug user. San Francisco, the symbolic AIDS capital of the United States, but with relatively few IV drug users, has seen hardly any cases of AIDS transmitted by heterosexual contact.

TAKING THE RISK

That modest rate may not last very long. In Africa, most AIDS cases are transmitted heterosexually. For some reason, no one is quite sure why, AIDS there is closely associated with two other venereal diseases, syphilis and chancroid. And since early 1987, there has been an enormous jump in the number of syphilis and chancroid infections in the United States, and particularly in New York City. Several scientists have recently insisted that AIDS is not caused by a virus like HIV at all, but by long-term, untreated syphilis, or syphilis acting perhaps in concert with a virus or another co-factor. Many of these new, syphilis-related cases have appeared in heterosexuals at high risk of developing AIDS. Whether that foretells a jump in the number of heterosexually transmitted AIDS cases here—whether AIDS will "break out" of the high-risk groups into the American population at large—it is too soon to say.

How quickly AIDS will spread in the 1990s depends in part on how many people regularly take the risk of exposure to the virus. And how large that group is may be anyone's guess.

Understandably, AIDS has already changed the sexual habits of many Americans. According to a study commissioned by Abbott Laboratories, a major pharmaceutical company, 75 percent of singles in the eighteen-to-thirty-four age group say they now avoid casual sexual encounters. About 45 percent report having had only one sex partner in the past year, and 36 percent say they are abstaining completely from sex with new partners. Fully 15 percent—more than one in six—say they have had no sexual relationship at all in the past year. In all, it is quite a change from the freewheeling sexual climate of the 1970s.

But other studies are less encouraging. According to the Centers for Disease Control, about 5 percent of men in the eighteen-to-twenty-nine age group still have more than ten sexual partners per year—enough to put them at significant risk of contracting AIDS. Some 60 to 70 percent of college students continue to have sex without condoms, and three in every thousand carry HIV, a rate nearly as high as among convicts. Considerably fewer than one-third of American couples polled in secret claim to be more than casually faithful to each other. The nation's prostitutes, many of them intravenous drug users, entertain tens of millions of clients each year. And four out of five teenagers are sexually active before the age of nineteen; few use condoms.

As 2000 approaches and the number of AIDS-related deaths climbs well into six-digit numbers, many more adults will opt for monogamous relationships or none at all. But by then it could be too late. In all, somewhere between 25 million and 50 million people— up to one American in five—may be at risk of catching and transmitting AIDS. Many will have done so long before AIDS vaccines reach the market.

In 1986 the National Academy of Sciences forecast that there would be about 270,000 cases of AIDS by 1991, when the disease would add about 10 percent to the nation's death tolls. If today's average holds good, that means some 10 million Americans then will carry the deadly virus. If just half of those people actually contract AIDS and die within ten years after infection—current evidence suggests that in the long run the number will be closer to ten out of ten—the death rate will easily pass 500,000 per year before we reach the turn of the century.

Even that will not make AIDS our leading killer; cardiovascular disease kills roughly 1 million Americans per year. But in all the wars America has ever fought, just over 650,000 of its citizens have died in battle. And with all the uncertainties that surround the incidence and transmission of AIDS, the real toll could well double or triple the 500,000-per-year death rate. In that case, by the mid-1990s, America's population will actually be shrinking for the first time in history.

All this assumes that we will not soon find a vaccine to prevent the spread of AIDS or a drug to cure it. Any breakthrough in prevention or treatment in the next few years could slow the spread of AIDS and reduce the number of patients who will die in the mid- to late 1990s. But while scientists have made enormous progress in understanding AIDS and a wide variety of possible treatments are under development, there are still so many things we do not know about AIDS that it is difficult to predict how long it will be before effective therapies are generally available.

A PUZZLING VIRUS

Most scientists believe that AIDS begins with a virus called *human immunodeficiency virus,* or HIV. When HIV enters the body, usually during sexual intercourse, unsterilized needle use, or a blood transfusion, it finds a variety of congenial places to hide. Some virus particles take up residence in the nerves of the brain, causing neurological symptoms that range from Alzheimer's-like disintegration of the mind to outright hallucinations. Some colonize bone cells. A few find refuge in the cells of the intestines, where they cause diarrhea and severe weight loss. But the majority make their home, with exquisite irony, in the "helper" T-cells and macrophages of the immune system—the very cells designed to fight off infection. Slowly, with little sign that anything is wrong, the virus destroys the helper T-cells and weakens the body's defense against disease. Eventually, the patient finds himself in the position of the famed "bubble boy," who was born without a working immune system and was condemned to die if he ever left his sterile plastic tent: he loses the ability to fight off infection and eventually dies of an illness that others would have found harmless.

AIDS is astonishingly difficult to contract. So far as anyone knows, it can be transmitted only by an exchange of bodily fluids, during gestation, sexual intercourse, a blood transfusion, or the use of an infected hypodermic needle. AIDS cannot, for example, be caught by kissing; in the laboratory, at least, a healthy man's saliva kills the AIDS virus very efficiently. The regular sexual partner of an AIDS victim requires, on average, two years to contract the disease. Even among the babies of AIDS patients, exposed continuously to their mother's blood for nine months, half are born free of the virus. It should be noted that there has *never* been a documented case in which a family member of an AIDS patient caught the disease, save through sexual intercourse.

Once someone has become infected, it takes six to ten years for an adult patient's illness to make itself known; in children, the first symptoms can appear in as little as two years. But once the disease presents recognizable symptoms, the patient can expect to die in a year or two—and even that is uncertain. Some patients, however, perhaps as many as one in ten, survive for years. A few who were diagnosed as early as 1981 and 1982 are still alive. The chances of long-term survival—for, say, five years—are vehemently debated among AIDS researchers. But no one seriously entertains the idea that any AIDS patient stands a chance of permanent recovery.

That is the orthodox view of AIDS, and no one doubts how hard the disease is to catch, or how slim are the chances of recovery. But as regards the cause of AIDS, there is another view. And while this revisionist theory will likely prove wrong, it does point up how little we really know about this disease.

In the 1960s and 1970s, molecular biologist Peter Duesberg was a giant in his field. His specialty was the study of retroviruses, a group that includes HIV. In 1970, working with colleague Peter Vogt at the University of California at Berkeley, Duesberg discovered the first oncogenes, fragments of genetic material that, when they malfunction, seem to be the ultimate cause of cancer. In 1986, the brilliance of his work won him membership in the prestigious National Academy of Sciences; it is as high an honor as an American scientist can receive, short of a Nobel Prize.

Dr. Duesberg's reputation has suffered since then, because he has gone head-to-head with some of the most powerful members of America's scientific establishment over an issue that most AIDS researchers consider settled. In the summer of 1986, at the height of his renown, Duesberg declared that, whatever causes AIDS, HIV isn't it. And when his fellow scientists ignored his message, he took it public.

In fact, the evidence that HIV causes AIDS seems pretty compelling. Using the most sensitive tests available, the virus can be isolated from nearly all AIDS patients. When AIDS appears in a new country, HIV has always gotten there first. And transfusion recipients have contracted AIDS from blood donations contaminated with HIV when no other explanation could be found.

But, as Duesberg points out, there is a lot about AIDS that remains unexplained:

For one thing, when other viruses similar to HIV cause disease, the blood is full of them; some patients with retroviral infections carry a trillion virus particles in a few drops. But even at the height of an AIDS patient's illness, his blood contains so little HIV that the most sensitive tests yet developed can hardly find it.

That is even more puzzling than it sounds. Unlike other organisms, viruses have no reproductive mechanism of their own. To multiply, they insert their own genetic programs into the DNA of their victim's cells and force their host to make new virus particles. In many viral diseases, we grow sick because our cells become so jammed with virus particles that they swell up and burst. That happens in laboratory cultures of HIV; the virus multiplies inside helper T-cells until it destroys them. If it happened in AIDS patients, their

T-cells would be jammed with virus particles, and their blood would swarm with them.

But, as Duesberg points out, in AIDS patients the virus is active only in one helper T-cell in 10,000; some estimates put it closer to one in 100,000. That is not nearly enough to destroy all the cells that vanish with AIDS, and no one has yet explained convincingly how HIV can destroy vastly more cells than it infects. Exaggerating to make his point, Duesberg says that "a man loses more T-cells when he cuts himself shaving than when infected with HIV."

Further, most viruses cause disease before the immune system can defend against them. When someone becomes infected with HIV, the immune system suppresses it almost immediately; clinical AIDS does not appear for months or years afterward. It is true that a few viral disorders lie hidden in the body for years after the infection that caused them; shingles and genital herpes are two common examples. But the delayed onset of AIDS is one more puzzle that scientists have yet to explain.

Finally, there is the problem of "Koch's postulates." In the late nineteenth century, Robert Koch, the founder of modern bacteriology, laid out three requirements that a microorganism must meet before doctors can safely say it causes a given disease: it must be found in all patients; a sample must be taken from one of the patients and made to grow in the laboratory; and the microbe must cause the same disease when given to another animal. So far, AIDS has fulfilled the first two requirements. But it has not passed the third test. Though HIV can be grown in chimpanzees, only human beings get AIDS, and for obvious reasons no scientist is going to infect someone with a possible AIDS virus just to prove that it makes him sick. Yet until researchers can find an animal that contracts AIDS when dosed with HIV, they will not have proved that HIV causes the disease—at least according to the standards that bacteriologists have followed for more than a century.

Most scientists would argue that there is so much other evidence against HIV that it can be declared guilty even without satisfying Koch's third postulate. But to Peter Duesberg, all those puzzles add up to one thing: the case against HIV has not been proved, and probably never will be. Animals do not get AIDS from HIV, he believes, because the virus has little or nothing to do with the disease.

That conclusion has not endeared him to AIDS researchers who like to see themselves as leaders of the crusade against a fearsome disease. The co-discoverers of HIV—Dr. Robert Gallo, of the National Cancer Institute, and Dr. Luc Montagnier, of the Pasteur Institute, in Paris—declare flatly, "Evidence that HIV causes AIDS is now as firm as that for the causation of any other human disease." Writing in the journal *Science*, Nobel Prize–winner David Baltimore, of the Whitehead Institute of Biomedical Research, in Cambridge, Massachusetts (whose work in cancer genetics is built on Duesberg's pioneering efforts) called Duesberg's criticism of AIDS research "irresponsible and pernicious." The American Foundation for AIDS Research even set up a combination debate and kangaroo court in which eight leading researchers, using tactics more common in political campaigns than in science, did their best to discredit Duesberg's views even when they could not disprove them.

But Duesberg's arguments bring up a frightening possibility: if AIDS is caused by something other than HIV, much of the work now going into vaccines and drugs could be wasted.

So far, it seems unlikely. Though HIV has proved a difficult virus to attack, scientists have made rapid progress in developing both drugs to treat existing patients and vaccines to halt the infection of others. And when they attack the virus, AIDS symptoms ease. The few success stories to date have been so widely publicized that there is little point in retelling them here in detail. Nevertheless, they are worth noting, if only to get some idea of how much farther AIDS will spread before effective treatments reach large-scale use.

PROMISES, PROMISES

At the moment, drugs offer the best hope of conquering AIDS. Scientists have nothing to suggest that might actually sweep the virus from the body; in fact, they now believe it will be difficult or impossible to eliminate the virus that hides out in the brain and bone. But they have been testing some drugs that might halt the growth of the virus, relieving some of the patient's symptoms and preventing any further deterioration.

The best known of these is *zidovudine,* or AZT. It blocks reverse transcriptase, a key enzyme that HIV uses to insert its genetic programming into the DNA of human cells, and so prevents the virus from taking over the cell's reproductive machinery. Human trials of AZT began several years ago, and soon gave promising results. In one test with 280 AIDS victims, half of the patients received AZT, and half went untreated. At the end of six months, nineteen of the untreated patients had died; only one of the patients given AZT failed to survive. In March 1987, the federal Food and Drug Administration, bowing to public pressure, approved AZT as a prescription drug for severe HIV infection.

Most doctors now believe that patients who took the drug every day could live out reasonably normal lives. Unfortunately, taking AZT for long periods has proved nearly impossible. In relatively short order, zidovudine makes people sick. In the long run, it attacks the bone marrow and causes severe anemia.

More recently, researchers have begun to test three new drugs that may work against the AIDS virus: *ddC* (2,2'-dideoxycytidine), *AME* (amphotericin methyl ester), and *abaerol.* Each works in a different way, so it may be possible to combine one or more of them with AZT to heal more effectively than any of the drugs alone. In fact, in preliminary tests of each drug with AZT, all three combinations seemed more effective than AZT alone. In particular, treatment with AZT and ddC on alternating weeks produced striking improvements in brain and peripheral nerve function of AIDS victims, without causing anemia. It will still take several years to figure out which combination of drugs works best.

Several other experimental AIDS treatments work by blocking the virus particles at other critical moments in its development. HIV infects helper T-cells, macrophages, and a few others because those cells carry an uncommon protein called CD4 on their surfaces. A protein on the virus particle, called *gp120,* binds to CD4, holding the virus and cell close while the next steps in the infection process are carried out. Some researchers are trying to develop genetically engineered antibodies that will bind to gp120 on the virus particles and prevent them from infecting human cells. Others are using a compound called *dextran sulfate* for the same purpose. The most promising binding-blocker at the moment is artificial CD4. Given by injection, it circulates in the blood, binding to virus particles before they reach susceptible cells. Coated with CD4, the viruses float harmlessly in the blood until cleared away during the body's normal "housekeeping." So far, it is too early to tell how effective these drugs will be. Only CD4 has reached human testing.

Another drug that may help combat AIDS is a protein called *peptide T,* developed by pharmacologist Candace Pert, working at the National Institute of Mental Health. Dr. Pert, who achieved fame in the 1970s for the discovery of the opiate receptor, began by comparing the chemical structure of gp120 with the structures of human proteins. Eventually she discovered a sequence of amino acids—the building blocks from which proteins are made—that is found in both gp120 and a normal human hormone called *vasoactive intestinal peptide* (VIP). VIP plays important roles in the intestines, in the nerves of the brain, and in the immune system—all the cells that AIDS hits hardest. Dr. Pert suspects AIDS makes people sick at least in part because the virus particles bind to the cells where VIP belongs and prevent the hormone from getting in. Other researchers have confirmed that nerve cells, at least, die when gp120 binds to them and blocks their supply of VIP.

To test her idea, Pert and her colleagues created peptide T, an artificial version of the structure common to gp120 and VIP. In the laboratory, peptide T prevented HIV particles from binding to human immune cells. Early human tests have been even more encouraging. Four of the first patients reportedly were near death when they received peptide T; three survived for eight months, and a fourth was still alive more than a year later. The drug also improved their digestive-tract and nerve functions. There were no adverse side effects.

After the instructions for building new virus particles have been translated from HIV's genes into the DNA of a human cell, the next step is to make the required proteins. The cell does it by the process described in Chapter 11, first building a template from RNA, and then assembling single amino-acid molecules on that framework to form the protein. Like cancer cells, some parasites, and other viruses, HIV could be stopped in its tracks by anti-sense DNA that blocks protein production. It works in laboratory cultures of HIV-carrying T-cells, but it will be years before scientists find ways to get anti-sense DNA into the cells of living patients and find out for sure whether this new kind of drug lives up to its promise.

Even if effective drugs are found to save the lives of AIDS victims, they will not stop the spread of the disease. AIDS patients will still be capable of transmitting the disease, and there will always be sexually active AIDS victims who have not yet discovered their illness. The only way to stop AIDS from spreading is to create a vaccine against it.

Unfortunately, developing a vaccine against HIV has proved uncommonly difficult. One reason is the structure of the HIV particle. The body's defense mechanisms work by attacking foreign proteins. We reject transplanted organs, for example, because the immune system recognizes some of their proteins as alien. Vaccines work by getting the patient's immune system to attack one or more viral proteins. The proteins that lie exposed on the surface of the virus particle are usually the best candidates for vaccine development; the body can't "see" proteins deep inside the virus particle, so the immune system cannot attack them. But in HIV, the surface proteins carry an "umbrella" of sugar that shields them from outside scrutiny. This makes HIV much more difficult to deal with.

Another problem is that the virus mutates constantly, changing even inside the patient. Researchers at the University of Alabama at Birmingham and at the University of Miami recently studied the DNA of AIDS viruses taken from two patients; in three samples they found up to seventeen different forms of the virus. This variation could make it impossible to develop an effective defense against infection, because a vaccine developed from one strain of HIV might not ward off infection by other strains. It might not defend against the same strain a few months later. It might not even kill all the virus in the patient from whom the original sample was taken.

Despite these difficulties, at least a half-dozen vaccines have been reported ready for testing in the last few years. Three have already undergone their first clinical trials, each with some success.

Early in 1987, French immunologist Daniel Zagury found himself on television around the world after announcing in a research paper that he had inoculated several volunteers—himself among them—with a vaccine against the AIDS virus. At the time, other AIDS researchers suggested that Zagury had moved too quickly; he had been foolhardy and, worse, guilty of sloppy science. A year later, it appeared that his gamble had paid off: after several booster shots, he and his fellow guinea pigs showed high levels of antibodies against AIDS. In the test tube, at least, their white blood cells were capable of destroying HIV very effectively.

The second researcher to test an HIV vaccine was well accustomed to the television camera. He was Dr. Jonas Salk, developer of the first effective polio vaccine. Again, after several booster shots, his volunteers showed a strong immune response against the AIDS virus.

The third group, led by Dr. Anthony S. Fauci, is based at the National Institute of Allergy and Infectious Diseases (NIAIA). Their HIV vaccine was successful in raising an immune response in about one-third of the people who received it.

Each of these vaccines has some advantages going for it. Both Zagury and the group from NIAID have made their viruses by gene-splicing a protein from HIV into a harmless virus. Zagury used the cowpox virus, which was used by Edward Jenner in the first vaccination, against smallpox, early in the nineteenth century. The scientists at NIAID used another harmless microbe called a *baculovi-*

rus. By making their vaccines from a single protein extracted from HIV, rather than from the whole virus, the scientists made sure there was no chance their product could transmit AIDS, which theoretically can occur with whole-virus vaccines. And because the protein seems to occur in most or all strains of HIV, these vaccines should be active against most potential infections.

Salk, in contrast, built his vaccine from whole killed viruses, just as he had done in developing his polio vaccine three decades earlier. Early evidence suggests that this vaccine, like the others, may be effective against many strains of HIV, not only the one from which it was developed. And Salk's choice also offers a benefit in that he believes it will wipe out the virus in patients who have already become infected. The other vaccines will not.

All three vaccines are a long way from widespread clinical use. Now that the French vaccine has been tested in human beings and shown to have some effect, Zagury is trying it out in chimpanzees. With the animals, he has been able to take the next logical step— injecting the vaccinated chimps with AIDS virus to see whether the vaccine actually protects against infection by HIV. In the first tests, it seemed to work. Salk has already completed that step and is proceeding with larger human trials.

Even if they are successful, there is no way to hurry any of these vaccines into general use before the mid- or late 1990s. By then, it seems likely that the worldwide AIDS epidemic will already be nearing its peak.

BUTCHER'S BILL

At this point it seems that AIDS will be under control by the turn of the century. Yet AIDS is one of the pivotal issues for the year 2000, and it has often proved uncomfortably hard to predict. In its brief history, people who had reason to consider themselves experts have forecast both that AIDS would remain confined to the few high-risk groups in which it first appeared and that it would spread through heterosexual America almost overnight. They have predicted both that a cure would soon be found and that, because of its genetic mutability, no effective treatment would be possible. And they have made innumerable forecasts of the number of AIDS patients to appear by a given date. Too often, their forecasts have been too low. Clearly, the coming impact of AIDS is one subject in which predictions require all the caution we can bring to them.

Even without an unforeseen increase in the spread of AIDS, the disease will sorely strain America's already creaking health-care system. Corporate health-care planners fear that because of AIDS their total benefit costs in 1990 could be nearly four times as high as they were only three years earlier. Chairman James D. Watkins of the Presidential Commission on the Human Immunodeficiency Virus Epidemic projects that at least 450,000 cases of AIDS will be diagnosed by the end of 1993. Based on that relatively modest figure, he estimates that an adequate testing and treatment program for AIDS would cost over $3 billion per year. According to the federal Centers for Disease Control, in Atlanta, overall medical costs associated with the care and treatment of AIDS could total as much as $12.4 billion by 1992. Where that money will come from, no one knows.

Ethically, AIDS could be just as trying. So far, no one has collected statistics on the rate of suicide among AIDS victims. Repellent as many find the idea of self-inflicted death, it is not easy to argue that AIDS patients should be compelled to suffer the drawn-out misery that their illness often brings. Will the AIDS epidemic lead America closer to the Scandinavian model, where a quiet suicide when life becomes less than enjoyable is regarded as being a matter for personal choice? Might it even help to legitimize euthanasia? We can only wait and see.

What about government spending policy? In 1988, the cost of medical care for AIDS patients was $4 billion per year; by 1993, it will reach at least $10 billion per year. If there are "only" 1.5 million AIDS carriers in the United States, we can afford to deal with the disease. But what if AIDS spreads dramatically in the coming years? Will it prove so expensive that federal medical expenses bankrupt other programs? Will the Strategic Defense Initiative, the NASA space station, and other easily canceled programs find their funding cut off in the mid-1990s because the money is urgently needed to provide life support for AIDS victims? And what will happen to Social Security if 10 to 20 percent of working-age Americans are suddenly unable to contribute to the fund because they are too sick, or are already dead?

And foreign policy? The United States now has more diagnosed cases of AIDS than any other nation in the world. China and the Soviet Union report—believably—that they have seen almost no cases at all, and those few only in people who have had contact with the West. Will Americans become unwelcome in foreign lands unless they have been tested for AIDS infection? Will the economic, technical, and human demands placed on us by AIDS significantly weaken the United States against its international competitors? Or will we simply become so preoccupied with our troubles that we turn inward and forget our global commitments, as we have done so often in the past?

Grim questions all, and we have no good answers. So let us close with one last speculation, a scenario that, though *highly* improbable, is nonetheless troublesome:

The AIDS virus is just one of many that mutate rapidly. And it, theoretically, could exchange genes with other mutable viruses. Influenza, too, is caused by a family of viruses that find it easy to pass around their genetic material. Now picture the viral community deep within the tissues of an AIDS patient who contracts the flu, the jostling of AIDS and flu viruses together . . . the passage of a few critical genes or gene sequences from one pathogen to the other. If something this unlikely *did* occur, by 2000, we would face a true plague caused by AIDS viruses that have learned to move, flu-like, from one victim to their next—in a sneeze.

In that case, all forecasts are canceled.

SAVING THE

ENVIRONMENT

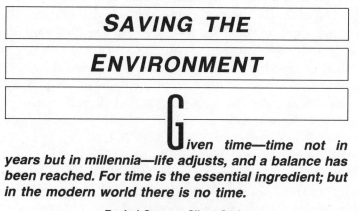

iven time—time not in years but in millennia—life adjusts, and a balance has been reached. For time is the essential ingredient; but in the modern world there is no time.

–Rachel Carson, *Silent Spring*
(Houghton-Mifflin, 1962)

Remember when all we had to worry about was an occasional depression, drugs, and the threat of nuclear war? These days it seems that after surviving for 4.5 *billion* years, the world itself is falling apart under us. And it's all our fault.

Look at what happened in a single bellwether year, 1988:

Waste gases from aerosol sprays and air conditioners were found to be rotting holes in the atmosphere's ozone layer, which protects life from cancer-causing ultraviolet light. Medical waste washed up on beaches, both in the United States and in Europe. A three-month drought killed crops and livestock throughout much of America, raising fears that so-called greenhouse gases are at last warming the planet, with dire climatic implications. In the North Sea, thousands of seals died of pneumonia, at least in part because pollution had weakened their immune systems. The Environmental Protection Administration issued a national radon health alert warning that the radioactive gas may contaminate one in three homes in the United States. The Department of Energy admitted that its bomb-grade uranium factories had been spewing radioactive waste into the environment for decades. And the good ship *Pelicano* finally found somewhere to dump the fourteen thousand tons of toxic incinerator ash that it had carried from Philadelphia to ports around the world for more than two years, without finding anyone willing to accept it; most onlookers suspected the captain had illegally jettisoned the waste at sea. There is little prospect that any of these environmental problems will get much better before 2000. Dramatic change on this scale will require more time than a single decade.

Yet we do believe that by the turn of the century, at long last, the United States will begin to heed the warnings of the environmental prophet Rachel Carson, and will spearhead a worldwide cleanup that will last well into the twenty-first century, though we must admit that for the moment that belief remains more an act of faith than a reasoned analysis of the evidence. The United States remains the world's unchallenged champion at coping with problems three minutes before it's too late, and with regard to the environment, one minute may be entirely more accurate.

As we see it, America faces three environmental problems we can solve on our own, one that will strike the United States specifically and may have no solution, and at least three closely related problems that require international cooperation:

GARBAGE GLUT

By far the most pressing problem for most Americans is not radon or holes in the ozone layer; it's where to throw the trash—not even toxic waste, but simple household refuse. In 1989, 80 percent of the nation's garbage wound up in one of only six thousand landfills, one-third fewer than there were in 1983.

The problem is, America just throws too much away each year: some 16 billion disposable diapers, each destined to clutter the earth for some five hundred years before it disintegrates; 2 billion razors and razor blades, 220 million tires, more glass and aluminum than existed in the entire world prior to World War II, and, of course, all the hospital waste that now floats up on East Coast beaches in the summer—160 million tons of flotsam in all, and that does not count the millions of tons of treated sewage that just the states of New York and New Jersey dump into the Atlantic every year. The United States creates twice as much garbage per person as any other industrialized nation, and the total is expected to grow by 20 percent in the next ten years.

So far, we have not done much about the problem. Only 10 percent of our trash is recycled; only ten states have mandatory recycling laws. Western Europe, in contrast, recycles nearly one-third of its trash, Japan more than half. The only major federal legislation in this area in recent years prohibits dumping of sewage into the ocean after 1990; it does not suggest where the sewage should go instead.

This inertia cannot last much longer. By 1993, two thousand more landfills will have been shut down. By the year 2,000 nearly three-fourths of America's major cities will have nowhere to dump their trash.

There is nothing complicated about solving the garbage problem; all we need do is adopt the recycling that most of the United States has neglected for so long. A dozen years from now we will have followed Japan and Europe in doing so. Most Americans—virtually all but those who live in the least populous rural areas—will have grown used to separating bottles from cans, paper from noncombustible hard plastics. Nearly all states will have enacted bottle laws as well, and the deposit on returnable bottles will have risen from a nickel or less to between ten and twenty-five cents. Most of these materials will be reprocessed for use in a new generation of bottles and cans.

Most combustible trash *could* be recycled to useful products, and at least some paper and cardboard will be reprocessed into packing materials and similar products. But most common garbage, along with tires, some plastics, and most other combustibles will be burned in new, efficient municipal incinerators, equipped with emission-control devices to prevent air pollution. The ash left from the process will be trucked to landfills sealed with plastic or impermeable clay to contain metals and other toxic contaminants.

This issue will inspire bitter controversies throughout the country during the 1990s. Whenever a new incinerator or landfill is proposed, the local NIMBY ("not in my backyard") contingents will be out in force. But they haven't a chance. With garbage mounting ever higher in city streets, politicians will at long last be able to tell irate constituents that they will have no choice but to dispose of trash as close as possible to where it is produced. As the long, desultory voyage of the *Pelicano* showed, no one wants our garbage any more than we do. So, in future, we will all be responsible for cleaning up our own mess.

TOXIC TIME BOMB

America will also be indirectly responsible for cleaning up the messes of the past. For more than two hundred years, American industry has been turning out huge quantities of toxic chemical wastes: sulfuric acid and mercury from pulp and paper factories, organic dyes and chlorine from textile plants, heavy metals used in pharmaceuticals synthesis, and cyanide-laced sludge from electroplating vats. And throwing most of it into landfills, holding ponds, and abandoned wells, where it soon leaks into the surrounding community. The Environmental Protection Administration has compiled a list of 1,200 such sites that desperately require decontamination and concedes that the total will soon exceed two thousand. Others say that ten thousand sites may eventually require cleanup at a cost of over $300 billion—three hundred times the current annual budget for such work. Making these toxic-waste dumps safe will be America's most costly environmental commitment, well into the twenty-first century.

Much of this work will be done at the taxpayers' expense. The Department of Energy alone will have to spend at least $53 billion in tax money, and perhaps as much as $92 billion, to clean up toxic materials and meet environmental, safety, and health standards at forty-five of its facilities. Another $1.8 billion per year will go to fund continuing programs designed to prevent further contamination. Of the forty-five DOE installations examined in a recent study, thirty-one were found to violate federal standards for air emissions, liquid discharges, and solid waste; thirty-seven require cleanup of contamination by toxic and radioactive substances. Defense-related programs require a $22-billion waste-management program. Cleaning up just one nuclear weapons facility, at Hanford, Washington, will cost $46.5 billion.

So far, U.S. efforts to combat toxic waste win mixed reviews. In the 1980s the country made a good deal of progress in cutting the amount it produces. In 1982—the peak—American factories were turning out some 77 billion pounds of poisonous glop every year. Since then, they have managed to reduce that output by more than half, and have cut the amount going into landfills by 65 percent. This is not as impressive as it sounds—Holland and Denmark destroy or recycle all their toxic wastes—but it is significant progress. By 2000, we should equal the success of heavily industrialized West Germany, which manages to detoxify nearly 90 percent of its hazardous waste.

Unfortunately, America's record on cleaning up existing waste sites has been less impressive. Of the 1,200 sites on EPA's list, only forty-three had been decontaminated as of early 1989, more than eight years after the cleanup effort began. And in most of those, the waste had simply been buried under impermeable clay and plastic, to contain it on-site, rather than being removed and destroyed.

That is not good enough, because even the best toxic-waste dumps are far from reliable containers for hazardous materials. One Texas community disposed of waste by pumping it into an unused well nine thousand feet deep; it soon resurfaced in the neighborhood drinking water. And a study in 1982 found that state-of-the-art landfills, which imprisoned toxic waste far more securely than federal standards require even today, often leaked badly within two years after they were built. There is little reason to hope that EPA's current attempts to contain toxic waste on-site will be any more successful. One experimental technique that may successfully contain waste where it lies is *in situ* vitrification, which uses electricity to heat the ground, fusing the contaminated soil into an inert, impermeable glass. Unfortunately, the method costs at least as much as digging up the waste and hauling it to a safer disposal site.

To date, America's anti-waste effort has been based on two programs: EPA's "Superfund" and the Resource Conservation and Recovery Act. They have not measured up to the task.

The Superfund got its start in 1980 as a response to New York's Love Canal waste-dump debacle. The plan was to clean up the nation's most dangerous toxic-waste sites and bill the dumpers for the cost. The program was first given $1.6 billion and four years to spend it, then renewed in 1987, with another $8.5 billion to be spent over five years. By early 1989, the forty-three dumps cleaned up under the program already had cost more than $4 billion. Little of the money had been recovered from the companies that dumped the waste.

In January 1989, a House Appropriations subcommittee and the General Accounting Office independently criticized EPA's handling of the $8.5-billion program. The House subcommittee charged that

EPA had failed to press private companies to clean up waste dumps, spending federal money instead, and turning the Superfund into a specialized pork-barrel program for private contractors; that EPA had not sought to recover cleanup costs from private companies; that the agency had used endless preliminary studies of sites to delay cleaning them up; and that it had failed to develop cost-effective cleanup technologies to treat waste instead of merely moving it from one dump to another. GAO also pointed out EPA had missed at least half of the cleanup deadlines set by Congress. It can take well over five years for a cleanup to begin, even after the site has been accepted for the program. Worse, when EPA finally does get around to acting, it usually takes the cheap way out, trying to contain the waste where it lies rather than digging it out and destroying it. In 1986, Congress amended the Superfund program to require that waste dumps be removed and the waste detoxified wherever possible. To date, there is little evidence that EPA has changed its policy.

A recent report from the Congressional Office of Technology Assessment was just as critical. The agency says that EPA has so badly mismanaged the Superfund program that its budget should be cut by several hundred million dollars per year, pending an overhaul. In 1988, congressional investigators were so unimpressed by EPA's management that Congress cut $175 million from the year's spending.

The Resource Conservation and Recovery Act has not been much more successful. RCRA required EPA to ban the disposal of 450 regulated toxic wastes unless they first underwent detoxification treatment, but allowed the agency to grant two-year exemptions when detox facilities were inadequate. As of January 1989, dumping had been banned for 134 such wastes, including the most toxic and largest-volume poisons. Wastes containing solvents and dioxins were granted exemptions, which expired late in 1988. Since 1986, most dioxin-containing waste has been stored, pending approval of advanced incinerators authorized to burn them. At this point, RCRA has run out, and congressional staffers are predicting a drawn-out battle over whether to reauthorize the act.

A proposal in one version of the reauthorization bill would encourage recycling by placing a seven-dollar-per-ton fee on the use of virgin material for packaging. The estimated $500 million per year collected by the fee would go to support state solid-waste programs also required by the bill. Other measures include a national goal of reducing municipal solid waste by one-fourth in four years and by 50 percent in ten years; air emission standards for municipal waste incinerators and tighter antipollution standards for garbage and ash landfills; tougher controls on the export of solid waste; a mandate for states to develop municipal solid-waste management plans; and EPA guidelines for regulation of infectious wastes and other material not now under the agency's jurisdiction.

In the 1990s, America will devote much of its environmental effort to rebuilding the Superfund program and toughening the RCRA; but by 2000, the federal government will follow California's lead. At the end of 1987, California had 186 hazardous-waste surface pond facilities, some with more than one impoundment. However, the state's Toxic Pits Cleanup Act has forced most of California's companies to close down hazardous-waste surface ponds. Some, including those within half a mile up-gradient from potential sources of drinking water or within five feet of the water table, were forced to close. Others could have shut the ponds temporarily, pumped them out, and rebuilt them to meet stringent containment standards. But most chose to close their waste ponds rather than go to the expense of keeping them open. Many of those companies have opted to detoxify most of their waste and have installed aboveground storage tanks for the rest. Others have chosen to ship their waste to states where ponds are still legal and disposal is cheaper. By 2000, federal law will close that loophole. Dumping of toxic waste in open ponds will be illegal throughout the United States.

In the end, companies deprived of cheap dump sites may find that their hazardous waste turns out to be a neglected resource. The reason is a process known as *chlorinolysis,* which breaks down such hazardous chemicals as DDT and PCBs into useful materials. Dow Chemical, in Pittsburg, California, has stopped putting waste into its ponds, instead reusing the waste streams from its agricultural chemicals plants as raw material for a nearby chlor-alkali plant. Chlorinolysis is used to break down organic contaminants in the mixture. In West Germany, Farbwerke Hoechst uses the process to digest its wastes into a variety of salable products. The process turned out to be so profitable that when its waste-treatment plant ran out of capacity, the firm built a much larger one, so that it could buy valuable "waste" from other companies.

RADWASTE

As America enters the 1990s, the nation's 106 operating nuclear power plants are storing something over fifteen thousand metric tons of spent nuclear fuel in huge pools of water. With most of its fissionable uranium already "burned," the material is no longer useful; yet it will remain dangerously radioactive for the next ten thousand years. By 2000, there will be nearly fifty thousand tons of what is known as radwaste in storage. We *think* it will be on its way to safe storage by then.

The site has already been chosen: Yucca Mountain, a six-mile-long ridge of geologically stable ground in southern Nevada, adjacent to the government's Nuclear Weapons Testing Site. If all goes according to plan, in 1998 miners will dig into the mountain and build a waste repository capable of holding seventy thousand tons of spent fuel rods one thousand feet below ground level and about one thousand feet above the water table. The first radwaste will move into its final home five years later. By 2030, the dump will be full, and the tunnels leading into it will be refilled.

Any doubt is more political than technical. It is possible to argue that some major climatic change, earthquake, volcano, or other unpredictable event could release the radwaste from Yucca Mountain before it has decayed to a safe level of radioactivity, but that is also true of any other possible interment site. Many such hazards could be dealt with by improving the containment of the radwaste—say, by vitrifying the waste (turning it into impervious glass) rather than by simply packing it in corrodible cans.

In fact, such technical concerns have very little to do with whether Yucca Mountain, or any other possible repository, ever gets put to use. The key question is who might be willing to host the site; the answer is, no one. While Yucca Mountain was under consideration, Nevada representatives lobbied hard to keep the facility out of their state. "The proposal is an act of naked aggression by the people of several states against a state which is smaller and which has less power," stormed Senator Harry Reid. There is at least an element of truth in the charge. Nevada *does* have less political power than some other states where possible waste sites were under consideration. That being the case, it seems unlikely that any amount of lobbying will delay construction of the Yucca Mountain waste repository for very long.

Before 2000, we believe the controversy over what to do with radwaste will be resolved, not by scientific data or technical arguments, but by pure common sense. Even for the most fervent antinuclear activist, it is too obviously silly to suggest that the United States should continue to store tons of nuclear waste aboveground in populated areas in preference to burying it far from human habitation. Not long after the turn of the century, approximately on schedule, Yucca Mountain will receive its first load of reactor waste.

Of course, that will not end the radwaste problem. In the end, the only way to deal effectively with reactor waste is to avoid making it. And that requires a new generation of reactor that is not only safer than current models but produces less waste. An ideal candidate is a relatively little-known design called the actinide-nitride reactor. The device would be far safer than today's light-water reactor, because it can operate only under such extraordinarily artificial conditions that any malfunction would simply shut it down. And it would burn up roughly 99 percent of the radioactive fuel it received, leaving next to no radwaste to be disposed of. So far, no one has built an actinide-nitride reactor, but the essential components were adopted for a nuclear fuel-reprocessing facility that operated briefly—until shut down for political reasons during the Carter administration—in North Carolina. It worked perfectly. Unless America is willing to do without the electricity that nuclear generators offer, actinide-nitride power plants offer the best answer to the problem of radioactive waste. The first could be in operation by the turn of the century, if work on them began today.

WATER, WATER... WHERE?

Deep beneath the Great Plains lies the Ogallala Aquifer, a vast reservoir from which Nebraska, Kansas, and parts of Colorado, New Mexico, Oklahoma, and Texas draw most of their water. Since the end of World War II, irrigation systems pumping water up from the Ogallala have turned the Dust Bowl of the 1930s into a farming center that grows much of the nation's corn and wheat, sorghum and cotton—crops worth more than $20 billion a year in all. Thirty years ago, the Ogallala contained roughly as much water as Lake Huron. But far more water is drained from the aquifer every year than rainfall restores, and today the supply is drying up. In parts of Texas, New Mexico, and even Kansas, the water table has dropped more than one hundred feet since the mid-1950s.

Farmers in the region are already working to cut back their water consumption. Some have stopped growing corn, which requires a huge supply of water, and turned their fields over to cotton, wheat, and sorghum, which do not. Many have turned to water-conserving irrigation methods and graded their fields billiard-table flat, so that desperately needed water does not run off. But in the end, these techniques can only slow the depletion of the Ogallala, not stop it. By 2000, many Great Plains farmers will have had to go back to dry-land farming, working harder to eke out smaller crops. By 2020, the six states that depend on the Ogallala will have lost more than 5 million acres of irrigated farmland, an area the size of Massachusetts.

The only alternative: import vast quantities of water up to 1,100 miles *uphill* from Arkansas, Missouri, and South Dakota, at an estimated cost of well over $25 billion. At the turn of the century, that grandiose, expensive scheme may well seem more acceptable than allowing the Great Plains to return to the near-barrenness of the Depression years.

The Great Plains are not the only region of the country facing water problems. At the turn of the century, California's fertile San Joaquin Valley almost surely will face a catastrophe of another kind. Today the valley is one of the world's most productive farming areas; by 2000, agriculture there could be a thing of the past. The San Joaquin Valley gets too little rain to support most crops, so farming there depends on irrigation every bit as heavily as in the Great Plains. As California's population grows, people are beginning to compete for the water that now keeps plants alive. What is more important, the same water that sustains the otherwise arid valley also carries in mineral salts and deposits them in the ground. Bit by bit, the soil is becoming so salty that few crop plants will grow. A decade from now, San Joaquin harvests will be dropping rapidly. Ten years after that, it will be nearly impossible to survive as a farmer in the valley.

In theory, there is a way to repair this environmental problem. It is simply to flood the affected lands with water, and let it wash the salt into the rivers and out to sea. In practice, this would take far more water than is available. So there are only two ways out: either biologists must develop genetically engineered crops capable of living in the otherwise toxic soil, or physicists will have to find some way to desalinate ocean water so cheaply that farmers can use it to launder the San Joaquin fields. Otherwise, this once-fertile valley could remain nearly barren for many decades to come.

LIFE IN THE GREENHOUSE

When the great drought of 1988 left crops parched and dying through much of the United States, it seemed a taste of things to come. The six warmest years in recorded history occurred in the 1980s, and 1988 was the warmest of all. Perhaps, it seemed, all the pollution that cars and industry had spewed into the atmosphere for the last century had at last warmed the Earth beyond its ability to adapt. Perhaps this near-desert was the America of the future.

In fact, it probably will be. But not by the year 2000.

The theory behind the greenhouse effect is simple. Carbon dioxide, nitrogen oxide, methane, the chlorofluorocarbons used in aerosol cans, and a few other gases absorb heat from the sun and hold it in the atmosphere. Trees, which naturally absorb carbon dioxide, are being cut down all over the world, reducing the planet's ability to cope with this pollution. The combination of more gas with less opportunity to get rid of it causes the Earth to become warmer. And when the planet becomes warm enough, local climates will change dramatically all over the world. The central United States will become hotter and drier, bringing semitropical weather to Kansas and Nebraska and destroying much of American agriculture. The polar ice caps will melt, raising the oceans enough to inundate much of the coastal United States.

It does seem to be happening, slowly, but faster as the decades pass. Though the numbers are far from firm, most scientists now believe that global temperatures rose about one-quarter degree Celsius between 1780 and 1880, a full degree between then and 1950, and more than half a degree since then—exactly in line with what scientists would expect, given the amount of greenhouse gases poured into the air during each period.

Where this trend will leave us is still unclear. At the current rate of warming, by the turn of the century the seas theoretically could rise by almost a foot over their mean level in 1980. Yet an increase of only a few inches is more likely. It is not until 2050, when the Earth will be anything from 1.5 degrees to 8 degrees warmer—many of the factors that shape such estimates are still impossible to forecast—that the oceans will wash over much of our coastline. But southern Louisiana is already losing its land to the Gulf of Mexico at a rate of one acre every sixteen minutes. And if the 1980s are any indication, we could already be in for a long period of hotter, drier summers.

Though the pollution responsible for planetary warming is undeniably a global problem, the United States bears a disproportionately large part of the responsibility. American cars and industry emit nearly one-fourth of the carbon dioxide produced in the world each year, and significant fractions of the other greenhouse gases. Cleaning up our own act could delay catastrophic changes in the world's climate for many years.

One small step will be the gasoline tax hike soon to be enacted to help balance the federal budget deficit. Though the initial increase that we anticipate, from nine cents per gallon to fifteen cents, will do little to cut the amount of gas that Americans burn each year, the levy is likely to rise slowly throughout the 1990s. By the time the gas tax reaches twenty-five cents per gallon, Detroit will again be feeling the pressure to build more economical cars, as it did in the OPEC oil embargoes of the 1970s.

Ultimately—before 2000—the nation is likely to enact a federal antipollution law similar to the one now being considered for the Los Angeles basin, home of the worst air in America. The plan, to be implemented in stages over nineteen years, would require carpooling and ban trucks during commuting hours, phase out the use of gasoline in favor of less polluting fuels, eliminate solvents from paint and furniture finish, scrap gasoline-powered lawn mowers, and place emission controls on dry cleaners. The proposed switch from gasoline to alcohol and natural gas has met with opposition because low-pollution fuels are far less efficient than gas and could double overall fuel costs for Los Angeles residents. When it comes to a vote, they are likely to decide that clean air to breathe is worth the price.

For the global warming, the law will be a mixed blessing. The carpooling requirement and truck ban should go a long way toward reducing production of the major greenhouse gases. But while burning alcohol and natural gas produces less nitrogen oxide, it may actually raise levels of carbon dioxide. On balance, it should be a worthwhile trade, but we will have to wait for actual results to be sure.

Making a dent in industrial pollution will be a lot harder. The worst offenders are coal-fired electric generating plants, the primary source of acid rain and a major threat to the global climate. In 1988, the Reagan administration created a $2.5-billion research fund to find ways to burn coal without pollution—a gesture to the Canadian government, which correctly blames its growing acid-rain problem on generating stations in the American Midwest. Just how much good the program will do for the greenhouse problem remains unclear. Previous research into cleaning up coal has concentrated on sulfur dioxide and nitrogen oxides, and it has been notably successful. Modern scrubbers can cut sulfur dioxide emissions by up to 90 percent, and technologies still under development could cut them by as much as 99 percent and reduce nitrogen oxides by up to 40 percent. But these methods do nothing for carbon dioxide emissions. In fact, because scrubbers make generating stations up to 17 percent less efficient, utilities must use more coal and produce more carbon dioxide. In all, we expect researchers in the 1990s to develop some practical way to burn coal without releasing huge quantities of CO_2, but it seems unlikely that they will go into use before about 2010.

Until then, the United States will rely on greater energy efficiency to reduce the amount of coal it needs to burn. The major-appliance efficiency standards that have just taken effect should trim electric consumption by some 30,000 billion watt-hours by 1995, equivalent to more than a dozen large generating stations. Another 500 billion kilowatt-hours will be saved by legislation now pending that will require fluorescent lights sold in the United States to use the most efficient ballasts available. According to one estimate, such energy-saving measures could cut our national demand for electricity by up to 20 percent. And that will dramatically reduce the amount of greenhouse gases that American power companies dump into the air.

One last thing America will do in 2000, and for many years thereafter, should have environmentalists dancing in the streets: In an effort to save energy and purify the air, we will plant trees by the tens of millions. According to one study at California's Lawrence Berkeley Laboratory, planting only three trees near a light-colored home can cut air-conditioning demands by as much as 44 percent—yet another way to cut our use of costly, CO_2-producing coal. The study estimated that planting trees on commercial and residential properties could save the United States enough energy to cut atmospheric carbon pollution by 18 million tons a year. More important, trees are to carbon dioxide what scavengers are to carrion. According to the Worldwatch Institute, planting an extra 120 million hectares of trees—about 46.6 million acres or 463,000 square miles—would clear from the atmosphere about 15 percent of the carbon dioxide produced in the world each year. The CO_2 would be released again when the trees died and decayed or were burned, but the delay would give us a much-needed grace period in which to develop other methods of coping with the problem.

HOLE IN THE SKY

To begin at the simplest level, life as we know it can survive on Earth because it is shielded from the sun's deadly ultraviolet light. The shield is the ozone layer, located ten to 30 miles above the planet's surface. Ozone is an unstable molecule consisting of three oxygen atoms, and it is very good at absorbing ultraviolet light. Even the small amount of ultraviolet light that penetrates the ozone layer is enough to cause sunburn, cataracts, and skin cancer. If the layer were to disappear, major ecological disruptions would surely follow. At the least, land animals would experience a plague of ultraviolet-induced cancers. Life itself would survive, but probably not without a period of mass species extinctions similar to the one that destroyed the dinosaurs.

And the ozone layer *is* disappearing. Scientists first discovered that fact in 1985, when satellite pictures revealed a "hole" in the ozone layer over the South Pole. The hole grows and shrinks with the seasons and the weather, but at times fully half the ozone layer has disappeared over a section of the Antarctic as large as the United States. Turbulent winds prevent formation of a similar bald spot over the North Pole, but ozone levels in the high northern latitudes have slipped by about 5 percent since 1972.

The Antarctic hole has scientists worried, because it may be a warning of things to come. If a similar hole appeared over a populated area, regular sunbathing would almost surely be followed by skin cancer. If the entire ozone layer were depleted, the excess energy from the sun would add four degrees to the global warming caused by the greenhouse effect, melting the polar ice caps and turning the central United States to desert.

The cause is *chlorofluorocarbons* (CFC), a group of chemicals used in aerosol sprays, air conditioners, foamed plastics, and the manufacture of microchips. Every time an air conditioner leaks or we break the plastic box a fast-food hamburger comes in, CFCs are released into the air. And there they stay, until the winds carry them up into the ozone layer. Then, no longer protected from ultraviolet light, CFCs break down, releasing chlorine and other chemicals. By a complicated process, one molecule of chlorine released into the ozone layer can destroy as many as 100,000 molecules of ozone. CFCs are also twenty thousand times more efficient than carbon dioxide at trapping heat, so even tiny amounts can greatly increase the greenhouse effect. According to one estimate, about 12 percent of global warming can be traced to CFCs.

The United States made the first move against CFCs in 1978, when it banned their use in aerosol cans. In 1987, representatives of forty-six nations met in Montreal and followed our lead, agreeing to cut production of CFCs in half by 1999. Britain, the Netherlands, and West Germany reportedly would like to make an 85-percent reduction, and the Nordic countries have asked to ban CFCs altogether.

One obstacle to that goal is the lack of substitutes for CFCs. A few candidate chemicals do exist, but most are far more costly than the compounds they would replace. Du Pont expects to spend $1 billion in the 1990s to develop an alternative to CFCs, a worldwide market worth at most $4 billion to $5 billion per year.

This is one environmental problem where America can do little more on its own. Two bills calling for a 95-percent reduction in CFC use have already been submitted to the Senate; one would also ban imports that contain CFCs. It seems unlikely that Congress will soon vote to destroy a $10-billion-a-year industry, but we believe that CFCs will be banned in the United States by the year 2000. Further progress on this issue will require a major international effort.

UNFRIENDLY SKIES

At this point, though Midwestern utility companies still like to quibble about technical data, much as tobacco companies like to quibble about the deadly effects of their products, there is no reasonable doubt about it: the acid rain that is killing aquatic life throughout much of the eastern United States and Canada comes primarily from coal-burning power plants in Ohio, Indiana, and their neighboring states. According to the ten-year National Acid Precipitation Assessment Program, begun in 1980 as a politically safe alternative to taking action on the problem, in 1985 power plants emitted 16.2 million tons of sulfur dioxide, the primary component of acid rain— 70 percent of the total SO_2 released in the United States that year. More than half of that was spewed out of smokestacks 480 feet or more in height, ensuring that it traveled long distances—to New York State, say, and Vermont and Quebec—before falling to earth.

The Midwestern power lobby has proved extraordinarily effective at blocking action on the acid-rain problem in Washington. In 1988, several major biological research projects concluded that it takes far less acid to destroy a lake than previously believed; that ecosystems can begin to recover almost as soon as the acid stops falling; and that full restoration of the original environment will nonetheless take hundreds of years. Despite those conclusions, Congress found itself incapable of passing a revised Clean Air Act that included measures to control acid rain. In the years to come, a new generation of environmentalists will find that cleaning up acid rain remains their most difficult problem.

In the end, the legislation that cures acid rain may not be aimed at this problem at all. Instead, the growing international fear of global warming will at last prompt governments all over the world to cut their nations' energy use and to install antipollution equipment to reduce carbon dioxide emissions. As long as that must be done, the equipment chosen will be designed to eliminate sulfur dioxide and nitrogen oxides as well, and the acid rain problem will at last be solved, almost as an afterthought. The process will be under way, but not nearly complete, by the year 2000.

WHOLE-EARTH ENVIRONMENTALISM

It clearly is not enough simply to clean up our own act. Acid rain, destruction of the ozone layer, and global warming are the ultimate in international problems. Sulfur dioxide emitted in the United States causes acid rain in Canada, and there is at least some evidence that Canadian emissions may to some degree add to our own problem. The world's largest user of CFCs is the Soviet Union, and although the Soviets have agreed in principle that the chemicals should be phased out, the enormous, rigid, inefficient Soviet economy makes it impossible for them to act quickly on this or any other issue. And in burning the Amazon rain forests, Brazil alone creates about 10 percent of the carbon dioxide that humanity adds to the world's atmosphere each year, and reduces the number of trees available to absorb excess CO_2. These problems in distant lands affect the United States as much as our problems affect our neighbors.

So far, there have been relatively few international efforts to control environmental problems, but these few point the way for efforts at the turn of the century. The Montreal Protocol to reduce CFC production was one tentative step. Another was a private environmental group's deal with Bolivia, in which the organization paid off $650,000 of the nation's debt, and Bolivia agreed to create a 4-million-acre tropical forest preserve. And the World Wildlife Fund bought up $1 million worth of Ecuadoran debt from Banker's Trust, paying only $354,000 for it. The Fund now receives the loan payments and passes the money on to a sister organization in Ecuador to support national parks and wildlife preserves. Many more such efforts should be in place by 2000.

But in the end, far more sweeping measures will be needed. The root cause of many environmental problems is that there are more people than the world economy is yet prepared to support in a clean, ecologically safe way. Any nation serious about curing environmental problems must in the end deal with that fact. That means doing everything possible to encourage birth control in the Third World, a cause rejected by the Reagan administration. It also means funneling massive aid to Third World countries now attempting to better themselves in the only way available—by ripping minerals and other raw materials from the ground and working them in pollution-causing smelters and factories, often fed by coal-burning power plants, just as Western nations did when building up their economies. That will require more than one huge cooperative program supported by all the developed nations, spending billions of dollars each year until the Third World has achieved an adequate standard of living. The task will hardly have begun when the new century arrives.

PART IV

Business at the Turn of the Century

BIMODAL ECONOMICS:

THE DECLINE OF

THE MIDDLE

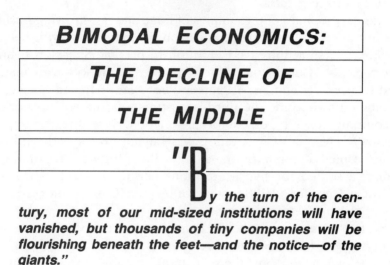

"**B**y the turn of the century, most of our mid-sized institutions will have vanished, but thousands of tiny companies will be flourishing beneath the feet—and the notice—of the giants."

Not so long ago, you could sum up the American business world with a song lyric: "The rich get richer, and the poor get poorer." Large companies prospered; some grew into giants. Small firms quietly stagnated until they either went under or were bought by a larger competitor.

The country does not work that way anymore. It hasn't for nearly ten years. In the new corporate economy, the rich still get richer, but the poor—or at least the small—are flourishing as well. It is the mid-sized company that is rapidly disappearing.

This "bimodal distribution" of institutions is one of the most pervasive trends in the American economy today, and one of the least noticed. In the next dozen years, it will dramatically change the scenery of the business world, not just in the United States but throughout the industrialized nations. By the turn of the century, most of our mid-sized institutions will have vanished, but thousands of tiny companies will be flourishing beneath the feet—and the notice—of the giants.

It is easy to find good examples of huge and fast-growing business institutions. On Wall Street, Shearson combined first with Lehman Brothers, then acquired E.F. Hutton to become Shearson Lehman Hutton. Coca-Cola accounts for 40 percent of the soft-drink market, and PepsiCo for another 30 percent; last year 7-Up and Dr. Pepper combined to become the third-largest manufacturer of soft drinks, accounting for 14 percent of the market. Just three years ago, Humana Hospitals Corporation was buying up formerly independent hospitals at a rate of one a day, while Hospital Corporation of America settled for five acquisitions per week. And in the auto industry, Chrysler's 1988 buy-out of Jeep AMC is still another example of the big getting bigger.

So far, none of this should come as any surprise. Larger firms always enjoy the advantage of economies of scale. Raw materials are cheaper when you buy them in multi-ton lots instead of by the pound; personnel costs per unit are lower when your salespeople sell your product by the thousand instead of one at a time; insurance companies cut better deals when you have thousands of employees to cover instead of just a few. Today's information economy is giving them one more advantage: those who have information—and use it in a timely fashion—succeed; those who can't find information and use it efficiently soon fail. Large companies generally can devote more time and effort to gathering information and turning it into business stategies.

Because of their size, larger firms can afford the latest and most sophisticated computers and telecommunications equipment. It gives them one more edge over their smaller competitors. In addition, a larger firm can cut costs when it takes over a smaller company by retaining a single set of well-paid top managers and administrative staff. New information technologies allow one executive to oversee the work of twenty or more employees, rather than the six or seven that would be possible under traditional methods. This often permits companies to flush out whole layers of middle management, resulting in further savings.

Deregulation, lenient antitrust policies, and the tax reform legislation of 1986 have also helped companies to consolidate. Deregulation of the airline industry in 1980 removed many of the obstacles that prevented large carriers from absorbing their competition. The Reagan administration has since extended this policy to many more industries, prompting mergers in every field that deregulation has touched. The administration's minimal antitrust efforts quickly eased any fears that mergers would run much risk of triggering government intervention. Most important, the change in tax laws enabled businesses to deduct the interest on money borrowed to finance hostile takeovers. That made it cheaper for corporations to grow by absorbing their competition, and even unrelated businesses, than by building their existing operations. Thus, the wave of corporate take-overs in the late 1980s was all but inevitable.

But that is only half of the economy. Tiny manufacturers and service firms surely cannot cut costs the way a corporate giant can. How is it that they, too, are flourishing?

The answer is that one segment of American business has escaped bimodal distribution: the consumer. As noted in Chapter 1, if you look at individual human beings instead of companies, you'll find a prosperous and fast-growing middle class. By 2000, three-fourths of American families will include two wage earners whose combined salaries add up to an attractive family income. They are long on funds but short on time, so businesses that offer personal services, such as housecleaning, childcare, investment management, and travel planning, will prosper. Many of these services represent markets that larger companies find it difficult to tap.

Just as important, the literate, moneyed middle class is finding itself increasingly surrounded by automation. In reaction, they look for what futurist John Naisbitt calls the "high-tech/high-touch" approach from the companies they deal with. The more they rub up against sterile, hard-edged technologies, the more they seek to add a human element to their lives. As computers further dominate their working days, people will become more interested in paintings, handmade furniture, tailored clothes, tailored services, and tailored advice that sets them apart from the pervasive machines and reasserts their identities as human beings. For a computer operator who spends his day staring into a terminal and processing abstract data, a home full of human handicrafts, plants, music, and other soothing reminders of the living world is necessary therapy. And when the time comes for a vacation, the group tour of tourist Europe is out; hiking, canoeing, helicopter skiing, and "adventure" tours of distant, computerless jungles are in.

Huge corporations can't meet that need; they specialize in turning out vast quantities of identical products and services—exactly the sterile uniformity that tomorrow's information workers are trying to escape. That is fine for products or services that are inherently uniform; no one asks for much creativity in a fifteen-minute oil-change and lube operation. But the closer a product or service is to the buyer's personal life, the more objectionable that necessary homogeneity becomes.

So the demand for one-of-a-kind products and individualized services is being met by people who work for themselves or for small, highly responsive companies. Many of these services handle chores that people would automatically have done for themselves even a decade ago. Many are entirely new. How many people would have imagined in, say, 1980, that someone could make a living doing other people's shopping for them? Or organizing their closets? Both small-scale services are flourishing among the affluent, harried two-income families of major cities. This trend toward highly personalized businesses is sure to grow throughout what is left of the century.

Consumers are fueling the spread of bimodal distribution in yet another way by buying from both ends of the spectrum. They go to luxury resorts for fantasy vacations or to elegant Victorian bed-and-breakfasts for a return to the gentility missing from their everyday lives, but on the way there they sleep at economy motels owned by giant chain operators. They have dinner at elegant restaurants—after all, what good is having two incomes if one of you has to cook dinner every night after a hard day at work?—but they have lunch at the fast-food stands near the office. Or they drive Mercedeses and BMWs but fill their own gas tanks and wipe their own windshields.

For the moment, these examples are all symptoms of yuppie culture. Yet they have already had a major impact on American business, and they are spreading quickly throughout society. Large companies with inexpensive products and services get some of the consumer's money, and small firms with high price tags—but style and quality to match—also receive their share. It is the mid-sized companies with mid-priced, *ordinary* products that get left out.

The mergers that have driven bimodal distribution are concentrated in industries where government regulations either have been relaxed or were not a significant obstacle to begin with. Examples include the following:

Airlines. Merger activity has been at its heaviest in the airline industry, where government regulation was most rigid in the pre-Reagan years. As this book goes to press, Pan Am and Northwest are negotiating a merger. In 1986 alone, there were four large mergers in this industry: Northwest Airlines bought Republic Airlines, Delta bought Western Air Lines, United Airlines bought Pan Am's Pacific division, and Texas Air bought Eastern, which in 1989 again came on the block. In all, nearly $3.15 billion changed hands. Today, ten domestic carriers control 80 percent of the market. Of these airlines, only the largest and most efficient will survive. By 2000, we expect that only three or four major domestic carriers will remain in existence. The rest will have succumbed to a combination of inflated payrolls and cost- and fare-cutting by their larger competitors.

At the lower end of the business scale, small "feeder" airlines have proliferated rapidly since the early 1980s. In many areas, the most successful commuter airlines have been absorbing their smaller competitors, closely mirroring the consolidation in the national airline market. Both of these trends will continue as long as a strong business climate encourages air travel.

Department Stores. These offer another example of the trend to bimodal distribution. Last year, the takeover of Federated Department Stores by the Campeau Corporation was the biggest merger in retailing history and created the largest department-store chain in the United States; it was just one of many that have consolidated the nation's successful full-price, full-service marketers in recent years.

A wide variety of smaller stores are also flourishing. At the bottom of the price and service scales, discount and convenience stores offer savings in either time or money. In some areas it seems impossible to drive more than five blocks without encountering a 7-Eleven, and independent convenience stores have set up shop across the country in all but the smallest hamlets. At the other end of the spectrum, specialty boutiques offer unique, unusual, or original products and a high level of personal attention. The same trend can be seen in the world of mail-order, where merchandisers cater to "niche" markets, often with remarkable success. Witness the spectacular growth of Patagonia, in sporting goods and sportswear, and Brookstone, one of the earliest merchants of odd-but-useful tools. In the new world of harried, price-conscious, and style-conscious consumers, all are raking in record profits.

It is difficult, however, to find mid-scale stores that are making money, or even surviving. Woolworth's and Montgomery Ward have both tried to make it as mid-scale stores and have admitted defeat. Both are in the process of scaling down their operations to the discount/savings bracket. Even giant Sears has recently been forced to mark down its prices in hopes of competing with other marketers.

Restaurants. Bimodal distribution is particularly easy to see in the restaurant business. McDonald's, Pizza Hut, and other well-run fast-food operations take a growing share of the market every year, while major companies have found that it no longer pays to run a "meat and potatoes" family restaurant. Many of the independent Howard Johnson restaurants—those without motels to help sustain them— have been forced to close. Some mid-size restaurants make ends meet by catering to specialized tastes; Cajun-style and other trendy ethnic cooking can still draw crowds in some areas. But in order to survive, most mid-size, mid-price restaurants have either cut prices or offered better food and more service. Once-successful chains like Friendly's, Farm Shop, and the International House of Pancakes have come in for hard times.

In these last years of the twentieth century, the very large or very fancy restaurants where people go for special occasions will have to turn away customers. With more women working and both spouses often working overtime, when husband and wife or husband, wife, and children have time to go out together, they go to New York's Tavern-on-the-Green or to Chez Panisse in Berkeley. With two incomes, they are earning more, and since the rest of the time they are either skipping lunch or grabbing a fast-food meal, they feel no qualms about indulging themselves.

Health Care. The health-care industry is second only to defense in the U.S. economy. As we progress to the third millennium, we expect a consolidation of this industry into large, multi-hospital systems. Within these systems, more technologically intensive and specialized hospitals will provide lengthy treatment for serious illnesses and perform such complicated major surgery as open-heart operations and kidney transplants. Ambulatory-care centers—surgicenters or "doc-in-the-boxes"—will provide services from diagnosing infections and setting broken bones to plastic surgery and cataract removal.

In this field, the trend toward consolidation is accelerated by the efforts of government and business to control escalating health-care spending in the early 1980s. Faced with declining profits, hospitals have been forced to specialize, expand their services, and keep their eyes on the bottom line. The change has made them ripe for takeover. In 1984, more than 1,200 hospitals were owned or operated by for-profit hospital-management corporations, more than twice as many as in 1976. Over seven hundred hospitals—10 percent of all the hospitals in the United States—are expected to close by 1995; many of the rest will merge. By 2000, we expect just twenty unified health-care systems to provide medical and hospital care and health insurance to over half of all Americans. Sixteen of them will be profit-making multi-system conglomerates; the four remaining chains will operate on a nonprofit basis. For consumers this should mean added efficiency, because a single corporation will coordinate all parts of their health-care program. But it may also mean that people have less opportunity to shop for lower hospital fees or better services.

As large, single-unit hospitals merge or die, ambulatory care centers, emergicenters, surgicenters, and walk-in clinics are experiencing monumental growth. This is understandable, since by demanding payment in full at the time of service and by foregoing expensive, specialized equipment, they cut their operating costs dramatically. As a result, these centers can charge as little as one-fifth of what the same care would cost in a major hospital.

The first ambulatory-care center in the United States appeared in 1973. By 1985 there were three thousand such centers, charging 45 million Americans almost $2 billion a year for their services. Today a new clinic opens every day, a rate of growth that should continue at least through 1995. By 1990, there will be 5,500 ambulatory-care clinics in the United States. By 2000, some ten thousand such facilities will corner one-fourth of the national market for primary health care.

Thus, Americans will increasingly utilize both ends of the health-care industry, frequenting the smaller centers for less serious afflictions and returning to the hospital—part of a nationwide chain—for more dangerous complaints.

Hospitality. When was the last time you stayed in a hotel or motel that was neither a small, family-run operation nor part of a giant chain? If it was at all recently, you are part of a dwindling minority. Howard Johnson and the other mid-priced hotel operators have been watching their occupancy rates decline for several years, while mid-sized independent hotels go out of business. Yet discount hotel chains like Econo-Lodge and Sleep-Cheep are making record profits. New York City's famed Algonquin is booked solid for up to three months in advance, and New York's Plaza, Boston's Ritz-Carlton, and San Francisco's Drake—all founded as independents but now owned by chains—are doing nearly as well. By 2000, the process will be virtually complete: bimodal distribution at its clearest.

Big hotel chains can afford the extra amenities, training programs, and efficient computer systems that give them the edge over their mid-sized competitors. The top twenty-five chains now control about half of the hotel rooms in the United States. They experienced a growth rate of 149 percent between 1970 and 1985. Today these chains are buying up properties, both on a case-by-case basis and by the mini-chain, as the field consolidates. In the not-too-distant future, three or four chains—Marriott, Hyatt, and Sheraton almost certainly, and perhaps one more—will dominate the industry.

This does not mean that our choices will soon be limited to the large chains, however. There is still room for independents strong on personality and personal service. Bed-and-breakfasts, often family-run, are popping up as never before. They offer quaint settings, antique furnishings, and homemade, family-style meals unavailable at either the luxury resorts or the economy motels of their giant competitors. Other hotels cater to niche markets with a taste for "Wild West" reenactments or mystery weekends where guests solve a fictitious murder. Like gourmet restaurants and fashionable boutiques, these businesses offer style and personalized service that provide a sorely needed break from the automated, high-pressure 1980s. More and more of us will be able to afford them as the next century dawns.

Agriculture. Farming is one of the most publicized instances of the trend to bimodal distribution. The huge commercial farms are prospering. Most of the small, part-time farms are at least surviving. But the mid-sized farms show up in the nightly news stories about farmers forced to sell their ancestral homes.

Part-time farms, with less than $100,000 per year in gross sales and annual profits usually under $20,000, survive because their owners usually earn more net income off the farm than on. Fully 93 percent of small farms have at least one person holding down an outside job, and more than half have two. For these farmers, agriculture is a preferred lifestyle and route to personal accomplishment, not an economic necessity. In 1986 there were 2 million of these small farms producing 35 percent of the nation's crops and earning 15 percent of the farm profit. By 2000, one-fourth of America's vest-pocket farms will have disappeared—but 1.5 million will remain, a better showing than television-news horror stories would lead one to expect. The survivors will account for 15 percent of the nation's crops. Because of their relatively high costs, they will receive only 5 percent of our farm profits. Yet if a small farm makes it to the year 2000, its continued survival will be almost assured. By then, rising pay from outside jobs will more than compensate for any loss of farm income. Debts that now threaten them will have been paid off. And the most imaginative small farmers will have found new profits in the growing specialty-produce market. For most, the risk of failure will have passed.

Large commercial farms, predictably, are in even better shape. Operations with substantial investments in agribusiness and more than $500,000 in gross farm sales each year are flourishing throughout the country and in all facets of agriculture. Like any other huge business, giant farms have advantages over their smaller competitors. They can buy their raw materials at prices 10 percent lower than small farms must pay, and sell their produce at prices 5 percent higher. And, because they have more profit to spend, they can afford to adopt computers, biotechnology, and similar high-tech innovations as soon as they become available. In 1986 there were 23,000 farms of this size, growing 25 percent of the nation's crops; they raked in fully half of the farm profits that year. By the turn of the century, large commercial farms will more than double their numbers, to fifty thousand. They will grow two-thirds of our crops and, because of their lower cost-per-unit, they will soak up fully three-fourths of the farm profit.

Moderate-size farms have none of the advantages of their competitors, and they will reap none of the rewards. In 1986 there were 250,000 farms with sales between $100,000 and $250,000 per year; they grew 40 percent of U.S. agricultural products and took in one-third of the farm profits. A few of these farms—the best managed—are gradually working their way up into the $500,000 category, where they will at last find prosperity. Yet by 2000, there will be only 100,000 farms left in this size range, accounting for 20 percent of the nation's farm products and profits. With too much work to permit taking on an outside job and too little "pull" to win favorable prices from suppliers and buyers, they simply cannot compete in the modern economy. Most of these farms will eventually be absorbed by large commercial agribusinesses.

Changes in Washington's farm policy will hasten this trend in the 1990s. There is a growing movement in Congress to reduce federal spending for farm subsidies; eventually, despite strong opposition from farmers, it will succeed. Large farm corporations will absorb the loss with little pain; though they receive by far the largest part of government assistance, for them it represents little more than a windfall profit. Mid-sized farms, already hard pressed, may not survive the loss. The Reagan administration showed Washington's power and willingness to destroy independent farms when, a week after the 1988 presidential election, it mailed out foreclosure threats to some eighty thousand delinquent farm-loan recipients.

Bimodal distribution will remain a major force in the American economy at least until the latter half of the 1990s, particularly if Republicans continue to occupy the White House through 1996. In that case, companies bent on merger need not fear tighter antitrust enforcement.

Large corporations will continue their merger activity, as long as interest rates remain affordable and tax breaks favoring debt remain in place. Mergers and acquisitions involving a common product or service—so-called synergistic deals—show no sign of declining. As William Loomis, general partner at the Wall Street investment firm of Lazard Freres & Company, puts it, "Now in takeovers you will see not only capital but industrial expertise involved—logic is prevailing instead of simply an excess of capital looking for a home."

Hard as this process is on many companies and displaced managers, by the turn of the century American consumers will be the better for it. They will continue to buy from both ends of the market, providing the ultimate justification for bimodal distribution. Discounters will continue to prosper in all the retail industries, because people with middle-class incomes have grown to prefer saving money in some areas so they can splurge in others. High-ticket "boutique" businesses will flourish by indulging the urge to buy quality merchandise and personal service; as a result, we will have a much wider selection from which to choose. And, barring another major revision in the tax code, the United States' citizenry will continue to evolve into one large middle class well able to afford what the boutiques have to offer. We will still have problems that remain to be addressed, but by and large we'll be better off than ever.

THE STRUGGLE FOR

ECONOMIC SUPREMACY

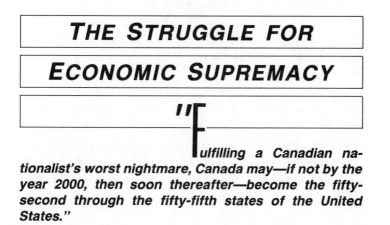

"**F**ulfilling a Canadian na-
tionalist's worst nightmare, Canada may—if not by the
year 2000, then soon thereafter—become the fifty-
second through the fifty-fifth states of the United
States."

Can the United States still compete effectively with other nations in
the years ahead? Or will its enormous trade deficits grow steadily
worse as overseas competitors systematically dominate world markets and reduce American firms to scrabbling for whatever scraps of
business fall from the tables of international giants with names like
Mitsubishi and Hyundai?

The answer is that the United States *must* be able to compete in
order to maintain the standard of living to which most Americans
have become accustomed. And in the 1990s it *will* again compete
effectively for export business. It will not be easy. The competition
for world trade markets will grow more intense, not less so, in the
final years of the twentieth century.

THE DECLINE OF JAPAN

In the short run, the United States may benefit from a windfall
unwillingly granted by its chief competitor. One of the world's most
prosperous trading nations may soon collapse, leaving the United
States with the dual mantle of political *and* commercial leadership.

Unless Japan is lucky as well as skillful and determined, by the turn of the century it will have fallen from the world's second-largest trading nation to between the fifth and tenth. The causes of this precipitous descent are already apparent today. Japan is losing its traditional markets to Korea, Taiwan, and Hong Kong. Some of its companies are even losing out to American companies they once bested; since the decline of the dollar on world foreign-exchange markets, Japanese firms have actually been importing specialty steels from the United States.

In its glory days, from 1980 through 1985, Japan's economy was growing at a rate of more than 4 percent per year; it has not reached 3 percent per year since 1986. As a result, unemployment has been on the rise. Admittedly, its current unemployment rate of 4 percent is low by American standards, but in Japan the goal of full employment—a place in society for every Japanese—is a fundamental national value. Virtually any unemployment at all represents a failure of the social structure. Government efforts to stimulate the economy—a retroactive tax cut and $40 billion public works program in 1987 and further prodding since then—have produced a temporary boom in consumer spending and housing starts. But this is only a brief reprieve from what will soon become a state of permanent recession.

Meanwhile, Japan is facing a population that is aging even more rapidly than that of the United States. By 1990, more than one-fifth of the 1985 working population will be retired on pensions that pay 80 percent of their final salaries. At the same time, the workforce that supports the pensioners will continue to shrink, and there is every evidence that the younger generation has far less interest in long hours and sober living than its parents did. In short, the Japanese business empire could find itself looking forward to hard times by the beginning of the next decade.

THE FUTURE OF ASIA

Needless to say, Japan has not resigned itself to that fate, or to the loss of export markets that might result from the unification of Europe and the productive confederation between the United States and Canada. For both of those reasons, and also because of a growing sense that Japan should take on the regional leadership role that befits its economic status, the once-insular Japanese have begun to look to their neighbors for mutual support. Both Japan and the newly industrialized countries (NICs) of South Korea, Taiwan, Hong Kong, and Singapore recognize that they must act quickly so as not to be frozen out of the huge European and North American markets.

One likely response is the formation of an Asian economic bloc, but support in the East is growing for an Asian-Pacific organization, which would include the United States, Canada, and other non-Asian nations. The pan-Asian group would be anchored by Japan, operating in concert with the NICs and with considerable participation from such emerging economies as Malaysia and Thailand. China, potentially the biggest market of all, would circle at the periphery.

In recent years, Japan has been acting more like a regional leader. It has increased its foreign-aid spending dramatically in the 1980s; it now surpasses even the United States as the world's largest donor. Japan's economic relations in Asia changed abruptly in 1985, when the era of the cheap yen came to an end. Before then, the Asian nations had developed individual relationships with the United States, while devoting little attention to their economic relations with one another. Since then, they have turned to each other and begun to develop a regional division of labor. Japan's motives for direct investment in their neighbors' economies shifted in the late 1980s, as high-cost Japanese society suddenly needed cheaper places to make "Japanese" products.

After years of stagnation, Japan's imports from its smaller neighbors have picked up considerably. Japan recognizes its former self in its new trading partners. It fears that the "four dragons" will imitate Japan and hold on to trade surpluses until pressed to open up their markets. They, too, will tend to have overvalued currencies. But, having learned from the error of Singapore's ways, the other Asian nations will do their best to maintain low wage scales. When they find that wages must rise, as they surely will in a more democratic South Korea, they will adopt automation as quickly as possible. Much of the factory equipment to do this will come from Japan, so Japan will continue to enjoy a trade surplus with them. The downside for Japan will be an invasion of its home markets by its neighbors' products.

This vision of Asian regional harmony neglects one major factor: the deep-seated hostility toward Japan harbored by countries throughout the Pacific. Japan dominated or occupied all of these countries during the Second World War, and it ruled with an iron fist. In Korea especially, the hatred that still remains thirty-five years after Japanese occupation will not be easy to overcome.

Japan's foreign competitors will gain from the country's willingness to play in global markets by the same rules as other OECD members. Japanese companies will be more willing to go into joint ventures as they diversify into relatively unknown territories. Japanese industries will provide increasingly stiff competition as they become even leaner and more aggressive, more willing to transfer technology to offshore subsidiaries and trading partners, and more willing to put increasingly brutal pressure on suppliers, including those in foreign lands. Margins on sales to Japanese companies will shrink from the wafer-thin to the microscopic.

In the mid-1990s, 30 million free-spending Japanese tourists will flock to the fleshpots and playgrounds of Southeast Asia. They will fuel a boom in infrastructure and facilities in those countries the likes of which Japanese construction firms have not seen in decades.

Growth will be higher and inflation a good deal lower than for other OECD countries. Those who can will shift production abroad. Defense spending will, after years of American pressure, rise by a real 6 to 7 percent annually through much of the 1990s.

As for North and South Korea, there is at least a chance that they will unite by the turn of the century. Already, during the 1988 Olympics in Seoul and the presidential election that preceded it, many hints could be seen that the two Koreas would eventually be one. South Korea's young people harbor emotional yearnings for unification, less out of affection for North Korea's harsh communist regime than out of growing South Korean nationalism. The major question here is the fate of North Korea after power passes out of the hands of President, General Secretary, and old-fashioned strongman Kim Il Sung. If the North Korean Communist Party can build what little power it possesses under the aging dictator into effective control of the country, reunification will be relatively simple to accomplish. If power descends—Duvalier-style—to Kim's son, as seems likely, it may yet be ten to twenty years before the two Koreas become one. With unification, Korea will have an even stronger economic base. The potential for growth brought on by reunification will give Korea more economic power, both within the East Asian community and throughout the world.

By 2000, East Asia's aggregate gross national product will be comparable to that of Western Europe or North America, about 22 percent of the world's total. In 1960, it was half the size of Europe's GNP and only one-third the size of America's. So far, Japan is the region's only member of the OECD club of industrialized nations. South Korea is already richer, per capita, than OECD members Portugal and Turkey.

For the United States, all this will rate as bad news—unless it joins in a pan-Pacific trading bloc, a move that seems only mildly probable. An Asian economic combine competing against the United States could soon make today's balance-of-trade deficits seem very small. A combine that joins the United States with its most aggressive, efficient competitors could quickly bring America new prosperity far beyond that envisioned in our first chapter.

THE NEW EUROPE

From the gloom of the 1970s, Europe has emerged as a region awash with optimism. Growth has been running at more than 3 percent per year—equal to that of Japan, the United States, and the rapidly expanding countries of Southeast Asia. The decision to unify the European market by 1992 has restored a sense of purpose to Western Europe. Indeed, "1992 fever" is sweeping across the continent, capturing the imagination of the average citizen as much as that of the Brussels-based Eurocrat.

The notion of a United States of Europe, a "Eurocracy" with 325 million consumers, is a heady thought. In fact, many American economists worry that it is likely to become considerably more than that, as a number of countries that do not now belong to the European Economic Community join the new confederation: Switzerland, Norway, Denmark, Sweden, Finland, Yugoslavia, and even East Germany. By 2000, Europe will be a single enormous market, with over 400 million consumers. Compare this with the U.S. market of some 250 million people or Japan's 125 million, and it becomes clear just how much economic and political power could shift toward the formerly weak Continent.

Fear that the newly united Europe will erect trade barriers will spur outside investment in the Community. Mergers and acquisitions are already progressing at a fast pace, both inside the Common Market and out. European conglomerates, flush with cash, have recently taken over a number of American concerns. American industrial giants have stepped up their European investments in return.

Japan, whose relations with Europe today are difficult at best, is also worried about its trade prospects in the post-1992 Common Market. Like their American counterparts, Japanese companies have been on a buying spree, scooping up companies and establishing joint ventures with European partners. Their eagerness to participate in the integrated market will worsen an anti-Japanese backlash in Europe.

As the twenty-first century approaches, European, American, and Japanese companies will weld their respective economies into one closely linked entity as they attempt to build a base for their operation within the newly structured market. By the turn of the century the process will be nearly complete.

For the East Bloc, this transformation could not have come at a worse time. Just as economic walls between the East and West are being dismantled, COMECON will be forced to adapt to the new reality of Western Europe's unified market, and productive capacity. There is little hope that COMECON's inferior consumer goods will find outside markets in the face of such stiff competition.

The Third World nations will be even more vulnerable to the global market shakeup. Faced with crippling external debts, low prices for their raw materials exports, and, in many cases, serious political problems at home, they will by and large be left out of the economic bonanza.

United markets and common legal and economic institutions will create manifold opportunities, not only for huge companies but for individuals with entrepreneurial spirit. The opportunities for translators and 1992 consultants are endless; many such specialists are already offering their services. But there will also be losers. Farmers in France, for instance, could find themselves competing for francs on their home turf with produce from Spain, a country whose lower wages make it possible to sell at lower prices. At the same time, more highly skilled Northern Europeans have already begun to descend on the south. Socially conscious Italian "yuppies" are already going to German dentists. Southern artisans, designers, and others steeped in Old World traditions of craftsmanship will prosper in the north.

The Europe of tomorrow, with goods and services flowing freely across borders and with uniform standards for products everywhere, has much to do in the transition. Today's Europe distinguishes itself by sheer numbers of idiosyncratic standards, but a true common market implies a commitment to uniformity. The task is a daunting one on a continent with fourteen kinds of electrical plugs, three electrical voltages, seven television broadcasting and reception systems, four incompatible cellular telephone systems, six standards for cardiac pacemakers, at least three sets of automobile pollution-emission laws, and a vast array of conflicting standards for foods, industrial safety, and product labeling.

These separate sets of standards were originally conceived to protect domestic producers. With 1992 about to arrive, Europe must consider an alternative approach to the wholesale dismantling of national standards: mutual recognition. Under a system of mutual recognition, a product approved for sale in one country would be accepted as safe by other Common Market countries. The alternative is a mammoth endeavor. More than three hundred committees within the Community are already working on the issue of standardizing electrical systems.

This leads to the most important, and also the most interesting, task for the 1990s. The Community will have to develop an institutional framework for the EEC. The members must establish some way to define the areas of policy that indisputably belong to the Community as a whole, and those that are retained by the individual member nations. The resulting chaos will make the American "states' rights" cries heard by the Southern states during the Civil Rights Movement of the 1960s look tame by comparison.

THE RUSSIAN REVOLUTION REVISITED

Some of the brightest trading opportunities, both for America and for its competitors, will come from the huge, almost untapped consumer market of a nation that has been virtually closed to outside development, not merely since 1917, but throughout history.

In the 1990s, the process of *perestroika,* begun by General Secretary Gorbachev, will still be young and frail. Confronted with low export prices for its oil and continuing shortages of hard currency, Soviet leaders will have no alternative but to sell off more of the country's gold reserves. Hard-pressed as they will be to meet their citizens' demands for high-quality consumer goods and services, they will be less and less able to cope with their troublesome trade and political relations with their COMECON neighbors. Political difficulties will occupy most of the Soviet leadership's energies, as the nationalist movements in the Baltic states and Azerbaijan show no signs of fading.

Despite these difficulties, or perhaps because of them, Gorbachev will continue working to relax tensions with the West. Call it *glasnost* or just glossy public relations, the Soviets are wooing Western corporations for joint ventures and other forms of economic cooperation on a scale and with a sophistication that make the economic detente of fifteen years ago pale by comparison. From billion-dollar petro-chemical partnerships and food-processing factories to pizzerias and sleek Finnish fashions, the Russians are wheeling and dealing.

Recognizing that foreign earnings and know-how offer the quick-est—in fact, the only—route to fiscal reform, Mikhail Gorbachev has made a point of inviting Western business leaders to consider the Soviet Union as their new land of opportunity. Transactions between American multinationals and their Soviet counterparts could mark a watershed in East-West relations. Until now, trade has been a trickle; the Soviet Union accounted for barely 1 percent of America's for-eign trade in 1987. By the turn of the century, this will grow dramati-cally.

THE AMERICAN BLOC

One of the most important factors in America's future prosperity was decided not in Washington, but north of border. When Can-ada's voters went to the polls in November 1988 to elect a Prime Minister, the decisive issue in their minds was the historic free-trade agreement with the United States. Opponents of Prime Min-ister Brian Mulroney argued that the price of lowering trade barriers with Canada's giant southern neighbor (already one an-other's largest export markets) would not be natural resources, but Canada's very soul.

Canada's intellectual and artistic leaders have roundly criticized the accord, which was passed by the Canadian Parliament on Decem-ber 31, 1988. Most of the business community supports it, in part because it strongly supports free enterprise instead of state control of industry. Previous Canadian governments often passed laws lim-iting or impeding foreign investment. The new accord reverses that policy. "It's the best guarantee that Canada will not behave like a banana republic again," says Lloyd C. Atkinson, chief economist at the Bank of Montreal.

Between 1975 and 1986 the value of Canadian direct investment in the United States—well over half of Canada's foreign invest-ment—soared from $5.6 billion (Canadian) to $39.9 billion. Can-ada's assets in the United States now include Bloomingdale's department store, Harris Bankcorp (the largest bank holding com-pany in Illinois), and 21 percent of Du Pont. The leading dairy producer in New York, the largest jewelry retailer in the United

States, and the largest school-bus operator in North America are all now Canadian-controlled.

Seagram, one of Canada's established multinationals, had nearly 72 percent of its total assets in the United States by early 1987; since then the group has added Tropicana, the up-market American fruit-juice maker, and Martel brandy to its holdings. Since 1977 the value of Northern Telecom's American assets has gone from $145 million (Canadian) to $4.2 billion. This tariff-lowering free-trade agreement is likely to raise Canadian investment in the United States even further.

Canadian novelist Mordecai Richler explained the nature of Canadian paranoia about the United States in a *Newsweek* article shortly after the pact was ratified. "French Canadians," wrote Richler, "[are] fearful of being culturally overwhelmed by English Canadians, who are even more terrified of being swamped by America."

Richler does not minimize the concerns of the pact's opponents, who fear that the United States will deplete the resource-rich and sparsely populated country's oil, natural gas, lumber, and fresh-water reserves, even as it dismantles Canada's universal Medicare and pension systems for the elderly. Despite those fears, the accord passed because it makes great economic sense for both countries.

Canada faces another problem during the 1990s. Fertility rates there have fallen to below the replacement level, signaling a possible loss of population. That, in turn, reduces that nation's potential economic growth. Most Canadians are relatively complacent about their shrinking families and falling population. They believe that immigrants will continue to arrive in such large numbers that the low birthrate hardly matters.

They are wrong. The Canadian population is currently 26 million; immigrants number only 125,000 per year. In the 1980s, half of all immigrants to Canada came from Asia, Africa, and the West Indies; only 10 percent arrived from Britain, and less than 2 percent from France. When the Canadians who leave each year—mostly to the United States—are subtracted, net immigration fails to balance the declining birthrate. This is disastrous for a country with a population density lower than that of Saudi Arabia, enormous resources to develop, and too few hands to do the work.

The problem also threatens Canada's driving urge to retain its distinct national identity. Canadians are among the most racially tolerant people on earth, but their tolerance has its limits. Rumblings of resentment over newcomers from the Third World are already being heard in such terms as "political refugees." A substantial rise in the number of hard-to-assimilate immigrants, coupled with a decline in the number of Canadians of European stock, would risk a political backlash that could force the government to restrict immigration.

French Canadians, for example, once made up one-third of the national population. They are now down to 25 percent and will decline to 20 percent before the 1990s are out. Quebec businessmen, however, welcome the opportunities offered by the trade accord. Separatists, too, talk of opportunity; they believe that Canada's closer ties to the United States will make it easier for Quebec to secede from Canada and establish its own nation.

In fact, the other provinces may well secede first, leaving Quebec to fend for itself. Once the free-trade agreement with the United States takes full effect, the next logical step will be to accept politically what has already happened economically—the integration of Canada into the United States. By the end of the 1990s, Puerto Rico will already have become the fifty-first state in the Union. And fulfilling a Canadian nationalist's worst nightmare, Canada may—if not by the year 2000, then soon thereafter—become the fifty-second through the fifty-fifth states of the United States. Canada's western provinces—Alberta, Manitoba, Saskatchewan, British Columbia, the Yukon Territory, and the Northwest Territories—will be compacted into two states; Ontario and the eastern provinces—Newfoundland, Nova Scotia, New Brunswick, and Prince Edward Island—will combine into two more. Politically, the new American states will be evenly divided: the resource-rich, development-minded western states will join the Republican camp, while the urbanized eastern states will tend to vote Democratic. Quebec will at last receive its wish and become an independent nation, if in name only. Economically, it will remain wholly dependent on its neighbors for survival.

In fact, incorporating most of Canada into the United States will do neither nation any great good beyond, perhaps, the psychological benefit of recognizing reality. The 1988 free-trade agreement will accomplish far more. Though Canada's population represents a relatively small market compared with Japan, France, or Germany, the guarantee of unrestricted access to both Canada's people and its raw materials will give American manufacturers a safe haven from which to support their other trading ventures. In a world quickly being divided between huge, competing trading blocs that might conceivably erect barriers against nonmembers, some such haven is badly needed. By the turn of the century, free trade will dramatically increase the profitable flow of products between the Siamese twins of international commerce.

JUNE 1990

In the months since the first edition of *American Renaissance* appeared, Canada has taken giant steps toward dissolution. This time, the question of secession hinges on the 1987 Meech Lake accord, which would recognize Quebec as a "distinct society" within Canada; with this status go far-reaching powers, formerly reserved for the central government, to protect French language and culture. The deadline for ratification is now June 23, and Quebec says that if the accord is voted down it will secede, a move that 60 percent of the province's citizens now support.

There is little chance that English-speaking Canada will accept the Meech Lake plan. The poorer provinces want to preserve the power of the central government, which grants whatever benefits they receive for being part of the confederation. New Brunswick and Manitoba, both thinly populated, fear that Meech Lake will invalidate their own language plans and cause their French speakers to leave for Quebec. The premier of Nova Scotia has already said in public that his province's best option may be to join the United States.

By the time this edition appears, the results of the vote will be known. We suspect that they will extend the deadline and Quebec will agree to remain in the confederation while negotiation continues. Such a truce cannot long survive.

In the end, it will not matter. If Quebec declares independence, the deed will have been done at last. If the other provinces grant Quebec's demands, it will cripple the central government and Balkanize the nation. And if Meech Lake is voted down but Quebec remains in the confederation—the least likely course of events—the Separatist push will merely begin again with much greater support than in the past.

In any case, the breakup of Canada now seems all but inevitable. And once the nation has lost its richest province and one-fourth of its population, the remaining provinces will soon wonder whether there is any reason to prolong Canada's existence.

A NEW SYSTEM OF WORLD TRADE

While politicians wrangle over tariffs and quotas, business is busy breaking down the barriers between countries. Unlike traditional multinationals, which grew by spawning subsidiaries abroad, these behemoths form strategic alliances with overseas competitors to penetrate every major economy. The reason for extending their global reach: no one country, not even the United States, offers a market big enough to allow many crucial industries—from aircraft manufacturing to telecommunications—to operate profitably. The trading nations of the world are now inextricably linked to one another, receiving an average of one-fourth of their gross national product from exports. Fully half of those export profits come from the operations of the multinational giants.

In theory, the growing interdependence between the American economy and those of Europe and Japan should prevent a repetition of the trade wars that destroyed the international economy after 1929 and plunged the world into the Great Depression. In such an interdependent world, where an all-American "manufacturer," such as IBM, relies on foreign production for some 40 percent of its personal-computer parts, trade wars become so obviously self-destructive that they are bound to occur less frequently. And the growing number of international investments, including those made by foreign firms buying into American companies at record rates, will militate against any severe or prolonged trade war.

In practice, governments tend to embrace protectionism as readily as most economists renounce it. The cause is political. If you tell an American or a British worker that there is no need to allow more competitive imports from abroad, he will vote you into any office in the land.

The self-destructive nature of tariffs and other trade barriers would be obvious, even if national economies were not so impossibly tangled. Such protective measures raise prices in the domestic market, placing a needless burden on consumers. They also prop up inefficient companies or industries that, on the basis of performance, should be allowed to die. Jobs are temporarily preserved, but at an absurd cost that, in the end, leads to even greater unemployment. According to the World Bank, the cost of preserving jobs in Britain's auto industry through restricting imports is much too high. In 1983, the bill for each job came to four times the annual wage. Losses that large make it cheaper to dismantle trade barriers and pay the losers *not* to work. The economy as a whole would be much better off.

Although it is hard to dispute the logic of free trade, interest groups in countries throughout the world are doing their best to sabotage efforts toward global economic integration. Witness the state of the current "Uruguay Round" of global trade talks under the auspices of the General Agreement on Tariffs and Trade (GATT.)

Two years ago, for the eighth time since the organization was established in 1947, representatives of the nearly one hundred GATT members met at the seaside resort of Punta del Este, Uruguay. Failure of the talks, which will be completed in 1991, could lead to a new wave of protectionism, and failure seems entirely possible. Predictably, the major sticking point is an American proposal to do away with costly, unproductive agricultural subsidies. The negative reaction from members of the European Economic Community and from Japan has been thoroughly predictable. Two other areas of contention in the GATT talks are trade in services and intellectual property rights. The lines of battle are drawn between the wealthier industrial nations and the developing world, which is seeking preferential access to patents, copyrights, and computer software.

Meanwhile, the twelve-member European Economic Community banned the importation of American beef, which had been treated artificially with hormones. Playing hardball, the United States retaliated with an often-used tactic: it imposed duties on Common Market agricultural products roughly equal to the beef sales American producers would forfeit under the ban—approximately $100 million per year.

There is a real danger that a cycle of retaliations could sabotage the GATT talks. In that event, protectionist fever could spread worldwide. The nations of the world would become further entrenched in regional trading blocs. For the United States, a breakdown in the mechanism of trade would make it overwhelmingly more difficult to reduce the country's trade deficit.

SELF-INFLICTED WOUNDS

In fact, however, America's success in world trade will probably depend a good deal less on protectionism and other external factors than on its own internal government policies. There are two key factors to consider: technical proficiency and trade policy. The United States can make progress in both areas during the 1990s, but it must make major changes to do so. The technical changes may well be the easier to make, if only because they depend less on what is politically expedient.

In the mid-1980s, the conventional wisdom held that America's balance-of-trade problems were due to the artificially high price of its dollar on foreign-exchange markets. With the dollar so high, American products were too expensive to attract customers in overseas markets, while imports were too cheap for American consumers to resist. Bring the dollar down, and all would be well, save perhaps in those few industries already too sick to recover.

And, in fact, it almost worked that way. The last time the dollar had fallen, Japanese manufacturers had plenty of warning, so they shipped a full year's worth of products into the United States at the old expensive-dollar/cheap-yen prices; their sales never faltered. This time the dollar dropped so quickly that they had little time to prepare. The price of Japanese products soared. The price of American products fell. (An exception was General Motors, whose short-sighted leaders seized the chance to make a little more money per car and ignored the rare opportunity to recover some of their lost market share.) The result was predictable: American exports soared from $230 billion in 1986 to over $320 billion in 1988. As many as 750,000 new manufacturing jobs appeared in the United States. By the end of 1988, American factories were running at nearly 90 percent of their capacity, even in industries once thought beyond saving.

But the change did less for the U.S. balance-of-trade deficit than most economists would have anticipated. Americans continued to buy Japanese goods, even when comparable native products were cheaper. And the cost advantage lasted only a year. When it was over, the price of Japanese goods was again comparable to that of products from the United States. (In some cases they are a good deal cheaper. Japanese cars are about $1,500 less expensive than the American equivalent.) Japan's remarkable cost-cutting did little to slow American exports, but at home their sole market advantage was gone. Dollars still flow toward Japan at a rate of more than $50 billion per year.

(Manufacturers in Korea, Taiwan, and Singapore were largely left out of this process. Their currencies are closely tied to the dollar in the exchange markets and fell as the dollar fell. They emerged from the process with little net gain or loss of competitive advantage.)

This is a stunning triumph for Japanese manufacturers. Their costs per unit product were already among the lowest in the world, yet they had managed to squeeze them still further—enough to compensate for the near doubling of the cost of the yen on exchange markets. Few American firms could have come close to duplicating that achievement, as they had proved when the dollar was at its peak.

The reason is modern manufacturing methods. Japan has adopted them. So have the fast-growing economies of Korea and Taiwan. To a large extent, the United States has not. With only half the American population, Japan uses nearly five times as many robots as the United States. Most major Japanese factories are well supplied with so-called flexible manufacturing systems (FMS), fully automated production lines that can be reconfigured with little effort to make whatever part or product is asked of them; only fifteen such systems were installed in the United States in 1987. And many Japanese companies have adopted "just-in-time manufacturing" (JIT), an inventory-control technique that drastically cuts manufacturing costs by reducing the amount of expensive parts and raw material stocked in the factory. At most, perhaps 5 percent of American companies that could use JIT have adopted it.

Yet the benefits to be derived from these new methods can be significant. A good example comes from AT&T's giant factory in Shreveport, Louisiana, which makes business phone systems, pay telephones, and a host of plugs, connectors, and other small parts. Each product the facility produces is configured to the customer's special needs. There are around three thousand variations in all, containing some forty thousand different parts, all built in the 1.2-million-square-foot facility. Until 1986 the factory was organized along traditional lines, a separate shop for every process. Then local managers reworked the plant, setting up six separate FMS lines and retaining only those few special-purpose shops that could not be eliminated. They set up a JIT inventory system as well; some suppliers deliver materials to the plant twice a day. The result: it used to take six weeks to ship a business phone system after the order arrived; now it takes about three hours. And the number of defective systems has fallen to less than 1 percent.

Similar methods allowed the once-moribund American textile industry to stage a dramatic comeback in the late 1980s. But such success stories are rare in the United States. They will have to become much more common if American industry hopes to compete in world markets in the 1990s and beyond.

But that is only one part of the problem. Modern manufacturing methods will do very little for the U.S. economy if American companies do not adapt in other ways to the astonishing speed of change in the modern business world. By and large, they have not kept up.

Products are like living organisms; they have a clearly defined life cycle from conception to maturity. (For a well-managed company, the senescence and death of a product should be unimportant; obso-

lete products should be a small, expendable part of their business.)
The key steps are "the four I's"—idea, invention, innovation, and
imitation.

The idea is the fundamental science on which many products can
be based. For example, the most fundamental idea behind digital
computers is the mathematical concept of binary notation, the idea
that any number can be represented as a series of zeros and ones.
Computers are machines designed to give practical form to those
theoretical "bits," and then manipulate them in useful ways.

Invention is the step most of us know best, if only from American
folklore: the condensation of a theoretical insight into a working
machine, a prototype that proves the concept can work. These days
the inventor is far more likely to be a team of salaried engineers in
a corporate R&D department than a lone genius working in obscu-
rity, but the process is the same.

Innovation is the creation of a product from the rough prototype—packaging the crude invention in a way that will appeal to
consumers. Henry Ford's first car was not a salable product, and
therefore not an innovation. His first Model T was.

Imitation finally gets the innovation to most of the customers who
want it. At this stage the product is spreading through its market; the
original developer builds new models for customers who want something bigger, faster, fancier, or cheaper than the first marketable
product, while competing companies bring their own versions to
market. Look at the history of photocopiers, personal computers, or
VCRs to see this at work.

It used to be that a product's life cycle was decades long. The first
great flowering of synthetic chemistry occurred in the 1880s; the vast
chemical industry that eventually sprang from it did not begin to
grow up until World War I, and reached maturity only in the 1920s,
some forty years later. At that rate, anybody could play the product-
development game. But the long climb from idea to imitation has
been shrinking steadily. By the 1970s, research scientists were setting up biotechnology companies to exploit genetic discoveries that
they and their colleagues had made barely five years before.

With that kind of competition, a company must be fast on its feet
to profit from research. In just six years, Control Data Corporation
reconfigured one of its factories to make large disk drives, small disk
drives, tape drives, printers, and a variety of other computer add-ons.
As a rule, American companies have not been nearly that flexible.

For better or for worse—mostly for worse—the United States has
specialized in the early stages of the product-development cycle. No

one can boast as many new ideas as American scientists; they have won forty-three Nobel Prizes in physics, twenty-nine in chemistry, and fifty-seven in physiology and medicine, just since the Second World War. And Americans have built a host of major corporations on inventions and innovations, from IBM and AT&T through Polaroid and Xerox to Apple Computer. It's an impressive list.

But ideas and inventions—research and development—are expensive, and innovation can be even more so; for every product that succeeds in the marketplace, several more vanish instantly, taking their creators' investments with them. It is imitation that wins international markets, and American manufacturers have systematically left that step to others.

In too many cases the United States has failed to capitalize on ideas and inventions that could have brought it huge new international markets. In others it has made key breakthroughs, then allowed itself to be outrun by others in the race to exploit them. Examples are easy to find.

As long as thirty years ago, Henry Kolm, of the Massachusetts Institute of Technology, invented the magnetic levitation train. A network of "maglevs" could hypothetically shuttle passengers between American cities at up to 350 miles per hour, using far less energy than air travel. Yet once Kolm's small models had proved that maglev trains could work, the federal government refused him further funding. Today, Japan is the undisputed leader in maglev development. Its first maglev trains should be in regular operation well before the end of the 1990s.

Superconductivity may prove to be an even bigger loss. The boom in superconductor research is, at this writing, only a few years old. It was early 1987 when Dr. Paul Chu, of the University of Houston, announced the discovery of a family of superconductors that functioned at much higher temperatures than other materials known at that time. These superconductive qualities were evident previously only at low temperatures that could be achieved mainly under laboratory conditions, which obviously restricted their usefulness. Superconducting power lines could save utilities billions of dollars per year in electricity that is simply lost in overcoming the resistance of normal metal cables. Superconducting computers would require less power and work more reliably because they would generate less chip-destroying heat, and might even work far faster than today's machines. And, of course, maglevs superconducting magnets would be even more efficient than current train models, and cheaper to build as well. Yet, in just two years, Japanese manufacturers have taken a dramatic lead in superconductor research, filing more than fifteen times as many patents in the field as their American colleagues.

A more ambiguous but potentially more important case is that of high-definition television. By the late 1990s, according to current plans, American viewers will be watching "fortysomething" on wide-screen sets with pictures as bright and detailed as a 35-millimeter photo, and listening to a soundtrack with the clarity of a compact disk. The televisions will be built in Japan, and chances are that they will operate on Japanese standards. Japanese electronics firms are already supplying HDTV studio equipment and prototype sets. The Federal Communications Commission recently established its own basic standards for HDTV, which are incompatible with the best of the Japanese technology, but given the history of consumer electronics, there seems little reason to hope that American manufacturers will (uncharacteristically) find any way to salvage from their overseas competitors an estimated $145 billion worth of market share over the next two decades.

Yet America's worst failing is not one of bad technological judgment or of merely being slow to capitalize on new developments; it is unrelievedly bad *business* judgment. In case after case, American manufacturers have willingly handed key technologies to their competitors, asking little in return. Take just three examples:

The first VCRs were invented by American and British engineers in 1954. American companies spent nearly twenty years reducing those huge, million-dollar prototypes to household appliances. Then they sold rights to the products to Japanese and Korean imitators and allowed themselves to be driven out of the market by competitors they had virtually set up in business. Today, not a single American manufacturer builds VCRs. They almost literally gave away a market worth $15 billion in 1987, and one that is still growing.

In the 1970s, American companies virtually owned the world market for microchips. Instead of pursuing their advantages, they licensed their technology to overseas competition and once more have found their market share shrinking rapidly. In 1988, Japanese chip makers owned about half of the world market, as much as the United States and Europe combined.

The most recent example of this self-defeating policy comes from General Dynamics, whose F-16 is the most successful jet fighter plane ever built. The Japanese want to use it as the basis for a new-generation fighter called the FSX. Japanese manufacturers also want to employ the proprietary technology that makes the F-16 such a capable warplane. So General Dynamics has agreed to license the technology to Mitsubishi Heavy Industries, retaining a small contract to build parts for the Japanese jets. The subcontracting agreement will bring the company about $500 million, roughly 7 percent of the estimated value of the technology Mitsubishi will receive in return. For this, and the promise of some lesser technologies of uncertain value, General Dynamics has agreed to give its competitors its knowledge, which represents one of the main products the company has to sell.

As this is written, President Bush has just approved the F-16 deal while congressional officials study the military and economic effects of giving $7 billion worth of advanced fighter technology to a highly competitive ally with an unfortunate habit of taking over America's high-tech export markets.

Whether the F-16 deal will eventually go through is yet to be decided. If it does not, it will be a welcome exception to a long-standing rule, under which American manufacturers have regularly abandoned profits that might otherwise have helped keep their nation's economy healthy.

REPAIRING AMERICA'S TRADE PROBLEMS

The United States has already made two giant steps toward repairing its trade problems: reducing the exchange value of the dollar and negotiating its free-trade agreement with Canada. But to date these measures have been able only to slow the flow of American dollars to its trading partners, not to stop it entirely. More is clearly needed.

Fortunately, more is in the works. The process began under the Reagan administration with several measures to promote product-level research and development and to fast-track new technology into practical use. These efforts included easing antitrust regulations, passing legislation allowing universities to patent the results of federally funded R&D work, and creating more R&D limited partnerships. All these measures were designed to help American business meet the challenge of Japanese Manhattan Project–type research efforts in such critical fields as artificial intelligence and superconductivity.

The newly renamed National Institute of Science and Technology (formerly the National Bureau of Standards) should help in this undertaking. It was established to promote the transfer of new technology from the laboratory to practical use, especially in such fields as synthetic materials, biotechnology, and factory automation. The new institute will soon take on the role of coordinating similar problems in forty-two states. If all goes well, the effort should lead to a dramatic increase in American manufacturing efficiency in the 1990s.

In 1988, Congress created an extension service on factory automation, similar to the U.S. Agriculture Department's successful extension program. The automation procedure will conduct technical audits for struggling manufacturers, provide help in modernizing factories and manufacturing methods, and help American companies find markets for their goods.

And yet, *more* is still needed. For one thing, the United States may be falling behind in the very area it has long dominated: basic scientific research. Rather than providing extra money for product-level research, recent government efforts have simply reallocated the funds available for all research. Today, basic research accounts for only one-eighth of total American R&D funding, $125 billion in all. Nearly $10 billion comes from federal coffers, while corporations channel only $3 billion toward it. Nonprofit organizations supply the rest. But while other countries have been raising their commitments to research, the United States has barely held even (in real, post-inflation terms). For the first time since World War II, America is spending less than half of the world's research outlays. Japan now spends 25 percent of all research money, twice what it spent ten years ago. If this trend continues, turn-of-the-century America could find that it has lost the one competitive edge that has kept the nation's export trade afloat. Any serious attempt to repair the balance-of-trade problem must begin by making sure that basic research has all the funds it can use.

We dealt with the shrinking supply of scientists and engineers in Chapter 4. For now, let us just repeat the obvious: no one can compete in the world market without top-flight scientists and engineers. Japan has spent nearly twenty years showing us the truth of that. As things are going, the United States will be desperately short of both long before the new century arrives. It must dramatically increase its supply of scientists and engineers, either by finding some way to lure its brightest, most dedicated students into these crucial fields or by importing trained technical personnel from other countries. One way or the other, we believe it will be done.

> # THE SHIFTING ECONOMIC BALANCE
> ## OF THE 1990S

Inevitably, the political changes of 1989 have transformed the economic outlook for the turn of the twenty-first century. Virtually everything we said above holds true, but the picture is now even brighter than we imagined.

One reason is that the European Economic Community has made some decisions that will work to America's benefit. A year ago, it was still possible that the Common Market would build a wall around the Continent, making it difficult for the United States and other nations to benefit from the economic unification of Europe. Instead, they have made it unexpectedly easy for America to participate in the coming boom. In four key areas of high technology—electronics, aerospace, chemicals, and pharmaceuticals—the EEC has adopted standards based closely on those of the United States. What it means is that American multinational corporations can buy firms in Europe, or set up joint ventures with them, produce goods that differ little from those sold at home, and buy goods for export to the U.S. with few legal or regulatory restrictions. Doing business with the Common Market is about to become dramatically easier, not just for the European trading partners, but for the United States as well.

An added boost, of course, is the spread of capitalist democracy throughout Eastern Europe. While not so vast a market as the EEC, the former communist dictatorships represent an enormous pent-up demand for both capital goods and consumer products that the West is in a good position to fill. Though Japan and the other Pacific Rim nations will compete in this arena, the prestige of the United States throughout the Iron Curtain countries places it in a unique position to build profitable trading relationships with the newly freed nations. The opportunities can only grow as the nations of Eastern Europe privatize industries long under state control.

How Americans capitalize on those opportunities will vary from one country to the next. In Hungary, Czechoslovakia, East Germany, and parts of the Soviet Union, we expect to see joint ventures. On the other hand, Bulgaria, Romania, Poland, some other parts of the Soviet Union, and Albania—if and when Albania joins in the transformation—will be "Irelandized"; in these nations, Western corporations will open up their own plants and hire local people to work in them. Which procedure is chosen will depend on the stability of the country and the regulations that govern the retrieval of profits to the United States.

Though the fall of the Iron Curtain will bring overwhelming benefits, not all of its results will be easy to digest. One of the most disruptive economic and political changes will be the gradual expulsion of so-called guest workers from their host nations. This will be especially troublesome in West Germany, where roughly 11 percent of the work force has been imported from Yugoslavia, Italy, Greece, and Turkey, and foreign workers will soon be replaced by East Germans. Not all of these guest workers will be returned to their homelands, because many have married German citizens, but the migration will still be substantial. German industry will suffer, though briefly, from the transition. The nations that have supplied guest workers will be harder hit by the loss of income that workers have long sent home to their families.

Another problem will be the difficulty of getting hard currency in Eastern Europe. Trade agreements that allow Western companies to take their profits in the form of local products will ease the burden on former COMECON nations, but hard—read Western—currency will still be required to pay for much-needed imports. Where factories are directly owned by Western companies, a popular tactic will be to require payment of salaries in hard currency and then sell government-owned houses to the people who live in them, requiring payment over time in Western currency. This will be easiest in the former East Germany, where nicely convertible Deutschmarks will soon be the native medium of exchange.

Changes elsewhere may work to America's benefit as well. In the next decade, Australia will be one of the world's fastest growing economic powers. Where once the island continent earned its living by selling such mineral resources as iron ore, titanium, copper, and bauxite, it has begun to do its own manufacturing. In the 1990s, this trend will grow rapidly, bringing new prosperity to an already prosperous nation.

The United States will benefit directly, as it always does when its trading partners grow more able to buy its products, but it will gain indirectly as well: The largest customer for Australian minerals has long been Japan, whose prosperity depends in part on the availability of cheap raw materials. As Australian manufacturing grows, those resources will stay at home, forcing Japan to pay more for its supplies and raising the cost of its products in world markets. Thus, American products, made largely with native materials, will find it easier to compete for export sales, and the nation's trade balance will shift in its favor.

In addition, the fabled "peace dividend," the money freed from the military budget by the easing of tensions in Europe, will be far larger than the Bush Administration has found it convenient to admit. In the near future, the United States will reduce its troop strength in Europe from some 300,000 men to 50,000 and perhaps fewer. Their return home will bring savings of some $130 billion and will be devoted to four sorely needed causes: Some of it will go to pay the medical bills for the 37 million Americans who have no insurance at all. Some will supply catastrophic health insurance for the elderly. A portion will be used to fund the education and job training programs described in Chapter Four. And the rest will be used to pay down the national debt while making good—more or less—on the promise of "no new taxes."

An added boon will come in the form of the soldiers themselves. Most are both literate and "computer literate," and most are trained in technical skills. No longer needed in Europe, they will return home to take up civilian jobs. The sudden influx of sorely needed workers will ease a growing shortage of technicians that might otherwise begin to stifle American high-tech industries just when vast new opportunities are opening up for them.

With markets and resources, money and personnel, the peaceful revolutions of 1989 have brought the United States far closer to solving the problems that beset its economy and its society. As the next century dawns, America will be a far more prosperous and stable land. Ironically, it will owe much of its new wealth to Mikhail Gorbachev and Lech Walesa, rather than to its own leaders in Washington.

16

WINNERS AND

LOSERS

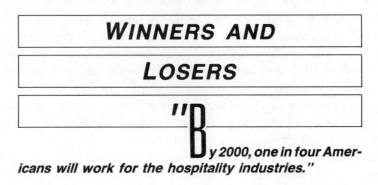

"B *y 2000, one in four Americans will work for the hospitality industries."*

Throughout this volume, we have dealt with factors that will shape the future of American industry. Early chapters forecast the rapid growth of an affluent, leisured middle class, eager for goods and services; the aging of the Baby Boom generation, with its growing need for personal conveniences and medical care; and the repair of the federal budget, which will lift several handicaps from the economy. Our discussions of microelectronics, biotechnology, and medicine amounted to blueprints for explosive growth in those industries. And the last three chapters have focused specifically on factors that will rebuild twentieth-century business to fit the new millennium. Now it is time to look at specific industries that will prosper or perish in the years ahead.

Accounting and Financial Planning. As the nation makes its transition from a product-oriented economy to one based on information and services, and as automation raises manufacturing productivity and cuts the price of goods, Americans will all make far greater use of the services now largely reserved for the well-to-do. Accounting and financial planning are two of the most obvious fields to benefit from the coming growth in disposable income. There was a shortage of accountants even before the Tax Reform Act of 1986, but the bill gave the profession a little-needed boost by making income tax rules so incomprehensible that not even the Internal Revenue Service truly understands them. The continuing growth of small business has added to the demand; every new company needs an accountant to set up and maintain its books. The number of accountants in the United States is growing at a bit less than 3 percent per year. Demand for them is growing at a rate of 6 percent annually, a trend that seems likely to continue far beyond 2000.

Advanced Materials. What could you do with a substance that conducts electricity without resistance or loss? With a ceramic tougher, lighter, and cheaper than aluminum, yet able to withstand higher temperatures? With a reinforced plastic composite stronger than steel? Or with a thin film of diamond that could be deposited on the surface of other materials? Some of the answers engineers have proposed include the magnetically levitated trains mentioned in the preceding chapter, all-ceramic auto engines, and diamond-coated knives that take almost forever to wear out. Superconductors, advanced ceramics and plastic composites, and diamond coatings are all available now.

As an industry, advanced materials are in much the same position that computers were in the early 1950s. Most of them are still research items, obviously promising for the marketplace but not yet there. The companies that finally bring these materials to market clearly will make a staggering profit. But there will be relatively few such firms. On an aggregate basis, the real profits will flow not to the large companies making these basic discoveries in materials science, but to the many smaller firms established to exploit new materials. By the turn of the century, those companies will have started to appear.

Aerospace. Like other defense industries, those segments of the aerospace business that depend on the Pentagon for their prosperity may find their profits unaccustomedly small in the early 1990s, as the military budget shrinks by 2 to 3 percent per year in real terms. That will not last long, however. The old "red menace" argument that we need an ever larger military will no longer wash, so defense planners will stress the need to replace the aging B-52 fleet when they are pushing for a delayed commitment to the $500-million-a-copy Stealth bomber. And Star Warriors will continue to argue that a space-based nuclear defense is the only hope we have—short of total disarmament—that the thaw in Soviet-American relations will never enter a new ice age, bringing a new threat of nuclear war. They will be successful. As soon as the federal deficit falls to acceptable levels, defense spending will begin to inch its way up again. In the long run, though, defense contractors will try hard to reposition themselves as high-tech generalists and take on nonmilitary product lines. By 2000, they will have made considerable progress in diversification.

With commuter airlines growing rapidly and national carriers modernizing their aging fleets, the civilian aerospace industry already knows it will not face major cutbacks in the foreseeable future. At the end of 1988, manufacturers of airliners faced a record backlog of more than one thousand orders, and the assembly lines were booked up through the mid-1990s. Their only worry in this century is that the struggle to keep up with demand will raise their costs and eat into profit margins.

As we near the new century, there is at least a chance that space exploration and development will finally recover some of its early-1960s energy. It will have the Soviet Union to thank. More than twenty years ago, when it became clear that American astronauts would beat Russian cosmonauts to the moon, Soviet space planners announced that their real long-term goal was to put the first men on Mars before the end of the twentieth century. They have worked on that plan steadfastly ever since, and so far as outsiders can tell, they are still on schedule. Even if the late-1950s fear of Soviet militarism is at last dead, the recognition that another country is about to beat us to another planet could so wound American national pride that Washington will at last free NASA from its perennial starvation budgets. A commitment to put Americans back on the moon—this time to stay—could give aerospace manufacturers a dramatic boost in the year 2000.

Automobiles. The American auto industry will be alive and well in 2000, but it will look even less like the Detroit oligopoly of the 1950s than today's global competition does. In 1988, Ford,

Chrysler, and General Motors had their best year ever. Industry profits totaled $11.2 billion, up 18 percent from the year before. But that was their peak, at least for the foreseeable future. After five good years, demand is starting to slip at last.

But that is a relatively small part of the picture. America's native automakers have not quite gone out of the automobile manufacturing business, but they are buying more and more parts from foreign manufacturers and placing their labels on cars built by Mitsubishi, Honda, and others. In short, America's car companies are rapidly turning themselves into wholesale distributors for their overseas competitors. This is one trend that will continue unabated until the turn of the century.

Another is the decision by foreign automakers to build their cars here. Hardly a major manufacturer in the industry has failed to build American plants. Honda has even taken to exporting its American-made cars to Japan. More foreign-owned auto plants will spring up in the United States each year throughout the 1990s. More of the profits from cars "made in the U.S.A." will be sent home to Tokyo and Seoul.

One last trend almost sure to continue is GM's shrinking share of the auto market. It need not happen. In fact, if it weren't for a shortsighted policy, General Motors could still be selling more than 50 percent of the cars made by American manufacturers. But whenever the dollar falls against the yen, driving up the price of Japanese cars, General Motors throws away the chance to regain its lost market share. Instead of keeping its prices down to win more sales, it raises the price of its cars in order to make a few dollars more on each sale. According to one estimate, in the mid-1980s, this strategic blunder, repeated at every opportunity, cost GM roughly $1 billion in sales—roughly one-third of our foreign trade deficit. Expensive as that is, we see no reason to hope that General Motors will soon change its ways.

Education and Vocational Training. Poor as America's schools have become at the task of educating the young, it is clear that they can do better (as we saw in some detail in Chapter 4). But, as in health care, one key to success lies in having enough trained people to handle the job. With school enrollment declining, that will not be a problem in the nation's grammar schools, but there are already shortages of high-school teachers in such fields as mathematics, the sciences, and foreign languages, and college-level engineering instructors are always in short supply. As the Spanish-speaking population continues to grow in the United States, it will be increasingly difficult to meet the demand for bilingual teachers in all fields.

Teachers of job skills will be in high demand as well, owing to the quick obsolescence of professional skills in technical fields, necessitating frequent retraining. According to one estimate, the average engineer today will need retraining every five years throughout his career. Another is the growing recognition that vocational-school training makes more sense than today's college programs, both for many students and for their communities. Florida has one of the nation's best voc-ed programs, and computer companies and other high-tech employers have hung out "help wanted" signs all along Route 4 from Orlando to St. Petersburg. Fortune 500 companies are heavily represented, and hundreds of small start-ups have followed. The reason: Florida's vocational-school system is the best in the country, so companies have no trouble finding well-trained people to get their work done.

In all, it adds up to a major market for the nation's colleges, vocational schools, and consulting firms that specialize in business training. Even today, American companies spend almost $250 billion per year to train their employees—much of it to make up for the deficiencies of public schooling. Roughly one-third of that goes to some 300,000 outside instructors, consultants, and writers of course materials. By 2000, America's corporate training budgets will triple, and companies will need at least 250,000 more instructors. Individuals, too, will demand more professional training as the practice of building second and third careers becomes increasingly common. Companies that can meet this demand will find business training a wide-open field. We expect it to be a major growth area at the turn of the century.

Farming. Michael Dukakis nearly got laughed out of the 1988 presidential campaign when he suggested that American farmers might survive by switching their fields from corn and wheat to Belgian endive. Yet, by 2000, many small farmers will have found that endive and other high-profit specialty crops are their ticket to survival. In the affluent, novelty-hungry America to come, once-rare fruits and vegetables will find a ready market.

That will be one bright spot in a picture that otherwise remains fairly bleak. At the dawn of the twenty-first century, American agriculture will still be pulling itself back together after more than a decade of bad news. By 2000, the trend toward bimodal distribution will have run its course in this crucial industry. Some 500,000 small family farms will have disappeared, along with another 150,000 mid-sized operations. Only the giants will have prospered, and making a profit will not be easy even for them.

By 2000, the cost-cutters in Washington will have eliminated most farm subsidies in the United States. Budget reductions will be only one reason for the long-needed change. In part, it will also be a response to the consolidation of the European Economic Community in 1992. Though individual European governments will resist fiercely, they will first reduce and then eliminate subsidies to their own farmers, a key part of their agreement to remove all trade barriers between the Common Market nations. Once those subsidies are gone, the United States will dismantle its own agricultural welfare system in order to gain access to the vast European market.

How well farmers survive this loss of income will depend largely on the size of their operations. The giants, backed by large capital reserves, will have no trouble, in part because the opening of European markets will bring greater competition for their produce. Neither will most small farms, where agricultural profits are supplemented by outside income. But for some mid-sized American farms, this will be the final blow; after a decade of bare survival, their owners will at last sell off their land and find other employment.

In all, we would rather write about the future of American farming than have to live through it.

Hazardous-Waste Disposal and Pollution Control. If the defects in our educational system are the number-one problem the United States must solve by 2000, environmental pollution will probably run them a close second. Cleaning up toxic waste, asbestos removal, radon testing, and countless other forms of pollution control will be one of the major growth industries at the turn of the century. Asbestos-removal services alone are expected to earn $65 billion by the year 2000. Radon elimination may do nearly as well.

How quickly this field will grow depends too much on politics for anyone to make accurate estimates. Look at the fate of the $1-billion so-called Superfund meant to pay for cleaning up the worst industrial waste sites. For years, the Environmental Protection Administration has had a list of one hundred sites intolerably polluted with toxic chemicals. Yet the Reagan administration had grudgingly paid to clean up only two of the most dangerously polluted dumps. The rest stand as festering sores, many of them near populous city neighborhoods. Our guess is that the administrations of the 1990s will be more willing to do their environmental duty than those of the 1980s have been. In that case, high-tech garbage disposal could be one of the biggest growth industries of the year 2000.

Health Care. It is hard to believe that any industry that already soaks up more than one-tenth of our gross national product could still be growing rapidly. Yet health care is among the most explosive growth segments of the American economy. According to the Bureau of Labor Statistics, fourteen of the thirty-six fastest-growing job categories are in this single industry.

The causes for this astonishing expansion are reasonably obvious. One is the growth of the United States itself. The American population expands by roughly 1.9 million people each year; the more people it has, the more medical personnel are needed to take care of them. The need for medical care grows with age as well, and people over seventy are now the fastest-growing age group in the United States. By 2000, there will be more than 100,000 Americans over the age of one hundred. And research creates new demand for special services with each new diagnostic instrument and therapeutic technique; all those body scanners, artificial limbs, and transplantable organs build their own markets as soon as doctors and their beleaguered patients learn they are available.

By far the fastest-growing segment of the health-care industry will be the ambulatory-care centers and surgicenters, which even now are popping up on street corners and in shopping malls all across the country. The number of ambulatory-care centers in the United States will double in the 1990s, thanks largely to their promise of high cost-efficiency in a country desperate to get its medical bills under control.

Hospitality. For business and pleasure, the prosperity of the mid-1980s made travel an indispensable part of many American lives, and the booming hotel and travel industries show it. This entire business group—hotels, motels, and resorts; restaurants; travel and transportation; and so on—has been one of the most expansive sectors of the economy throughout the 1980s. We believe its best years lie ahead.

The reason is a combination of economics and demographics. With more people working in the information-based services, more of us will be traveling for business. With two-paycheck families becoming even more common, and with more low-income families finding their way into the middle class, more of us will have the money to travel for pleasure. And as America ages, more people will find the freedom that comes when the children grow up and start their own families just as their parents reach their peak earning years. That translates to boom years, both for hotels and resorts and for the airlines that carry people to them.

And, as we noted in Chapter 14, dual-earner households tend to have too little time for shopping and cooking and too much money to deny themselves the comforts of prosperity. Going out to dinner several times a week is quickly being transformed from a luxury to a normal part of middle-class life. Even in small-town America, restaurants will prosper throughout the years to come.

The last decade of this century and the first decade of the next will bring super-growth to a super-industry. By 2000, one in four Americans will work for the hospitality industries.

Law. Inevitably, the legal profession seems destined to grow almost as fast as accounting. But this may say less than we would expect about the future of the world's most litigious society. Attorneys take the blame—rightly so—for many of the ills of American business, and especially for the exorbitant cost of liability insurance throughout American industry. One former presidential economic adviser jokes that he has the solution to America's balance-of-trade deficit: for every hundred cars the United States imports from Japan, the Japanese should be made to take ten American lawyers; their productivity will plummet and their prices soar, while ours improve dramatically. But before 2000, Congress will finally act to limit liability in such industries as medicine and light-aircraft manufacture. With that trough closed to greedy snouts, many of the attorneys and legal assistants who join the field in the 1990s and the early twenty-first century will go into such relatively benign specialties as contract law and real estate.

Personal Services. We can expect the same growth in a host of personal services, taking care of chores that people used to do for themselves. With the increase in two-income families, people no longer have time to clean their houses, walk their dogs during working hours, or even care for their children. What they do have is the money to pay others to handle these necessary tasks. So housekeeping services, public and private day-care centers, lawn-care and home-maintenance services, and a host of similar businesses will flourish in the years to come. So will more-personal services, such as fitness training, diet counseling, and shopping. In general, these industries seem likely to develop along the lines of today's lawn-care services: most will be small, localized concerns, many of them a single individual with just a few clients. But there will also be opportunities for regional franchise operations. By 2000, most areas will have at least one franchised chain of day-care centers and one of home-maintenance services substantial enough to advertise on local television.

Real Estate. As this is written, we are starting to hear that real-estate values are about to hit the skids. In much of the Northeast, the great 1980s boom in home prices seems about over. In Texas, where depressed oil prices sent real-estate values through the floor, home prices have recovered only a little of their losses. Only Southern California is still chalking up price rises of 20 and 30 percent per year. Throughout most of the country, housing starts are off and are expected to decline further. Massive overdevelopment of commercial space has produced office vacancy rates of 25 percent or more in many American cities. And with forecasts that mortgage interest rates will touch 12 percent in 1990 and beyond, developers are starting to wonder where their next million will come from.

We are not likely to hear many stories like these in 2000. The small generation maturing in the 1990s will not require all the small "starter" homes their parents did, but continuing expansion of the middle class will create a steady demand for housing of all sorts late in the decade. The vacation-home market will heat up as Baby Boomers reach their peak earning capacity and seek the luxuries that go with near-wealth. And the proliferation of small, information-based service businesses will go a long way toward soaking up the excess office capacity in our cities.

Though populations will grow fastest in the South and Southwest, one broad region in the North will offer turn-of-the-century profits in real estate: cities along the chilly border between the United States and Canada. The coming boom in trade between America and its neighbor to the North will stimulate local economies in the Bellingham, Washington, area and from International Falls, Minnesota, to Presque Isle, Maine. By 2000, trade figures will be climbing rapidly, and prices for traditional one-family houses will rise with them.

Look for a cheap alternative to today's budget-breaking homes, however. For years, builders in Florida have been turning out comfortable, well-built houses at little more than half the price charged by hammer-in-hand contractors; recently the trend has been spreading to other fast-growing regions. The secret: build the houses in factories, and assemble them on site. By the early 2000s, major high-tech companies will be molding customized houses out of foam-insulated fiberglass on robotic assembly lines. Cast-in-place conduits will carry plumbing, electric lines, and fiberoptic data links, while bathrooms, major appliances, and similar built-ins will be plug-in modules. Thanks to automation, each house will be customized to fit the buyer's taste and made to look like anything from traditional wood construction to stone and mortar; yet they will cost only one-fourth as much as on-site construction. At first the homes will be trucked to the buyer's lot and assembled on site, just as today's modular homes are. Soon they'll be delivered by cargo blimp and bolted to the foundation in one piece. Our bet is that carmakers hit by declining profits will diversify into this fast-growing new business. Cars like the Pontiac Fiero—37 percent fiberglass—have already given them the needed experience in high-volume production of plastic composites.

Steel. After years of decline, the steel industry has been picking up of late. The antiquated smelters that once doomed American producers to low quality and high prices have been replaced by modern, efficient plants. More to the point, the Reagan administration slapped tight import quotas on foreign steelmakers, salvaging the American market for native firms. Without them, foreign companies, particularly Korean smelters, would still have a strong advantage in bulk steels, but, since the dollar dropped against the yen in 1988, even Japanese manufacturers have found it worthwhile to buy high-performance specialty steels here. These factors should all work to the advantage of American steel producers throughout the 1990s. By 2000, this once-moribund industry should again be a strong competitor throughout the world.

Utilities. America's troubled utilities seem set to prosper in the early 1990s. But they may well find themselves struggling through the rest of the decade, and toward the turn of the century, some of the weakest may go under.

For the next few years it should be fairly easy to make a profit by generating electricity. The government forecasts 2.4 percent annual long-term growth in the use of electric power; efficient producers will keep their bottom lines solidly in the black. And if the long, hot summers of recent years turn out to mark a fundamental change in weather patterns, as some climatologists suspect, the nation's air conditioners could lift the growth rate to 5 percent per year.

But there are two devastating problems ahead:

One is the age of our nuclear generating stations. There are now more than one hundred operating reactor units in the United States. All were designed for a useful life of about twenty-five years. More than half have passed that design life; some are rapidly approaching forty years in service. It is time they were retired, and by 2000 it will no longer be possible to ignore the fact. Unfortunately, there is no cheap or easy way to "decommission" a reactor. You can disassemble it and move its radioactive parts to a long-term containment facility—at least you could if the United States *had* a long-term containment facility; you can shut it down and post guards around it to make sure curious neighbors do not accidentally expose themselves to radiation; or you can fill it full of concrete and walk away, secure in the knowledge that any harmful materials will stay put for the next few thousand years. Estimates of the long-term cost of all these options range from $100 million up for a full-sized power reactor. This huge expense will materialize just as utilities must invest in a new generation of smaller, safer reactors to meet the growing demand for power. So much for the bottom line.

The other problem is acid rain. Though many power-company officials would like to deny it, there is no longer any doubt that coal-burning electric plants in the Midwest are killing the lakes and streams of southern Canada, New York State, and much of New England. The Reagan administration "handled" the problem by perpetually claiming that it needed more study. After candidate Bush's campaign promises to defend the environment, President Bush's administration is not likely to take the same way out. Still, we do not expect dramatic action on this issue until about 1997, when his successor will take office. At that point, power companies could face huge bills for antipollution equipment and low-sulfur fuel, and liberal legislators are not likely to allow the entire bill to be passed on to consumers. Profits will tumble as a result.

EIGHT SUPER-GROWTH MARKETS

Cellular Telephones. Today's million-phone market will expand to 10 million by the mid-1990s and keep growing thereafter. By 1995, cellular telephones will be standard equipment in luxury cars, common options in most other models.

Fax Machines. There were 1.3 million fax machines in use at the end of 1988. By 2000, manufacturers will sell 20 million to 25 million more.

High-definition TV. This will be a $13-billion market (including Hi-D VCRs) by the turn of the century, $150 billion by 2008. Alas, most of the manufacturing profit will go to the Far East.

Home Satellite Dishes. Drive through some rural areas, and it seems that almost every home in the country must already have a satellite dish. In fact, there are only 2.4 million of the metal mushrooms installed. Nearly four times that many more will be sold by 1993. But by 2000, this market will be saturated.

Generic Drugs. As patents on expensive brand-name drugs expire in the 1990s, less costly generic equivalents will replace them. Generic sales, on the order of $250 million today, will soar to $25 billion by 1997. Three years later they will account for 25 percent of the drug market.

Laptop Computers. There were 1.2 million in use at the end of 1988. In only four years, that number will climb to 8 million. After flat color screens become available, super-portable computers will begin to replace desktop PCs for all but the most high-powered applications. By the turn of the century, the process should be nearly complete.

Storefront Hospitals. Outpatient facilities—walk-in clinics, surgicenters, and emergicenters—will become a $2.5-billion industry by 1990, up from virtual nonexistence a decade earlier. We see nothing to slow their growth in this century.

No-calorie Food Products. Procter & Gamble's fat substitute, Olestra, will be a $1-billion product by the mid-1990s, while NutraSweet's left-handed sugars—as sweet as natural sugar, but indigestible—marketed under the name Simplesse, will do almost as well.

THE GREAT JOB

SHAKEOUT

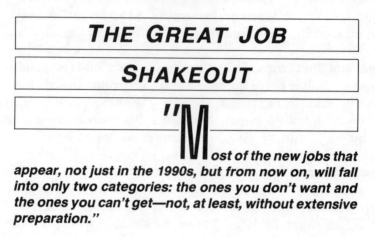

"**M**ost of the new jobs that appear, not just in the 1990s, but from now on, will fall into only two categories: the ones you don't want and the ones you can't get—not, at least, without extensive preparation.**"**

The 1890s were known as the Mauve Decade. For the 1990s, the color is pink, as in "pink slip." By the year 2000, half of the manufacturing jobs in the United States will have disappeared, as will many of the remaining farm jobs and two-thirds of the openings for middle-level executives. The Great Job Shakeout, described in our previous book, is at hand.

The good news for turn-of-the-century job-hunters is that new jobs will appear ever faster throughout the 1990s. An estimated 21 million jobs will appear in the next decade, even as the old ones vanish. By the turn of the century, the transformation will be complete; obsolete jobs will be gone, and new jobs—whole new occupations— will be created faster than ever before. America at the turn of the century will be stronger and more prosperous for the changes.

But for many of us, getting there will be a struggle. Perhaps we should face the problems before looking at the benefits to come.

The bad news is the price Americans must pay for those new jobs at the turn of the century. Few of the people who find themselves unemployed in the chaos of the 1990s will ever get another job doing the work they know. In the past, companies failed, taking specific jobs with them. This time, whole job categories will disappear. Nothing like the change to come has been seen since the rise of the automobile wiped out the market for draymen and buggy-whip makers early in this century. But this time the impact will be felt in all areas of industry. Many of the remaining auto manufacturing jobs will go as the assembly lines become still more automated. In printing, typesetters and compositors are almost gone already. What is left of America's textile, clothing, and shoe industries will lose on the order of 500,000 jobs. Even gas-station attendants are being displaced by computerized pump-it-yourself systems. In short, if it can be done by a machine, it soon will be.

Most of the new jobs that appear, not just in the 1990s but from now on, will fall into only two categories: the ones you don't want and the ones you can't get—not, at least, without extensive preparation. There will be plenty of bottom-end service jobs flipping burgers at the local fast-food restaurants. And thousands of well-paid professional openings will go begging for people with the good basic education and months or years of specialized training required to fill them. Missing will be all those earn-while-you-learn jobs in manufacturing and trades that used to give high-school grads, and even the occasional dropout, a route into the middle class.

For a vision of what the 1990s will be like for those caught unprepared, look at the Rust Belt assembly-line workers who lost their jobs during the early 1980s. It was a purge with few precedents in American experience. Between 1979 and 1985, Caterpillar, the Peoria-based heavy-equipment manufacturer, slashed its workforce from 89,000 to 53,000 and closed one-third of its factories. Since 1982 the entire steel industry has used the same ax to cut its operating expenses by 35 percent and raise labor productivity by 38 percent. USX (the old United States Steel), for example, closed seven of its dozen mills, cutting its workforce from 75,000 steelmakers to only twenty thousand. Salaried employees were hit harder than hourly workers. Going into the reduction, USX employed thirty thousand executives, plant foremen, and the like; when it was all over, only five thousand were left. Similar stories were repeated throughout manufacturing.

Today, the worst of that contraction is over. Automation and management reforms have cut production costs. The dollar has come down, the yen has risen sharply, and American manufacturers are winning more foreign sales than at any time in the 1980s. Unemployment is down, and new jobs are appearing. Indiana suffered an unemployment rate of 12.6 percent in the worst days of 1982, and things were far worse in some cities; today the rate statewide is only 4.8 percent. Ohio's rate has dropped from 12.5 percent to 5.9 percent in the same six years. And manufacturing employment is climbing throughout the region at between 3 percent and 5 percent per year, thanks largely to the growth of American exports since the fall of the dollar on exchange markets following the October 1987 stock-market crash.

But those encouraging figures mask less cheerful realities. One reason the Rust Belt states have improved their employment rates is that their populations are growing so slowly. In 1970, the eighteen states from Maryland to Maine, from New York to Illinois, were home to just over 100 million people; sixteen years later the region's population had risen only to 104 million. The South and West grew from 106.2 million to 137 million in the same period. There is little prospect that this trend will soon end. By 2000, the population of the South and West will reach 157 million; only 110 million people will live in the Rust Belt—and that includes prosperous New England, which should grow by nearly 10 percent in the 1990s. In the states that were hit hardest by the manufacturing crunch, the population will grow by less than 2.5 percent. All this makes a small improvement in employment look much better than it is. In fact, the Northeast and Midwest have lost 2 million manufacturing jobs since 1979, most of them in the core Rust Belt states.

The renaissance in manufacturing has done little good for the workers fired during the bad years. Even today, far fewer than one in three has ever been invited back to the plant. One-third eventually found work in local fast-food franchises and other bottom-of-the-market industries, where they earn perhaps half as much as they did at their old factory jobs. The remainder either fled to sunnier economic climates or have never worked again.

Machines have taken their place. Even with the help of the new, low-profile dollar, American manufacturers can't make it in the world market if they continue to build their products by hand. True, the competition in Japan, Taiwan, and Korea benefits from low employment costs; workers overseas are willing to accept salaries far lower than Americans are used to. But their real advantage today is in their factories—the newest, most automated equipment technology has to offer. Computer-aided design and manufacturing—computer-integrated manufacturing—lets them turn out better products on tighter schedules, and at much lower prices. American companies that want to survive in the world market have had to follow their lead. And today the world market is the only market there is.

Automation is not limited to the assembly lines. In the executive suites, traditional management structures are being replaced by information flow. Using standard management techniques, one executive can oversee about six workers; computer-literate executives can coordinate twenty or more. As firms become information-based, they stop hiring people with generalized management skills and sign on specialists to work in task-focused teams. In the past, a company that wanted to set up a new automated production line would probably have delegated people from all the departments involved: production, computing, procurement, and so on. Each would have reported back to his superiors, they to their bosses, and so on up the line. Today the team is more likely to act on its own, reporting directly to top management. Information flows freely from front-line workers to the ultimate decision makers.

As a result, large, top-heavy companies have been eliminating whole tiers of middle managers and salaried office personnel. AT&T is transferring some three thousand administrative workers into more productive positions. Xerox has already cut more than six thousand white-collar workers. Honeywell fired four thousand in 1986 alone. Du Pont has cut its white-collar payroll by 15 percent, Mobil by 17 percent. IBM has shifted about seventeen thousand administrators and staff workers into sales, programming, and similar money-making areas. Ford has, on aggregate, fired middle managers in all but one quarter for the last three years. And Chrysler is eliminating one-fifth of its white-collar positions.

This is virtually unavoidable, since, in the competitive global economy, divisions and departments that must wait for information to percolate up through corporate layers or for strategic decisions to filter down from an oligarchy of managers will be left in the dust. But it is hard on executives who once thought their careers were secure.

In the 1980s an estimated 4 million executives lost their jobs as a result of this kind of corporate restructuring; some put the figure much higher. "Middle managers have become insecure, and they feel unbelievably hurt," comments management expert Peter Drucker. "They feel like slaves on an auction block."

We talked about bimodal distribution in Chapter 14. Like mid-sized companies, middle managers have also been losing out to merger mania. Mergers are very cost-effective, because the high-salaried workers—upper and middle management—of the acquired company are usually replaced with the top management of the acquiring company. (The lower-end workers of the acquired company—the ones doing the actual work—usually get to keep their jobs.) Alternatively, many companies require both sets of managers and workers to reapply for jobs in the combined organization, subjecting both groups to the threat of joblessness. In either case, where once there were two accounting, purchasing, and planning departments, only one is left; if product lines are similar enough, sales staffs may be combined as well. A major purge is all but inevitable.

Unfortunately, it is the mid-sized companies that employ the most people to get a given amount of work done. Smaller companies tend to be more efficient, their employees more productive, than in mid-sized firms. So closing a corporation with $100 million in annual sales is likely to put more people on the streets than closing, say, ten $10-million concerns. The giants can afford to automate, and need still fewer people to get a given job done.

Farms are one good example. Small family farms can seldom afford to hire much in the way of help, and they don't really need it. So when a small farm dies, chances are that only the immediate family has to go looking for work; and today one or two members almost surely have outside jobs to cushion the blow. The giant agribusinesses benefit from automation, wholesale mechanization, and the ability to manage their farms with a single, integrated corporate staff. This keeps the workforce smaller than it would be if huge farms merely scaled up the methods of small ones. It is the mid-sized farms that require the most help. They need more than a single family's hands to bring in the crop, yet do not rake in enough profits to pay for the high-tech tools of the corporate empires. So when a mid-sized farm gets plowed under, loss of jobs is at its worst. The same principle applies to companies in all types of business.

By 2000, the mid-sized companies will either have vanished or grown into giants in their own right; automation will continue to replace human managers for perhaps another decade after that. According to Peter Drucker, the typical large business in 2010 will have fewer than half as many levels of management as do similar firms today, and only one-third as many managers. Throughout the next twenty years, this flattening of the corporate pyramid will leave many mid-level executives looking for jobs or going back to school to learn more marketable skills.

As the trend to bimodal distribution nears completion, technology will still be in the early stages of its revolution. And if technology has eliminated millions of jobs once performed by well-paid human beings, it has also created employment. By the turn of the century, it will be the single greatest source of new jobs in America. For all the glamour of computers, aerospace, and the other high-tech industries, they will not all be good jobs, and they will not all be well paid. Above all, they will not be permanent. Yet for most of us, high-tech training will be the most certain route to a good career.

Technology produces two kinds of jobs. Both will be available in abundance by the year 2000.

One kind, one we seldom think about, is what writer Barbara Garson refers to as the "electronic sweatshop." In these dismal jobs, computers take the need for intelligence and creativity out of work and closely monitor how quickly and how well the unavoidable human employees churn out their labor. Think here of the unskilled employees on the cash registers—really computer terminals tied into the restaurant's data-processing equipment—at McDonald's; they can be trained for their jobs in half an hour and replaced as quickly. Think also of the operators on the reservation desks at any major airline. They spend their days parroting rigidly formularized inquiries, punching up information on their terminals, and recording any reservations in the thirteen seconds allowed them between calls. And they are monitored constantly, both by their computers, to see that they don't waste any time, and by human supervisors, who eavesdrop on their calls to make sure their salesmanship is up to the company's standards.

Not everyone who now works in an electronic sweatshop started in one. Many found challenging, satisfying professions and then hung on while their jobs changed around them. Garson cites as an example the social workers in Massachusetts and nearly two dozen other states. Armed with idealism and college degrees in sociology, they started their careers by visiting clients, counseling teens headed for trouble, and guiding people through the maze of the welfare system to get the help they needed. Today, many state welfare departments have been computerized, and former social workers— now known, at least in Massachusetts, as Financial Assistance Workers—find themselves locked into their offices, pushing papers a clerk could handle and struggling to meet production quotas more rigid than on any assembly line. The same trend is at work in every business where computerized systems can eliminate human judgment.

In 2000, sweatshop jobs will be available for anyone desperate enough to tolerate them. They will pay a little bit better than they do today, because the entry-level workforce has begun to shrink, and it will be harder for employers to fill their openings. But they will still be as tedious, pressured, and grim as in any basement factory where undocumented aliens turn out cheap clothes at half the minimum wage. And they will be the only taste of technology available to anyone without both a good basic education and vocational training. For those who are both determined enough and lucky enough to find a way out, sweatshop jobs will be only a way to get by while learning the skills needed for better work. For the unlucky ones, life in the twenty-first century will turn out to be a cycle of soul-destroying labor punctuated by brief searches for a new job when the last one has grown intolerable.

Back to the good news:

The other kind of high-tech job calls for skilled professionals—scientists and engineers to develop new products and services based on computers, genetics, advanced materials, and the like; technicians to make the products and deliver the services; repairmen to keep all the complex hardware working; and writers and teachers to supply the manuals and train workers and consumers to make and use the wonders of technology. These jobs provide the challenge and sense of accomplishment needed to keep people interested through a long career. And they pay very well.

Good jobs will be as easy to find as bad ones, for those who can qualify. Much of the credit goes to America's research-and-development community. American scientists do more and better research than anyone else in the world; no fewer than eighty Americans won the Nobel Prize in physics, chemistry, and physiology and medicine between 1965 and 1987, out of 143 science prizes awarded. Only four Japanese scientists won Nobels during the period; one of them carried out his work at MIT. And American research is not all theoretical. The first practical videotape recorder was invented by the hardware division of Bing Crosby Associates! It was Americans, too, who after nearly twenty years of work, shrank the bulky, $10,000 device to videocassette recorders cheap enough for home use.

As 2000 nears, it no longer takes two decades to turn a proof-of-concept prototype into a job-creating product. The entire development cycle is going a lot faster than it once did. It used to be that forty years went by before industrialists turned their discoveries into products and got them to market in quantity. Today the time is down to five years and still shrinking. The first microchips had been around for nearly a decade when the two Steves—Jobs and Wozniak—brought their first Apple computer to market. When Intel's more powerful 80286 chip was introduced, the first computers built around it took nearly four years to reach the customer. The first 80386 machines took little more than a year to reach the market once the chips became available. And the next generation of personal computer, based on the 80486 microprocessor, is expected to enter the stores within weeks after the chip reaches production. New jobs built around new products and services will appear ever faster as the new century approaches; some of the jobs that open up in the year 2000 will grow out of basic research that has not yet been imagined, much less carried out.

Many of them will be found in small, fast-growing firms. In the last half-decade, new businesses have been starting up at a record rate of 100,000 per year. An estimated 95 percent of the new jobs created since 1982 have appeared in half a million or so of these entrepreneurial companies. Bimodal distribution will bring even more opportunities on the small end of the corporate scale.

But the giants will be growing rapidly as well. By the turn of the century, corporate America will have trimmed all the fat it can find. Virtually every function that can be automated will have been. Megacompanies that want to continue growing will have to recruit and train new people to do the work that only humans can handle.

From now on, nearly all the jobs created in America will appear in service industries; by 2000, nearly 90 percent of American workers—more than 120 million—will hold jobs in the service sector. This is not necessarily bad. Though many service jobs fall into the minimum-wage, dead-end category, many others offer far better prospects. For several years the clothing and textile industries in and around New York City have been creating thousands of new jobs in importing and in wholesale and retail sales; according to one estimate, they pay roughly twice as well as the manufacturing jobs lost from the region during the same period. Fifteen of the two dozen fastest-growing jobs today offer average starting salaries of $15,000 or more per year; thirteen pay $25,000 or better at mid-career, and three average $50,000 and up. All are service jobs. People who can retrain for positions in such high-tech, largely service-oriented industries as computers and data processing, tele-communications, and health care will find that a wide variety of openings are going begging for someone qualified to fill them. In the end, they may well earn more at their new service jobs than they did in the blue-collar careers they once counted on for a good living.

Where will the best jobs appear? Obviously the fastest job creation will occur in the rapidly growing industries we looked at in the preceding chapter: computers and data processing, telecommunications, and health care. Other bright spots in tomorrow's employment market include biotechnology, advanced materials, hazardous-waste disposal and pollution control, education and vocational training, and the thousands of personal and business services demanded by an aging and increasingly affluent society.

Let's look at some specific jobs in greater detail:

Computer Console and Equipment Operators. This trade is a step above typing on an old manual typewriter, but the basic skill required is the same, and the demand is stronger than in almost any other segment of the computer job market. After all, someone has to get all that data into the computers and back out. These are strictly entry-level jobs, the least demanding and least well paid in the computer industry. But with more than 500,000 openings available in the next decade, they represent the quickest, easiest way to break into a field that offers many other opportunities.

Computer Programmers. Look into the help-wanted pages of almost any metropolitan newspaper today, and one of the largest sections will be for computer programmers. They will grow larger as the years pass. More than 250,000 programmers will be needed by 2000. At today's rates, programmers' salaries start at around $20,000 per year. Mid-career salaries are about twice that, on average, and people with good experience in desirable specialties are regularly earning $70,000 or more, with a few reaching six figures. But it takes at least two years of training to break in.

Computer Service Technicians. With computers rapidly becoming almost as common as people, someone has to keep all the hardware working. Nearly 100,000 new openings will appear in this job category by 2000. Salaries for computer service technicians now begin at about $18,000 and still top out at less than $30,000 unless the worker can make the transition to management. We expect these figures to climb faster than the inflation rate for the remainder of the century.

Computer Systems Analysts. Systems analysts are the planners of the computer software world, figuring out just what new software should do, how it must operate, and how it must fit in with existing systems. It is still possible for programmers to work their way up into systems-analyst positions, but someone deliberately entering this profession will need more technical education than programmers start with; most have a college degree in computer science, and many have advanced training. In return, pay scales start at more than $25,000, and mid-career salaries of $50,000 are not uncommon; they will grow faster than salaries of less-skilled computer professionals. Some 260,000 will be needed in the next twelve years.

Telecommunications Workers. By the turn of the century, online database providers and other teletext services will hire nearly 300,000 people. Telemarketers will employ up to 400,000 more, with most openings coming near the turn of the century. Job-hunters in 2000 will find these industries a ready source of opportunity for people with a wide range of skill levels.

Hazardous-Waste Technicians. These are the hardy souls who clean up land, air, and water that the rest of us find too dangerous to tolerate. Unless the Bush administration defaults completely on its promised concern for the environment, at least 400,000 hazardous-waste technicians will be needed by the end of the next decade; if the government's Superfund program ever goes into practical operation, that could climb to well over 1 million. Training for these positions is both necessary and, at the moment, nearly impossible to find. Look for programs that turn out certified industrial hygienists, and then try to locate courses in the specialties that most interest you. Salaries still begin at less than $20,000 per year and seldom top $30,000 unless you work your way into a management position. They should rise sharply when the national cleanup gets properly under way. We expect it to happen at last in the 1990s.

Teachers. After a decade of shrinking school enrollments, communities across the country are again finding themselves short of teachers, particularly in such fields as mathematics, engineering, and the sciences, and in such languages as Japanese and Russian. And the continuing growth of the Spanish-speaking population in this country will create demand for bilingual teachers, particularly in the grammar and high schools of the South and West, and in some Northern inner cities. Starting salaries in many communities remain low, so new teachers with families to support will find it hard to get by. This should pass as the decade progresses and the dearth of specialized educators makes itself felt.

Accountants. For precise, detail-oriented people, there is no better job than accounting. In 1985 and 1986 the nation added some 1,500 new workers with college degrees in accounting, bringing the total supply to nearly sixty thousand. More than 3,600 new accountants were needed. And the proliferation of small businesses in the last five years has added still more demand for people capable of setting up and maintaining their corporate books. As a result, major accounting firms now plan to increase their hiring for entry-level employees by 15 percent. By 2000, there will be more than 1 million accountants tapping their calculators in the United States.

Hotel Managers and Travel Agents. Both of these jobs will flourish amid the rapid growth of personal and business travel. For travel agents, chances for advancement are relatively limited, but high demand makes this one of the easier industries to enter, and income is limited only by your skill and willingness to work.

Career hotel workers may have more to look forward to. Even today, Cornell University's School of Hotel Administration reports that graduates with a bachelor's degree leave school with four or five job offers carrying starting salaries of $20,000 or more. In major chains, advancement is rapid, even for those without a degree. By tradition, most hotel chains still promote from inside, and good workers often rise from small hotels to large ones, from tiny wages to solidly middle-class salaries, and even into management positions. According to the Bureau of Labor Statistics, openings for hotel desk clerks will grow by 43 percent from 1986 to 2000. We would put the demand considerably higher.

Legal Assistants. God knows, there are plenty of lawyers in the United States. But after all, they are expensive to hire, and there are many legal chores that do not require four years of law school. That is where legal assistants, or paralegals, come in. Become a paralegal, and you can find yourself performing real-estate title searches, drafting corporate benefit plans, preparing cases for court, and even working with clients. According to the Bureau of Labor Statistics, this will be the single fastest-growing job category in the nation, at least through 1995. There were 61,000 legal assistants in 1986, up by 15 percent in two years. By 2000, legal assistants will number at least 125,000.

Personal Service. As two-paycheck families continue to dominate the American economy, more and more people are finding they lack the time to keep house, mow the lawn, or even pick up the groceries. What they do have is the money to pay someone else to handle these chores. In the years to come, a growing number of small, local businesses will be formed to service this market. They will provide a steady demand for relatively unskilled workers. Few of us will want to make a lifetime career of personal-service jobs like these. Pay scales will be low, chances for advancement slim to nonexistent, and few such occupations are likely to offer much in the way of job satisfaction. But they will be available to all who need work in the year 2000.

Nurses. At the end of 1987 there were roughly 1.4 million registered nurses in the United States, and 631,000 licensed practical nurses. Just two years from now, according to U.S. Department of Health and Human Services estimates, there will be a shortage of nearly 400,000 registered nurses. By 2000, 2 million RNs and nearly 870,000 LPNs in hospitals, corporate medical offices, neighborhood clinics, nursing homes, and health maintenance organizations will be needed—and even more will be self-employed. Though average salaries are relatively modest nationwide, in major cities RNs already can earn $40,000 per year, LPNs more than $25,000. Those salaries will grow by 50 percent in the next decade.

Geriatric Social Workers. The so-called "old old," people over age eighty-five, now make up the fastest-growing segment of the American population. And as their numbers grow, so do their needs. By the turn of the century, an estimated 700,000 trained people will be required to care for the nation's aging population. At that, the demand for geriatric social workers will only have begun to grow. The giant Baby Boom generation will not even start to reach retirement age until 2010. Look for rapid growth in this field at least through the year 2025.

Biomedical Engineers and Technicians. Someone has to turn new medical techniques discovered in the laboratory into practical hardware ready for clinical use. That is the task of biomedical engineers. An estimated fifty thousand of them will be required in the coming decade—vastly more than the projected supply. Another ninety thousand technicians will find jobs maintaining and repairing the machines the engineers design.

Paramedics and Emergency Medical Technicians. Fifteen years ago, most paramedics had trained as battlefield medics in Vietnam. Today that supply of experienced personnel has long since found its way into civilian health care, and new paramedics receive much the same premed courses as doctors-to-be. The shortage of doctors and nurses in some rural areas and the continuing development of big-city emergency medical services have added to the demand for paramedics. By the end of this century, there will be jobs for some 400,000 of these journeyman primary-care providers.

HELP-WANTEDS FROM THE YEAR 2000

★   **CORPORATE ETHICIST**   ★

Prestigious Fortune 500 employer needs experienced corporate ethicist with Ph.D. in philosophy or history and five years' practice in medical or technological field. Mid-$70s.

★   **ECOLOGICAL RESTORATION SPECIALIST**   ★

Leading trout–stream-restoration consultants require experienced ecological restorer for two-year project in Idaho. Limnology degree helpful, chalk stream experience a must. State salary requirements.

★   **GAL/GUY FRIDAY**   ★

For small, growing database marketer. Familiarity with financial service industry. Experience in voicewriter editing, OCR scanners, computer communications. Type 65wpm. Low-$30s.

★   **GENETICIST**   ★

Require Ph.D. and three years' experience in DNA synthesis for custom yeast cultures. Pharmaceuticals background preferred. State salary.

★   **RADON TECHNICIANS**   ★

Have five openings for radon technicians. Home and small-factory experience preferred, but will train. To $35K.

★   **SECURITY GUARDS**   ★

Find a career in the fast-growing personal security industry. American Safety Industries has openings for up to two hundred physically fit men and women with pristine, non-criminal backgrounds throughout the eastern United States. $32K–$35K.

**EDUCATION FOR
TOMORROW'S JOBS**

SCHOOLING REQUIRED	TODAY'S JOBS	NEW JOBS
8 years or less	6%	4%
Some high school	12	10
High school diploma	40	35
Some college	20	22
College or advanced degree	22	30

Data from the Hudson Institute.

THE FASTEST-GROWING JOBS, 1985–95

JOB TITLE	PERCENT GROWTH 1985–95	NUMBER NEEDED (in Thousands)	1995 STARTING SALARY (in Thousands)	1995 MEDIAN SALARY (in Thousands)
Paralegal assistant	98%	–	$10	$18
Computer programmer	72	258	22	40
Computer systems analyst	69	260	29	51
Medical assistant	62	–	8	16
Computer service technician	56	93	21	32
Electrical or electronics engineer	53	367	25	38
Actuary	51	–	15	34
Electrical or electronics engineering technician	50	359	14	16
Computer console and equipment operator	46	558	11	21
Health service administrator	44	220	22	57
Travel agent	44	52	11	21
Physical therapist	42	34	19	31
Physician's assistant	40	10	21	25
Podiatrist	39	12	25	57
Financial services sales	39	–	–	–

THE FASTEST-GROWING JOBS, 1985–95 (*continued*)

JOB TITLE	PERCENT GROWTH 1985–95	NUMBER NEEDED (in Thousands)	1995 STARTING SALARY (in Thousands)	1995 MEDIAN SALARY (in Thousands)
Engineer	36	–	–	–
Attorney	36	487	24	68
Accountant or auditor	35%	1047	$19	$29
Correctional institution officer	35	103	14	29
Mechanical engineer	34	237	23	32
Registered nurse	33	1302	16	23
Public relations	32	131	14	36
Computerized-tool programmer	32	200	14	23
Occupational therapist	31	–	17	25
Medical records technician	31	20	14	26

Data from the Bureau of Labor Statistics and Forecasting International.

24 LARGEST JOB CATEGORIES

JOB TITLE	NUMBER NEEDED 1985–95	1995 STARTING SALARY (in Thousands)	1995 MEDIAN SALARY (in Thousands)
Food service worker (commercial cook)	4436	$ 8	$23
Secretary or stenographer	3490	10	14
Sales worker, retail	3300	8	16
Sales clerk, retail	2435	7	16
Truckdriver	2275	19	31
Bookkeeper	1904	11	19
Computer software writer, general	1830	23	34
Housing rehabilitation technician	1750	16	25
Waiter or waitress	1700	8	14
Assembler	1670	9	23
Teacher, elementary school	1600	19	–
Cashier	1554	14	19
Energy conservation technician	1500	15	30
Hazardous-waste-disposal technician	1500	17	32
Farmer or farm manager	1485	–	–
Registered nurse	1302	16	23
Blue-collar-worker supervisor	1300	18	22
Teacher, secondary school	1243	21	–
Farmworker or supervisor	1218	15	25
Auto mechanic	1197	10	16
Carpenter	1185	18	32
Accountant	1047	19	29
Typist	1023	9	14
Sales representative, wholesale	1001	21	38

Data from the Bureau of Labor Statistics and Forecasting International.

MEDIAN SALARIES IN THE YEAR 2000

JOB	1988 (in Thousands)	2000 (in Thousands)
Accountant	$30	$48.3
Biomedical engineer	33.6	54.5
Carpenter	33.6	54
Cashier	20.4	33
City manager	58.8	95.2
Collection clerk	15.6	25.2
Computer programmer	32.4	52.5
Correctional officer	30	48
Economist	30	49
Electronic mail operations specialist	19.2	31
Farmworker	26.4	35
Firefighter	24	38.9
Genetic engineer	45.6	73.8
Housing rehabilitation technician	28.8	46.6
Legal secretary	21.6	34.9
Medical laboratory technologist	25.2	40.8
Office machine servicer	18	29
Registered nurse	24	38.8
Robot technician	26.4	42.8
Sales clerk, retail	16.8	27.2
Security guard	21.6	35
Social worker	31.2	50.5
Teacher, high school	28.5	49
Teletext computer specialist	48	77
Vocational counselor	31.2	50.5

Data from the Bureau of Labor Statistics and Forecasting International.

P ART V

Values at the
Turn of the Century

A NEW ORDER

COMES OF AGE

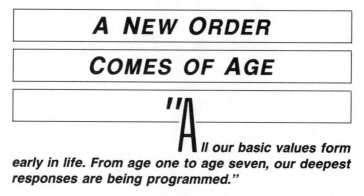

"**A**ll our basic values form
*early in life. From age one to age seven, our deepest
responses are being programmed."*

—Gloria Wasserman

As the year 2000 approaches, the United States is going through yet
another transfer of power from one generation to the next. In past
centuries, this was an almost imperceptible process, adolescents turning into young adults, putting away childish things, accepting adult
roles, until by the time they inherited their parents' authority, they
had so thoroughly adopted their parents' values that the succession
made few lasting changes in society. In the twentieth century, the
differences between generations have been very real, though often
obscured by war and technology. By the turn of the century, the
differences between the generations of the 1930s and 1940s and
those born after World War II will radically alter the basis of American society.

"You are when you were born," comments University of Colorado sociologist Morris Massey. If you know anyone who grew up during the Great Depression, you probably have seen the proof firsthand. In the poverty of the early 1930s, wasting hard-earned food was a sin barely more acceptable than armed robbery, and perhaps harder to understand or forgive. Wasting money, when any could be found, was almost beyond thinking. The scars of those grim times remain with all whose habits were formed during the prewar years. It is almost impossible for anyone of that Depression era not to clean his plate; to be seen wasting food, to *throw food away,* is unendurably embarrassing. No matter how wealthy this generation has become in the decades since then, it will always fly coach, never first class—if it flies at all.

Contrast this with the Baby Boomers—the nation's leaders at the turn of the century. This generation grew up amid plenty, and their values show it. They shop in designer boutiques, eat in the best restaurants, vacation in the trendiest resorts. The best is none too good for them, whether they can afford it or not. One typical Baby Boom woman buys cheap shoes, eats at McDonald's, and reads used magazines in order to pay for her turbo Porsche!

VALUE PROGRAMMING

Values like these—all our basic values—form early in life. From age one to age seven, our deepest responses are being programmed. From cradle to sandbox to sandlot, we watch the adults around us and absorb everything they do—not just their actions, but the values they imply. From nine to thirteen, we are modeling. Adolescents build their future characters around the behavior of their heroes—if there are any available; it's not as easy for today's sophisticated children as it was in the days of Amelia Earhart and Lucky Lindy, or in the days of Joe Dimaggio. From age thirteen to nineteen years old, heroes are out, peers are in. It is during these years that we finally learn to deal with others. For most of us, that pretty well completes the process.

By the age of ten, 90 percent of our personality has been formed; by the age of twenty, 95 percent of our values are all but unalterable. We may change our haircuts or our taste in clothes, but our basic personalities remain the same until the day we die—unless we go through some experience with searing emotional impact. Getting fired from a job may change the way we behave at our next, just as an electric shock tells a laboratory rat which part of a maze is off limits, but the effect probably would not carry over into other parts of our lives. The emotional trauma of spending a year in Vietnam could transform someone's entire life; for thousands of American men, it did.

For some of us, there is one last step that shapes us: professional training. As people, we are when we were born, but as doctors, scientists, and engineers, our careers are rigidly shaped by when we graduate. Professionals may go back to school for regular retraining, learn to use new equipment and new techniques, but their basic thought processes remain locked firmly in the habits developed during their graduate work. Difficult as it is to imagine, fifteen years after programmable calculators appeared and more than a decade since the birth of the personal-computer age, some veteran engineers still cling to their ancient slide rules for most day-to-day work. "No one ever really accepts a new theory," one scientist commented. "It's just that the older generation dies off, and people who grew up with the idea take over."

CATEGORIES

Morris Massey divides the American population into several age groups, each with characteristic habits and values. They correspond very closely to the tradition-directed, outer-directed, and inner-directed people defined by David Riesman in his classic study, *The Lonely Crowd.*

Massey classifies people now in their fifties and sixties as "Traditionalists." Shaped by early memories of the Great Depression and the Second World War, they put a premium on institutional leadership and a strong social order. They feel a puritanical discomfort with sex and all forms of intimacy. "It's not that they didn't have fun," Massey comments. "They just didn't talk about it." For Traditionalists, work is a means of staving off the poverty they knew in childhood; change is a frightening threat that life will take a turn for the worse. Things—houses, cars, patios with swimming pools, and backyard barbecues—mean a lot to this generation, because they were deprived of them as children.

Most "Rejectionists" are now in their twenties and thirties, though the oldest have already passed "the big four-oh." In Chapter 7 we looked at some of the major influences that shaped their values: the civil rights movement, the deaths of John and Robert Kennedy and Martin Luther King, Jr., the Vietnam War (whether they protested it or fought it), and Watergate. Inevitably, these experiences have turned these children of the Baby Boom generation into Riesman's inner-directed people. They value individual initiative, performance, and above all the will to question authority.

It sometimes appears that Rejectionists value possessions above all, but these are no second-generation materialists. They are bored with things; they've had them all their lives. Rejectionists are sensualists. They "dropped acid," flocked to Woodstock, and made a religion of casual sex, not merely to reject their parents' values, but for the stimulation of the experiences. Ten or twenty years later, a BMW is not a "thing" to Rejectionists; it's the exciting experience of fast, precise driving. Unafraid of a poverty they never knew, they view a job as one more experience, to be made as pleasurable as it can be. Change may be risk, but it's also exhilarating; change is opportunity.

Conflicts between such disparate value systems are inevitable. Sometimes they can even be funny. Massey tells of one Southwestern college where Traditionalist administrators decided to show how much they valued students' participation in campus life by letting them vote on what to them were major issues: the football team's colors and mascot. The Rejectionist students, few of whom could even find the stadium, opted for uniforms of pink and white. The school mascot, had college administrators accepted the vote, would now be an artichoke.

Fortunately, between the Traditionalists and the Rejectionists there is a generation that understands both sides of such conflicts. "In-betweeners," in their forties, are Reisman's outer-directed people. In-betweeners have never been quite sure what is important. They have lost faith in the values that sustained the Traditionalists, but cannot quite bring themselves to accept the freewheeling lifestyles of the Rejectionists. They know belongings are not the meaning of life, but there is something disquietingly rootless about unrestrained sensuality. In-betweeners tend to follow their parents' lifestyles—steady job, good home, with children and dog—and buy dozens of self-help psychology books to find out why they are not satisfied and what they can do about it.

Massey summarizes the differences between these generations with an observation he made in 1969 and 1970 while doing market research for the President's Commission on Obscenity and Pornography. "What we found was that Traditionalists had it, but hid it up in the attic," he reports. "Rejectionists found it and did it. And the In-betweeners missed it and bought stacks of it."

In the 1990s, the In-betweeners will be taking over the top positions in business and politics from the Traditionalists who have held them since the 1970s. America may be more peaceful for the change, because In-betweeners are life's great compromisers. They understand both Traditionalist and Rejectionist values and hold few beliefs of their own so firmly that they become blind to the ideas of others. When Traditionalists and Rejectionists clash, In-betweeners make effective mediators.

THE REAL GENERATION GAPS

Since the 1960s, the tension between the generations has been one of the most powerful and divisive factors shaping American society. By 2000, it will be resolved in favor of the Baby Boomers. Nearly all of their parents will have retired from American business and public life, and the young inevitably will have won by the simple expedient of outlasting their opponents. The transition has already been felt in nearly all parts of our lives.

Look at the changes we have seen in the last few decades in two deeply felt values of the past: institutional leadership and social order. Both are expressions of the heartfelt wish for stability.

Even after Vietnam and Watergate and the televangelist scandals, the over-fifty generations by and large still believe in their leaders. If the President says we should help the Nicaraguan Contras, he must have good reason. If the Church says that abortion is legalized murder, then it is unquestionably true that millions of American women will be transgressing Church canon by aborting fetuses. These are the generations that echoed the saying, "What's good for General Motors is good for America." It was not even quite what GM's "Engine Charlie" Wilson said, but it's what millions of Americans fervently thought he should have said. It is what millions of older Americans still believe: If we can trust our leaders, then we need not fear another depression or world war. Our lives are secure. And after a lifetime repeatedly scarred by the unexpected, that is just how the over-fifties want it.

That is also why they value social order: If everyone knows where he stands in society, life becomes very predictable, and that is comfortable.

Contrast that with the attitudes of their children and grandchildren, whose values jelled when the old mores were at last coming apart. The under-forty crowd know in their hearts that conservative—read Traditionalist—political and business leaders learned their ethics from W.C. Fields: "Never give a sucker an even break." Social order is just as suspect, because it once barred the righting of all manner of wrongs. If people had obeyed the social order, blacks would have remained disenfranchised, women would have remained shut out from professional careers, the Vietnam War would have been fought without dissent, the environment would have been raped even beyond the dreams of the Reagan administration, and all the other pet causes of the Baby Boom generation would have died on the vine. More than that, they grew up in a world where change is rapid and unending. They actually like change. Stability bores them. No wonder the 1960s and 1970s were so turbulent.

There are other differences as well. Many are less contentious, but all will help to shape the year 2000 in crucial ways.

Take work and money. If there is an ultimate value for the over-fifty group, it's cash. Not that they are greedy; they just grew up without money, and they know from experience that life is a lot easier when they have it. And because of that, they have always valued work. Work provides the money they need to live well, so they grew up believing that a good job was almost infinitely valuable. In the end, work became internalized, a moral value in its own right. Work validates older-generation people. It provides a sense of meaning and of position within society. They do not just build houses, design turret lathes, and organize sales campaigns; they *are* carpenters and mechanical engineers and marketing managers. Their jobs are a major part of their identity.

Not so the Baby Boomers. Their parents, on average, did such a good job providing for them that as a generation they don't know what poverty is. Money is a readily available source of pleasure, hardly worth worrying about. Thanks to television, even those who grew up less well off have absorbed much of the Boomers' casual attitude toward money. All this goes a long way toward explaining why Americans have been saving only 2 percent of their income in recent years.

It also explains the disdain that under-forties seem to feel for most jobs. Shielded from poverty, they never invested work with the sense of righteousness that inspires their parents. Work can be a satisfying, creative part of life, but most jobs are chores to be endured only out of necessity. The older generation used to ask, "If you're not making any money and you aren't having any fun, why do it?" The younger asks simply, "If you aren't having fun, why do it?"

There is another difference here. For the older generation, money means *cash*. When they were growing up, no one dealt with checks. Their first employers most likely paid in greenbacks, and they prefer to do the same. As for credit cards, according to the American Bankers Association, probably 70 percent of the over-forty crowd virtually never use plastic. But things have changed for their children and grandchildren. These generations can hardly remember whose picture is on a five-dollar bill. By 2000, they may well learn the hard way the meaning of debt.

Massey points to one other difference between the generations: their response to problems. The older generations love problems. They teethed on problems. Big problems. They had to escape the Depression, win the Second World War and fight the Korean War, and then build a world-dominating economy capable of giving an entire nation the highest standard of living man has ever seen. When a problem comes along, the over-fifties know just what to do: form a committee. They may never solve the problem, but they will come out of the effort secure in the knowledge that they have done the right thing.

The younger generations don't worry much about problems. They have seen too many of them solved, all in one hour, minus time for commercials.

"Rejectionists do not like problems, but they love causes," Massey comments. "Give them a cause, the bigger the better. The less they can do about it, the better they like it. They love big things that they have absolutely no impact on. It's fun to worry about the big issues. They'd a whole lot sooner do that than stay home and clean out their closets."

We have all seen ample evidence of that characteristic. It will be a guiding feature of American life in 2000.

THE NEW ERA

For business and government, the transition from a mixture of Traditionalists and In-betweeners to an overwhelming population of Rejectionists will bring both problems and unexpected benefits in the 1990s.

It has already changed American foreign policy. For at least the next thirty years, America will never go to war unless directly attacked on its own soil. Patriotism was a major value for the generation that grew up in World War II; any good American was willing to fight for his country, whenever and wherever his country found it necessary, even if the reason was a bit obscure. Americans learned in Vietnam how much of that patriotic fervor remains in the post–World War II generation. Even where military action is clearly required—say, following some particularly heinous act of terrorism sponsored by a foreign government—they will not support it; they are far more likely to feel that their own government somehow asked for trouble. Backing a counterrevolution in Nicaragua, no matter how well it might be justified by the standards of an earlier period, is out of the question.

Insofar as this pacifism prevents Americans from dying for obscure causes in foreign lands, it may be a positive force in our national life. But our obvious reluctance to fight for our policies will make it difficult for American negotiators to take a hard line with belligerent nations. The day may come when an opponent, assuming that our posturing is as meaningless as usual, will do something to make military conflict inevitable. In that case, we could lose more casualties than we have saved by avoiding lesser hostilities.

The rise of the Baby Boom generation will bring other changes to government as well. As we saw in Chapter 7, and have seen in daily life for some twenty years, these people do not worry about any possible evils of big government; they are too accustomed to bending Washington to their will. What does bother them is any failure by their elected representatives to meet their demands. So far, legislators have had it relatively easy. They could balance the demands of the Baby Boomers against those of other generations, perform studies, and generally stall when faced with a demand they chose not to meet. The causes and effects of acid rain were clear some fifteen years ago; the first tentative countermeasures are still in the planning stages. By 2000, that kind of delay will no longer be possible—not if elected officials hope to remain in office. Baby Boomers are not shy about making demands on government, and they certainly aren't patient.

In business, the changes will be equally profound. A generation or two back, there was nothing more important than loyalty. If the machines on your production line broke down, you stayed overtime to fix them; your loyalty to your company and co-workers demanded it. If your boss made a mistake, you covered for him, as he most likely would have done for you. Loyalty. That is how the older generations still live, and many forty-plus executives still play the game, even if for them it carries less moral authority. But to a large extent, the Baby Boomers have replaced loyalty with personal advantage. Broken machine? "When the whistle blows, I'm outta here!" Boss goofed? Drop a word to his supervisor's boss, and you might wind up with his job and a hefty promotion. The generation of whistle-blowers, in the above sense of the term, is at hand.

In compensation for—or perhaps because of—this inability to identify with the institutions and people that helped give earlier generations their sense of fulfillment, the Baby Boomers have an independence and dedication to performance and achievement beyond those of their parents. And they bring to their careers the same impatience they display when dealing with the government. There is little tolerance in them for make-work, rubber-stamp committees and old-boy-network clubbiness. If an organization or system does not produce the results they want, and promptly, they will rearrange it until it does.

The process has begun already. Business consultant Thomas L. Brown has identified nearly two dozen key workplace issues on which the under-forty generations clearly reject traditional viewpoints. These new attitudes are rapidly changing both our relationships with our employers and our jobs themselves.

In many companies, management powers once reserved for mid- and high-level executives are being distributed to everyone. This is happening not only because computers make it possible to manage a business with fewer people, but also because that is how New Age workers think it should be. It used to be that only managers made decisions. Today more and more decisions are being made by the people closest to the work; in many highly automated factories, anyone on the assembly line can shut down the entire operation in order to solve a quality-control problem. Teamwork is quickly replacing the lone worker of yesteryear; individual employees still carry out a single, repetitive operation on many auto assembly lines, but many car manufacturers have at least begun to experiment with work teams that see one car through the entire process. And instead of leaving it up to managers to look after the customer's needs and watch the bottom line, companies are making sure that everyone understands both what customers need and what the individual worker can do to build customer satisfaction.

New-generation managers are also bringing their activist sense of ecological systems to the office. Old-style managers thought the "big picture" was for top managers; everyone else should pay attention to whatever job he or she was assigned and leave policy to their appointed leaders. Under-forty managers want to understand where everything fits—where they fit in the business and how the company contributes to society—and they believe that every employee should be able to share that vision.

In part, this all grows from a novel recognition that workers are human beings, even from nine to five. Where once only senior employees were treated with individual care, modern managers now value everyone in the organization, and let them know it. Where once employees were expected to get to work on time and do their jobs efficiently, managers are now trying to build enthusiasm and team spirit in their employees. They reward participation not just with a paycheck and an occasional promotion—in the new "flattened-pyramid" companies, there are too few promotions to go around—but offering personal recognition at every opportunity. Everyone is challenged, everyone helped to learn and grow, both as workers and as people. And companies are trying hard to help workers fit their jobs into their personal lives with a minimum of disruption. This is one reason many firms are setting up on-the-job day-care facilities. Companies that treat new-generation workers as "meat machines" suffer high employee turnover and low productivity.

Business and society can adapt to all these changes; they have been doing it for years now. But the Baby Boomers may have unique problems with a handicap that all generations share—the "you are when you graduated" syndrome. Until recently, it has been relatively easy for professionals to retain the thinking habits they built in training for their careers. By the time new technology had made them totally obsolete, their working years were just about over. But as we have already seen, a technological revolution is now reshaping American life faster than we can absorb the changes. Coping with new technology, making the best possible use of it, will be one of America's most pressing needs during the 1990s and far into the future. That may well mean we must find a way to update not just our professional knowledge, but the deep-seated ways in which we think about it. This is one challenge Americans have not met, or even considered. By 2000, it may be recognized as the most fundamental problem of our time.

THE NEWEST GENERATION

All this leaves us with one puzzling group to consider: the generation now in their adolescent and teen years and putting the finishing touches on their value systems. Massey calls them the "Synthesizers." Superficially more conservative than their rejectionist elders, they are very different from any of the generations that have gone before.

For one thing, they are more confused. They learn Traditionalist values from the most powerful people in the country, Rejectionist values from their parents—and no values worth mentioning from the endless procession of packaged sports figures and rock stars that has replaced the heroes of earlier generations. Somehow, from this array of conflicting messages, they are having to synthesize a coherent value system of their own.

They are also more frightened. The Synthesizers are the first generation ever born who have grown up with the worry that they will not live as well as their parents did. After all, they have had it drummed into them since birth that the world is running out of resources, that first inflation and now the federal budget deficit are destroying the economy, and that robots are taking over the jobs they should have grown into. And the rest of life is no more comforting. Underarm deodorants will soon destroy the ozone layer and give us all cancer. Nuclear power will cover the earth in radiation.

TRADITIONAL VALUES	NEW VALUES
Self-denial ethic	Self-fulfillment ethic
Higher standard of living	Better quality of living
Traditional sex roles	Blurring of sex roles
Accepted definition of success	Individual definition of success
Traditional family life	Alternative families
Faith in industry, institutions	Self-reliance
Live to work	Work to live
Hero worship	Love of ideas
Expansionism	Pluralism
Patriotism	Less nationalistic outlook
Unparalleled growth	Growing sense of limits
Industrial growth	Information/service growth
Receptivity to technology	Technology orientation

Adapted from Plummer, The Futurist, *January–February 1989.*

Some idiot in Washington will kill us all in a nuclear war; it's inevitable. Never mind that most of this is silly. Their Rejectionist parents value "openness" a lot more than critical thinking.

If the Synthesizers have several strikes against them, they also have what may prove to be an enormous advantage over the rest of us: this is the first generation to grow up with computers. Just as the Rejectionists take for granted the jet airliners that some Traditionalists still refuse to board, Synthesizers who belong to middle-class and wealthy families could hardly imagine life without computers. Computer professionals from the Traditionalist and Rejectionist generations feel they are doing well if, over the duration of a large programming project, they produce an average of five lines of software per working day. There are thirteen-year-old children today who can sit down at the keyboard and write a three-hundred-line program off the top of their heads and have it run perfectly the first time.

In all, Synthesizers are shaping up to be one of the most interesting and least predictable generations this century has produced. By 2000, they may begin to wield more influence in American society than their numbers would suggest. But this early in their development, it is impossible to guess exactly how that influence will make itself felt.

ETHICS IN THE WORLD OF
CUSTOM-TAILORED LIFE

Living is not the good, but living well; the wise man, therefore, lives as long as he should, not as long as he can. He will always think of life in terms of quality, not quantity.

–Seneca

If you become seriously ill today, doctors will do their best to cure you. If you cannot afford the treatment, by and large Medicare or Medicaid will pick up the tab. You need not fear that your doctors will take it upon themselves to decide that your life is no longer worth saving. While you have any chance to survive, doctors today will not opt to end your treatment or "put you out of your misery." In the twenty-first century, that may no longer be true. Many of the rights we now take for granted will soon become privileges, subject to loss under conditions we cannot control.

The same technologies that will save thousands of human lives in the year 2000 are bringing with them some of the thorniest ethical problems that society will ever have to face. Many were not even theoretically possible only two decades ago. Many threaten such basic concepts as the right to life and what it means to be a human being.

It is a long list of questions to be faced. In the 1990s, gene therapy will finally offer practical cures to some hereditary illnesses—if we can take on the responsibility of tampering with the human genome. Genetic testing will identify these conditions and dozens of others for which no effective therapy is available—but to what end? So that defective fetuses can be aborted? What of aborted fetuses? Transplants of fetal tissue could ease or cure a number of grave disorders; should we allow fetal-tissue transplants at the risk of encouraging abortions? Old ethical problems, too, will hang on in search of some resolution that society can agree on: Have the terminally ill a right to "death with dignity"? And with state-of-the-art medical technology growing ever more costly, who should be granted access to limited resources? Who should decide?

These questions, and more like them, will present the most profound legal dilemmas of the coming years. And in the legal sense, most will have been resolved by the turn of the century. By then a variety of Supreme Court rulings and a mounting body of case law will have staked out the judiciary's position on each of these issues. That will not end the debate, however. As in the case of abortion, controversy over the new bioethics will remain with us for many years to come.

PLAYING GOD (1)

Begin with the most basic of high-tech dilemmas: There is very little in life that we will not be able to change with the genetic engineering methods now in use and under development. But what right have we to tamper with the stuff of life?

We looked at gene therapy in Chapter 11 and saw the wonders this almost miraculous technology offers. By 2000, somatic-cell therapy should make it possible to give patients a missing gene and relieve such horrible disorders as Lesch-Nyhan syndrome and phenylketonuria. Almost surely, germ-cell therapy will allow doctors to cure such defects, not in the patients themselves, but in all their descendants on into eternity. It is hard to imagine any greater blessing that science could offer the victims of these capricious illnesses.

But it is also difficult to imagine any product of modern biology that presents thornier problems of ethics. Most doctors and medical ethicists view somatic-cell therapy as no more controversial than any healing drug; it spares the patient a life of misery, but has no effect on others. The same cannot be said of tampering with the germ cells. Alter human reproductive cells, and it would change not only that baby but his descendants for all the rest of human history.

There is no guarantee that we will always use that power to good ends, or even for any serious purpose. In principle, germ-cell therapy could be used to change the unborn in any way their ancestors today fancy. Would you like to give your descendants a life expectancy well into their nineties? The kind of muscles that make for great baseball players? Or simply blue eyes? It can be arranged, if not today, then when we learn a little more about which genes control which of our features—a task that should be nearly complete as the human genome project reaches its climax early in the next century. Whether you believe that man was created by evolution or by the beneficence of an almighty God—we soon will have the power to overrule the decisions that shaped us.

Despite the obvious benefits of eliminating a congenital disease, some medical ethicists would ban any change in the germ cells, no matter what the reason. Others see no problem with ridding a family of hereditary disease, and would leave that decision in the family's hands—but would draw the line at an attempt to breed Olympic-caliber athletes or any other form of superman. And for a few, the real problem with gene therapies is not what to permit but who will pay for them. This is, they point out, one more high-tech medical procedure that the wealthy could soon be able to buy, while the poor must do without.

We will not have to make any immediate decisions about germ-cell therapy, at least here in the United States. American researchers, already burned by too many controversies, are avoiding the field in droves. But in countries where controls on experimentation are not so strict, these techniques are sure to be developed and, once developed, perhaps exported. This is an issue we will meet again, probably soon after 2000.

Gene Testing

Thirty years ago, when a woman was pregnant, she pretty well had to accept whatever baby the fates sent her. A woman might have an illegal abortion if she simply did not want a child—even a legal one if the woman's life was in danger—but there was no way to foretell the birth of a child with an inherited disease. So the question of aborting a pregnancy to avoid a genetic defect did not arise.

That changed with the development of amniocentesis in the late 1960s. In this test, doctors insert a long needle into the abdomen of the mother-to-be and withdraw fluid from the womb. Fetal cells can then be examined for abnormalities. So far, only a limited range of defects can be found with amniocentesis—Down's syndrome, Tay-Sachs disease, and a few other diseases, as well as the sex of the infant. (A blood test that does not require fetal cells can also detect spina bifida—incomplete formation of the spine—which can cause birth defects that range from minor disability to severe retardation.) Amniocentesis cannot be performed until about the sixteenth week of pregnancy, and it takes about three weeks to get the results. So even if the test uncovers a genetic disease, abortion is not possible until well into the third trimester of pregnancy. At that point it is so harrowing, both emotionally and physically, that few doctors would recommend abortion, save to avoid the most seriously defective births. Yet 91 percent of women whose fetus carries Down's syndrome terminate their pregnancies.

In the next ten years, two more changes will make prenatal diagnosis quick and easy and open a huge new variety of genetic disorders to the procedure. Abortion will become a practical, if not ethically acceptable, means to avoid the birth of children with even minor defects. Some of the most difficult bioethical battles of the late 1990s will be fought over this issue.

One reason is a technique called *chorionic villus sampling* (CVS), an easy alternative to amniocentesis that can be performed as early as the ninth week of pregnancy. Instead of impaling the patient with a needle, CVS uses a thin plastic tube inserted through the vagina and into the uterus. Rather than sipping liquid from the womb, the technique removes a tiny piece of the placenta and examines its cells. Results are usually back in a week, allowing plenty of time for a first-trimester abortion.

The other change is the rapid development of new genetic tests for a variety of hereditary diseases. Already, doctors can detect such disorders as cystic fibrosis, hemophilia, Huntington's chorea, and Duchenne muscular dystrophy, a wasting disease of the muscles that eventually kills one in every 3,300 boys. Medical researchers believe they have found genetic markers that could predict the development of Alzheimer's syndrome, manic depression, and heart disease, though it will be several years before tests based on them are ready for use. In the long run, there probably is nothing to prevent the development of tests for all the three thousand or so heritable diseases that afflict us.

But the same gene samples that reveal curable diseases will disclose other ills that cannot yet be cured, and many of those pregnancies will be terminated. In some cases it is difficult to argue that a child should be made to endure a life of suffering and an agonizing death, when there is no treatment for a genetic disease and an abortion arguably would be a merciful release. What of a fetus with Lesch-Nyhan syndrome, who, if brought to term, will spend his short life compulsively biting his limbs, tearing his hair, and clawing his face to blood-soaked tatters? And what should be done for parents who, having already had one child with a genetic disorder, cannot face the prospect of having another?

But once genetic testing is possible, there is nothing to prevent it from being used for purposes many of us would find trivial. Even today, no test is easier than determining the sex of the fetus. And that opens the possibility that couples who want, say, a boy and are about to have a girl may simply abort and try again. In 1973 the National Center for Health Statistics found that 49 percent of married women preferred sons, while only 19 percent preferred daughters. More recently, a poll of college students found that nearly all hoped their first child would be a boy; in a nation of one-child families, that leaves little room for girls. There is little indication that these preferences will soon change; some parents-to-be will find it hard to ignore an opportunity to make a choice where chance once reigned.

That thought worries some medical ethicists, and even some genetics researchers. Dr. Jorge Yunis, of the University of Minnesota, has developed a test that, rather than studying the chemical details of the DNA, uses a microscope to search for tiny variations in its physical structure. He has spent the last decade correlating his findings with a wide variety of personal characteristics, from blue eyes to susceptibility to many kinds of cancer. There is no reason his work could not be applied to fetal testing tomorrow. He habitually offers to forecast the medical future of friends and acquaintances, a suggestion that many decline, because his predictions are so frighteningly accurate. Yet most of his research remains locked in a desk drawer. "I am very much afraid to release this material and find that people use it to abort pregnancies because they want a child with blond hair or blue eyes instead of brown," he explains.

Many others echo his fear, and perhaps with good reason. In a recent poll by Dr. John C. Fletcher, of the University of Virginia School of Medicine, one-third of the medical geneticists surveyed said they would tell a couple the sex of their unborn baby, even if they knew the prospective parents would abort the pregnancy simply to try for a baby of the opposite sex. Another third would not do the test themselves, but would refer the parents to another practitioner who would perform it.

Does it really make sense to deny couples the results of gene testing when the law sets forth no specific guidance for those seeking abortions? So far, most medical ethicists hold that testing, and possible abortion, is acceptable in order to avoid a disease that would condemn the fetus to a life of misery. Nearly as many would test in order to spare the parents an overwhelming burden. Very few would accept testing for any less important reason.

By 2000, we believe most states will have turned that consensus into law.

Fetal Tissue

It is an ugly thought, but aborted fetuses today usually wind up in the hospital trash. That seems a waste, since transplants of fetal tissue theoretically could save patients from Alzheimer's disease, Huntington's chorea, Parkinson's disease, and a variety of devastating diseases. In all, several million people could benefit from fetal tissue each year in America alone.

What worries antiabortionists is that people might be encouraged to terminate a pregnancy if they knew that some good would come of it. In a country where there are already upwards of 1.7 million abortions each year, that seems unlikely to make much difference. But they also suggest that wealthy Americans in need of fetal spare parts could pay women in underdeveloped countries to become pregnant specifically to undergo an abortion, and that may be more probable than it sounds. At least three women here in the United States already have sought the help of doctors in arranging transplants of fetal tissue, which they would have supplied by deliberately becoming pregnant. One hoped to cure her father's Alzheimer's disease, another sought to cure her husband of Parkinson's disease— in the latter case, their daughters had volunteered to supply the abortus—and the third hoped to cure her own diabetes. None found a doctor willing to perform the operation.

Though these women's ethical standards may not be acceptable to many, there are others whose sad indifference to human life leaves no room for speculation. For several years now, there have been persistent rumors that several Olympic-level athletes have deliberately become pregnant and undergone abortions because they believed—correctly—that the hormonal effects of pregnancy would improve their stamina during competition. While no one in the sports community has been willing to name any names, there seems little doubt that the rumors are true. If even a small minority of American women share that casual attitude toward pregnancy and abortion, the wealthy would not have to leave the country to find donors-for-dollars.

Ethicists have already staked out their positions in this field clearly. Abortions to further athletic careers would leave most of them gasping in horror, but fetal-tissue transplants to cure disease would not. In December 1986, a gathering of medical ethicists at Case Western Reserve University proposed three guidelines for these procedures: (1) the decision to have an abortion should be clearly separated from the decision to donate the tissue for transplant; (2) although law requires only the mother's permission for the transplant, some independent body should also pass on the decision; and, (3) to be sure that no one terminates a pregnancy in order to help a sick relative or friend, women would be forbidden to donate tissue for any specific patient.

Again, we believe that by 2000 these guidelines will be law in most of the United States.

Babies Without Brains

A closely related issue is anencephaly, a condition in which most of the cranial nervous tissue fails to develop. Anencephalic babies are born with only the brain stem, the most primitive part of the brain, which controls only the basic bodily functions. The cortex, the "human" part of the brain where personality, awareness, and thought reside, is missing; for all practical purposes these are babies without a brain. Nearly all such infants die in the first week of life, the remainder soon thereafter.

Technically, anencephalic infants are almost perfect organ donors. They carry healthy, well-developed hearts and kidneys and livers, but have no possibility of using them. There is no hope at all that they might survive to become even the most retarded of human beings.

Ethically, however, there are problems. Anencephalics die because, without the higher brain to oversee the stem, they "forget" to breathe. This happens intermittently, so that the organs are progressively damaged by oxygen starvation. By the time the baby dies, the organs are useless for transplantation. So the only way to preserve the organs for use is to put the infant on a respirator until they are needed—and then pull the plug on what outwardly looks like a healthy baby. That is even harder to accept than it sounds, because some anencephalics appear to experience pain, and putting them on the respirator may prolong their suffering.

If that were all there was to it, using anencephalic organ donors would amount to a grisly sacrifice of one more or less human being for the benefit of another—clearly unacceptable under our ethical traditions. But when doctors at California's Loma Linda Medical Center transplanted the heart from one such donor to a Canadian girl who otherwise would have died, more than fifty families of unborn anencephalics called, pleading to donate their babies' organs. It was the only way to give meaning to their own children's brief and otherwise futile existence.

Medical ethicists are still divided over this issue. Some, recognizing that anencephalics have no chance to live and almost surely have no awareness of their own existence, hold that such infants should be declared dead at birth and their organs used as needed. Others believe that we know too little about them to make any valid ethical decision; therefore we must let them die naturally, as their "fates" prescribe, no matter how sorely their organs are needed.

There is no easy way out of this issue, but we believe an answer will be agreed upon before 2000. In the end, society will conclude that it is more important to save the lives of children who can grow up to become whole, functional adults than it is to preserve the rights of anencephalics, who cannot. The deciding factor will be the parents of anencephalic infants, who find in donating their babies' organs the only solace available for one of the most painful situations they will ever face.

Abortion

There is little point in dealing with the issue of abortion here at length. We all see the abortion battle played out nightly on the news, and we could easily write several books on the topic without adding anything new to the debate. But here is one thought to ponder:

Between now and the turn of the century, the ethical problems of abortion will grow more difficult, not less so. The reason is medicine's rapidly growing ability to keep premature infants alive until they can survive at home. In the best neonatal intensive-care units, preemies weighing less than two pounds can be popped into incubators that amount to artificial wombs and maintained until ready to go home with their parents. In the coming years, the age at which babies can be successfully delivered and kept alive will fall dramatically. Sooner or later, neonatal life-support systems will be able to sustain a first-trimester fetus until it reaches full babyhood. Our guess is that it will happen before the year 2010. At that point the only difference between a premature baby and an aborted fetus will be whether the parents want it—whether it goes into an incubator or into the trash. That development will make it very difficult even for the most ardent "pro-choice" advocates to argue that a fetus lacks the rights automatically granted to any baby.

And yet—another guess, not a true forecast—we doubt that even a Supreme Court dominated by conservative Republican appointees will reverse *Roe v. Wade,* the case that in 1973 legalized abortion during the first six months of pregnancy. As strongly as antiabortion lobbyists feel about their cause, and as powerfully as they influence some Washington circles, abortion is too much a part of the American scene to be discarded, even for the best of reasons. By the turn of the century it will have had ten more years in which to become business as usual.

PLAYING GOD (2)

By 2000, the terminally ill in all fifty states will have the right to refuse medical treatment that could, however temporarily, save their lives. Though the right to die remains controversial, thirty-eight states and the District of Columbia already recognize "living wills," which make it known that in case of terminal illness one would prefer to die without benefit of so-called "heroic measures," and that doctors should merely try to make the patient comfortable while nature takes its course. During the 1990s, most of the remaining states will enact similar legislation. If one has neglected to make out a living will and cannot voice a preference, most states will let his next of kin or a court-appointed trustee make the decision for him.

So far, this policy remains carefully limited. Dying patients or their next of kin may ask that physicians remove them from life support equipment or withhold food or water. Physicians may not actively end the patient's life. The American Medical Association maintains that taking positive action to hasten death is "contrary to the most fundamental measures of human worth and value," yet concedes that in some cases it may be ethical for physicians to cause a patient's death by stopping treatment. Even the Catholic Church would permit physicians to disconnect life-support equipment in some circumstances.

Yet the distinction between allowing someone to die and actually killing him remains enormously controversial. To many people, it sounds much like the rationalization of the Thai fishermen who, as devout Buddhists, are forbidden to kill: they argue that they merely take the fish out of water; if the fish prefers to die rather than live on land, that is its own decision. So-called passive euthanasia thus will remain controversial for as long as abortion does.

Beyond their dismay at the immediate loss of human life, many opponents of both abortion and the right to die are moved by a fear that could soon prove justified. Once we accept abortion and "passive euthanasia," they reason, we invite further erosion of our traditional belief in the sanctity of human life. The logical next step is for physicians to aid the terminally ill in actively ending their lives when and how they wish. After that, how long will it be until we accept outright euthanasia, whether patients have expressed any wish to die or not?

At that point we will be far down one of those "slippery slopes" that abound in legal discussions. If doctors may kill the terminally ill, why not those who will survive for many years, but will live in such misery that the end can only come as a merciful release? Why not the profoundly retarded and severely handicapped? How many others can we add to the list?

Even if we can hold the line at suicide by the terminally ill, how can we guarantee that they will not be subtly pressured by relatives to stop being a burden to those around them? Can we guarantee that not a single overworked doctor or nurse will give in to the temptation to add pressures of his or her own? It is not easy to answer such questions optimistically.

The United States would not be the first nation to accept the right to choose the time and manner of one's death, or even a physician's right to decide when patients should die. Since 1984, doctors in the Netherlands have been allowed to prescribe a fatal mixture of drugs when patients request it; the only restriction is that patients must accept professional counseling to clarify their motives and make sure that suicide really is their preferred way to deal with their illness. Despite powerful Catholic traditions, Uruguay and Peru have decriminalized homicide when the victim is incurably ill and has asked to die. And Dr. Christian Barnard, the famed South African surgeon who performed the world's first heart transplant, reports that for several decades he has routinely, on his sole judgment, administered lethal drugs when he believed that patients—white as well as black—could no longer hope to recover an adequate quality of life.

Even here in the United States, there is strong support for medically assisted suicide, at least for patients who are terminally ill and in pain. The AIDS crisis will make voluntary suicide an even more pressing issue in the coming years. According to a Louis Harris poll in 1987, 84 percent of Americans now believe that doctors should obey a living will, and more than half hold that physicians should assist in euthanasia upon request. In contrast, two-thirds of doctors themselves said that it would be wrong to help a would-be suicide under any circumstances.

We do not believe the United States is ready to sanction mercy killing, nor will it do so by 2000. But in the years to come, a growing number of individuals will help terminally ill friends and relatives to end their lives, and in many states juries will grow less and less inclined to inflict harsh penalties on them.

Yet at the same time, the right to commit suicide seems a policy whose time has almost come. It almost surely will be enacted first in California, where a proposed initiative supporting euthanasia almost made it onto the 1988 ballot. Whether any of the United States will have sanctioned medically assisted suicide for the terminally ill by 2000 is still uncertain. But we would not bet against it for 2010.

PLAYING GOD (3)

The reason is economic. The United States now spends 11 percent of its gross national product on health care, and the figure is growing rapidly. Per year, $2 billion is spent to save the lives of premature infants who twenty years ago would have died—more than $150,000, on average, for each baby in the neonatal intensive-care unit—and 15 percent of the survivors carry permanent physical or mental defects. Another $2 billion per year goes to fund dialysis treatments for about sixty thousand patients with kidney disease. And roughly one-third of Medicare funds—on the order of $150,000 per patient—go to support people in the last six months of their lives, many of whom have little or no chance of recovery. By contrast, fewer than 40 percent of impoverished Americans get any Medicaid coverage, and upwards of 35 million people—two-thirds of them working poor—lack any health insurance at all.

Proposals for a comprehensive health-care program—British-style "socialized medicine"—will not solve this problem, because of their enormous cost. Britain has coped with the problem by denying medical care to patients who in the United States would be accepted for treatment without question. For example, kidney dialysis centers all over the United States routinely accept patients in their sixties and seventies. In Britain, kidney disease over age fifty-five is almost an automatic death sentence. And for elective surgery, the waiting list can be years long. We do believe that a comprehensive health-care program will be enacted in the United States before the turn of the century. We doubt that it will turn out much better than its British model.

The ugly fact is that America can no longer afford to provide adequate medical care for all its citizens. That means that some people will miss out on care they need. Some will die. And the problem will grow worse, not better, as the giant Baby Boom generation reaches its years of declining health. Deciding how to allocate increasingly scarce medical resources will be one of the most pressing and difficult ethical challenges the United States faces in the 1990s and on into the twenty-first century.

So far, attempts to cut the cost of health care have gone far less well than their backers would have us believe. The first took form as Medicare's Prospective Payment System, adopted in 1983. Under this plan, illnesses are classified into 467 "diagnosis related groups," or DRGs. Hospitals are paid not for the care a patient actually receives, but for the average amount of care that Medicare planners believe should be needed, given the patient's illness and condition. If the patient can be sent home sooner than average and with less treatment, the hospital makes an extra profit; if he remains longer than average or requires more treatment, the hospital makes less and could even lose money. The idea was to encourage hospitals to provide more efficient treatment; the result has been to cut service to patients who need it. Medicare officials, hospital administrators, politicians, and even the American Medical Association deny the existence of widespread "dumping" of patients, but many of the doctors who must actually decide whether someone is ready to go home say privately that they are pressured to get patients out of the hospital within the DRG guideline, whether they are ready to go home or not.

So how can we allocate medical care fairly? How can we decide who will receive the chance to live and who must die? There are few possibilities.

One is "first come, first served": take patients as they arrive, young or old, rich or poor, and give them whatever care they need. What could be more fair? Of course, it does little to hold down health-care costs. When any given year's Medicare budget runs out in September, either Washington must pass a supplemental appropriation, or doctors wind up telling their patients, "We'll just have to hope your pancreas holds out until January." Obviously, no one is likely to accept that idea.

Then there is "you get what you pay for": the rich have the best chance of living to a healthy old age, because they can afford whatever treatment they need. The merely well off can protect themselves against most ills, but the need for an organ transplant will do them in. And the poor die young, just as our ancestors did. This is, after all, the natural state of affairs. Even today, someone who can afford to pay for, say, cancer chemotherapy will get the treatment he needs, even if government programs fail to pick up the tab. But Medicare and Medicaid were devised to bring needed treatment to those whose pockets were not so deep, and in a nation where a poor man's vote carries as much weight as a rich man's, we will not abandon that goal.

That leaves two alternatives. Neither is pleasant.

"I'm sorry, but you are too old." That is largely how the British medical system stretches its resources. No matter what his condition, anyone over age fifty-five is "a little crumbly," as one British physician put it, and therefore is not really a good prospect for treatment. American doctors already use that principle in some cases; if three patients each need a kidney transplant and only two donor organs are available, the oldest will probably have to make do with dialysis. At least one prominent medical ethicist, Daniel Callahan, of New York State's Hastings Institute, believes that we should extend that principle to all medical care. After patients reach "a natural lifespan"— Callahan has yet to choose his cutoff point—he believes that doctors should concentrate on relieving their suffering and forget about helping them to survive. Few practicing physicians agree. Neither does the American Association of Retired Persons, the most powerful lobby in Washington. Neither will most members of the Baby Boom generation as the first group begins to reach retirement age around 2010.

Finally, there is the bean-counter's approach to allocation: "I'm sorry, but saving your life would not be cost-effective." In this approach, medical planners weigh the benefits expected from each possible use for every health-care dollar and fund those programs that, in their terms, promise to be most productive. This system can seem attractive, because it sounds so rational. The $2 billion now spent each year on the nation's dialysis patients would buy prenatal services for every woman in the country, with money left over. In years to come, such measures would ensure that millions of children were born healthy. Infant mortality rates could be cut substantially and many billions of dollars saved in medical and social services. The drawback is that today's sixty thousand dialysis patients would soon die, as would all those other people whose kidneys will someday fail in the future.

A case in point: In 1987, Oregon Medicaid officials decided to stop funding transplants and put the money instead into prenatal services. They were backed by a public-interest group called Oregon Health Decisions, which specializes in medical-resource allocation. That December, seven-year-old Adam "Coby" Howard died because the state's Medicaid program refused to pay for the $100,000 bone marrow transplant that would have saved his life. Coby's parents had tried to raise the money privately but were still thousands of dollars short when the end came.

There will be many cases like Coby's in the years to come, not only in Oregon but throughout the country. For those who believe that human life should be subject to cost accounting, that is not too large a price to pay for a rational allocation of limited medical resources. We believe America is doomed to follow this approach in what remains of this century. By 2000, it will be standard operating procedure.

A NEW VIEW OF LIFE

All these ethical decisions, from the woman's right to abort an unwanted pregnancy to the death of Coby Howard, speak of a fundamental change in our view of human life. Unable to resolve the conflicts between a pregnant woman's right to her body and her unborn baby's right to life, between the need to restrain medical costs and the almost endless need for medical care, we are taking what may be the only way out: we are redefining what it means to be a human being.

Or, rather, we are beginning to distinguish between being human and being a person, between the body and the functioning individual who may—or may not—inhabit it. And the rights we once granted to all humans are now being limited only to persons.

Humanity is an easy standard to meet. A fetus or a coma victim is human because it inherits human genes. It is human from conception and remains human until death. So long as we retain humanity as the standard for granting individual rights, we must grant them to all. In this case, abortion is intolerable, except to save the mother's life.

From a person we require more. Persons are more or less rational beings, aware of themselves and of their surroundings. Within broad limits, they can choose their circumstances and actions, and they can make commitments about their future actions. Above all, they have the capacity for moral awareness. Persons, in short, are autonomous beings. With personhood as our standard, we can distinguish between humans; we can grant to some the full rights of a person, and to others no rights at all.

Driven by the conflicts we have considered throughout this chapter, more and more ethical theorists are revising the Declaration of Independence. The rights to life, liberty, and the pursuit of happiness no longer apply to all who take the form of human beings, but only to those who function as independent persons. Merely being human earns us only the right we grant any innocent organism—the right not to be subjected to needless suffering.

A fetus, an anencephalic infant, and an adult in an irreversible coma are all human, but none is an autonomous being. By its definition, none is a person. And under the new rules, none is entitled to the rights granted a person. We may abort a fetus, scavenge the anencephalic for transplantable organs, and remove the coma victim from life support without violating the autonomy of a fellow person. Similarly, a person retains those rights we grant to any organism: the terminally ill may ethically opt for suicide so as to avoid needless suffering. It may even be the doctor's duty to "put them to sleep."

This is a frightening, post-Huxleyian new world in many ways, but most frightening because it will often require individual judgments. Though many of us still defend the old standards, as a society we have already ruled on the acceptability of abortion and "passive euthanasia" for humans who either are not yet persons or have lost their personhood. In those cases, general rules are possible; we may not like them, but we know where we stand. Yet there are gray areas that can never be resolved by categorical decisions; they must be approached on a case-by-case basis. And eventually the case may be our own. Under the ethics of the twenty-first century, the day will almost surely come when others sit in judgment over our claim to a person's right to medical care, and perhaps other rights as well. We can never be sure they will make the decision as we would want it made. Few things could be more frightening than that.

How defective must a newborn be before it can be allowed to die, or aided in doing so? How retarded may a human being be before he loses his personhood, and with it his right to life? How old may a person grow before his rights begin to slip away, and doctors need no longer attempt to heal, but merely to comfort? We will still face these questions, and more like them, in the year 2000 and for many years thereafter.

AN UNETHICAL SOCIETY?

*I*t seems that hardly a segment of American life today is free of ethical problems. To pick just a few high—or low—points from the last decade: In government, we have watched the unfolding of the Iran-Contra affair and seen more than one hundred of President Reagan's appointees driven from office by charges of corruption. In politics, two candidates, Joseph Biden and Gary Hart, left the 1988 Democratic primaries after incriminating revelations, one for plagiarism, the other for sexual misconduct. In sports, there were the Olympic steroid scandals, rampant drug abuse, extramarital sex among the Boston Red Sox, and the 1986 Boston Marathon winner who lost her title when it was found that she had run much of her race on the subway. In business, insider-trading schemes netted billion-dollar profits before being exposed, and corporate raiders daily line their pockets at the expense of workers who lose their jobs when their employers are forcibly merged with other companies. Even religious leaders, like Jimmy Swaggart and Jim and Tammy Bakker, fell to charges of sexual and financial impropriety. The question is not whether there are more such scandals to come, but who will be caught and under what circumstances.

The lives of average Americans are just as marred by unethical conduct. About 25 percent of children in the United States today are born out of wedlock, and the number is growing. More than half of the high school class of 1987 reported having used marijuana; 15 percent had used cocaine. And an estimated 1 million Americans inhabit the nation's jails, three-fourths of them imprisoned on drug charges.

If these issues were as complex and unsettled as those of biomedical ethics, it would be easy to understand how even our leaders could get caught on the wrong side of a personal choice. But these are lapses from widely accepted standards of behavior. Some who matured in the permissive sixties and seventies might uphold Gary Hart's right to an extramarital affair; few would grant him license to lie about it while seeking his party's presidential nomination. Some might accept the idea of having a child out of wedlock—but only as a deliberate choice of parents who are prepared to care for the baby; few unwed parents can take proper care of themselves, much less a child. And there is very little sympathy in America for drug abuse, either by sports heroes or by the nation's young. How is it that so many Americans get themselves entangled in such obviously unethical behavior?

One answer may be our value-free school system. In their eagerness to be "nonjudgmental," America's teachers have long declined to participate in the ethical training of their students. But parents, too, have abdicated this role. Thus, children grow up without an ethical compass beyond an ill-defined sense that some things are "wrong"—if they develop even that.

We believe this long-standing neglect of ethics must soon come to an end if the United States is to remain a viable society. And we believe that it will. As part of the national effort to reform their schools, Americans will at last begin to establish an ethical curriculum designed to help young people develop the ability to live responsibly in a complex society. A few school systems have begun this effort already. By 2000, it should be a basic part of American education.

RELIGION FACES

ANOTHER THOUSAND

YEARS

F or we must consider that we shall be a city upon a hill. The eyes of all people are upon us, so that if we shall deal falsely with our God in this work we have undertaken, and so cause Him to withdraw His present help from us, we shall be made a story and a byword through the world.

–John Winthrop, from
A Model of Christian Charity, a sermon
delivered on board the *Arbella*
while en route to the
New World, 1630

In one of the most famous speeches delivered by an American colonist, the Puritan governor of the Massachusetts Bay Colony pictured the new land as a shining citadel, guided by the love of God toward a life of moral purity, personal industry, and contentment. Somehow it has not quite worked out that way. But as the millennium arrives, a growing number of Americans will devote some unaccustomed attention to their religious roots.

For American religious institutions, the last three decades have been a time of ferment; the turn of the century will be no less so. We expect to see few changes in the trends now well established: a dramatic return to faith by formerly irreligious Americans, a preference for conservative, authoritarian creeds, and a growing demand that women receive a broader role in ecclesiastical affairs. In addition, the Catholic and Jewish faiths will continue to have unique problems of their own.

A RETURN TO FAITH

We have seen this trend grow strong in the 1980s. The generation that once embraced the illicit joys of sex, drugs, and rock and roll is finding its way into church, and many of today's college students are joining them. Where church membership dropped from 64 percent of the U.S. population in 1960 to 59 percent in 1980, it has not lost a point since. And in sheer numbers, churches have grown dramatically. They could claim only 114.4 million members in 1960; their ranks have grown to nearly 143 million today. If that trend continues, more than 170 million Americans will claim membership in a formal church by the year 2000.

There is nothing particularly surprising about this abrupt recovery of clerical influence. In part, it reflects the generally conservative shift in society, both reflected and promoted by the Reagan administration. But on a deeper level, religion is now moving to fill a spiritual void that has been building for more than half a century, and the drawing to a close of a monumental century may by its very passage promote an even more forceful return to religion. The generation that fought World War II found its faith strained by the horrors of battle and the death camps, then watched as many of its children rejected virtually all their traditional values for the hedonistic life prevalent in the 1960s. Social structures that had lasted since the Civil War were torn apart by the civil rights movement in the late 1950s and early 1960s. Baby Boomers grew up under the perceived threat of nuclear war, then found themselves almost constantly at odds with the bedrock values of earlier generations; drugs, the sexual revolution, and above all the war in Vietnam divided them from their own upbringing. By the time the Baby Bust generation arrived, the core of shared American values that once sustained their forebears had been leached away. For too many, all that is left is a perpetual now, a world of MTV-like mass-media entertainment and accelerating technological change without solid foundations in the past and without direction for the future.

Harvard's Francis Peabody said it some eighty years ago: ''We do not know whence we come or whither we go, and what is more important, we do not care; what we do know is that we are moving faster than anyone ever moved before." It could have been a motto for the last three generations. Under the circumstances, a return to the comfort of religious faith was all but inevitable.

RIGHT-WING RENAISSANCE

Yet rapid growth has not blessed all denominations equally. The liberal Protestant churches suffer the handicap of being liberal in an age when liberalism is no longer fashionable. They aligned themselves early with the forces of change. Their ministers preached for civil rights and against the war in Vietnam. They endorsed women's lib and, some of them, the right to abortion. Church members marched in parish-sponsored picket lines. In a society bending increasingly toward the right, this is cause enough for many potential members to seek other religious affiliations. Perhaps even more important, these denominations clearly were not the place to turn for relief from the turmoil of the 1980s. Since 1965, these orders have watched their memberships drop at a rate of nearly 5 percent every five years. We expect this exodus to slow as the turn of the century approaches, but it will not stop in the foreseeable future.

Though hard figures are less easy to come by, a similar trend appears to be making progress in the Jewish world. The generation that once largely abandoned traditional Judaism for the middle-class American mainstream has come back to rediscover its Jewish heritage. And while formerly non-observant Jews are returning to all three major branches of Judaism, many are bypassing Reform congregations to follow the more traditional teachings of Conservative Judaism and even the stringent dictates of Orthodox sects. Again, this trend seems likely to outlast the next decade.

In contrast to the turmoil which has beset Catholic and liberal Protestant denominations and Reform Jewish congregations, the deeply tradition-minded Protestant churches have managed to hold most worldly troubles at bay for decades. The Mormons have maintained firm control over their Utah home and branched out to proselytize vigorously in places as distant as West Germany, Korea, Taiwan, and Japan. Among Southern blacks, the Baptist church has always remained strong, and unlike largely white denominations it has gained strength because of social activism; Baptist churches, after all, act on behalf of their black members in coping with the dominant white majority. And throughout the United States, but particularly in the rural South and West, the fundamentalist evangelical movement has hung on, largely unnoticed by the American mainstream since the 1920s. When the conservative 1980s arrived, these unchanging faiths were waiting.

In an uncertain world, they offer a safe refuge for the terminally future-shocked. There are very few doubts in the lives of devout Mormons, Baptists, and evangelicals. There are few ambiguities, and there will be no changes likely to shake anyone's understanding of their place in the world or belief in the meaning of their lives. For all three denominations, life is a constant struggle between good and evil, between the temptations of sin and the strength of their faith. And if their faith is strong enough, they will be saved by their acceptance of Jesus as their Lord and Savior. The worldly chaos that surrounds them carries little more importance in the eternal scheme of things than the Hindu world of *maya*—illusion—from which one will eventually escape if one's life has been sufficiently pure.

Combined with this shared fundamentalist dogma is a conservative social agenda that also promises a return to America's past and to safety from the difficult issues that confront us daily. Evangelicals will suffer no drug or alcohol problems, because temperance is their rule. They will never find themselves in isolation, because a devotion to community joins them with each other. They need not doubt their government, because a deeply felt patriotism binds them to their country. And their families will never suffer the disintegration so often seen on the nightly news, because their traditional, American family values remain strong.

These are simple, compelling messages, and they have received a warm welcome from all parts of American society. The two fastest-growing churches in the United States are the Southern Baptist Convention and the Church of Jesus Christ of Latter-Day Saints—the Mormons. In the early 1960s, there were about 1.8 million Mormons in America; today, their numbers have more than doubled. More than 250,000 adults are baptised into the Mormon church each year, many of them converts from more traditional denominations.

But with the aid of television, the evangelical Protestant organizations as a group are expanding even more rapidly. About 40 million Americans now call themselves evangelical Protestants, up 8 percent in the last five years. And this trend has moved through all parts of society. In 1960, evangelicals were only one-third as likely to have attended college as the average citizen; today they have virtually caught up. The sex scandals that disgraced televangelists Jim Bakker

and Jimmy Swaggart did nothing to slow the growth of the evangelical movement as a whole. They merely prove that good and evil
compete for the human soul, and evil sometimes wins out. In this,
they confirm the fundamentalist worldview.

The disorienting pace of change that has driven many of us to seek
a fixed truth in our lives will accelerate, not slow, as the next century
begins. Millions of Americans will be displaced from their jobs by
automation and bimodalism. Most will be forced to learn new skills
long after their traditional school years have passed, and many will
leave their homes for regions with more active economies. They will
discover in themselves a need for spiritual security that they may
never have felt before. Many will be attracted to the fundamentalist
churches as much by their social conservatism as by their underlying
theological content. And at least 2.5 million Americans will have
been trained for the devout life almost from birth; that is how many
students are now enrolled in the nation's fifteen thousand private
evangelical schools. Inevitably, the spiritual migration toward that
old-time religion will be just as strong in 2000 as it is today.

JILL IN THE PULPIT

The divisive, often bitter controversy over the role of women in
religious affairs cuts across sectarian lines more than almost any other
issue. We hear about it most, of course, in the Catholic church, where
rebellious nuns and priests have been agitating for female ordination
for some twenty years. But the debate is just as heated in liberal
Protestant denominations and in some segments of Judaism.

Until recently, the argument over ordaining women clergymen
has seemed nearly deadlocked. The first Reform Jewish synagogues
accepted female rabbis in the 1970s, but even in these congregations, arguably the most liberal religious institutions in America, the
vast majority of rabbis still are men. That will probably not last long,
however. More than one-third of the rabbinical students attending
Hebrew Union College are now women. No similar trend can yet
be seen in Conservative synagogues, however, and there seems no
possibility at all that Orthodox sects will accept any but male rabbis
in our lifetimes.

American Catholics remain divided from their leaders in the Vatican over the role of women in the Church. A 1985 Gallup poll found
that Catholic parishioners overwhelmingly favored ordaining

women as permanent deacons; two years later, a follow-up survey found that between 50 and 60 percent would ordain women as priests. In his visit to the United States in September 1987, Pope John Paul II heard impassioned pleas for female ordination throughout his trip, yet he strongly reaffirmed the Church's traditional stand on women priests. Soon after, he released an Apostolic Letter condemning sexual discrimination, but reiterating that women cannot become priests, because Christ chose only men as his apostles. Women, he declared, have a choice of two vocations: motherhood and virginity. In either case, their fulfillment as women is to be found in "maternal" service to others. There is no prospect whatever that this position will change before the millennium.

Among Protestant denominations, only the Episcopal Church has been open to clerical feminism. The first women priests were ordained illicitly, in unsanctioned ceremonies in 1974. The practice was officially approved by the Episcopal General Convention two years later, and the denomination now boasts several hundred female priests. In this, American Episcopalians have proved far more open-minded than their sister faiths elsewhere. Twenty of the world's twenty-seven autonomous Anglican churches forbid ordination of women priests, and the 450-year-old Church of England, parent body for the American Episcopal Church, has rejected the idea pending the outcome of a long study begun only in 1987.

Late in 1988 the Episcopal Church took the obvious next step, electing its first woman bishop. A year earlier, a poll of ten thousand Episcopalians in southern California had found that 56 percent said they were "open" to appointment of a woman to the post left open by the death of Bishop Robert Rusack. Yet actually appointing a female bishop set off an unprecedented controversy in the Episcopalian ranks. One reason was the candidate herself, fifty-eight-year-old Barbara Harris of the Massachusetts diocese, a former public-relations executive, divorced and widely known as an outspoken member of the church's far left wing. The vehement attacks on Harris herself obscured any objections to raising a woman into the church hierarchy, but it seems certain that any other woman would have drawn fire as well.

The appointment also caused a split in the 65-million-member world Anglican community. Though Harris's elevation was hailed by the few other Anglican churches that accept the ordination of women, Archbishop of Canterbury Robert Runcie declared that until church law changes, no member of the Church of England may recognize either Bishop Harris or any priest she ordains.

It is easy to make firm forecasts in this area. By 2000, women rabbis should be an accepted part of Reform Judaism; that much seems certain. Even more surely, the first woman will not be admitted to the Catholic priesthood in the next decade, or even the next century; it may well be several hundred years before the Catholic Church ceases to be a men's club. On the other hand, we would not be surprised to see the world's Anglican churches follow the American lead and open their priesthood to women. In that case, resistance to female bishops in the American Episcopal Church could soon vanish.

CRISIS IN CATHOLICISM

If the Vatican has been slow to give women a broader role in the Church, it has been no quicker to accept any other change. On a variety of doctrinal issues, American Catholics have found themselves at odds with Rome for many years. Despite an unyielding Vatican ban on contraception, most American parishioners practice birth control without hesitation. A growing number accept divorce and continue to attend Mass, ignoring the church orders that even today automatically excommunicate them. During his trip to the United States in September 1987, the Pope defended the traditional bans on contraceptives, divorce, and abortion, and a month later, he urged eighteen visiting American bishops to persuade couples to reject abortion and contraception. It is difficult to imagine that any of these positions will change before the twenty-first century arrives. But on these and other traditional issues, the Word from Rome has become nearly irrelevant.

In sharp contrast, for problems that afflict the Church hierarchy, the Vatican position remains almost unquestioned law. Here, too, Rome has been slow to adapt to a changing world, a tardiness that has begun to cost the Church dearly.

One of its most pressing internal problems is the grave loss of morale among Catholic clergymen. Overworked, lonely, often sexually troubled, Catholic priests live a hard life. Many feel themselves trapped between Rome and their parishioners on such key issues as divorce and birth control. More difficult still is the problem of priestly celibacy. The Roman Catholic insistence that priests never marry is unique among major Christian sects; even the Orthodox churches require celibacy only for bishops. More than one thousand men leave the priesthood each year in America alone; most cite the problem of celibacy as a major cause of their departure. At least 70 percent of dropout priests will marry within five years. About 40 percent marry former nuns. And there are many of them. Hartford Seminary's Center for Social and Religious Research estimates that the number of Catholic priests, roughly 53,500 today, will plummet 40 percent by the turn of the century.

In recent years, AIDS has made the issue of priestly celibacy even more pressing. At least four Catholic clergymen have died of AIDS in Boston, as well as three in New York, and one parish priest and four lay brothers in Chicago. Many others are known to be suffering from the disease. One Houston physician says that he is currently treating nearly a dozen priests who have AIDS. People close to these cases report that priests who contract AIDS often are ostracized by their clerical colleagues, but others say that some priestly AIDS patients have received sympathetic care, though the nature of their illness has been "hushed up" to avoid embarrassing publicity, since homosexuality has never been acknowledged as an issue or problem by the leaders of the Catholic Church.

The AIDS problem even shows signs of undermining the long-standing Vatican position on birth control. In 1987, American Roman Catholic bishops voiced hesitant approval of public health campaigns that provide information about condoms in an effort to slow the spread of the dreaded illness. At Vatican insistence, their letter was recalled and rewritten. But a year later Jean-Marie Cardinal Lustiger, a pro-papal conservative whom Pope John Paul II himself appointed Archbishop of Paris, gave his implied endorsement to the use of condoms—he avoided using the word itself—by people "who carry the virus and cannot live in chastity."

There is little sign that the Vatican has any help to offer its followers, either in this matter or in any of the other problems that now confront American Catholics. There is just as little evidence that American Catholics will soon resign themselves to life under the traditional rules.

Rome and the United States debated the issue of priestly celibacy throughout 1988. Early in the year, Pope John Paul II issued a twenty-page letter asking priests to make themselves "eunuchs for the sake of the kingdom of heaven." Celibacy, he affirmed, remains a crucial part of priesthood. The National Federation of Priests' Councils responded with a declaration that celibacy should be optional and asking that resigned, married priests be readmitted to the clergy. Some months later the Vatican issued yet another statement defending its position. This is one of many Catholic conflicts that will not be resolved until well after 2000.

All this has undoubtedly had some impact on the number of Catholics in the United States. Yet it is all but impossible to see that impact clearly. In calculating its membership, the church hierarchy assumes that all children born to Catholic parents are Catholic as well. Thus, the official census of its faithful has grown from 50.4 million in 1970 to more than 52.6 million in 1986. It seems safe to guess that if only churchgoing adults were counted, the number would be considerably smaller, and shrinking.

WHO IS A JEW?

The controversy that nearly split the Jewish world after the 1988 elections in Israel will surface repeatedly in the years to come. Orthodox and Reform Jews have been increasingly at odds over the Law of the Return, the statute that grants Israeli citizenship to all Jews who wish to claim it. The key question is, who is a Jew?

There are several answers. Orthodox laws nearly two thousand years old define a Jew as a person born of a Jewish mother. Reform congregations also accept as a Jew anyone whose father was Jewish and who was raised as a Jew. By Orthodox standards, these people would not qualify for Israeli citizenship. Israeli civil law agrees; children of a Jewish father must qualify for citizenship as any Christian or Moslem would, by applying for naturalization after living in the country for three years. It is a point that rankles even Jews who have no interest in emigrating, and one on which neither side is willing to compromise.

Even more contentious is the problem of conversion. So far, Israel accepts any converted Jew under the Law of the Return. But according to Israel's more-Jewish-than-thou Orthodox sects, only an Orthodox rabbi can preside over a valid conversion; no one converted by a Reform rabbi, or even a Conservative one, can be accepted as a citizen of Israel under the Law of the Return. Their price for joining the Likud Party in forming a coalition government after the 1988 elections was to amend the Law of the Return so that only Orthodox converts would automatically be admitted to Israel.

An estimated 500,000 American Jews either were converted by Reform or Conservative rabbis or are the children of such converts. Fewer than two dozen emigrate to Israel each year. Yet the question of their status under the Law of the Return goes to the heart of what it means to be a Jew. If these people are not Jews, then by implication neither are the rabbis who performed their conversions; neither are the Reform and Conservative branches to which they belong. "Make no mistake about it: the revision is being pushed for one primary reason, to invalidate the Conservative and Reform movements," declared Avraham Weiss, Orthodox rabbi of the Hebrew Institute of Riverdale, New York.

For the vast majority of American Jews, that is a substantial threat and an overwhelming insult. Orthodox Jews make up only 10 percent of the American Jewish population; the remainder belong to Conservative or Reform congregations or claim no firm allegiance to any particular branch of Judaism. Imagine that some fundamentalist clique in the Vatican had conspired to excommunicate 90 percent of American Catholics, and you will begin to understand the sense of betrayal with which many American Jews greeted the "Who is a Jew?" debate in Israel.

Though temporarily put on hold, this controversy already has changed the relationship between American Jews and their spiritual homeland. Though contributions from the United States to Israeli organizations continue to rise each year, American donors reportedly no longer give their support automatically; they now ask tough questions about the recipient's policies. It has also made them more willing to intervene in Israel's governing process. Even the United Jewish Appeal, which has a long-standing prohibition against interfering in Israeli politics, joined with several dozen other American Jewish organizations to lobby against the Orthodox legislation.

It has also brought renewed efforts to reconcile conversion practices among the three branches of Judaism. In 1988, for example, Rabbi Ronald D. Price, executive director of the Union for Traditional Conservative Judaism, circulated a detailed proposal that would establish an interbranch council to oversee conversions and set uniform standards. Yet neither this effort nor others like it have received any perceptible welcome among the most Orthodox sects, who must sign on to any compromise.

This issue has the power to divide the Jewish world into armed camps, much as the Reformation divided Christianity in the sixteenth century. We do not believe that it will do so, because we believe that Israel's fractious Labor and Likud parties will cooperate to deprive the far-right sects of the power they nearly wielded in 1988. If that uneasy detente fails, Israel could lose the support of American Jews, who would in turn find themselves without a spiritual homeland. There seems little reason to hope that the question of who is a Jew will be resolved by the year 2000.

THE THIRTY-TWO-HOUR

WORK WEEK

"**A**s we approach 2000, people will still work hard, but the frenetic competition of the 1980s 'yuppies' to work the longest day and pull down the highest income will be replaced by a healthier enjoyment of life and family and a desire for 'quality of life.' If the eighties' motto was 'Live to work,' the goal of the nineties will be 'Work to live.' "

One of the steadiest trends of this century has been the shrinking work week. A generation ago, from the offices of New York to the assembly lines of Detroit, Americans worked a forty-hour week; the only exceptions were farmworkers, who labored from dawn to dusk, and men working overtime to fatten their paychecks. Today the work week has contracted to slightly more than thirty-five hours, and it is still shrinking. By 2000, Americans will spend just thirty-two hours each week at work, a full day less than their parents did. This and other changes—in the work week, in their methods of working, in benefits, and in their attitudes toward their jobs—will bring most Americans fuller, more satisfying lives in the years to come.

FLEXTIME, FLEXPLACE

As the work week has shrunk, it has begun to change in other ways as well. Already, many employers are experimenting with alternative work schedules. Gone for many American employees is the traditional work week of five equal days spent at the office or factory. Instead, "flextime" lets us set our own work schedules, so long as we work enough hours overall and the job gets done. "Morning people" may choose to get up before the sun and go straight to work. "Night people" may show up after noon and stay until the wee hours. Workers on the same project may seldom see each other, communicating instead by leaving messages on one another's desks or in computerized message centers accessed by telephone. In the idiosyncratic world of computer scientists, such odd workstyles already are almost commonplace.

"Flexplace" takes the process a step further. Not only can we choose our own hours, we need not even show up for work. Instead, we can work at home, or sometimes in a local branch office, rather than at company headquarters. By 2000, up to 20 percent of the American workforce will opt to work at home, communicating with the office by telephone, fax, and computer terminal. Among information workers—roughly 44 percent of the labor force at the turn of the century—up to half will be able to work wherever they find it most convenient.

Many other options are also gaining popularity. These include "job splitting," in which two or more persons share a job that ordinarily would employ one; compressed work weeks, in which people work four long days each week instead of five of normal length; a sabbatical leave for federal civil servants; the chance to trade portions of one's annual salary for added vacation time; and the rapid growth of permanent part-time jobs that provide career opportunities.

Social pressure for more individual choice in balancing work and leisure is growing rapidly. In national surveys, the number of American workers citing problems with "inconvenient or excessive hours" rose from 29.5 percent in 1969 to 33.5 percent in 1977. It is a safe guess that the same poll today would turn up at least that many dissatisfied employees, despite the new freedoms that some companies already provide. Traditional work schedules cause problems for one-third of all workers in the United States, says Stanley D. Nollen, of Georgetown University's School of Business Administration.

In fifteen years or less, such policies as flextime, flexplace, and job splitting will have become standard practice at many companies. The key word for corporate recruiters at the turn of the century will be "flexibility." If there is any way to adapt a job's hours, working conditions, or benefits to fit the individual worker's needs, the adjustment will be made.

CAFETERIA BENEFITS

As we escape the fixed office and the rigid work schedule, we will shed some of the other ties that traditionally have bound us to our jobs. Workers of the future will no longer have to qualify for benefits yet again whenever they change employers. They will carry their own insurance, health, retirement, and other benefits with them from job to job. Each employment contract will include an agreement that specifies how much of the employee's fringe-benefit package the employer will pay as part of the overall compensation.

As we move toward individually held, fully portable benefits, companies will increasingly offer a "cafeteria" of benefits from which employees can choose according to their individual needs. Working couples will divvy up fringe benefits to make certain all their needs are covered: one will take family psychiatric and dental coverage, while the other signs up for catastrophic medical care and legal services. When the time comes, both will take parental leave.

Benefits will grow more lavish as the supply of skilled young workers tightens and employers struggle to retain highly valued employees. Future benefits may include daycare at the office or factory for workers' children, expanded maternity and paternity leave, wellness programs for workers, and even health-care benefits for the workers' elderly parents. In a survey of more than one hundred U.S. companies, *Personnel Journal* found that 70 percent of personnel directors recognized that "eldercare" affects workers' productivity, absenteeism, turnover, and morale.

One company where many of these policies are already in effect is Perkins Geddis Eastman, architects and interior designers in New York City. Workers there enjoy both male and female parental leave when a child is born, followed up with a flexible work policy that allows them to work at home one or two days a week, to ease the transition. This flexible policy was established to reduce the turnover rate among the firm's workers and to enable valued employees to build a strong home life.

The first three employees at Perkins Geddis Eastman to take advantage of the flexible work week were men. Each took an unpaid three-week paternity leave and, for about a year after that, worked out of his home at will. As women began starting families, the policy was modified to allow for longer leaves. It continues to evolve. According to partner Barbara Geddis, "Now as the kids get to be two or three years old, we see people want their flexibility in different ways. They want flexible hours instead of working set days, and they want to know they can bring the child to work if they need to."

The freedom to work part-time, while retaining the security and benefits of a full-time job, does come at a price. Those people who have chosen to work a three- or four-day week have frozen their responsibilities temporarily; they are not likely to get a promotion or a raise until they return to their normal schedule. Women at law firms who work only nine-to-five hours to be with their children often are put on a so-called "women's track," which guarantees them employment, but lower salaries, without hope of promotion to a partnership. It is a price that many couples with strong family commitments are willing to pay. They have found one way to improve their lives at a crucial time and have few doubts about accepting the consequences. Many more of us will follow their lead in the years to come.

THE CHANGING WORKFORCE

This transformation from "off-the-rack" jobs to custom-tailored employment grows directly from the inevitable technological, demographic, and philosophical changes that will overtake the United States as the twentieth century reaches its close. We have already touched on many of its causes in previous chapters.

In large part, members of the Baby Boom generation can take credit for these de-homogenized workstyles, not by virtue of anything they have done, but because of what they haven't. They have not had many children. So before the 1990s are out, there will be more work waiting to be done than there are hands to do it. Employers will be all too eager to offer potential employees whatever comforts it takes to get them to sign on and stay on the job.

Students and retirement-age workers will fill at least some of the openings left by the tiny "Baby Bust" generation. Though most are available only for part-year and part-time jobs, they are potential workers that business cannot afford to ignore. (Witness those McDonald's television ads that star post-retirement hamburger clerks.) So more and more businesses will find ways to fit part-time and temporary workers into their offices and factories.

They will be hiring ever more women as well. Thirty years ago, a woman's place still was generally in the home. The changing economy made that social tradition obsolete. In the past two decades, many women have begun careers out of necessity, but more and more of them have found themselves eagerly climbing the corporate ladder. Today the question for most young women is not whether they will have a career, but what it will be. Some 63 percent of the new job-seekers entering the labor market between the years 1985 and 2000 will be women.

They will have a choice of jobs that in many cases are likely to be better suited to the kinds of skill that traditionally have been women's specialties. In an economy based on manual labor, many jobs required more muscle strength and muscle stamina than women could bring to them; and even pre-robotic assembly lines were largely a man's domain. But with experience in typing and some computer literacy, women can be expected to run many of the robots on tomorrow's assembly lines. This will help to raise women's salaries to within 10 percent of men's wages by 2000.

Yet to make the best use of this valuable labor pool, employers will be forced to offer women more than money. Many mothers are available for part-time jobs; others can work a full week if offered flexible schedules. Without those options, many would have to choose between pursuing a career and rearing children, and many would take themselves out of the job market, at least for several years. Companies desperate to get their work done will try to help them do both at once. If that means hiring two part-time employees instead of one full-time worker, letting women work at home until the children are old enough for school, fitting their work schedules in around the school day, or setting up day-care centers at the office, employers large and small will do it.

The need to cater to women and part-time employees has also made it easier for men to choose their working conditions. As women have joined the workforce, two-career families have grown common, and families have shrunk. These changes both raise family income and reduce financial needs, so that men can cut their working hours, even at the cost of lower earnings. Husbands can thus spend less time at the office and more time with their families.

Over the next ten years, as more and better day-care centers are established, the conflict between home and career will ease, and the pressure to adopt flextime and flexplace will wane. But by then these policies will be permanent features of the American workplace.

THE SERVICEABLE COMPUTER

All that tells us why flexible workstyles are desirable. What makes them possible is the continuing evolution of our economy from its foundation in agriculture and manufacturing to the new world of computer-based services.

In an economy built on agriculture or manufacturing, none of the arguments for flexibility would have mattered. Agricultural workers have no choice about where they toil, and very little about when; fields of corn will not make their way, like Birnam Wood to Dunsinane, to the door of a farmhand who prefers to work at home, and cattle must be milked morning and night, without exception. Similarly, manufacturing offers few opportunities to adapt to personal wishes; every step in the process is choreographed like a ballet, and, of necessity, the worker who cannot make his curtain call will have to find other employment.

But flexibility comes easier to the service industries that will employ 88 percent of the labor force by 2000. Some 20 million new service jobs will be created in that time. Business and finance, legal services, and the retail trade are all based on the flow of information; such "hands-on" personal services as health care, hotels, and restaurants have large information-based components. Even in manufacturing, large-scale automation is replacing many of the old manual activities with specialized forms of computer programming and other information-based skills. And to a large extent, information can be processed when and where people find it most convenient.

This sudden evolution from the Industrial Age to the Information Age applies to office jobs in all industries— management and support functions are always based on information—and it is only just beginning. So far, relatively few executives have learned to use computers productively, in large part because computers are not yet bright enough to bend to their ways of working. People talk; executives spend more than 90 percent of their time talking with other people, either over the phone or in meetings. Today, computers take orders only from competent typists. But by 2000, digitized voice-recognition and voice-synthesis systems will allow computers to speak and be spoken to.

In the future, the executive suite will be dominated by computer-wise decision makers aided by artificial intelligence and expert systems. These computer programs will work independently to compile reports and statistical profiles on demand. And when artificially intelligent computers become commonplace, they will also understand and do our bidding—by listening to our words, not by interpreting typed commands.

Office productivity will take a giant leap as these new machines are adopted, and workers will get their jobs done in less time. This growth in output per worker will make it easier for employers to shorten the work week.

In the short run, computers have caused widespread dislocation among white-collar workers who once thought they could not be automated out of their jobs. As we saw in Chapter 17, the growing emphasis on information flow is flattening the traditional corporate command structures. Computerized management techniques allow a single executive to oversee more than three times as many employees as traditional methods, so middle management is now being replaced by the desktop computer. An estimated 4 million managers already have lost their jobs, and the trend has just begun. The introduction of voice-activated computers in the 1990s will carry this purge to secretaries and stenographers as well.

But this is strictly a transitional phenomenon. In very few years, our fast-growing economy and shrinking workforce will bring new openings for virtually any experienced executive who wants them, while the best secretaries and office managers will move up the ladder, learning new skills to manage the sophisticated gear that does the actual work of managing information. And these new jobs, unlike the traditional positions they replace, will offer shorter hours and flexible working conditions.

TELECOMMUNICATIONS

In a world increasingly interwoven with optical fibers and other data links, it makes less and less difference where the information originates and where it is processed. Two people need not be near one another to work together on an information-based product that can flash electronically around the globe in seconds. In the new, information-driven office, this means that aides need not be near their bosses; they may be in the next room or the next country.

We will take advantage of that freedom in ever-increasing numbers. By 1990, fully 10 million employees out of a total of 130 million in the national workforce will be "telecommuting" from home workstations, linked to main offices via computer terminals. And by 2000, fully 22 percent of all employees will be working at home, using information technology.

Joining the telecommuters are the "worksteaders," small entrepreneurs working from a home office. The U.S. Chamber of Commerce reports that in 1990, 15 million people will list a home address as their principal place of business. The majority of these businesses are built around microcomputers, either for their product or service or for the fast, accurate record-keeping that makes them profitable. More and more of these small businesses are headed by women. In a mass "homecoming," these feminine entrepreneurs are leaving traditional jobs to build businesses they can operate even while rearing children.

Telecommuters and worksteaders report that they are able to get more work done at home because they suffer fewer interruptions and can thus concentrate better on their work. They also benefit from a greater sense of control over their work, more flexible scheduling of their home lives, improved communications both in their private lives and in their jobs, and savings on food, clothing, and transportation.

Business also benefits, and not only because telecommuters require little in the way of costly office space. Companies enjoy greater staffing flexibility, because they can recruit highly qualified people who live too far from the office to commute, but may still telecommute. As employers offer their workers the alternatives of flextime and flexplace, they establish an environment of individual responsibility, initiative, and accountability. And when companies act on the principle that they are paying employees to get the job done, not merely to put in time, they find measurable productivity increases, lower unit labor costs, and overall improvement in operating effectiveness. In trusting employees with more control over their working hours, companies are discovering renewed organizational flexibility and responsiveness—key ingredients in today's increasingly competitive environment.

Telecommuting also offers a solution to at least one major problem of society in general: it may relieve the traffic gridlock many commuters experience daily. According to a 1988 report by the California Transportation Commission, commuters there already waste an estimated 400,000 hours and $500 million each year because of stop-and-go freeway conditions. The slowly moving cars also spew needless tons of pollution into the air each day. Already, California legislators are beginning to wonder how they can encourage tele-commuting as an alternative to covering ever larger portions of their state with pavement. The question will occur to many state and local governments as the suburbs grow ever more crowded and commuting becomes increasingly nightmarish.

FROM WORKSTYLE TO LIFESTYLE

As we saw in the first chapter, more Americans each year are finding enough economic security to turn some of their attention away from their jobs and toward more personal rewards. As we approach 2000, people will still work hard, but the frenetic competition of the 1980s "yuppies" to work the longest day and pull down the highest income will be replaced by a healthier enjoyment of life and family and a desire for "quality of life." If the eighties' motto was "live to work," the goal of the nineties will be "work to live."

One of the most important measures of a "high-quality" life is the amount of time people can spend with their families and on personal interests. Telecommuting will give us more time for both. In the coming years, more and more of us will find new, often creative ways to earn an adequate living without having to shape our lives around our jobs. Save for vacation travel, we may seldom leave home.

Aging Baby Boomers are new to this "cocooning" lifestyle. After having spent years "married" to the office, they are finally starting families and trading some of their chances for income and career advancement for a better home life. And as former hard-hitting executives seek to slow down and find a balance between jobs and family, the boundaries between the two will become increasingly blurred. Men and women will find themselves sharing responsibilities and goals to an ever-greater degree. By 2000, this somewhat elitist trend will have penetrated much of the American workforce.

This will be one factor that promotes the continuing flight from cities and the most crowded suburbs toward rural America, particularly in the South and West, where good weather encourages outdoor recreation. Many will choose to live in luxury developments built around a special-interest leisure facility, such as a golf course or a small airfield for amateur pilots. With the rise of telecommuting, people will no longer have to go job-hunting when they make such a move; the terminals in their home offices will link with their employers' computers just as easily from a home outside Santa Fe as it did from a condo in Scarsdale.

Even those stuck in the cities will attempt to revert to a small-town way of life. They will insist on more personalized services, such as closer relationships with the family doctor, lawyer, and banker. Others will fix up their homes and spend time in the garden, even if it is planted on a city rooftop or terrace.

With their leisure hours and disposable income, Americans will seek out one-of-a-kind furniture and handicrafts to decorate their homes. They will spend more time in quality recreations: dining in fine restaurants, going to the opera or ballet. (Hard as it is to believe, in 1986, for the first time, Americans actually spent more on the performing arts than on sports—$3.4 billion versus $3.1 billion.) Above all, they will travel.

Yet none of this means that they will begin to neglect their jobs, which, in fact, will be focused on more than ever. As a people, Americans are becoming more interested in job satisfaction than in either job security or a bigger paycheck, according to a national survey of corporate personnel officers. Work is no longer something done because someone else tells Americans to do it, or even because they need the money. Rather, Americans work for themselves, motivated largely by a sense of responsibility for performance. So instead of simply putting their time in, they will work harder—in those hours that they choose to spend working—to see that their jobs are done right.

A major part of their "spare time" will be spent in training, either to do their jobs better or to equip themselves for some new line of work. To help people remain productive in an ever-changing environment, new education and training programs will encourage the development of "flexpertise," the skill of learning a new career quickly. As the work week shrinks, Americans will spend much of their new free time in school. This lifetime of education eventually will grow into the single largest demand on nonworking hours.

AN UPWARD SPIRAL

These parallel trends—toward automation, more flexible workstyles, greater leisure, a higher quality of life, and constant retraining in off-hours—will quickly prove self-reinforcing. Each will add to the efficiency of the economy; that will raise the standard of living and quality of life; and better lives will make Americans more willing, efficient workers, in a spiral of rising productivity.

Flextime, flexplace, and job-sharing are all key components in this future. When people can share available work time, they spread jobs among more persons. They also share the limited number of desirable positions among an increasingly skilled workforce. Thus, qualified people who might otherwise be out of work are able to support themselves, and their employers gain the skills and creativity of people whose talents would otherwise be lost to them. The nation becomes more productive as a result.

With automation, future relations between employers and employees will be based on continuous flows of information in a network fashion. Organizational charts will be redrawn weekly. The traditional pyramid will be replaced by interactive circles in an organic system that is able to respond quickly to changes in its environment. Individuals will have high degrees of autonomy, yet be bound together by information and communications systems. The best of these new-age companies will be less authoritarian, more streamlined and decentralized, and ready to abandon old products and old ways as soon as their markets show any sign of weakening.

New emphasis on training and education will bring productivity gains to every sector of the economy. Today, adult illiteracy costs the United States $225 billion per year in lost industrial productivity, unrealized tax revenues, welfare, crime, prisons, and related social problems. The American workforce is one of the least literate in the industrialized world, with some 45 million job-holding adults who are either illiterate or only marginally able to read and write. The shrinking work week will allow for more time to repair such deficiencies; and business, facing a growing shortage of new workers, will do all it can to help Americans take advantage of that opportunity.

For most Americans, the result will be greater affluence, personal freedom, and satisfaction with their lives as America reaches the early years of the twenty-first century.

THE END-OF-CENTURY

PHENOMENON

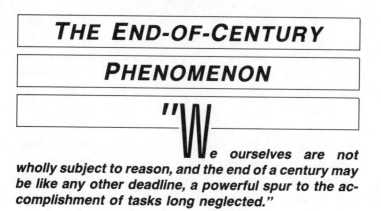

"**W**e ourselves are not wholly subject to reason, and the end of a century may be like any other deadline, a powerful spur to the accomplishment of tasks long neglected."

Throughout *American Renaissance,* we have dealt with tangible forces. We have looked at technology and economics, and have calibrated the changing balance of world power. Now it is time to deal with *in*tangible forces. The topic of this chapter is a sort of magic.

More for emotional reasons than for any logical cause, the end of one century and the beginning of another is a time when creativity flows with special freedom. At such moments the relative predictability of human events seems to fray at the edges, letting in a spontaneity whose expression even the best forecasters can seldom guess in advance. These moments can occur in the adolescence of a century, or in its middle age, but when a century nears its climax we can be sure that such a time is again at hand.

As the clock ticks its way through the tenth of ten decades and begins its next hundred-year cycle, the themes that have shaped human affairs since the last great transition somehow seem to reach their zenith and conclusion, while the themes that will dominate the coming years begin to take shape. Like the Cheshire Cat, these new themes and ideas often seem to materialize from thin air, but in reality spring from the human spirit.

There is nothing particularly rational about this coincidence of centennial and creativity. Neither is it entirely surprising. We ourselves are not wholly subject to reason, and the end of a century may be like any other deadline, a powerful spur to the accomplishment of tasks long neglected. The deadline is no less powerful for being a matter of tradition and symbolism, rather than practical import. In fact, that may be the key. Faced with a call to action, but no mandatory focus for it, our minds are free to move almost at random in a pattern of creative chaos, following the random impulses from which true novelty is made.

We see this "end-of-century effect" in nearly all fields of creative endeavor. Sigmund Freud wrote his seminal books and papers between 1893 and 1906, the same years in which Frank Lloyd Wright was creating his architectural revolution. Beethoven, Picasso, and Einstein all did their formative work during the last five years of one century and the first five years of the next. So did a vast number of less talented people whose contributions have been forgotten. It was during the 1890s that Vladimir Illyich Ulyanov, later known as Lenin, finally dedicated his life to the cause of a Marxist revolution in Russia. With luck, it may be in the 1990s that his successors at last unexpectedly begin to clean up the worldwide chaos that Lenin's efforts left behind. If so, the theme of conflict between communism and capitalism, set at the turn of the twentieth century, may be replaced—exactly on schedule—by a theme of cooperation between former enemies for the betterment of humanity.

Ideas have taken root more quickly of late, and change has moved faster, thanks to the development of modern communications networks. In the past, say before the late eighteenth century, the grand movements of history clearly grew from local events whose influence their creators seldom could accurately conceive. And they grew slowly. Before that, an isolated school of artists might blossom in one country; a few religious zealots might conclude that the Second Coming was at last at hand and begin whatever preparations they considered appropriate. But there it ended, often for years. One idea might inspire other local artists to change their work, and then the artists of neighboring cities, and finally those of distant lands, traveling no more quickly than word of mouth; another idea might become a minor joke, good for a laugh at the local inn. Mass movements and rapid change could not exist when innovators had no efficient way to spread their views to other susceptible minds.

By 1795, more efficient ways had begun to appear: the postal network in the new United States was so well developed, traffic across the Atlantic so busy, that people learned of events in other states in a few days, and of developments abroad in weeks. A century later, the telegraph, railroad, and steamship had knit the world together ever more tightly, and the Gay Nineties ended with a burst of creativity in art, music, science, and popular culture the like of which has seldom been seen. Decades of change were compressed into a few short years.

This time we have television to spread the word, computers to offer new opportunities for creation, and the end, not merely of a century, but of a *millennium* to celebrate. In music, art, literature, and popular culture, we can expect the coming years to bring forth an outpouring of exotic new styles and movements ricocheting instantaneously from computer network to TV screen around the world in hours. Ideas will spring forth so quickly that it will be almost impossible to tell where they originated. Most will be evanescent. Some may endure. All will add their increment of influence to the shape of the future.

CENTURIES PAST

In this case, the past truly is prologue. We can see the turn-of-the-century effect throughout much of history. Let us begin at one historical turning point, the final years of the fifteenth century.

It had been a busy century already. This was the age of Machiavelli, the Borgias, and the first of the Medici; of Joan of Arc, Martin Luther, and the Grand Inquisitor Torquemada; of Gutenberg; of da Vinci and Dürer. England and France spent the first fifty-three years of the century fighting the second half of the Hundred Years' War. No fewer than seven kings held the throne of England, most dying violently.

But in the 1490s there came a flowering of creativity that would reshape the world, not just for the next century, but for all the centuries to follow. In the performing arts, ballet was born in the Italian courts. In literature, the modern profession of book publishing arose and divided itself into its three separate trades—type founder, printer, and bookseller—some forty years after Gutenberg printed his Mazarin Bible. In art, Leonardo da Vinci created his *Last Supper;* Michelangelo began his career under the sponsorship of Lorenzo de Medici and then moved to Rome, where he sculpted his *David* and *Pietà.* In science, Copernicus studied astronomy at the University of Cracow, the beginning of a line of thought that eventually changed man's view of himself and the universe. In technology, da Vinci created the first conceptual aircraft more practical than wax-and-feather wings. And in medicine, a Swiss pig gelder named Jakob Nufer performed the first Cesarean operation on a living woman.

In 1492, Columbus set sail for the Far East, and discovered the New World. He was followed by John and Sebastian Cabot, Vasco da Gama, Amerigo Vespucci, and the world as we know it. The fifteenth century would be the age of exploration.

One century later, in the 1590s and early 1600s, we find a time of scientific discovery, attempted conquest, and the greatest literary outpouring in history. It was the time of Galileo's first works and Giordano Bruno's last, of Tycho Brahe and Johannes Kepler. When the 1590s began, the Copernican revolution had languished for nearly a century. When it ended, no one could honestly doubt that the sun was the center of our solar system, and just one of countless stars.

The revolution in literature in the 1590s was just as historic. Above all, this was the time when Cervantes wrote the first part of *Don Quixote,* the first modern novel; when Edmund Spenser published *Epithalamion* and *The Faerie Queen;* and when Shakespeare wrote his sonnets (not published until 1609) and fully three-fourths of his plays over a period of fifteen years. Among them were virtually all of his greatest works, including *Richard III, The Comedy of Errors, The Taming of the Shrew, Romeo and Juliet, The Merchant of Venice, Much Ado About Nothing, Julius Caesar, Hamlet, Othello, King Lear,* and *Macbeth.*

One century later, in the 1690s, the focus had shifted dramatically. The era of Baroque music was reaching its height. As the decade opened, Henry Purcell and Alessandro Scarlatti dominated the scene; four years into the next, the young J. S. Bach wrote his first work at the age of nineteen. In 1690, John Locke published his two best-known works, *Essay Concerning Human Understanding* and *Two Treatises on Civil Government,* the wellsprings of our modern sense of human rights and in large part the inspiration for the American and French revolutions. Wars were still being fought throughout the Old World: between England and Ireland again, between the Turks and Hungary still, and between France and Germany. In the New World, William Penn's rights to his colony were briefly revoked, then restored, but not before the citizens of Pennsylvania developed a taste for life free of the Proprietors. In Virginia, the growth of vast plantations worked by slaves began to drive smaller farmers from their land, spurring the long migration west that eventually peopled the continent. In New England, Cotton Mather preached that even his stern Puritan faith must be ruled by reason.

In the 1790s, the arts and music still appear thoroughly classical, at least to modern sensibilities. Louis David painted his *Murder of Marat* in 1792, *The Rape of the Sabine Women* in 1799; Goya's *Maja Nude* and *Maja Clothed* and his portraits of the Duchess of Alba are all from this period. Haydn wrote his London symphonies, his two great oratorios, *The Creation* and *The Seasons,* and the best of his chamber music in this decade; Beethoven became his student in 1792 and a decade later had firmly established the romantic movement in music.

Yet, in politics, we come at last to a period that begins to look distinctly modern. In the New World, as the decade opened, George Washington had just completed his first year as President, Congress had sat for the first time, and the Supreme Court had heard its first cases. In 1792, Kentucky became the first new state admitted to the Union. In these years, the United States took the form we know today.

In the Old World, a single event was shaping the entire century to come: the French revolution. In 1790, it, too, was one year old. Within a few years, the Reign of Terror would thoroughly undo the Ancien Régime, with the guillotine claiming the lives of Louis XVI and Marie Antoinette, Danton and Desmoulins, Robespierre and St. Just, and thousands of unknowns. As the decade began, Napoleon was a student in military school; when it ended, he had carried out his campaigns against Italy and Egypt and been named First Consul. By 1814 he had been replaced by the Bourbon monarchy, which the Revolution had been intended to overthrow. On the surface, a small ocean of blood had been spilled without effect. Yet when the revolution began, France was still a largely feudal state. When it was over, the bourgeois were clearly the dominant power in society, the Code

Napoleon had introduced the concept of social justice to Europe, and the modern sense of nationalism had begun to appear.

At last we come to the 1890s: the "Gay Nineties," a time when, it is said, the sheer joy of living flowed in abundance (at least among those who could afford that luxury) and a sense of possibilities was in the air. In the United States, it was a time of world's fairs, particularly in Chicago, that presaged the rise of technology, science, and modern architecture in the twentieth century. The 1890s were also an era of flamboyant wealth, of Diamond Jim Brady and Gentleman Jim Corbett, of Andrew Carnegie and J. Pierpont Morgan. In England, the long, sober reign of Queen Victoria was drawing to a close, and society was shaped by the extravagant, amorous Edward VII, who would inherit sovereignty in 1901. The Empire spanned the world, its power reaffirmed by the Boer War at the turn of the century.

For science, it was the time when modern physics was born. William Röentgen discovered X rays in 1895. Before the decade was out, William Ramsay discovered helium, xenon, krypton, and neon; Ernest Rutherford found that electricity and magnetism were one; J. J. Thompson discovered the electron; and Rutherford elucidated radioactive decay. In 1900, Max Planck proposed his quantum theory, which still governs our understanding of the universe. And Albert Einstein was hard at work on the theory of relativity.

The essence of the age coalesced in Europe in one city: Vienna. The *fin de siècle* atmosphere of Vienna during the 1890s and the first years of the twentieth century—a period that combined decadence, wistfulness, and monumental creativity—is likely to reoccur in cities like Tokyo, Los Angeles, Hong Kong, and Beijing as the new century approaches.

Given the enormous social strife and political unrest that spread through China in the spring of 1989, the entire country, with its billion people and its suppressed intellectual community, will be a wellspring not only of political ferment but also of creative thought in areas as diverse as physics, painting, and literature. Given the repressed climate that is likely to continue in China for some years now, we can anticipate that leading Chinese dissidents will become as familiar to the American public as Solzhenitsyn and Sakharov were to a previous generation. The Chinese physicist Fang Lizhi has already assumed such a major international position, and he will be followed in the proceeding years by numerous other Chinese martyrs and intellectuals. To understand the forces that are likely to occur in a place like Los Angeles or Beijing, one must again return to Vienna.

In Vienna, during the concluding years of the nineteenth century, there was a restlessness with the old order and an apprehension with the imminence of modern culture and progress that combined to stir the arts and the intellectual roots of the city. This cultural phenomenon was unalterably linked, not only in Vienna, but somewhat less so in capitals like Berlin and Paris, with the *fin de siècle* or turn-of-the-century phenomenon. In Vienna, this intellectual ferment and cultural deracination manifested itself most clearly in the intellectual salons of the city; the movement produced not only a glittering social milieu that rejected the classical images of the nineteenth century in fields like painting and architecture, but also caused enormous class divisions and social tensions whose full effects would only be felt thirty and forty years later.

CREATIVE FIRES
THIS TIME

We do not really mean to give the end-of-the-century effect credit for the works of Shakespeare and Beethoven, or even for the French Revolution. Genius appears in its own time and, if genuine, will find some way to express itself; and so vast a purging as the French Revolution seems more the work of history itself than of the individuals who set it in motion. Yet perhaps the slaughter of the Bourbons makes the point: there are times when the atmosphere is thick with the potential for change, and works of genius or of madness have their best chance for a friendly reception. A disproportionate number have occurred when an aged century was about to give way to a new one.

Where will it strike this time? What unpredictable social and intellectual changes await America (and the world) as the twentieth century slips away?

Well, even if they are unpredictable, perhaps there is still something useful to be said beyond throwing up our hands. There are a few trends that may point the way. They affect not the things we have done, but the way we go about doing them, the way we think.

For one thing, there certainly will be unpredictable breakthroughs in the sciences. Some 80 percent of the doctors, chemists, engineers, physicists, and mathematicians who have ever lived are alive today. Most are still in their productive years. We have reached more than a critical mass in many fields.

For another, we have begun to break out of the rigid categories that for decades limited our activities. "Interdisciplinary studies" have at last become something more than a catchphrase used to justify grant applications by academics who have little to offer their own fields. The American space program remains a testimonial to the power of interdisciplinary work, threadbare after years of unconscionable neglect, but inspiring still. Biomedical engineering is combining fundamental biology, electronics, mechanical engineering, and a dozen other specialties to build a new brand of medicine that no one field could have produced. In many cases, this interdisciplinary approach unites people who ordinarily would remain separated. Some of the most advanced robots to date have combined electronics from Unimation, optics from MIT's Lincoln Laboratories, hydraulic and mechanical systems from Cincinnati Milacron, and computers from IBM.

So, in the 1990s, look to the boundaries, the places where seemingly unrelated disciplines rub together. We do not know whether the end-of-the-century phenomenon will bring us historical calculus, biochemical astronomy, subatomic sociology, or some other combination that today sounds comically improbable. But the flourishing fields of computer art and "space music" would have been equally inconceivable two decades ago. Some of the least predictable and most fertile developments of the next decade will emerge from this kind of cross pollination.

Finally—and we are almost reluctant to mention it—a new brand of philosophy seems to be developing in the United States, the effects of which seem as wholly unpredictable as anything in human activity: so-called New Age thinking. A combination of the human-potential movement of the 1970s with old-fashioned mysticism, of systems thinking with a kind of humanistic religious faith, it embraces everything from crystal healing to old-fashioned astrology. The New Age belief structure seems to us more than fuzzy-mindedness (or perhaps less), more than a willing suspension of disbelief; it seems a willful abandonment of critical thought in all its forms. Yet it has gained adherents in all fields, at all levels of society, and throughout Western Europe as well as the United States. We are aware that our response mildly resembles the outrage that met the first exhibits of Impressionist painting and the knee-jerk skepticism of physicists confronted with Heisenberg's uncertainty principle. We can see no future for the New Age. Neither can we wholly ignore it.

After all, this chapter was meant to deal in magic.

EPILOGUE:

A NEW STYLE OF

WORLD LEADERSHIP

The American position is a very special one. For all its economic and perhaps military decline, it remains "the decisive actor in every type of balance and issue." Because it has so much power for good or evil, because it is the linchpin of the western alliance system and the center of the existing global economy, what it does, or does not do, is so much more important than what any of the other Powers decides to do.

—Paul Kennedy, in *The Rise and Fall of Great Powers*

The era when the United States could, as Teddy Roosevelt advised, walk softly and carry a big stick is long gone. So are the halcyon postwar days when American business had so little competition in world markets that its companies could fatten themselves almost at leisure, like grazing cattle. And so is the time when, within the United States, a wealthy, powerful, white elite could use the state and federal governments to manage the country for its own private benefit. Americans have been struggling, often awkwardly, to adapt to those realities for more than twenty years. As we have seen, during the 1990s, the transformation to a new order will at last begin to take hold.

By the year 2000, the United States will be a wealthier and more tranquil nation. It will be more peaceful and less contentious largely because technology will have made it a more affluent and egalitarian society. The United States will also be a happier place because it will finally have adopted rational solutions to such problems as drug abuse and falling educational standards. As the tumultuous twentieth century yields to the twenty-first, we will live better in almost every way.

In a relative sense, the United States may also be a more powerful nation at the turn of the century. If so, it will have its competitors to thank. In the 1990s, and for many years to come, its great adversaries—Japan, in business, and the Soviet Union, in the sphere of domestic affairs—will have no alternative but to focus their attention on pressing internal problems. To the extent that they do so, they will cede to America an opportunity to prosper and to wield greater influence in world affairs. To the extent that they do not, they will steepen their own decline, ultimately giving the United States even more freedom from competition.

But the world's growing economic and political interdependence will mean that America must define its leadership role differently in coming years. American politicians and diplomats have long been in the habit of leading by *dictat,* restrained only by the need to curry favor with the voters at home. That policy will no longer work in the world of 2000. Imperial leadership will have to give way to corporate leadership, subject to the veto of an active "board of directors" of the industrialized powers. (If General Secretary Gorbachev's reforms take root in the Soviet Union, even America's traditional adversary may have a seat on the board.) But leadership by consent is leadership nonetheless. America will wield it throughout the first half of the twenty-first century, if only because no other country enjoys the combination of wealth, power, and prestige required to do so.

To some, accustomed to the old style of hegemony, any forecast of renewed prosperity and power must seem optimistic beyond all reason. It is difficult to recall the Vietnam War or the economic chaos of the Carter years without feeling that the United States then had clearly lost its way. Or to view America today—its economy burdened by unprecedented foreign debt and budget deficits, its productive assets being sold off piecemeal to owners in other lands, its young people poisoned by drugs and deprived of an adequate education—without feeling that the nation has made little progress since then. From there, it is a short step to the despair that moved Oswald Spengler to his disturbingly accurate forecast of doom in the Europe of the 1920s.

Yet in contemporary America, there is actually very little cause for despair. As we have seen, America's problems are not nearly as insoluble as they sometimes appear. Those that cannot be eliminated, such as AIDS and drug abuse, may blight individual lives, but they can be endured by society at large.

The cures and partial solutions that we envision for the turn of the century do require some measure of political will to accomplish them. That will has been lacking throughout the 1970s and 1980s, and it remains the only requirement that is missing. The United States finds it enormously difficult to build the national consensus that a democracy must achieve if it is to govern itself effectively. That nearsighted refusal to set aside partisan bickering in order to deal with America's many pressing problems is probably the strongest argument supporting the "America is doomed" school of forecasting.

Yet whenever a functional unanimity is truly needed in the United States, it usually appears—just before it is too late. Witness the early history of the Second World War, when most Americans resisted the obvious necessity of entering the war in Europe and a minority were eager to join the German cause. Even after Pearl Harbor, many people still hoped to confine U.S. hostilities to the Pacific and seek a rapprochement with Hitler after England and France had been defeated. Scant months later, such fantasies had been put aside, and the nation was all but unanimous in pursuing the annihilation of the Axis powers.

In the 1990s, the American people will at last recognize in debt, drugs, AIDS, and illiteracy the fabled "moral equivalent of war" and achieve the consensus that has so long eluded them. In part, the United States will accept workable solutions to its troubles because, as at Pearl Harbor, it has finally been backed against a wall: The social and economic cost of further delay has grown so high that desperation measures are becoming acceptable. In part, too, the long-standing American preference for politically convenient rhetoric over sorely needed results will come to an end because the Baby Boom generation will at last inherit control of the government from its parents, a generation that had greater patience, less interest in social activism, and less singleminded concern for getting things done.

The society that emerges from the strife-ridden twentieth century will be very different from the America of today:

Most important, and seldom considered in "futurist" tracts, the American people themselves will change. Their rapid evolution will be by far the most influential factor in setting the national agenda a decade hence. Americans will, as we have seen, grow older, on average, as the Baby Boom generation reaches middle age. And they will grow even less homogeneous, as the white majority of the past finds that immigration from Asia and South America, combined with its own low fertility, has made it just one more minority in a nation where no single ethnic group can dominate the rest. Accommodating these changes, and in particular absorbing several million new Americans, many of whom are poor and illiterate even in their native languages, will be one of the greatest challenges facing the United States in the years to come. Yet it will also be one of the great opportunities of this period. People who become Americans by choice rather than by birth have turned out to be among the most vital and productive segments of society. Recent arrivals from Korea and Cuba have maintained that tradition, even in the America of high technology and mass culture. Any honest, effective effort to assimilate the immigrants of the 1990s into American life will give the nation an economic and cultural transfusion that can only make it stronger.

Economic reforms will give all Americans, native and transplanted, a better chance at a comfortable and rewarding life. Eventually relieved of its government debt and international trade deficit, the United States will achieve a new prosperity based, not on the disguised Keynesianism of the Reagan era, but on the vigor of a healed economy. In this, it will be aided by the gradual decline of its chief rival, Japan, and by the growth of internal trade with the new states that once were Canada.

Private citizens will retain more of this wealth than they did during the peak-tax years of the 1970s, and the goods on which they spend it will cost less, thanks to the continuing rise of automation. Thus, their effective standard of living will begin to grow steadily again, as it has not done since the OPEC oil shocks nearly two decades ago.

In all these changes, and many others, two factors will play major roles: technology and education.

The technology that dominates most discussions of the future will provide some of the tools needed for more fundamental transformations. As the turn of the century approaches, large-scale automation will help a shrinking workforce outproduce the larger generations that preceded it. New medical therapies will give Americans longer and healthier lives. Computers and advanced communications equipment will streamline not only business, but the educational process as well.

Yet the make-or-break factor is education. When Tocqueville toured the United States in the 1830s, he estimated that fully 90 percent of Americans were literate. Today, not even the best public high schools can be relied on to turn out a large majority of graduates who can read, much less write, and do arithmetic without the crutch of a calculator. With so little training, young people can be expected neither to guide their own lives wisely nor to grow into adults who can manage a vast technological society in the face of competition from countries with far better schools. At heart, America's social and economic problems stem from trying to run a complex nation with simple people.

If we expected this problem to survive the 1990s, we, too, might despair. But for all the reasons we have cited in Chapter 4, we believe that America will repair its school systems: computers, educational software, and tailored curricula will make it easier to learn; business will contribute both personnel and money to help make the system work; a growing network of day-care centers will give the children of working mothers, and of parents who themselves were deprived of an education, the intellectual head start that the children of past generations received from middle-class nuclear families. And a frightened nation, recognizing that neglect of education is slow but certain economic suicide, will demand that its schools receive the support they need from Washington. In a sense, the United States of 2000 will be a nation on a war footing, much as it was in the early 1940s, with almost everyone working for the cause. But rather than building bombers and tanks, Americans will be working to give their young the education required for a productive life in an increasingly technological world.

Without educational reform, none of the other changes we anticipate can alone keep the United States prosperous and strong. But with an educated, creative, hardworking, and technologically sophisticated populace—and just a few policy changes in Washington—America will regain the prosperity it enjoyed in the 1950s and has been losing ever since. With this newly regained affluence, America will have less of a problem maintaining its diplomatic and military power in world affairs—a might for which it will have less and less need. It will also be able to spend more of its national income on education and research, the fundamental sources of wealth in a technological era. And thus the cycle will begin again. With renewed wealth, military strength, and the undisputed control of its own destiny, America will retain its influence over its neighbors—not the nearly dictatorial power it once enjoyed, but all the power it needs.

World leadership may be, as Paul Kennedy argues, unsustainable over a long period. The United States may eventually lose its economic supremacy, its world leadership, and its military security. Someday. But that day lies in the unenvisioned future. Even in its current troubled state, America retains more military strength than any other country on this side of the Iron Curtain, more economic power than any nation in the world, more prestige and moral force than any other participant on the global scene. In the worst of all possible futures, the United States—burdened by ever-mounting trade deficits, a decaying school system, the hapless victim of drugs and AIDS and international terrorism—would remain the world's leader for several more generations. It took, after all, more than a century of industrial decline and two world wars to erode the greatness and the glory of the British Empire. Mere decay would require much longer to reduce American might to a secondary role. With the changes to come in the 1990s, no force on Earth can do so.

For the next fifty years the United States will remain the most productive country in the world, the most powerful, the richest, and the most free. By the year 2000, few of us will have reason to doubt it.

APRIL 1990

A year ago, we believed that the United States was destined for a new era of wealth and power, though severe difficulties would remain to trouble it in the coming century. In that year, some of the most troubling international problems it faced have all but vanished. They have been replaced by a world of opportunity almost unimaginable before the recent tide of change swept across Eastern Europe. It is somewhat ironic that these developments have not sprung from the efforts of America's leaders, but instead have arrived almost as gifts from the first enlightened statesman ever to hold power in the Soviet Union, traditional archenemy of the Western democracies.

On all sides, the barriers which the United States has faced are falling rapidly. In politics, the communist dictatorships of Eastern Europe are being replaced by capitalist democracies as fast as their people can engineer the transition; of the two communist nations in the American hemisphere, one has disappeared, while the other is reluctantly coming to face the reality that it must find some accommodation with the prosperous giant next door; even in China, South

Africa, and the Soviet Union itself, democracy shows signs of awakening. In the economy, the coming "peace dividend" will soon reduce the budget deficit, while the new markets opening up in the former COMECON countries offer new prosperity to American exporters. And in society, this new wealth will be quickly translated into better schools and more effective social programs.

All this is not to say that problems have wholly disappeared. AIDS is still a modern plague for which no cure exists; America's leaders have found no credible, politically acceptable cure for the epidemic of drug abuse abroad in the land; the Middle East will be a trouble spot until Israel agrees to the formation of a Palestinian state in the Gaza Strip and on the Left Bank—a development that may well occur before the year 2000. But after decades of struggle in the post-Kennedy era, it seems that the United States has suddenly been transported into the best of all possible worlds.

For the moment, American policy makers are struggling to deal with these changes, much as one long crippled must adapt to restored mobility. They will soon recognize that the United States has gained both a new freedom to meet its domestic challenges and the chance to wield unprecedented influence in parts of the world that until recently were closed to it. Eventually, they will accept these opportunities, adjust their international and domestic policies, and so guarantee their nation's continuing preeminence in world affairs.

If there ever was a valid cause to doubt America's future, the last year has removed it. Long into the twenty-first century, the United States will remain first among equals in a world of growing freedom and prosperity, peace, and justice. Even today, few of us have reason to doubt it.

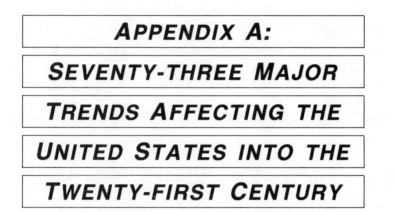

APPENDIX A:

SEVENTY-THREE MAJOR

TRENDS AFFECTING THE

UNITED STATES INTO THE

TWENTY-FIRST CENTURY

GENERAL LONG-TERM
SOCIETAL TRENDS

1. Economic prosperity-affluence, low interest rates, low inflation rate. (There may be a recession in 1990, but this will only be a perturbation. Our long-range forecast for the economy is good.)

- Economic growth will continue as technological gains in the manufacturing sector boost productivity, and as slow growth in the labor force is offset by workers who remain in the labor force longer.

- Per capita personal income increased 1.4% annually (1973–83); projected to average 1.8% annually (1983–2000).

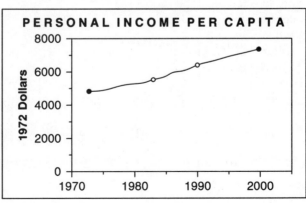

PERSONAL INCOME PER CAPITA

- Part of society's affluence rests on credit-card use or overuse; extension of excessive credit could result in government-imposed limitations.

- Intolerably high interest rates in 1981 have resulted in "managed" (by the Federal Reserve Board) low interest rates.

- An intolerably high inflation rate in 1980 has resulted in monetary policies that tend to assure low inflation rates.

- Monetary policies instituted by Federal Reserve Board Chairman Volker will be continued by Greenspan to keep interest and inflation rates in check.

2. Rise of knowledge industries and a knowledge-dependent society.

- About half of all service workers (43% of the labor force by 2000) will be involved in collecting, analyzing, synthesizing, structuring, storing, or retrieving information as a basis of knowledge.

- Half of these people will opt for "flextime," "flexplace" arrangements which allow them to work at home, communicating with the office via computer terminals.

- By 1995, 80% of all management will be "knowledge workers."

- There will continue to be vast opportunities within the computer industry for developers of hardware and software.

- "Expert systems" will issue reports and recommend actions on data gathered electronically without human intervention.

- Revenues from expert system off-the-shelf application software is rising exponentially, and is expected to continue.

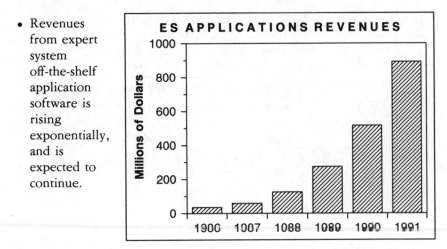

- Industries that will benefit from expert systems include insurance, investments and banking; manufacturing and process control; equipment diagnosis and quality control.

- By 2001, nearly all college textbooks and many high school and junior high books will come with computer disks to aid in learning.

- Computers will provide access to all the card catalogs of all the libraries in the world by the late 1990s. It will be possible to call up on a PC screen millions of volumes from distant libraries. Videodiscs will enhance books by providing visual and audio information and even recordings of smells, feels, and tastes.

- Many encyclopedic works, large reference volumes, and heavily illustrated manuals will be more economical to produce and sell through electronic packaging. Videodisc will fill this need.

3. Fewer very poor and very wealthy in our society.

- The number of households with annual money income over $50,000 (11.1–14.8% of total) *increased* 82% 1970–1986; those with income under $5,000 (6.8–8.5% of total) *increased* 25%, but inclusion of noncash benefits would reduce this figure.

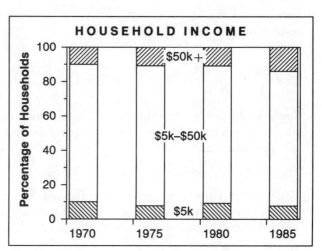

• The number of families with annual money income over $50,000 (13.4–20.7% of total) *increased* 71% 1970–1986; those with income under $5,000 (3.3–5.3% of total) *increased* 54%, but here, too, noncash benefits would reduce this percentage.

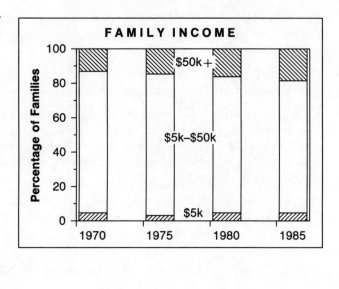

But the Tax Reform Act of 1986 will tend to reverse these trends:

• Fewer loopholes (such as the oil depletion allowance, accelerated depreciation allowances, alternate taxes for bond income) mean the wealthy will pay more tax.

• The burden for poorer taxpayers will be eased.

• The Social Security System will be reformed. Some of the reforms will be means testing, taxation of benefits, and ceilings (although all workers will still have to contribute).

4. Urbanization and suburbanization of rural land.

- Land in farms has decreased steadily since 1959 (1% per year, 1975–1985).

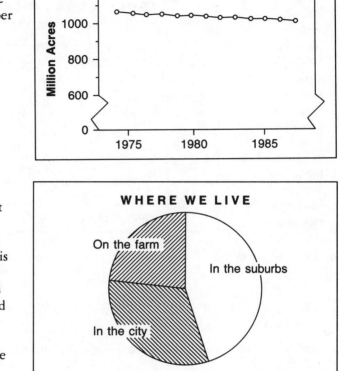

- Greatest development in suburbs (rather than cities): land is cheaper and road systems provide good accessibility. Currently, 44.6% of the U.S. population lives in the suburbs, 31.5% in the city, and 23.3% in rural areas.

- Suburbia itself is being urbanized as satellite cities grow outside the major metropolitan areas. Suburban "downtowns" are being created with the construction of office parks, shopping centers, and entertainment districts.

- Creation of "penturbia" as population expands beyond the suburbs into outlying towns and rural areas.

- "Superburbs" will connect cities in the South and West, where most of the population growth over the next decade is expected to occur.

5. Rise of the middle-class society.

• Fewer very poor/very rich (see number 3).

• Middle
three-fifths of
families have
received
52–54% of
money income
since 1950.
Noncash
benefits, which
would
primarily affect
the lowest
fifth, are not
considered in
this graph.

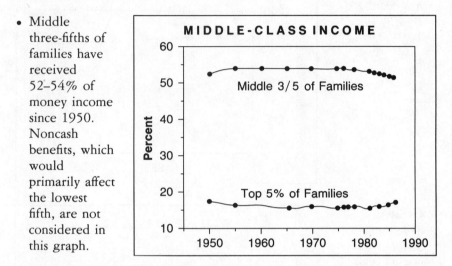

6. Growing acceptance of cultural diversity, resulting in the growth of a truly integrated national society.

• What we see and hear is a leavening influence; all Americans see the same movies and TV programs.

• Schools teach essentially the same thing across the country.

- New modes of transportation, better roads (especially the Interstate system) and accommodations, more leisure time, and greater affluence will allow more frequent travel. This will result in a greater interplay of ideas, information, and concerns.

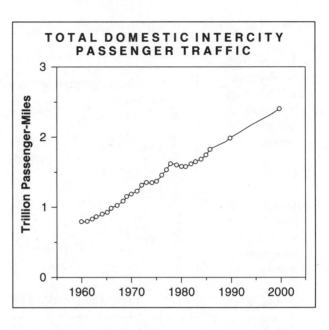

- Intermarriages tend to mix cultures geographically, ethnically, etc.

- Information technologies allow more far-reaching communication as people hook up with the same commercial databases and computer networks, or interact on two-way cable television.

- Regional differences, attitudes, incomes, and lifestyles are blurring as people shift from one region to another.

- Minorities will exert more influence over the national agenda as the population of Blacks, Hispanics, and Asians increases to 23–28% by 2000.

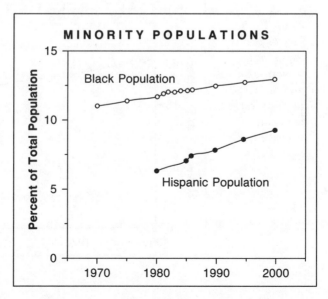

7. A static permanent military establishment.

- Except during
  the Korean
  and Vietnam
  war periods,
  military
  personnel
  strength has
  settled out at
  just over 2
  million, with
  slow growth
  since 1980. If
  superpower
  tensions
  continue to
  diminish, as
  we expect they
  will, force
  levels will tend
  to decline also.

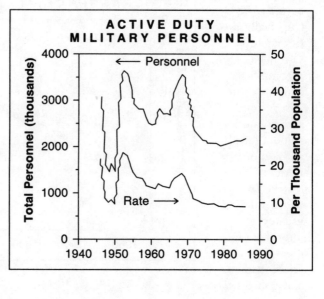

- "Smart" weapons may tend to reduce military personnel requirements.

8. Mobility: (a) personal, (b) physical, (c) occupational, (d) job.

- In the five-year
  period
  1980–1985,
  41.7% of the
  population
  moved. The
  annual
  mobility rate
  has been
  increasing
  since 1983.

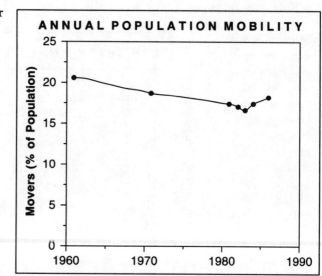

- Modular plastic housing will allow people to move more easily and frequently. People will simply pack up their houses and ship them to new locales.

- Dual-career families, perhaps working in different cities, affect personal mobility.

- Transportation systems are available and accessible to all. High speed, magnetically levitated trains will allow commutes of up to 500 miles.

- A constellation of satellites providing position fixes and two-way communication 24 hours a day will be in place by the 1990s. A person equipped with a mini-transmitter-receiver will be able to send a message anywhere in the world.

- Occupational mobility occurs as people increasingly retrain for new careers.

- The new information-based model for the organization (nonhierarchical, organic system able to respond quickly to environmental changes) fosters greater occupational flexibility and autonomy.

- Job mobility—i.e., changing location or firm but doing the same work—will increase. People will get more used to the idea of changing jobs several times in their lifetimes.

- Movement of jobs to Sunbelt states, right-to-work states (states that bypass the minimum wage), or coastal areas.

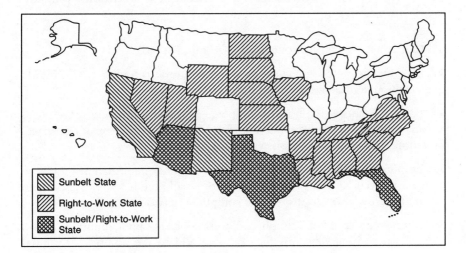

Sunbelt State
Right-to-Work State
Sunbelt/Right-to-Work State

9. International affairs and national security as major societal factors.

- More international travel for business and pleasure.

- More foreign student exchange programs/participation.

- More East-West observation/verification activity, e.g., NATO observers at Warsaw Pact war games (and vice versa), at missile bases, and at munitions manufacturing facilities.

- The Cold War will draw to an end by 2000; the United States and the Soviet Union will compete economically instead of militarily.

- More East-West cultural exchanges.

- More East-West television and radio satellite hookups.

- Growing influence of regional political and economic arrangements (such as EEC, OAS, COMECON).

- The first international treaty to reduce acid rain, approved by 27 nations, should go into effect in 1990; this will be the first step toward environmental cooperation on a global scale.

THE TECHNOLOGY TRENDS

10. The centrality and increasing dominance of technology in the economy and society.

- High technological turnover rate (see number 16).

- Many technological advances (e.g., computers, robotics, CAD/CAM) directly affect the way people live and work.

- Personal robots in the home will appear by 2000. Mundane commercial and service jobs, environmentally dangerous jobs, and repairs of space-station components in orbit will be done by robots.

- Computers will become part of our environment rather than just tools we use for specific tasks. Portable computers will give us wireless access to data wherever we go inside our computer network.

- "Wireless hookup" will simplify relocation of personnel, minimize delays in accomplishing new installations, and add to the ability of terminal equipment to travel with the individual by not forcing the user to travel to the terminal.

- By 2001, artificial intelligence will be in almost universal use among companies and government agencies to help assimilate data and solve problems beyond the range of today's computers. AI's uses: robotics, machine vision, voice recognition, speech synthesis, EDP, health and human services, administration and airline pilot assistance.

- By 2001, expert systems will be in universal use in manufacturing, energy prospecting, automotive diagnostics, medicine, insurance underwriting, and law enforcement.

- Superconductors operating at room temperature will be in commercial use by 2001, resulting in supercomputers the size of three-pound coffee cans, electric motors 75% smaller and lighter than those today, practical hydrogen-fusion power plants, electrical storage facilities with no heat loss, analyzers that can chart the interaction of brain cells, and 200 mph "maglev" trains that float on magnetic cushions.

- There will be much growth in the engineering, technology, and health industries; many new biotechnology jobs will open up.

11. Solutions to the specter of national gridlock in the air and on land will be found in technological advances in transportation.

- Rails, not trains, are on the way out as maglev trains replace the spokes (hops of 100–500 miles) of the airline industry's existing system of hubs and spokes.

- Planes will carry 1,000 passengers. New York, Tokyo, and Frankfurt will become common transfer points for passengers of supersonic planes.

- The average life of a car will be 10 years in 1990 and 22 years by 2000.

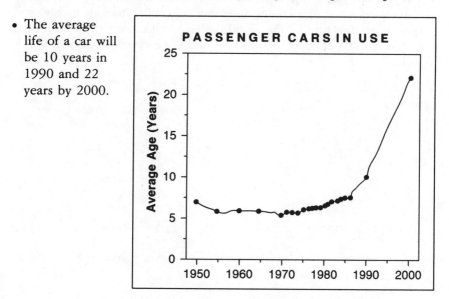

- Advances in automobile technology will give us the "smart car" (equipped with sensors, antilock brakes, computer-orchestrated fuel-injection systems, continuously variable transmission, active suspension, etc.), increasingly powered by batteries, light, and magnetism.

- However, the government will lag behind in bringing highway technology up to par. A White House initiative, "Car Wars," in 2000, will usher in new technologies that allow traffic lights and the roadbed itself to interact with cars.

- Separate lanes for trucks will be enforced.

- Airline crashes will be fewer, with fewer fatalities, by 2000, thanks to implementation of the Traffic and Collision Avoidance System (TCAS), use of satellites for both navigation and communication in transoceanic flights, safer seat design, and fire-resistant fuels.

12. Integration of the national economy.

- Gramm-Rudman-Hollings is forcing tradeoffs to be made across programs, e.g., a space shuttle versus food stamps versus aid to education.

- Arguments surrounding defense versus social programs will become more serious; there will be trade-offs.

13. Integration of the national and international economies.

- The assimilation of the U.S. into the global economy will continue as imports continue to increase, international capital markets merge, and buying patterns around the world coalesce. All these factors contribute to the interdependence of business and government decisions worldwide.

- Foreigners own $1.5 trillion in U.S. assets (one-fourth more than the value of assets the U.S. owns abroad).

INTERNATIONAL INVESTMENT POSITION

- Thirty-nine percent of parts used in manufacturing in the U.S. originate overseas; 37% of parts used by IBM are imported.

- Not limited to U.S.: Japan, like the U.S., must sell internationally to offset energy and scarce resource imports.

- Nationalistic self-interest will continue to yield to international trade cooperation. Both developing and developed countries will focus less on dominating economic competitors and, instead, will put efforts into liberalizing trade cooperation.

- Today $400 worth of health care is built into every Chrysler, $200 into every Japanese car, and $100 into every Korean car.

14. Growth of international economy.

- The 1987 stock-market crash bore witness to interactions among world's stock exchanges.

- The quality of products and services will be increasingly emphasized.

- Deregulation is spreading around the world.

- Trend is toward both national and international privatization, with national governments around the world selling off public services.

    In the United States, this could mean an end to the U.S. Postal Service's monopoly on regular mail service.
    Abroad, this means a transition from federal to private ownership of airlines, railroads, water, and electricity.

15. The growth of research and development as a factor in economy.

- R&D outlays, as percent of GNP (1982 dollars), has varied narrowly (2.1–2.8%) since 1960 and has been rising steadily since 1978.

**R&D OUTLAYS
(CONSTANT 1982 DOLLARS)**

Percent of GNP — years 1960, 1970, 1980, 1990

- R&D outlays are growing most rapidly in the electronics, aerospace, pharmaceutical, and chemical industries.

16. High technological turnover rate.

- The development cycle (invention, innovation, imitation) is steadily shortening; successful products must be marketed quickly.

- New production technologies will continue to be rapidly adopted.

- Computer-aided design in the automobile industry and others shortens the amount of time between idea and finished design.

- All the technological knowledge we work with today will represent only 1% of the knowledge that will be available in 2050.

17. The development of mass media in telecommunications and printing.

- Telecommunications removes geographic barriers; satellite-transmitted data can be set into a computer in a place like the Caribbean by two people at 50 cents per hour and transmitted back to the U.S. for less than $1.50, as compared to having one person set the data in the U.S. at $5 per hour.

- The "integrated information appliance" will combine a computer, modem, fax, and file cabinet in one unit.

- *USA Today,* relying on satellite communications, is printed simultaneously at multiple sites every day.

- Company-owned and industry-wide television networks are bringing programming to thousands of locations.

- Currently, 57% of homes have cable TV; this figure will reach 87% by 2000.

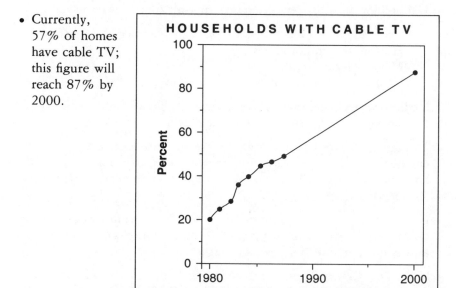

HOUSEHOLDS WITH CABLE TV

- Magazines in the year 2001 will be on floppy disks that allow the reader to interact, play with, and manipulate the information on his or her PC.

- Mass media will be more personalized as consumers use pay-for-view television to select movies and entertainment. Viewers will download their choices from a "teledelivery" service, paying for the program when they see it.

- A computer system will create a personalized newspaper by logging onto news-service databases at night, selecting stories, laying them out, setting the headlines in sizes that reflect their importance to the individual reader, and adding pictures.

- By 2001, new network architectures, operating synergistically with intelligence in terminal systems, will form the foundation on which an infinite variety of telecommunication services will be built. (This will require adoption of technically sound standards for the interfaces between users and the network, as well as among network elements.)

- Nearly unlimited bandwidth of fiber optics, coupled with evolving new network standards, and the ability to use software-defined networks, will result in new network topologies for transmission and distribution networks. Improved line-width lasers or dispersion-shifted fibers, multigigabit systems, coherent detection systems, LEDs for single-mode fibers, and integrated optical circuits will be in widespread use.

18. Major medical advances (see also numbers 51 and 52).

- $100 billion spent in genetic engineering by 2000 will result in:

  Artificial blood (which could replace the nation's blood banks).
  Human growth hormones.
  Memory-recall drugs.
  Newborns with particular disease immunities.

- Medical advances will have given us artificial blood, limbs (feet, hands, arms, legs), hearts, spleens, lungs, and skin.

- Technology makes possible organ transplants, artificial organs, genetic engineering, etc., but raises ethical/moral issues: surrogate motherhood, how to equitably distribute capabilities, when to terminate extraordinary life-support efforts.

- New, computer-based diagnostic tools will be providing doctors with unsurpassed cross-section images of soft and hard tissues inside the body, thus eliminating much exploratory surgery.

- "Bloodless surgery," using advanced lasers, will decrease patient trauma, decrease the length of hospital stays, and help lower medical costs.

- Brain cell and tissue transplants will be in the experimental phase by 2001 to aid victims of retardation and head trauma. Heart repairs will be done using muscles from other parts of the body. Transplanted animal organs will find their way into common use in humans. Laboratory-grown bone, muscle, and blood cells will be used in transplants.

- Pacemakers will have built-in fibrillators so that, if the heart stops beating, a series of shocks will be administered automatically to "restart" it.

- More and better bionic limbs and hearts, drugs that prevent disease and not merely treat symptoms, body monitors that warn when trouble is brewing.

EDUCATIONAL TRENDS

19. Expanding education and training throughout society.

- President George Bush advocates greater federal spending for education.

- Needed: an annual $5-billion increase in federal spending for programs such as Head Start preschool program, federal aid for disadvantaged children, Job Corps and Job Training Partnership Act.

- Half-life of an engineer's knowledge today is 5 years; in 10 years, 90% of what he knows will be on the computer.

- Eighty-five percent of the information in National Institutes of Health computers is upgraded in 5 years.

- A rapidly changing job market, along with the changing requirements of new technologies, will necessitate increased training across the board.

- Because of fundamental changes in the economy, there will be fewer and fewer well-paying jobs not requiring advanced training.

- Close to 6 million jobs will open up in the next decade in the highly skilled occupations—executive, professional, and technical.

- Up to 4% of the labor force will be in job retraining programs by the 1990s to upgrade skills and knowledge to keep pace with changing technologies and changing demands of the work place.

- Schools will train both children and adults around the clock: the academic day will be lengthened to seven hours for children; adults will be working a 32-hour workweek and preparing for their next job in the remaining hours.

- State, local, and private agencies could play a greater role in training by offering internships, apprenticeships, pre-employment training, and adult education.

- Growth in professional alliances between high school and college faculty.

20. New technologies will greatly enhance education and training.

- Job simulation stations (modules that combine computers, videodiscs, and instrumentation to duplicate job-work environments) will be used in training.

- Telecommunications coursework with another school district, state, or county opens up new vistas in education.

- Education becomes more individualized as new media (interactive computer/videodisc) permit students to learn according to their needs and abilities.

- Personal computers with ultra-high-resolution screens, 3-D graphics, high-level interactivity, and artificial intelligence will enhance gaming and simulations used in education and training.

21. Greater role of business in training and education.

- More businesses will be involved in schools, job-training programs, and community source programs.

- The investment by corporations in employee education and retraining, now some $80 billion a year, will double by 2001.

- Automation and computers eliminate low-literacy jobs but replace them with jobs requiring a high degree of literacy. Businesses will have to provide continuous training to their workers to keep up with the greater demands.

- By calling on private business to help direct the training of unemployed workers, the Job Training Partnership Act ($4.5 billion per year) allows greater communication between those who need jobs and those who need workers.

- Most new jobs are generated by small businesses that cannot afford to pay for training; one-half of all funding for formal training comes from 200–300 large companies in business and industry.

22. Education costs will continue to rise.

- Heavy pressure to control costs will emerge.

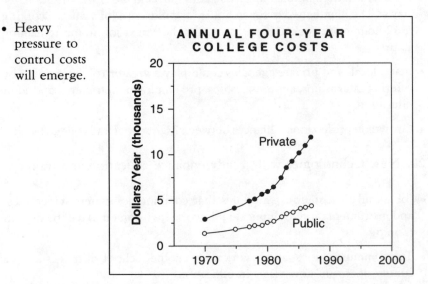

- Increasing costs may escalate to the point where they threaten to reduce the pool of college graduates over the next decade. The graduation rate could also be affected (see number 49).

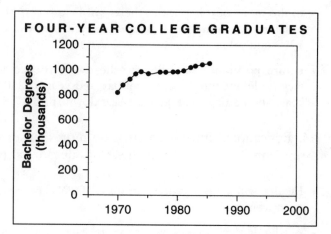

- Two-year colleges and associate degrees will grow.

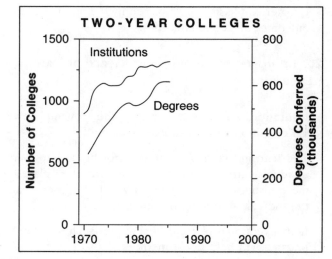

- Loans, rather than grants, will constitute the main source of student financial aid.

23. Educational *perestroika*.

- The information economy's call for skilled workers will necessitate educational reform.
- More students will be actively recruited by science and engineering schools.
- Lackluster performance of U.S. students on standardized tests will prompt inevitable reforms.

- In the midst of this reform, there will be a severe shortage of qualified teachers. An estimated 1 million new teachers will be needed between 1989 and 1993.

- Future possibilities to alleviate the overburdened U.S. school system include lengthening the school day and year to 210 seven-hour days a year, and cutting average class size down from 17.8 to 10 students.

24. Educational institutions will be more concerned with ways to assess outcomes and effectiveness of educational programs.

- Faculty will support efforts to assess their classroom performance and effectiveness.

- Academic departments will support assessment of their academic programs' results and effectiveness.

- Greater emphasis will be placed by the public and the legislatures on the outcomes of public education.

25. Improved pedagogy—the science of learning—will revolutionize learning.

- Institutions will increasingly apply the growing knowledge about individual cognition to educational situations.

- The learning environment will not be as important in the future: individuals will learn more on their own, the "places" of learning will be more dispersed, and the age at which things are learned will depend on the individual, not on tradition.

- Unconventional learning techniques such as sleep-learning and mental practice will help boost memory skills.

- Computer-supported approaches to learning will improve both techniques and allow a greater amount of material to be learned.

- The ultimate consequence may be a one-sixth reduction in learning time overall.

- Despite the new technologies and new approaches to learning, many students will still suffer from learning deficiencies.

- Alternative testing approaches will be widely used for learning feedback.

26. Universities will stress development of the whole student; the total university environment will affect that development.

- Faculty will receive greater support from the administration for class-related activities.

- Individual students will receive more support from faculty and advisors with decisions about academic programs and career paths.

27. Reduction in the size of higher-education institutions.

- By 2001 there will not be enough adolescents to sustain the current number of colleges and universities. Colleges will close their doors, merge with other schools in a federation, reduce faculty size and class offerings, and seek more adult students.

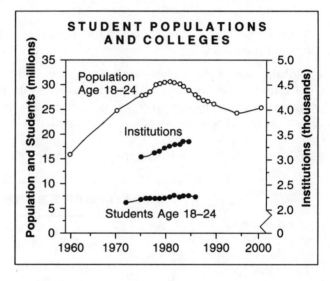

- Private commercial ventures will establish themselves as the proprietors of large electronic databases, eventually replacing university libraries.

- Students will adopt the scholarship mode of learning, learning by consulting books, journals, etc., as professors and Ph.D. candidates do today.

- College and university instructors will find employment at secondary schools, in business-based education programs, and producing educational electronic software.

- More and more businesses will conduct research.

TRENDS IN LABOR FORCE AND WORK

---

28. Specialization.

- Within professions (medical, legal, engineering, etc.) the body of knowledge that must be mastered to excel in a particular area precludes excellence across all areas.

- The same principle applies to artisans, too—auto mechanics, house builders.

- The information-based organization is dependent upon its teams of task-focused specialists.

- Globalization of the economy calls forth more independent specialists: for hundreds of special tasks, corporations will turn to consultants and independent contractors who will specialize more and more highly as markets globalize and technologies differentiate.

29. Growth of the service sector.

- The service sector, as percent of labor force, shows steady growth. The Bureau of Labor Statistics projects 73.5% by 1990, 74.4% by 1995, 77.4% by 2000, but we think the figure will be about 85% by 2000.

- Service jobs have replaced the many well-paying jobs lost in manufacturing, transportation, and agriculture. Low-paying and often part-time, these new jobs pay wages at half the level of manufacturing jobs.

- Approximately 1 million new jobs will be created in the less-skilled and "laborer" categories in the next decade.

30. Further decline of agricultural and manufacturing sectors.

- The growth and extraction industries (agriculture and mining), as a percentage of labor force, show a slow decline: 3.3% in 1990; 3.0% by 1995.

- There will be 1.25 million farmers in the U.S. in 2000; this is 900,000 fewer than today.

- Manufacturing jobs that disappeared between 1979 and 1985 totaled 1.7 million.

- As percent of labor force, the fabrication industries (construction and manufacturing) are expected to continue their steady decline: 23.2% in 1990; 22.6% in 1995; 19.6% in 2000.

- These are BLS projections. We think the figures are too high; for growth/extraction we estimate 2%, and for fabrication 13% by 2000.

- By 2001, percent of labor force in manufacturing will be 9.7, down from 18 percent in 1987. However, productivity will have increased 500 percent in those industries that have become more automated, added robotics, and remained flexible in their production.

- With the evolution of new materials and production technology (e.g., computer-aided design [CAD], computer-aided manufacturing [CAM], robotics, and semiconductors), unskilled and semi-skilled jobs in manufacturing will disappear.

31. Growth of information industries, movement toward an information society. (This is an outgrowth of item 2.)

- By 2000, we predict that 85% of the labor force will be working in the service sector. Of that 85%, 43% will be working in the information industry, 22% of which will be working at home.

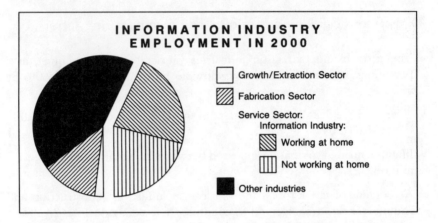

- Information is the primary commodity in more and more industries today.

- Computer competence will approach 100% in U.S. urban areas by the year 2000.

- Seventy percent of U.S. homes will have computers in 2001, compared with 18% now; more than three-fourths will be equipped to permit communication with the public switched network.

- Computers in the home mean that we will have vast new powers over information and services. These include education, work, health care, shopping, banking and finance, and reservations.

- The amount of information accessible through home computers (from telephone links and from disks with thousands of times the capacity of present-day floppies) will be so vast that we will require the services of artificially intelligent electronic assistants to sort through it.

- Interactive cable television means a need for electronic newspapers, electronic shopping, and electronic banking at home.

- Personal computers will be used for voting, filing income tax returns, applying for auto license plates, and taking tests such as college entrance exams and professional accreditations.

- Five of the ten fastest-growing careers between now and 2001 will be computer-related, with the demand for programmers and systems analysts growing by 70%.

- Users will be able to access terminal devices far more easily than they can today as local cubic arrays of co-processors in homes and offices access function-specific subnets via fiber-based fast-packet-switched channels.

- Data transmission and acquisition costs will come down as the public communications network evolves into a predominantly digital configuration, leaving behind the voice-oriented analog signal and the need for modems. Internationally agreed standards, ISDN (Integrated Services Digital Network), will be implemented concurrently, using much existing switching and transmission equipment.

- Telecommunication will become infinitely more transparent to the user while its complexity increases. Cubic-architectured local nodes sending and receiving fast packets over fiber loops in ISDN-like formats will serve as steersmen for not only basic voice and data communication, but also multiple expert systems, providing medical advice in advance of likely illnesses, execution of financial transactions proactively, travel and entertainment options before reservation limits are exceeded, and all forms of education.

- The major change ISDN will deliver by 2001 is to bring data capability to the relatively small user. ISDN will provide access to databases (real-estate listings, inventory, and financial information) at much less cost and over much greater distances.

- High-technology industries are being encouraged in many states' economic development plans, yet in reality these industries account for only 4–5% of the new jobs created annually. However, new jobs are opening up in businesses that use computers and other high technology equipment.

32. More women enter the labor force.

- Drivers: increasing volume of work can be done at home, expanding child-care facilities/services, and the economic need to have income from both spouses.

• Working
women, as a
percentage of
the female
population, took
a sharp turn
upward in the
mid-1960s; as a
percentage of
the total labor
force, growth
has been slower
but steady
since World
War II.

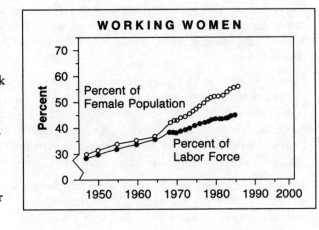

• Expect new demands for childcare as approximately 63% of new entrants
into the labor force between 1985 and 2000 are women.

• Businesses will seek to fill labor shortages with stay-at-home mothers by
offering childcare programs and job sharing.

33. Women's salaries become increasingly comparable to men's.

• Women's
salaries, as a
percentage of
men's, are
catching up.

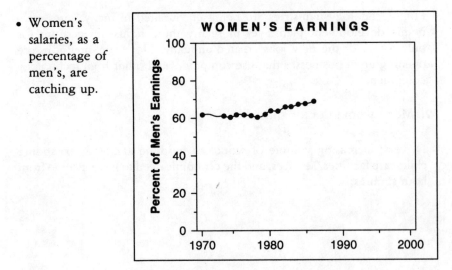

• We think this figure will be 85% or more by 2000.

• Historically, women's salaries in California and north of the Mason-
Dixon Line have been higher (currently 87% of men's); south of the Line
they have been lower (currently only 55%).

34. More blacks and other minority groups enter the labor force.

- Black workers are increasingly entering the labor force.

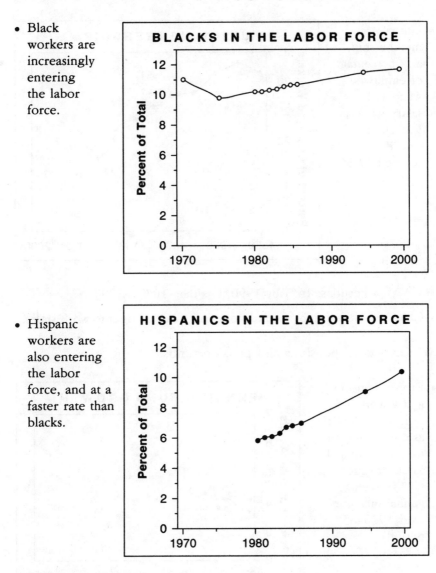

BLACKS IN THE LABOR FORCE

- Hispanic workers are also entering the labor force, and at a faster rate than blacks.

HISPANICS IN THE LABOR FORCE

35. Later retirement.

- Life expectancy is increasing (see number 62).
- Retirement age will rise to 70 by 2000.
- Military retirement age will be extended.
- Civil Service retirement plan will be converted to Social Security.

36. Decline of unionization.

- Union
  membership,
  as a percentage
  of employed
  wage and
  salary workers,
  is declining
  steadily. It
  reached 17.5%
  in 1986.

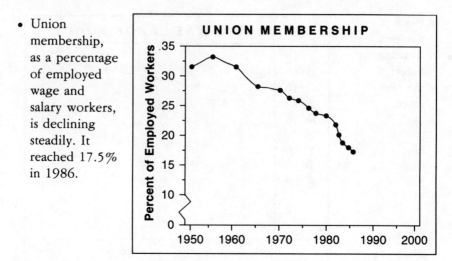

- UAW projections: 14% by 1990, less than 10% by 2000.

- Continual shift in jobs toward no-union states or right-to-work states.

37. Growth of pensions and pension funds.

- Private pension
  and government
  retirement funds
  as a percentage of
  total institutional
  assets are growing
  (2.7% average
  annual increase
  over 1970–85
  period).

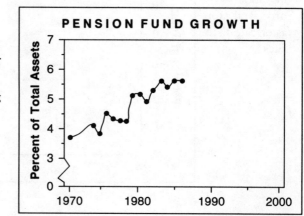

- There will be more people in the labor force for longer periods.

38. Movement toward second and third careers and midlife changes
in career.

- Career changes every 10 years, average.

- Lack of commitment to the job is illustrated by the results of a recent Louis Harris poll: only 39% of workers say they intend to hold the same job 5 years from now that they hold now; 31% say they plan to leave their current work; 29% don't know (see number 39).

39. Decline of the work ethic.

- Tardiness is increasing.

- Sick leave abuse is common.

- SAT scores have dropped.

- Job security and high pay are not the motivators they once were, because there is a high degree of social mobility and people seek job fulfillment (48% of those responding in a recent Louis Harris poll say they work because it "gives feeling of real accomplishment").

- Fifty-five percent of the top executives interviewed in the poll say that erosion of the work ethic will have a major negative effect on corporate performance in the future.

- Yet, two-thirds of Americans would like to see an increase in the length of the work week rather than shorter hours.

40. More two-income couples.

- Two-earners as a percentage of all married couples: 28.5% in 1960, 37.7% in 1970, 46.2% in 1980, 49.0% in 1985. We think the figure will reach 75% by 2000, BLS projections notwithstanding.

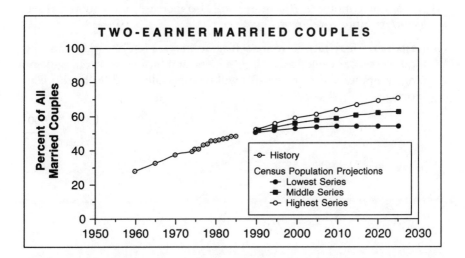

41. Shortage of labor, low wage-rate workers.

- The decline in the birthrate in the 1960s and early 1970s means a smaller number of young people entering the job market today. The number of jobs is increasing, creating entry-level labor shortages expected to increase in the 1990s, especially in the service sector.

- This may translate to more entry-level job opportunities for high school graduates as companies train them on-the-job.

- Institutions of higher education, business, and the military will all vie for youths 16 to 24 years old as this group shrinks from 20% of the labor force in 1985 to 16% in the year 2000.

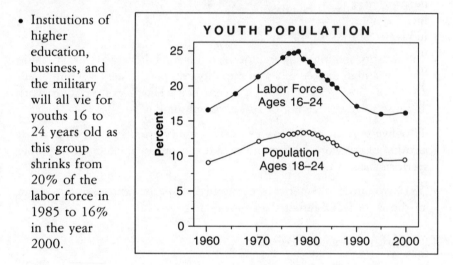

- The military (army and navy) has seen the education levels of recruits drop as competition from the private sector intensifies.

- Untapped resources include the retarded and handicapped, as well as stay-at-home mothers. Businesses will also increase automation and seek to attract more foreign workers.

- Restaurants may turn to more self-serve items. Hotels, restaurants, fast-food places, convenience stores, retailers, and businesses needing beginning computer and clerical skills will be especially hard hit by this labor shortage.

MANAGEMENT TRENDS

42. More entrepreneurs.

- Between 1950 and 1970, the number of new business incorporations jumped from under 100,000 to nearly 300,000 annually; in 1986 the number of new business start-ups hit a record 700,000.

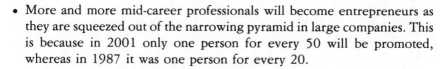

NEW BUSINESS INCORPORATIONS

- More and more mid-career professionals will become entrepreneurs as they are squeezed out of the narrowing pyramid in large companies. This is because in 2001 only one person for every 50 will be promoted, whereas in 1987 it was one person for every 20.

- More and more women are starting up small businesses. In a mass "homecoming," they are leaving traditional jobs to go home, open up businesses, and have children.

- During the decade from 1970 to 1980, small businesses started by entrepreneurs accounted for most of the 20 million new jobs created. In 1987, small businesses accounted for 1 million new jobs, versus 97,000 from larger companies.

- By the year 2000, 85% of the labor force will be working for firms employing fewer than 200 people.

43. The typical large business will be information-based, composed of specialists who rely on information from colleagues, customers, and headquarters to guide their actions.

- Decision processes, management structure, and modes of work are being transformed as businesses take the first steps from using unprocessed *data* to using *information* (data that have been analyzed, synthesized, and organized in a useful way).

- The advent of data-processing capacity has allowed this transformation of data to information.

- Information-based organizations require more specialists who will be found in operations, not at corporate headquarters.

- Upper management will clearly state performance expectations for the organization, its parts, and its specialists and supply the feedback necessary to determine if results have met expectations.

44. A typical large business in 2010 will have fewer than half the management levels of its counterpart today, and about one-third the number of managers.

- Middle management will all but disappear as information flows directly up to higher management for analysis.

- Computers and information-management systems enable the span of control to increase from 6 to 21; fewer mid-level managers are needed.

- With major firms "trimming the fat," the pyramid will be flattened, with the specialists on the bottom.

- Opportunities for advancement will be few because the opportunities will come within the narrow specialty.

- The process of finding top managers will be extremely difficult.

- As the information-based organization replaces the typical business of today, there will be a greater need to prepare professional specialists to be business executives and business leaders in these organizations.

- Thus, the values and compensation structure of business will have to change radically.

45. The command-and-control model of management will be a relic of the past as the information-based organization becomes the norm.

- Manual and clerical workers are being replaced with knowledge workers.

- Information technology is the driving force.

- Management styles will move toward more participation by workers on a consultative basis.

46. The actual work will be done by task-focused teams of specialists.

- The traditional department will assign the specialists, set the standards, and serve as the center for training.

- Research, development, manufacturing, and marketing specialists will work together as a team on all stages of product development rather than keeping each stage separate and distinct.

TRENDS IN VALUES AND CONCERNS

47. General shift in societal values.

- "Me" ethic→"we" ethic→family ethic.

  Family issues in the 1990s: long-term health care, day-care, early childhood education, anti-drug campaigns.
  Companies will be required to grant "family leave" for mothers and fathers of newborns, for newly adopted children, and for care of elderly or ill family members.

- A shorter work week is coming (Sweden is now at 36 hours; West Germany is at 37, headed for 35 hours).

- Promiscuity used to be inhibited by fears of "conception, infection, detection"; infection (e.g., herpes, AIDS) still stands, but the others have fallen, especially the social stigma associated with "detection."

- We used to live to work; now we work to live.

- Conspicuous consumption is passé; it has been replaced by downscaling.

- Middle age will be "in" by 2000; the "youth culture" will be "out."

- Narrow, extremist views of either the left or the right will be unpopular. Moderate Republicans and conservative Democrats will lead their consecutive parties.

- Some liberal views will be back in the mainstream in the 1990s, resulting from the 30-year Hegelian swing.

- Drugs may be decriminalized, with concomitant savings being used to treat addicts.

48. Diversity as a growing, explicit value.

- The old idea was to conform, to blend in with the group; this is giving way, especially among minorities, to pride in cultural heritage and a general acceptance of differences in all aspects of society. The interest and acclaim that Alex Haley's *Roots* generated is an example. Sexual preference is another.

49. Increasing aspirations and expectations of success

- Continued high emphasis on economic success; stress will keep step.

- Growing numbers of entrepreneurs (see number 42).

- Aspirations are there but the means may not be; only one in three high school graduates goes on to graduate from college.

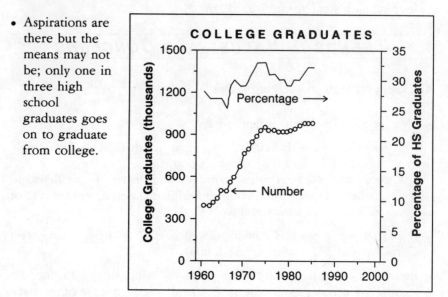

- Without higher education, expectations may never be met: in 1986, male high school graduates not enrolling in college were earning an average of 28% less in constant dollars than a comparable group in 1973.

- There are, in addition, more young people who report no earnings, up from 7% of all 20-to-24-year-old men in 1973 to 12% in 1984.

50. Growth of tourism, vacationing, and travel, especially international (see number 60).

- More disposable income, especially in two-earner families.

- Number of U.S. travelers to foreign countries (excluding Canada and Mexico) increased at a 5%-per-year rate, 1981 to 1985.

- Number of foreign overseas travelers to the U.S. increased at a 1.3%-per-year rate, 1981 to 1985.

- International currency exchange rates directly affect travel; now that the dollar has fallen, we can expect more foreign visitors.

- By 2001, air travel for both business and pleasure will be twice the 1985 rate.

- Tourism will be spurred as printed brochures yield to video as a source of information about vacation destinations. Programs include current, detailed information on accommodations, climate, culture, currency, language, and immunization and passport requirements.

- One of every ten people in the United States will be working for the hospitality industry by the year 2000.

- Multiple, shorter vacations spread throughout the year will continue to replace the traditional 2-week vacation.

51. General expectations of high level of medical care.

- Medical knowledge is doubling every 8 years.

- Catastrophic health care insurance plans will be approved by 1990.

- By 2000, 85% of doctors will be salaried.

- There will be more nurses available for community-based health care; salaries for nurses will rise.

- Physician assistants will be able to prescribe drugs in 38 states by 2000 (17 states grant this authority now).

- Medical costs will rise more slowly by 2000:

    Drug costs will decrease; 53% of drugs will be generic.
    Seventeen states will authorize druggists to prescribe drugs (only one state [Florida] grants this authority now).

- More local medical outlets (surgicenters, "doc-in-the-boxes," etc.) will make high-quality medical services available at the local level.

- There will be a surplus of 100,000 physicians by 2001. The result: Doctors will pay closer attention to individual patient care, office hours will be extended to evenings and weekends. Families will receive much additional medical information via home communication centers. Prescriptions will be written, transmitted, and filled via computer.

- By 1990, organizations such as Allied Respiratory Care in Miami, Florida, and similar organizations in New York, Pennsylvania, and Ohio will care for over half of AIDS patients at home and others in special AIDS wings in hospitals.

52. Growth of physical culture and personal health movements.

- Emphasis on preventive medicine will grow. By 2001, some 90% of insurance carriers will expand coverage or reduce premiums for policy-holders with healthy lifestyles.

- Personal wellness, prevention, and self-help will be the watchwords for a more health-conscious population. Interest in participant sports, exercise equipment, home gyms, and employee fitness programs will create mini-boom industries.

- Sixty-six percent of those polled in a recent Harris poll claimed to have changed their eating habits in the past two years. Americans today eat lighter fare than in 1976, consuming 15 pounds more chicken, a pound more fish, and 22 more gallons of low-fat milk per capita.

- Consumer purchases show a per capita decline in liquor consumption, from 2 gallons in 1979 to 1.8 gallons in 1984. There was a noticeable shift away from hard liquors to wines, beers, and bubbly waters.

- General trend toward nonsmoking: currently 35% of men smoke, down from 52% two decades ago; 29% of women smoke, down from a 34% peak.

- There are many more magazines on health care and fitness than in the past.

- People will be more inclined to take steps to control stress as they realize that 80–90% of all diseases are stress-related.

53. General expectations of a high level of social service.

- Adequate Social Security income if retirement age goes to 70.
- More services/accommodation for the deaf, blind, disabled, poor, infirm, and aged.
- $50 billion by 2000 for AIDS research and treatment.
- Every taxpayer will be paying $500 a year to care for AIDS patients in the year 2000.
- More psychiatric help for alcohol and drug abuse.
- Compulsory national service (2-years, male and female) is likely by 2000, with 3 options: military service, VISTA-type work with the disadvantaged, or Peace Corps.

54. Increasing concern for environmental issues. (However, a real environmental push may not occur until the Democrats return to the White House in 1996.)

- More activist Baby Boomers will call for redressment of major environmental problems such as air pollution, acid rain, loss of forests, depletion of the ozone layer, global climate change, toxic chemicals in our food and water, soil erosion, mass extinction of species, and pollution of beaches, oceans, reservoirs, and waterways.
- Zoos will serve as "Noah's Archives" as the extinction rate of animals increases.
- By 1990, more than half of U.S. cities will have exhausted their existing landfills and will need to develop alternatives for waste disposal.
- Warming of the earth's atmosphere caused by the greenhouse effect will result in a worldwide rise in sea levels; national governments will implement policies to require less use of CO_2-intensive fuels, develop more efficient energy technologies, and combat deforestation.
- A new breed of inherently safe nuclear reactors (small size, underground location, sealed fuel particles) will take the place of extinction-bound conventional nuclear reactors.
- Fusion reactors will appear after 2000; by 2020 they will be a major source of power.

- Power plants using only the energy of the oceans will produce both electricity and fresh water for island communities; more islands will be inhabited as a result.

- Concern for the indoor environment will increase. The quality of indoor air, the effects of building materials, asbestos, and radon gas will be controlled.

55. Growth of consumerism.

- More consumer agencies and organizations.

- Consumer information (e.g., unit pricing, content labels) will proliferate via packaging, TV, special studies/reports.

- With a wealth of information, consumers will be able to become smarter buyers. They will demand quality, service, dependability, and fair prices.

56. Growth of the women's liberation movement.

- "Good old girl" networks will become increasingly effective as women fill more positions in middle and upper management.

- An infrastructure is evolving that allows women to make more decisions and to exercise political power, especially where both spouses work. The effect will be:

  > More child-care services
  > Greater employment opportunities
  > More equal male-female pay rates (but we don't think the "comparable worth" concept has a future).

- One indication of the growing dependence on the wife's income: life insurance companies are selling more policies to women than to men.

FAMILY TRENDS

57. Decline in birthrates.

- The birthrate per 1,000 population shows a roller-coaster decline.

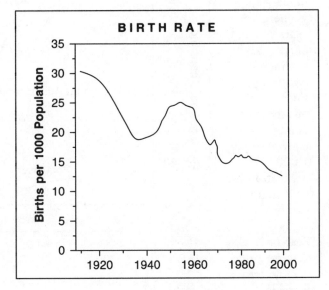

- Families are getting smaller. In 1987, the average number of people living in a U.S. household was 2.66, versus 3.67 in 1940.

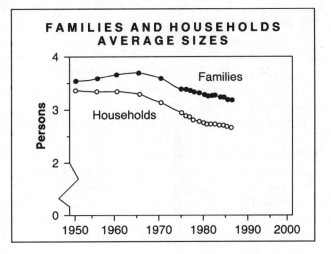

58. Increase in rates of family formation and marriage.

- Marriage rate per 1,000 unmarried women, 15 years old and older, has declined erratically since 1950, but the number of marriages per 1,000 population has held quite steady.

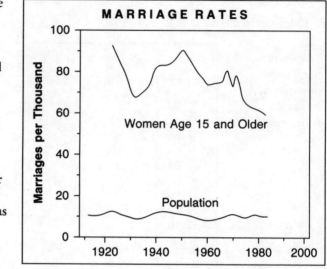

- Fear of AIDS may turn this decline into an increase.

59. Decrease in the divorce rate.

- After a steady rise in the 1970s, divorce rates have headed down.

- Fear of AIDS may cause a further decline. The real impact of AIDS will be seen in more stable marriages.

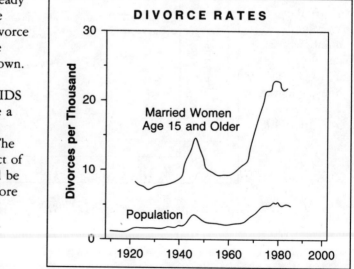

60. Growth of leisure.

- Automation and computer applications in manufacturing (specifically CAD/CAM and CIM) will result in a shorter average work week.

- Both spouses working, plus a smaller tax bite, means more disposable income to spend on leisure activities.

- As more people enter the labor force, the work week will drop to 32 hours, resulting in more leisure time.

61. Growth of the do-it-yourself movement.

- The high cost of hiring outside workers motivates people to do the work themselves.

- There will be more leisure time available to spend on do-it-yourself projects.

- Availability of more tools and supplies aimed at the do-it-yourself market will spur the movement.

62. Improved nutrition and wellness movement, with a consequent increase in life expectancy (an outgrowth of items 51 and 52.)

- The average child born in 1986 will live to be 74.9 years old (average male, 71.5 years; average female, 78.5 years).

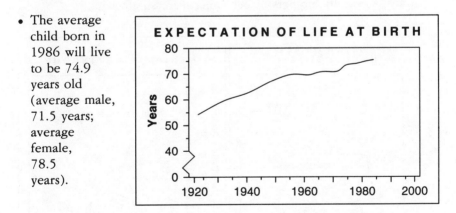

63. Isolation of children from the world of adult concern.

- Movement toward overprotecting children from the outside world and the consequences of their acts.

- More children are being placed in day-care centers and preschools. Many are near old-age homes where young and old can share a common bond.

64. Protracted adolescence.

• For social as well as economic reasons, young people are leaving the nest later than their parents did. Increasing age at first marriage is another indicator of this delay.

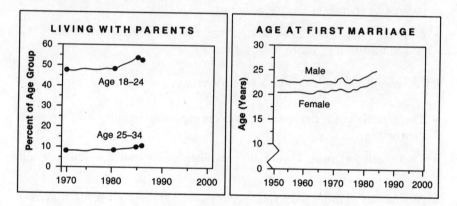

65. More single heads of households—the new poor.

• The number of family households with no spouse present has been increasing rapidly since the early 1970s. The economic burden on single parents, especially mothers, is becoming increasingly acute.

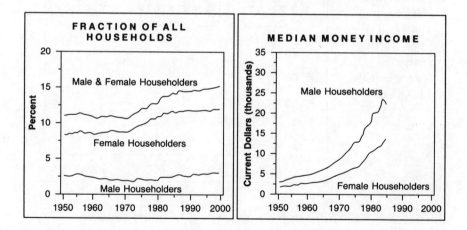

66. Growth of the already-large aged population.

- The
  percentage of
  Americans age
  65 and older
  will continue
  to grow. The
  percentage in
  Western
  Europe will
  grow even
  faster.

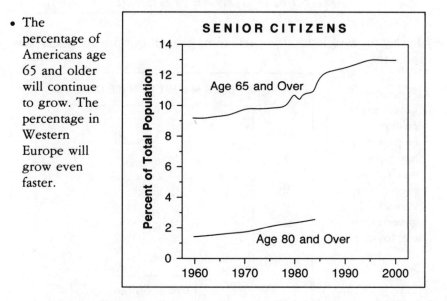

67. Replacement of the extended family by the nuclear family and other living arrangements.

- More older people retain their mobility and independence.

- Older person's family can be near, but not next door.

- Prefabricated (manufactured) housing will be cheaper than conventional construction, enabling older persons to afford housing where they want to live, in the suburbs, for instance.

INSTITUTIONAL TRENDS

68. Decrease of federal government; growth of state and local governments.

- Federal government civilian employment has grown much more slowly than has state and local government employment.

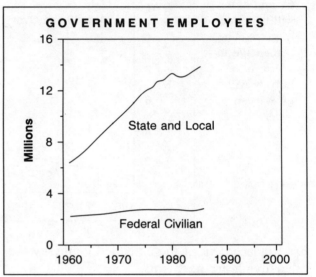

- More block grants are being given to state and local governments for administration by them rather than the federal government.

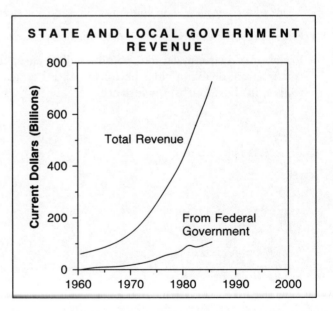

- Further deregulation will tend to increase the responsibilities of the private sector and/or state and local governments, with a corresponding reduction in federal government resources.

69. Growth of multinational corporations.

- We predict that the multinationals may be affected by the increasing number of AIDS cases in Africa and around the world, since many firms rely on indigenous workers.
- AT&T expects to have a worldwide 800 toll-free telephone number system in place by 1992.

70. More futures studies and forecasting.

- These will result from the need to know the consequences of expensive or irreversible acts before the decision is taken, and from the need to anticipate problems that could develop.
- Future-oriented organizations have moved forward steadily since the early 1960s, when they first appeared. The momentum developed in the 1970s can be expected to grow, and such organizations will have increasing influence on decision-making in government, business, and industry in the years ahead.
- A conservative estimate of the number of futurist groups in the world in 1975–76 by the World Future Society was 300; a spokeswoman from the Society believes the number of organizations has increased tremendously in the ensuing years.
- There is a congressional clearinghouse for futures research.
- The World Future Society reports a record membership.

71. Growing demands for accountability in the expenditure of public resources.

- Computers permit transaction information (i.e., audit trails) to be kept, facilitating accountability.
- Greater emphasis will be placed by the public and the legislatures on the outcomes of efforts in public education.

72. Growing demands for social responsibility.

- Union Carbide's Bhopal disaster is a classic case in point.

- Nuclear power plant controversies.

- Auto seatbelts (especially seatbelt-use laws).

- Testing for AIDS and drug abuse.

- Safety testing of children's toys.

- National resolve to attack social problems such as homelessness, AIDS, drug abuse, and the environment.

- Companies will be judged on how they treat the environment.

- Government intervention will supplant deregulation in the airline industry (safety and services), financial service industry (instability and costs), electric utility industry (nuclear problems), and the chemical industry (toxic wastes).

- With 5% of the world's population and 66% of the lawyers on the planet, U.S. citizens will not hesitate to litigate if their demands are not met.

73. A phenomenon of bimodal distribution of institutions is emerging: the big get bigger, the small survive, and the middle-sized are squeezed out.

- Ten domestic air carriers today control 80% of the market, leaving the smaller domestic carriers with only 20%. By 2001 there will be only three major domestic carriers.

- Currently there are 20 major automakers around the world with market shares ranging from 18.1% (GM) to 1.0% (BMW). By 2001, there will be only five giant automobile firms; production and assembly will be centered in Korea, Italy, and Latin America.

- By 2000, there will be three major corporations making up the computer hardware industry: IBM, Digital, and Apple.

- Today the manufacturer often sells directly to the dealer, skipping the wholesaler or distributor.

- The 1990s will be the decade of micro-segmentation as more and more highly-specialized businesses and entrepreneurs search for narrower niches.

- The above trend extends to:

    Stores: big chain department stores and, at the opposite end, discount stores succeed.
    Hotels: large hotel chains and, at the other end, economy hotels thriving with those in the middle being squeezed out.
    Restaurants: elegant dining and, at the opposite end, cheap, fast-food

restaurants making it at the expense of sit-down family restaurants in the middle.

Hospitals: growth in hospital corporations and, at the opposite end, walk-in medical centers.

Agriculture: the farmer making over $500,000 is flourishing; the farmer who makes under $100,000 is surviving; the middle-income farmer is going bankrupt.

Banks: growth of interstate and international banks and, at the other end, local banks pushing service.

Financial institutions: the recent merger of E.F. Hutton and Shearson-Lehman Brothers illustrates this trend, while, at the other end, the local broker is succeeding.

- The above trend leads us to believe that AT&T may be reconsolidated in the mid-1990s.

- What we see across the board with institutions is also happening within organizations as the traditional pyramid is flattened and middle management is squeezed out. (See number 44.)

PARTICIPANTS

IN THE FUTURE

What follows is a list of corporations, federal and state government agencies, foreign governments, and individuals for whom Forecasting International and Marvin Cetron have consulted:

GOVERNMENT AGENCIES

Annandale Chamber of
Commerce
Armed Forces Industrial College
Army Material Command
Army Research Office
Bolling Air Force Base Defense
Intelligence
Bureau of Government Financial
Operations
Bureau of Indian Affairs
Central Intelligence Agency
City of Dayton, Ohio
City of Framingham,
Massachusetts
City of New York
City of Zanesville, Ohio
Commonwealth of Virginia
Department of Education
Congressional Research Service
Connecticut State Library
Council of Governments
Defense Intelligence Agency
Department of Defense
Department of Education

Department of Housing and
Urban Development
Department of the Interior
Department of Labor
Department of the Treasury
Economic Development Division,
State of Utah
Energy Research and
Development Administration
Environmental Protection Agency
Fairfax County Chamber of
Commerce
Fairfax Housing Commission
Federal Judicial Center
Food and Drug Administration
Fort Myer Propulsion Society
Governor's Conference on
Tourism, Ohio
Grand Rapids Chamber of
Commerce
Hamilton County Trade Center
Industrial Development Research
Council
Internal Revenue Service

Investors Committee Institute
Joint Chiefs of Staff
Kentucky Chamber of Commerce
Library of Congress
Maritime Administration
Maryland Municipal League
Maryland State Council on
   Vo-Tech Education
NASA
National Academy of Sciences
National Bureau of Standards
National Defense University
National Highway Association
National Science Foundation
National War College
Naval Ship Research and
   Development Center
Navy Materials Command
Norfolk Naval Shipyard
Office of the Governor, Kentucky
Oklahoma State Department of
   Vocational & Technical
   Education
Small Business Administration
Social Security Administration
State Department

State of Hawaii
State of Louisiana
State of Michigan
Texas Society of Association
   Executives
Transition Team, George Bush
U.S. Army
U.S. Atomic Energy Commission
U.S. Bureau of Mines
U.S. Chamber of Commerce
U.S. Coast Guard
U.S. Corps of Engineers
U.S. Department of Agriculture
U.S. Department of Commerce
U.S. Information Agency
U.S. Intelligence Agencies
U.S. Senate
Veterans Administration
Virginia Attorney General
Virginia Department of Education
Washington Metro Area Transit
   Authority
Worcester Area Chamber of
   Commerce
Workers Compensation Fund of
   Utah

CORPORATIONS

ABC
Adolph Coors Company
Aetna Life & Casualty Insurance
   Company
Allstate Insurance
American Can Company
American Druggist Magazine
American Frozen Foods
American National Bank
Ameritech Services
Amway International
Apple Computer Company
Arthur Andersen & Company
AT&T

Atlanta American Feed Industry
Atlas Van Lines
Besser Company
BHS Securities Corporation
Bluegrass Area Development
   District, Inc.
Boeing
The Brookings Institution
Brown & Williamson Tobacco
   Company
Brown Shoe Company
Business People Inc.
Capital Holding Corporation
Care Enterprises

CBS
Christopher J. Hegarty &
  Company
Citibank
Clorox
CNN
Coldwell Bankers
Colgate-Palmolive Company
Com/Energy Services Company
Comprehensive Care Corporation
Conoco
Control Data Corporation
Creative Recruitment
Croften Publicity Company
Culligan International Company
Data Communications
  Corporation
Du Pont Corporation
Dynamac Corporation
Eberstadt Asset Management
Empire Blue Cross
Farmland Industries
Financial Planners Equity
Food Industry Association
Food Marketing Institute
Ford Foundation
FRAM Corporation
The Futurist
General Electric Corporation
General Motors Corporation
General Telephone & Electronics
Georgia-Pacific Corporation
Gordon & Breach Publishers
GTE Service Corporation
Gulf Power Company
Heck's Company
Hoffman-LaRoche
Holiday Corporation
Hospitals Magazine
Hyatt Corporation
IBM
Indiana Bell
Insilco Corporation
Institute of Industrial Launderers
Institutional Investor Magazine

International Fertilization Industry
International Schools Services
International Telephone &
  Telegraph
Joan Garber Associates for State
  Street Bank
John Hancock Insurance
John Muir Memorial Hospital
Johnson & Johnson
Kata Associates, Inc.
Kepner-Tragoe-Scantion
Levi-Strauss
Logican Corporation
Look Up Gaston Foundation, Inc.
Louisiana National Bank
Lutheran Brotherhood
Management Systems–Finland
Manufacturers Hanover
Marriott Corporation
McDonald's & Coca-Cola
  Convention
McGraw-Hill Corporation
MCI
Meeting Success
Merchandise Mart Properties, Inc.
Metrics Inc.
Michigan Bell
Monumental Corporation
National Investor Relations
  Institute
NATM Buying Corporation
NBC
Niarchos & Associates
Northern Plains Natural Gas
  Company
Northern Telecom
Northwest Airlines
Nursing '86
Omni
Orient/Pacific, Research &
  Development Company
Otis Elevator
OXY Occidental Exploration &
  Petroleum Company
Pacific Northwest Bell

Paramount Productions
Park Inn International
Partridge Group
The Pearson Group
Pepsi-Cola
Pharmaceutical Card Systems, Inc.
Pizza Hut
Podium Professionals
Price Waterhouse
R. J. Reynolds Development
  Corporation
Ralston Purina
Restaurant and Institutions
  Magazine
Rhone Poulenc
RJR Archer, Inc.
Rocco Corporation
Roche Labs
Rochester Methodist Hospital
SAI Communication Systems
Searle Pharmaceuticals
Seattle-First National Bank
Shari Medical Center
Shell Oil Company
Sheraton Corporation
Siemen's Public Switching
  Systems

Simon & Schuster
SITE International
Smith-Barney
Smith Company Medical Society
Sperry Corporation
Stuart Pharmaceuticals
Susan Hendley & Company, Inc.
Teledyne
Timex Corporation
Total System Services
Transamerica Occidental Life
  Insurance
The Travelers
Union Carbide
United Stirling, Inc.
United Technologies
University Computing Company
Volume Shoe Corporation
Volvo Corporation
Wang Laboratories
Weight Watchers Spa Reviewer
Weyerhaeuser Company
Why In The World
Xerox, Inc.
Young & Rubicam New York
Zanesville Community
  Corporation

ASSOCIATIONS

A. H. Robbins Pharmaceuticals
AASA (American Association of
  School Administrators)
Aetna Institute
AICPA (American Institute
  of Certified Public
  Accountants)
Airport Operations Council
  International
Alexander and Alexander
Aluminum Extruders Council
American Academy of Family
  Physicians

American Academy of Physician
  Assistants
American Apparel Association
American Association of
  Community and Junior
  Colleges
American Association of
  Equipment Lessors
American Association of Retired
  Persons
American Association of School
  Administrators
American Bus Association

American Chamber of Commerce Executives

American Consulting Engineers Council

American Council of Life Insurance

American Dental Trade Association

American Dietetic Association

American Feed Industry Association

American Feed Manufacturers Association

American Group Practice Association

American Hardware Manufacturers Association

American Home Economics Association

American Hospital Association

American Hospital Planning & Marketing Association

American Hotel & Motel Association

American Institute of Architects

American Institute of Certified Public Accountants

American Management Association

American Marketing Association

American Meat Institute

American Medical Association

American National Banking Association

American Pharmaceutical Association

American Red Cross

American Road and Transportation Builders Association

American Society for Hospital Public Relations

American Society for Industrial Security

American Society of Interior Designers

American Society of Landscape Architects

American Speech, Language & Hearing Association

American Trucking Association

Association County Commissioners of Georgia

Association of Field Service Managers

Association of Field Service Managers International

Association of Information System Professionals

Association of Investment Management Sales Executives

Association of Part-time Professionals

Association of Schools & Agencies for the Handicapped

Audio Visual Management Association

Automotive Parts Rebuilders Association

AVAS (American Vocational Association)

Bank Marketing Association

Blue Cross/Blue Shield

B'nai B'rith Women

Boehringer Ingelheim

Building Owners & Managers Association

California Grocers Association

California Pharmacists Association

Career Education Association

Ceiling & Interior Systems Construction Association

Center for Applied Management

Chemical Specialties Manufacturers Association

Chicago Food Brokers

Chicago National Office Products

College Bookstores

College of Pharmacy
Construction Industry
  Manufacturers Association
Copeland Corporation
Dairy & Food Industries Supply
  Association
Diet Food Marketing Institute
Dulles Area Board of Trade
Employee Relocation Council
Employment and Management
  Association
Federation of Societies for
  Coatings Technology
Financial Management Service
First Data Resources
Flexible Packaging Association
Footwear Industries of America
Franchesca Sisters for the
  Poor
Frank Russell Corporation
Gas Appliance Manufacturers
  Association
Hanover Trust
Honeywell
IEEE (Institute of Electrical &
  Electronic Engineers)
Independent Insurance Agents of
  America
Indiana Electric Association
Institute for Educational
  Leadership, Inc.
Intermountain Oil Marketers
  Association
International Association for
  Financial Planning
International Association of
  Refrigerated Warehouses
International Booksellers
  Federation
International Facility Management
  Association
International Oxygen
  Manufacturers Association
International Society for
  Technical Assessment

League of Savings Institute
Learning International
Life Communicators Association
Mechanical Contractors
  Association
Meeting Planners International
Merrill Lynch
Michigan Blue Cross/Blue Shield
  Management Association
Michigan Food Dealers
  Association
Michigan Food Processors
  Association
Michigan League of Savings
  Institutions
Michigan Social Service
Midwest Cooperative Education
  Association
Mortgage Bankers Association of
  America
National Agricultural Chemical
  Association
National Agri-Marketing
  Association
National Association for
  Ambulatory Care
National Association for Home
  Care
National Association of
  Aluminum Distributors
National Association of Bank
  Women
National Association of Casualty
  & Surety Agents
National Association of Chain
  Drug Stores
National Association of
  Convenience Stores, Inc.
National Association of Credit
  Management
National Association of Electrical
  Distributors
National Association of
  Elementary School
  Principals

National Association of Home
Economics

National Association of Hosiery
Manufacturers

National Association of Life
Underwriters

National Association of Printers
& Lithographers

National Association of Social
Workers

National Association of State
Boards of Education

National Association of Tobacco
Distributors

National Building Materials
Distributors Association

National Business Forms
Association

National Cancer Institute

National Candy Wholesalers
Association

National Cattlemen's
Association

National Center for Research in
Vocational Education

National Education Conference

National Electrical Manufacturers
Association

National Fisheries Institute

National Food Brokers
Association

National Food Distributors
Association

National Freight Transportation
Association

National Glass Association

National Grocers Association

National Knitwear Manufacturers
Association

National Office Products
Association

National Paint and Coatings
Association

National Pest Control
Association

National Petroleum Institute

National Pharmaceutical Council,
Inc.

National Shorthand Reporters
Association

National Structural Settlements
Association

National Vocational Education
Association

National Wholesale Druggist
Association

Natural Structured Settlement
Association

New York Auditors

New York State Bankers
Association

Northern Virginia Jewish
Community Center

Northern Virginia Youth Services
Association

Northwest Public Power
Association

ONI Users Group

Outdoor Power Equipment
Institute, Inc.

Pennsylvania Medical Society

Personnel Industrial Relations
Association of Wisconsin

Photo Marketing Association

Prudential Bache Securities

Rice Millers Association

Risk and Insurance Management
Society

S. E. Poultry & Egg
Association

Sacramento Business Council

Senior Executives Association

Smith/Bucklin Association
Management Firm

Society for Hospital Planning &
Marketing

Society of Incentive Travel
Executives

Society of Industrial and Office
Realtors

South Carolina Educational
  Association
Southeastern Electric Exchange
Southern Business Administration
  Association
Southern Deans Association
Sowell & Hopkins
Special Libraries Association
Spokane County Medical
  Society
State Street Bank
Stuart Corporation
Tampa Concrete & Masonry
Texas Cattle Feeders
  Association
Texas Cattlemen's Association
Texas Land Title Association
Textile Care Allied Trades
  Association, Inc.

3M
Toy Manufacturers of America
TSSI International
United Fresh Fruit and Vegetable
  Association
Urban Land Institute
Virginia School Boards
  Association
Washington Health Care
  Corporation
Western Association of State
  Highway & Transportation
  Officials
Wine & Spirits
Wisconsin Hospital Association
Women's Bank Association
World Future Society
Young Men's & Women's
  Hebrew Association

OVERSEAS CLIENTS

Australian Government
Brazilian Government
British Airport Authority
British Ministry of Defense
Canadian Government
Chinese Government
Danish Government
European Economic
  Community
Finnish Government
IIASA (International Institute for
  Applied Systems Analysis)
Indonesian Government
Irish Management Institute
Israeli Government
Istratypeset, Ltd.
Italian Government
Japan Industrial Planning
  Association
L. M. Ericcsson
  Telecommunications Inc.

Malaysian Government
Ministry of Citizenship
  and Culture, Ontario,
  Canada
MITI (Japanese Ministry of
  International Trade and
  Industry)
NATO
Norwegian Government
Peruvian Government
Royal Canadian Mounted
  Police
Singapore Government
South African Government
Swedish Government
Thailand Government
United Nations Industrial
  Development Organization
Vatican Council of Public
  Affairs
Yugoslavian Government

EDUCATIONAL INSTITUTIONS

American University
American Vocational Education
Arlington County Public Schools
Baltimore College of Notre
  Dame
Baltimore Hood College
Blue Ridge Technical College
Cleveland State University
College of Notre Dame of
  Maryland
Cornell University
Cornwall-Lebanon School District
Derry Township School District,
  Hershey, Pennsylvania
District of Columbia Public
  Schools
Fairfax Country Public Schools
Falls Church High School
Flatrock, North Carolina, School
  System
George Washington University
Georgia Tech
Green River Community College
Hershey Public Schools
Illinois Junior Colleges
Indiana University of
  Pennsylvania
Institute for Fiduciary Education
Jefferson Science & Technology
  High School
Lorain County Community
  College

Louisiana School for Math,
  Science and the Arts
Louisiana State University
Loyola University
Minnesota Department of
  Education
MIT
National School Board
Northwestern State University of
  Louisiana
Ohio Department of Education
Orange County Public Schools
Penn State
Pennsylvania Department of
  Education
Pensacola Schools
Pewaukee Public Schools,
  Pewaukee, Wisconsin
Prince George County Schools,
  Maryland
Rowan Cabarrus Community
  College
Saginaw Valley State
  University
St. Petersburg Junior College
Tampa Vocational Education
Tyler Junior College
University of Florida
University of Maryland
Utah State University
Virginia Polytechnic Institute &
  State University

INDEX

9486